Books by Ralph M. and Terry H. Kovel

The Kovels' Price Guide for Collector Plates, Figurines,
    Paperweights, and Other Limited Editions
The Kovels' Complete Antiques Price List
Know Your Antiques
American Country Furniture 1780–1875
Dictionary of Marks—Pottery and Porcelain
The Kovels' Complete Bottle Price List
Directory of American Silver, Pewter, and Silver Plate
Kovels' Collectors Guide to American Art Pottery
The Kovels' Organizer for Collectors

THE KOVELS'
Price Guide
for
Collector Plates, Figurines, Paperweights, and Other Limited Editions

THE KOVELS'
Price Guide
for
Collector Plates, Figurines, Paperweights, and Other Limited Editions

RALPH & TERRY KOVEL

CROWN PUBLISHERS, INC. • NEW YORK

Contents

wiley Rec 7/2/79

Weekly, Continental Mint, Cowboy Artists of America, Count Agazzi, Cowles, Creative World, Cristal d'Albret, Crown and Rose, Crown Delft, Crown Staffordshire, Curry, Cybis, d'Arceau Limoges, Damron, Danbury Mint, Daum, Davis, de Grazia, Dennis the Menace, Detlefsen, Downs, Dresden, Egerman, Eschenbach, Fairfield Collection, Fairmont, Fenton, Ferrandiz, Fischer, Fontana, Fostoria, Franklin Mint, Frankoma, Fujihara, Fukagawa, Furstenberg, Georg Jensen, George Washington Mint, Gibson Girl, Goebel, Golf Digest, Gorham, Gourinat, Grafburg, Grande Copenhagen, Grandma Moses, Granget, Greentree, Grossman, Gustavsberg, Halbert, Hallmark, Hamilton Mint, Haviland, Haviland & Parlon, Henry Ford Museum, Hibel, Historic Plates, Hudson, Hutschenreuther, Imperial Glass, Incolay, Indian Art, International Silver, Ispanky, Israel Creations, J & E Specialties, Jean-Paul Loup, Josair, Judaic Heritage Society, Juharos, Kaiser, Kate Greenaway, Keane, Keller & George, Kera, Kern Collectibles, Kilkelly, King, King's Porcelain, Kingsbridge, Kirk, Knowles, Kobycia, Kosta, Kramlik, Kurz, Lake Shore, Lalique, Lenox, Leyendecker, Lindner, Lincoln Mint, Walt Litt, Lladro, Lori, Lund & Clausen, Lundberg, Mallek, Manjundo, Mark Twain, Marmot, Mary Gregory, Meka, Metawa, Metropolitan Museum of Art, Mettlach, Michelsen, Mingolla, Moser, Mueller, National Trust, Noritake, Norse, North Dakota, Norwegian, Oma, Orrefors, Pairpoint, Palisander, Paramount, Pearl Buck, Pennington, Picasso, Pickard, Poillerat, Poole, Porcelaine De Paris, Porcelana Granada, Porsgrund, Puiforcat, Ram, Reco, Reed & Barton, Remington, Reuge, Ridgewood, River Shore, Rockwell, Roman, Rorstrand, Rosenthal, Royal Bayreuth, Royal Berlin, Royal Copenhagen, Royal Cornwall, Royal Crown Derby, Royal Delft, Royal Devon, Royal Doulton, Royal Limoges, Royal Tettau, Royal Worcester, Royale, Royale Germania, Sabino, Sango, Santa Clara, Sarna, Schmid, Schumann, Scottish, Sebring, Selandia, Seven Seas, Shenango, Silver City, L. E. Smith, Spode, Stanek, Sterling America, Stieff, St. Louis, Stromberg, Stumar, Svend Jensen, Tirschenreuth, Towle, Ukrainian, Ulmer Keramic, U.S. Historical Society, Val St. Lambert, Veneto Flair, Vernonware, Viletta, Vogel, Dante Di Volteradici, Washington Mint, Waterford, Wedgwood, Wellings Mint, Wendell August Forge, Westmoreland, Westminster, Wheaton, White House, World Wild Life, Zenith.

Preface

Someone once said that a limited edition is "an instant antique." The humor of that remark would be lost by the serious investor who thinks of limited editions only in terms of profit and loss. The collector who has been buying Christmas plates for years can understand exactly how the limited edition and the antique are related.

This book is a report of the limited edition market as it appears in the United States. Most of the manufacturing companies cooperated in every way, offering us pictures and information. A few companies absolutely refused to tell us anything about the quantity they made in some of their limited editions, or to describe their marketing methods. Some of the information that we wanted could not even be found in the manufacturers' offices because no records were kept of the original issue prices. No doubt, a few companies have been missed entirely. Although we tried to find them all, records of some of the older ones particularly seem to be nonexistent. A very small number of companies proved impossible to locate.

We have read dozens of articles about the investment possibilities of limited editions. A careful look at the issue and current prices in this book will help you make your own determination. Not all the claims are true, but many of the limited editions have become more valuable. Compare the listings with those in *Kovels' Collectors Guide to Limited Editions*, a 1974 price list. The number of limited edition manufacturers no longer making pieces is also part of the investing story.

June 1, 1978

Ralph Kovel *ASA Senior Member*
Terry Kovel *ASA Senior Member*

How to Use This Book

We have tried to use as few symbols as possible, but when a price list is written sometimes abbreviations are needed to conserve space.

Items are grouped by manufacturer. When the information was available we have included a very short paragraph that will furnish you with the location and years of production of the firm. Many of the limited editions are sold by one company and manufactured by another. This type of information has been kept a "trade secret" and was not always available to us. The first column of each listing gives the name of the item, and the name of the artist where it is important; the second column gives the year of manufacture. Column 3 contains the number of items in that particular edition. If the edition is limited to the number of orders before a special date we use the word "year." In many cases the exact number of the edition is released later. The next column tells the price at the time of issue. The last column gives the current range of prices for the piece. These prices were taken from advertisements, auctions, sales, and shops from January 1978 to June 1978. A SINGLE ASTERISK FOLLOWING AN ENTRY REFERS TO A BLACK-AND-WHITE ILLUSTRATION; TWO ASTERISKS REFER TO A COLOR ILLUSTRATION.

This book is divided into three chapters: Chapter 1, Figurines; Chapter 2, Paperweights; Chapter 3, Plates, Plaques, and Miscellaneous. Chapter 3 also includes Christmas ornaments and spoons. This book does not contain listings for any type of prints or paper limited editions, medals, ingots, or furniture. Bottles were not included because the full listing for modern limited edition bottles are to be found in the *Kovels' Complete Bottle Price List*. Some other limited edition items such as coronation or souvenir items may be missing. We have tried to include items that are most likely to be found in the United States. Limited editions made in other countries that have little interest to the American collector were not included. The limited editions included in this book date back to 1895 when the first Christmas plate was made. It was virtually impossible to find out about all limited editions since that date. We have concentrated on items made since 1965, and where it was possible, we traced the earlier editions made by these same companies. Information about original issue price and edition quantity has often been missing for some of the early editions, and for future books we would certainly welcome any added information from readers.

Acknowledgments

Cliff Hammeren
American Greetings, Corp.

Edward Babka
Antique Trader

Kurt Pousar
Arabia Co. of Finland

Ivan Glickman
Arista Imports

Dave Armstrong
Armstrong's

William Veroxie
Artisans in Glass

Thomas K. Riseland
Baccarat, Inc.

Baxter Sperry
Galt, CA

Joan Doyle
Bing & Grondahl

Blue Delft
New York, NY

Maryanne Wagner & Louise Crawford
Edward Marshall Boehm, Inc.

Hunter Haines
Bradford Exchange

Svend A. Knudsen
Britco & Vest

Carol B. Sammond
Burgues

Peggy Roberts & Rhoda Engelson
Calhoun Collectors Society

David Tolins
Certified Rarities, Inc.

Frank B. Knight
Collector's Weekly

S. Strachovsky
Creative World

Paul Jokelson
Cristal d'Albret

T. W. Brian
Crown Staffordshire

Bill Curry
Bill Curry Productions

Ida Julian
Cybis

Nancy L. Segreto
Danbury Mint

Anthony Clippen
Daum International

Jim Laford
DeGrazia of Scottsdale

A. L. Goeldner
Ebebling & Reuss

Mary W. Rosenberg
Ellis-Barker Silver

Malcolm Decker
Fairfield Collection

Frank Fenton
Fenton Glass Company

David Schreiber
Franklin Mint

John Frank
Frankoma Pottery

J. W. Frank
Georg Jensen

Ann Holbrook
Gorham Silver

Judy Sutcliffe
Greentree Enterprises

Judy Gura
Gura Public Relations

Frederick Haviland
Haviland & Co.

Earl D. Hartman
Henry Ford Museum

James Lerner
Hummelwerk

Stephen S. Barnet
Hutschenreuther Corp.

Carl J. Uhrmann
Imperial Glass Company

Cindy Haskins
International Silver Co.

James Stilliana
Interpace Corp.

Robert A. Borst
Jacques Jugeat

Joyce Adams
J & E Specialties

Matthew Brummer
Kern Collectibles

M. Blair
Koscherak Bros.

Karen M. Cohen
Lenox

L. H. Selman
Lundberg Studios

Dick Davis
Lunt Galleries

Kay Mallek
Tucson, AZ

Flo Tugwell
McCalla Enterprises

Joann McConnell
Metlox Potteries

Richard Dougherty
Metropolitan Museum of Art

Mr. Dupres
Noritake Design

Greg Tessitore
Paramount Classics

John David Hugunin
Pemberton & Oakes

Helen Brown
Pennington Pottery

Stuart Drysdale
Perthshire

Larry Smith
Pickard Inc.

Charles Dean
Poole Pottery

Brigitte Moore
Reco International

Patricia Johnson
Reed & Barton

Mel Atkin
Ridgewood China

Ed Gillies
Rivershore Productions

Howard Kranin
The Rockwell Society

Klaus Vogt
Rosenthal, U.S.A., Limited

Royal Crown Derby
Derby, England

Elizabeth Rice & Evelyn Clark
Royal Doulton Company, Inc.

Daniel Price
Royal Tettau

Joyce Hendlowitch
Royal Worcester Spode

Paul A. Schmid
Schmid Bros., Inc.

Bill Knecht
L. E. Smith Glass Co.

Hugh & Carolyn Smith
Smith Paperweights

Lars Flygt
Stromberg

Angela Kaufman & Erik Larsen
Svend Jensen

Arthur L. Roy
Towle Mfg. Co.

Tom O'Meara
Viletta China

Luella Powell
Wara Intercontinental

Claudia Coleman
Wedgwood

Myron Pred
Wheaton Commemoratives

J. H. Brainard
Westmoreland Glass Company

C. E. Kloos
Wildlife of the World

Ed Rohn & Bonnie Bishop
Edward Williams Co.

Pat Owens
Viking Imports

Clubs

Goebel Collectors Club, 105 White Plains Road, Tarrytown, NY 10591
Hummel Collectors Club, 1261 University Dr., Yardley, PA 19067
Rockwell Society of America, P.O. Box 176, Slatersville, RI 02876
American Limited Edition Assoc., Box 1034, Kermit, TX 79745
International Plate Collector's Guild, 260 Claremont Ave., Long Beach,
    CA 90803

Bibliography

Altman, Seymour and Violet. *The Book of Buffalo Pottery*. New York: Crown Publishers, Inc., 1969.

Bloch, Georges. *Picasso*. Berne, Switzerland: Kornfeld et Klipstein, 1972.

Clark, Eleanor. *Plate Collecting*. New Jersey: Citadel Press, Inc., 1977.

Cosentino, Frank J. *Edward Marshall Boehm, 1913-1969*. Trenton, N.J.: Edward Marshall Boehm, Inc., 1970.

Cybis Factory Publication. *Cybis*. Trenton, New Jersey, 1973.

Edward Marshall Boehm Inc. *Boehm Porcelain Objects of Art*. Trenton, N.J., 1976.

Edward Marshall Boehm Studio. *Porcelain Objects of Art 1950 to 1975*. Trenton, N.J., 1975.

Ehrmann, Eric. *Hummel the Complete Collector's Guide and Illustrated Reference*. New York: Portfolio Press Corporation, 1976.

Eyles, Desmond. *Royal Doulton, 1815-1965*. London, England: Hutchinson & Co. Publishers Ltd., 1965.

Krause, Chester L. *Guidebook of Franklin Mint Issues 1978 Edition*. Iola, Wis.: Krause Publications, Inc., 1977.

McGraw-Hill. *1977 The Bradford Book of Collector's Plates*. New York: McGraw-Hill Book Company, 1976.

Melvin, Jean S. *American Glass Paperweights and Their Makers*. New York: Thomas Nelson & Sons, 1967.

New Jersey State Museum. *Cybis in Retrospect*. Trenton, N.J.: New Jersey State Museum, 1970.

Owens, Pat. *The Story of Bing & Grondahl Christmas Plates*. Dayton, Ohio: Viking Import House, Inc., 1962.

————. *The Story of Royal Copenhagen Christmas Plates*. Dayton, Ohio: Viking Import House, Inc., 1961.

Palley, Reese. *The Reese Palley Boehm Collectors Handbook*. Atlantic City, N.J., 1974.

Platt, Dorothy Pickard. *The Story of Pickard China*. Hanover, Pa.: Everybody's Press, Inc., 1970.

Ramié, Georges. *Picasso's Ceramics*. London, England: Secker and Warburg, 1975.

Royal Copenhagen Porcelain Manufactory, The. *Plates from The Royal Copenhagen Porcelain Manufactory*. Copenhagen, Denmark: Gyldendalske Boghandel Nordisk AS, 1970.

Royal Worcester Factory Publication. *The Collector's Handbook of Royal Worcester Models*. England: The Royal Worcester Factory, 1969.

Sandon, Henry. *Royal Worcester Porcelain from 1862 to the Present Day*. New York: Clarkson N. Potter, Inc., 1973.

Selman, Lawrence H., and Linda Pope. *Paperweights for Collectors*. Santa Cruz, Calif.: Paperweight Press, 1975.

Steinke, Violette. *Original Royal Delft Christmas Plates*. Publisher unknown, 1972.

Witt, Louise Schaub. *Wonderful World of Plates, Annual, Christmas and Commemorative with Collector's Price Guide*. North Kansas City, Mo.: Trojan Press, Inc., 1970.

Worcester Royal Porcelain Company, Ltd. *The British Birds of Dorothy Doughty*. Worcester Royal Porcelain Company, Ltd. Worcester, England, 1965.

Magazines and Newspapers of Interest

Annual Bulletin of the Paperweight Collectors' Association. Paul Jokelson, P.O. Box 128, Scarsdale, New York 10583.

Antique Trader. Babka Publishing Co., Inc., P.O. Box 1050, Dubuque, Iowa 52001.

Collectors Editions Quarterly. (Incorporating Acquire).

Collectors News. P.O. Box 156, Grundy Center, Iowa 50638.

Plate Collector. P.O. Box 1041, Kermit, Texas 79745.

Introduction

The term "limited edition" became a part of the collector's vocabulary during the 1960s. Some plates, spoons, and figurines had been produced in limited quantities, but the idea of selling a stated number of pieces was new. An object must have clearly stated limitations of production to be considered a limited edition. Some pieces are announced as "limited to a production of 500." Some are limited in number, and the total number in the edition and the number of the piece are included (for example, a plate may be number 421 of an edition of 500). Many pieces, especially plates, are limited by design. A Christmas plate is produced for the year that it is dated; then, if it is limited, the mold is destroyed and no more are made. The final number of plates produced may or may not be announced by the company. Some firms never reveal their production figures. One set of plates, the Rosenthal Christmas series, was an unlimited series until 1971, when the company began making limited numbers of the year's plate.

The announced limits for a sculpture or paperweight sometimes is higher than the actual production. The time needed to produce 400 or 500 complicated porcelain figurines can be as long as ten years, so a factory might offer several hundred but make fewer, depending on the demand. In several cases a firm changed its marketing approach and reduced the size of a limited edition. If a firm raises the quantity of the edition after it is issued, it would adversely affect the value of the edition and not really be a limited edition.

Limited editions in this book include only plates, figurines, eggs, bells, spoons, forks, plaques, boxes, steins, mugs, urns, Christmas ornaments, and paperweights. Other objects that are in production can be made to announced limits and thereby qualify as limited editions. We have not included such limited items as medals, ingots, prints, books, medallion-like jewelry, or furniture.

History of Limited Editions

The first limited edition is the Bing and Grondahl Christmas plate, made by the Danish factory in 1895. Part of the Danish celebration of Christmas included serving a plate of cookies and perhaps the dish was meant as a special Christmas cookie plate. The factory produced a blue and white dish with the word "Christmas" written in Danish, and the date was part of the design. The next year it probably seemed impossible to sell an out-of-date plate so a new design with the new date was made and the old one was no longer produced. It is not known how many plates were made the first year. Some knowledgeable collectors have said as few as 400 were made. The plate sold for 50 cents, a high price in 1895. The plates sold well, but the Christmas plate idea was not copied by another firm until 1908 when the Royal Copenhagen factory of Denmark began its series. Porsgrund tried selling Christmas plates in Norway in 1909, Rorstrand in Sweden in 1904, and at least one other unknown Danish firm made Christmas plates before 1915. None of these proved successful. The Michelsen Christmas spoon and fork, also made in Denmark, started in 1910 and is still being made each year.

The idea of a limited edition, even one limited to a single year's production, remained a Danish idea. Collectors bought the plates, but owning all the plates in a series did not become a collector's goal until the late 1940s. A few antique dealers began offering older dates of the Christmas plates and some collectors began buying. The new yearly plate was not offered through stores in the United States until 1949. Back-issue plates were all offered at the same price until 1951 when the first price list appeared. Collectors soon began buying and selling; prices for each year were based on supply and demand. The antique collectors were interested enough so that in 1968 when the *Kovels' Complete Antiques Price List* first appeared, Christmas plates were included. Other antiques price lists did not notice the phenomenon until 1972.

The Boehm porcelain pieces made by Edward Marshall Boehm of Trenton, New Jersey, were the first limited edition American porcelain sculptures to gain prominence, made first in 1951. Early pieces were made in small quantities and not made again. It was not until the 1960s that the true limited edition concept was promoted. Edward Boehm died in 1960, but his designs are still being produced.

Several English firms began making limited edition porcelains in the 1930s. Special cups and plates were made to commemorate coronations and jubilees, but they still have not become part of what we now call the limited edition market. It was from 1931 to 1953 that the Royal Doulton factory of England began making a special series of wares in announced limited editions. Jugs and pitchers were made in issues of 1,000 or less and today collectors have begun searching for them to complete collections. Royal Doulton did not begin making limited editions again until 1971.

The Royal Worcester Porcelain Works began making limited editions plates in 1934. These were service plates decorated with birds from Audubon's *Birds of America*. Two editions were made each depicting different birds. The first limited edition figurines featuring King George V and Queen Mary were made in 1935. The edition was announced as 250 pairs, but when the king died, the edition was withdrawn at 72 pairs. The Dorothy Doughty-designed birds were their next limited edition. The first figurine, a pair of "American Redstarts on Hemlock" was made in an edition of 66. The second Doughty edition, "American Goldfinches," was made in an edition of 250. The success of these editions led to more limited edition figures from the factory. The war interrupted, but by the 1940s limited edition items became a regular part of the firm's production.

Paperweights were always produced in small editions because of the problems of manufacture. The Baccarat series, which started in 1953, is considered the first modern limited edition paperweight series. Baccarat sulphide paperweights were made in limits of about 200 for the overlay and 1,000 for the plain weight. Several designs were made each year and they were sold in all parts of the world. None of the limited editions was in great demand until the mid-1960s. Then a small group of collectors developed, so the prices rose, but slowly.

Lalique, the French glass firm, made its first annual crystal plate in 1965. Two thousand were made to sell for $25 each. The limited-edition craze had started and this was the first plate that was not porcelain. Soon other plates, figurines, paperweights, assorted porcelains, and metal objects were being made.

Medals and ingots had a brief flurry of favor in the 1970s. In 1974, when the first edition of this book was written, 46 companies were offering medals and 12 had ingots. Most of them were limited to those sold during a stated time period. The craze has faded, but there are still some medals and ingots being offered for sale in the limited edition market. Their resale market is weak and we have not included them in this edition. These medals differ from the limited type that have been produced by the French mint or the Society of Medalists that are bought by coin collectors. For some reason they have remained out of the volatile limited edition classification. Even inaugural medals have remained in a separate classification among collectors.

The limited edition market became specialized by the 1970s. Books appeared, and ads were placed in the antique trading papers in a special section just for limited editions. Clubs were formed. Conventions were held and special magazines devoted to the limited editions came into print. It was estimated that almost two million collectors were buying limited editions in 1975, over 4 million by 1978 (these figures are given by those making and selling plates). During this period of expansion and promotion, the market went through many stages. Poor-quality merchandise was promoted, sold, and disappeared. The secondary market in limited editions appeared, and older editions could be purchased and sold with ease. Auctions were held, dealers began specializing in limited edition plates, paperweights, figurines, or a combination of items. Many collectors approached the limited edition market as they would the stock market. Everyone had his own system or theory of how to make money in the limited edition market. What would be the next "winner"? What buy would make the most profit? Some sold at a profit and some at a loss, but unfortunately many buyers forgot that the primary reason for buying a limited edition was because of its beauty. The manufacturers never forgot the main reason for making a limited edition was profit.

The Financial History of the Limited Editions Market

Is a limited edition a good investment? Historically some limited editions have fared well and others have not. The porcelain figures by Edward Boehm and the Royal Worcester figures have been bought and

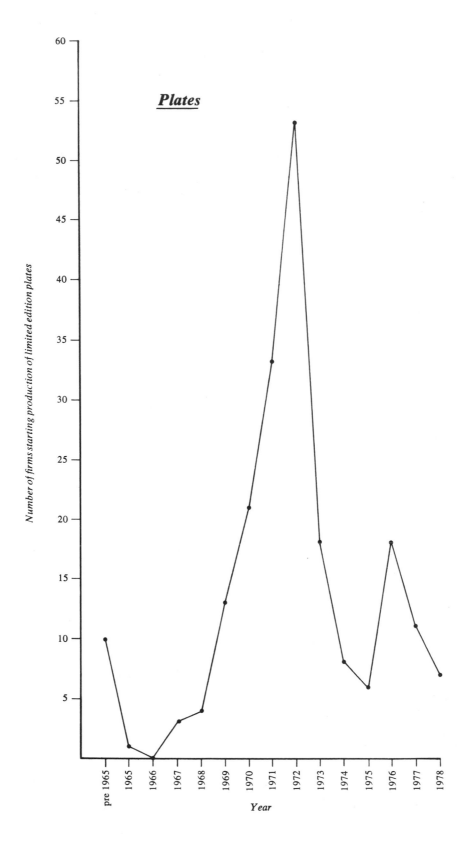

Plates

sold through many auctions, shops, and sales. Prices for some are up far more than expected, if compared with the present rate of inflation. ''H.R.H. Elizabeth riding Tommy,'' a 1947 edition of 100 issued at $275 by Doris Lindner sold in October 1977 for $13,200. Many of the figurines from the 1950s and 1960s have doubled in price. The 1962 edition of a quarter horse is an example. Five hundred of these figurines were issued at $400 each, and some are now selling from $850 to $1,100, depending on whether they were sold at auction or a retail shop. Royal Worcester birds by Dorothy Doughty have always sold well. The first figure, ''American Redstarts and Hemlock,'' is now selling at $5,500, and ''Appleblossoms,'' a 1941 edition of 250 issued at $400, is selling from $1,400 to $3,750. Most of the Royal Worcester issues listed in this book have at least doubled in price. Some have tripled or gone even higher. The

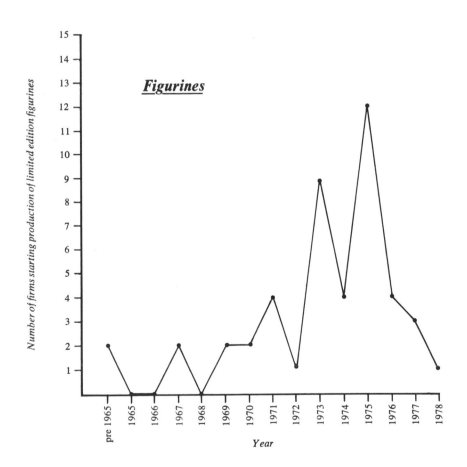

Edward Boehm porcelains show similar gains for the earlier models. In 1958, 500 "American Redstarts" were issued by Boehm and offered at $300. The same issue today costs from $1,600 to $2,750. The 1957 "California Quail" edition of 500 that sold for $300 now sells from $1,600 to $2,600. The "Common Tern," a 1968 series of 400 offered at $1,400, although the subscription is not yet complete, is bringing up to $6,000. The later editions may show no increase over edition prices because they are still in production and available at issue price. A 1970 figure may still be in production in 1978. It is only after the edition is completed that the prices tend to rise. The number of figures in the production of Ispanky, Burgues, Kazmar, Cybis, and others proves that buyer interest in current production is increasing. Many figures have not been available long enough for the secondary sales market to develop.

Paperweights have had a steadily rising secondary market with the increase in cost of new paperweights and the growing number of collectors. Baccarat weights, the first of the type we now refer to as limited editions, such as the 1954 Churchill overlay, of which only 81 were issued at $75, now sell for from $1,500 to $2,000. The Abraham Lincoln regular weights of 1954—1,291 weights at $25 each—now sell for from $300 to $350. The price of the new Baccarat weight is now $85 for the regular weight and $275 for the overlay. The earlier issue paperweights cost $25 for the regular and $75 for the overlay, so a normal rise in secondary market price for the old ones could be expected. Most of the other limited edition paperweights dating from the late 1960s and 1970s are still too new to show much increase in price.

Paperweights are sometimes made in very small numbers for a given design and not officially announced as limited. Many of these weights appear on the limited edition market, but they are really only limited by the number the artist can produce in a period of time.

The plate market appears to be the most favored by the limited edition collectors buying for investment only. Advertisements continue to appear suggesting that a 50-cent plate could be worth $3,000. The ads are truthful, but only part of the story is included. Check carefully before assuming that all limited edition plates are a good investment.

The 1970s brought a rush of plate manufacturers into the market. Plates were made of porcelain, pottery, wood, silver, gold, glass, copper, pewter, and combinations of these materials. The news media began reporting on the plate-collecting phenomenon. Articles in the *Wall Street Journal, New York Times, Time,* and *Forbes,* and syndicated investment columns suggested that plates have been a good investment and that they could be considered more than decorations for the home. Then, as might have been expected, the collectors began to realize that not all plates by all makers were desirable. A process of selection began and dozens of series of plates were discontinued because of a lack of buyers.

Part of the reason for rising prices in the limited edition market is the desire of the collector to own all of a series. When a series is stopped and no new buyers appear the demand is reduced and prices become lower. In the 1970s the established companies continued producing and promoting limited edition plates. Dealers and collectors began studying the supply and demand, and by 1974 the prices began to rise for the more desirable items. A few plates each year seem to be the investor's dream because they have doubled in value in a single year. The best of these are shown in the following table.

Plate	Date	Issue Price	Current Price
Bing and Grondahl Christmas	1895	$ .50	$3,000.00
Bing and Grondahl Mother's Day	1969	8.00	450.00
Franklin Mint Christmas Silver Rockwell	1970	100.00	350.00
Goebel Hummel Annual	1971	25.00	1,000.00
Haviland Christmas	1970	25.00	225.00
Haviland Parlon Tapestry	1971	35.00	240.00
Haviland Parlon Christmas	1972	35.00	200.00
Lakeshore's Rockwell Butter Girl	1973	14.95	95.00
Lalique Annual	1965	25.00	1,750.00
Lenox Boehm	1972	150.00	375.00
Pickard's Alba Madonna	1976	60.00	200.00
Porsgrund Christmas	1968	7.50	180.00
Rivershore's Lincoln No. 1 (Copper)	1976	40.00	160.00
Edna Hibel, Yasuko	1976	275.00	900.00
Royal Copenhagen Christmas	1908	1.00	1,500.00
Royal Doulton Mother's Day	1973	40.00	500.00
Schmid Disney Christmas	1973	10.00	125.00
Wedgwood Christmas	1969	25.00	250.00

How to Invest

Investing in limited editions, especially in plates, requires special information. Part of what appears to be an increase in value can be attributed only to inflation. As each new issue appears the original issue cost rises. This can push up the price of the older pieces to match new prices.

Some of the apparent increase in price is the result of the activities of the manufacturers and not the true demand of collectors. Several plate manufacturers have told us that they will buy back editions of their plates and resell them at a price they set. They deliberately control the secondary market prices. Many companies have asked us to list the plates in this book at their suggested price. (We did not. The prices contained in this book are reports of actual offerings in the marketplace.) There was concern in the limited edition figurine market in 1977 when a well-publicized auction of porcelains was attended by buyers who deliberately bid more than expected so the resale prices in the general market would be increased.

The National Association of Limited Edition Dealers is a business association of the dealers who specialize in selling limited edition pieces. Most of them sell only the current year's production plus any pieces left over from earlier years that are still in their possession. Many dealers make no major attempt to purchase back issues, but there are some dealers who specialize in back issues and will buy and sell in the secondary market. The association had a buy-and-sell list of plates for the members who thereby contacted others for limited editions at wholesale prices. A check of their 1977 listings showed very few plates that were wanted. Most plates listed were offered for sale. Those on the want list included selected years of the Bing and Grondahl Christmas plates dating from 1907 through 1967; d'Arceau Limoges Christmas, 1975; the Fenton carnival Christmas plate, 1973; Georg Jensen Christmas, 1975; Goebel Hummel annual plates, 1971 to 1973; Gorham DeGrazia 1975; Lincoln Mint, 1972 Mother's Day; Pickard eagle, 1974; Porsgrund Mother's Day, 1972; Rockwell Society Christmas 1974, 1975; Rosenthal Christmas plates, selected years from 1917 to 1948; the Royal Copenhagen Christmas plates from 1911 through 1973; Schmid Hummel Christmas 1971-1973. Of all the hundreds of plates listed in this book those mentioned above are the only more-than-one-year-old plates that the association dealers seemed to be actively buying. Apparently there are only a few plates that are not easily available in the resale markets. Others must be available or else are so scarce the dealers don't even bother to search for them.

It is not enough to just buy a plate and plan to resell it for a profit in future years. Every investor must remember that the new buyer will expect the plate to be in mint condition, preferably with the original box and the original papers. One recent ad offered $50 for the empty box to hold a 1971 plate. We can't help but imagine a collector with a living room featuring plates on the wall and shelves and an attic filled to the rafters with empty boxes.

Collectors usually buy at retail and resell at wholesale. This means that to be a good investment a limited edition must more than double. At best the wholesale price is 40 to 50% less than the retail.

A Few Hints about What Might Go Up in Price

The limited edition pieces such as Christmas plates, bells, spoons, and other seasonal items often go through a price cycle. When first announced for the year the retail price is asked by most dealers. A few will offer one or two items at a discounted price to lure new customers. In January, when another year's offering will soon be available, the price of last year's pieces often goes down. That does not mean that these same pieces may not again go up in price later in the year if the demand increases.

Most of the pieces, plates, figurines, and paperweights that have increased in value were made by well-known companies or were "firsts." The first glass plate, the first copper plate, the first Rockwell plate, the earliest figurines by Boehm, Ispanky, or Cybis, and the first Baccarat sulphide paperweights, and so on, have increased in value simply because the first is the oldest of the series. It could also be that the supply is the smallest the first year. Many collectors who begin their collection a year or two later want to own all back issues.

Never buy part of a set if a full set is offered at issue time. The Franklin Mint editions that are offered for sale over a period of years have almost no resale value until the final piece has been issued. If you stop buying in the middle of the series it is almost impossible to sell a partial set for anything but a loss. Never buy a damaged piece. The resale value is low. Expensive plates and porcelain should be checked with a black light to assure condition.

Investing Theories

There are many different theories about what makes a popular limited edition that will have a continually rising resale price.

Theory 1

Buy the first piece by any reputable, known firm that has announced it as part of a series. (This is the old "first-in-the-series-will-go-up-in-value" theory.)

Theory 2

A piece must have the correct limits. Not too large (over 15,000 for plates is too big a supply) and not too small (for a plate, under 2,000 is so small the demand will not develop). The rule about "too small" does not seem to apply to figurines or paperweights.

Theory 3

Buy it for its artistic value or because you like it. The problem with this is that the "most beautiful" or the "most artistic" is so subjective, determined only by an individual's taste. It is not a very reliable indication of what the average buyer may or may not want to own.

Theory 4

Buy from well-known manufacturers. This has been productive in many cases but there is always the exception and a few small firms have issued limited editions that grew quickly in value. The Edward Marshall Boehm pieces of the 1950s and 1960s were made by a relatively unknown artist, yet today because the company has gained in size and prominence, the early figures are sold for high prices.

Theory 5

Buy only numbered and signed editions. There seems little validity to this theory because the numbered, signed pieces that are often sold at a higher price at issue do not seem to go up on a percentage basis with any more regularity than unsigned editions.

Theory 6

Buy the best workmanship. This is valid because poor quality, badly designed editions have not retained value in the market. Buyers are aware of quality.

Theory 7

Buy the works of popular artists. A few artists have become the favorites of limited edition buyers. Some of the paperweight makers, the top four or five firms making porcelain figurines, and some of the plate artists seem to sell out each edition quickly. Edna Hibel, Lorainne Trester, Norman Rockwell, and Berta Hummel have been able to design top-selling pieces for several firms. Many buyers seem to favor these artists.

Theory 8

Buy the popular designs. For example, a figurine of a dolphin made by Gunther Granget appeared in 1970; it was an immediate success and rose in price. Since then other firms have made very successful dolphin figurines. Why? The dolphin is the symbol of the submarine service and many naval officers' clubs wanted to display the figurines.

Theory 9

The original price of the limited edition has little effect on the future percentage of increase or decrease. True.

It is certainly indisputable that you should never buy a piece that has not been produced. The finished limited edition could look very different from the proposed sketch. One silver plate that was to have been carved was merely acid engraved, some porcelain pieces were decorated with decals, not by hand, and some of the proposed figurines were advertised without the exact size.

Don't assume that a piece that is made from silver or gold has more value than one made from porcelain or wood. The melt-down value of the metal is usually a very small percentage of the purchase price. You are paying for the design, workmanship, promotion, and quantity issued.

Be wary of the pieces sold through high-pressure advertising and promises of dollar profits if you buy.

One company offered a plate with a guaranteed buy-back price. The U.S. Securities and Exchange Commission declared the plate to be a prohibited security when accompanied by a guarantee of increased market value. The SEC ruled that the plates, if offered with a guarantee that they will double in value, must be registered as a security under the Securities Act of 1933. The company then began to write about it as "the first plate offer ever declared a security, like stocks and bonds, by the U.S. Securities and Exchange Commission" and "it was even guaranteed to double in value until the U.S. Securities and Exchange Commission declared this to be a security." Other advertising compared the collector plate market to the securities market. All of this can be misleading if the advertising is not read with great care.

There are still some buy-back offers but these are so carefully worded in the offering they really mean very little to the investor.

Some are limited to a 15-day examination period; most require the original box and certificate to be returned.

No investment in art can be quickly converted into cash. Do not buy limited editions expecting to buy and resell in a short period of time, or even to sell after you decide you want to sell. To take advantage of the rise in market price a buyer must wait for the proper auction, or sale, or a buyer to be found through an ad. It is a slow process. There are no dividends on your investment as there might be when you buy stock or deposit money in the bank. Don't think about limited editions as investments in those terms. There is the cost of insurance, the danger of breakage and theft, the problem of storage and display, and many other related problems in buying limited editions.

Buy any of the limited editions that appeal to you and that you want to own and admire. The value of having beautiful objects in your possession can not be measured in dollars. Many of the limited editions are works of art. The promotion and investment possibilities are not the reason for their manufacture. Even if these pieces were in unlimited production there would still be a strong market.

Fakes

No one involved in making limited editions wants to suggest there might be fakes and forgeries. Two types of problem categories do exist: those involving changes in production quantity and actual fakes. There have been times when an edition was announced, the maker noticed the strong demand, and soon announced a second group of the identical item. Nothing was changed, but the manufacturer claimed it was a new series of the old edition. No suggestion was made in the first advertisements that a second series would be forthcoming.

Some fake plates have been made, and some of the reproductions are so good that they could fool a collector. We understand that this is true with a few of the 1940s Danish Christmas plates.

Some original plates that were seconds at the factory have been sold. These can be recognized by a scratch through the glaze over the mark on the bottom of the piece. They are worth less than a first-quality piece. A few fake Baccarat paperweights have been made and marked with the original mark. These are slightly different in size and quality than the originals. Porcelain figures do not seem to be faked often but a few pieces have been seen with well-known marks forged onto the bottom. Only the most unsophisticated beginner would be fooled by the quality.

Always buy art, limited editions included, from a reputable dealer. If there is any question of condition or origin a reliable dealer will refund your money. Beware of buying any limited editions that are priced too far below the market price. If they later prove to be stolen merchandise you lose not only the limited editions but your money.

Records

When you buy limited editions keep complete records of your purchases. The source, date of purchase, price, and any information about the edition should be recorded for your own purposes and for future use by your heirs or buyers. A photograph of the piece is also a good idea to complete your record. Any large collection should be covered by a special fine-arts insurance policy. Your regular homeowners insurance will not adequately cover your loss in case of fire, theft, or breakage. Try to display breakable figurines or porcelains behind glass. Fragile porcelain can be broken, metal or glass pieces can be scratched. Children and enthusiastic cleaning can do the most damage.

1. Figurines

Title	Issue Date	Number Issued	Issued Price	Current Price
Baccarat limited editions are made in France by La Compagnie des Cristalleries de Baccarat, located near Paris. The factory was started in 1765. The firm went bankrupt and started operating again about 1822. Famous cane and millefiori paperweights were made there during the 1860-1880 period. In 1953, after a lapse of 80 years, sulphide paperweights were again introduced. A series of limited edition paperweights has been made each year since 1953.				

See listing for Baccarat in Paperweight section

Baccarat, Owl

Baccarat Crystal Sculptures

Title	Issue Date	Number Issued	Issued Price	Current Price
Cat, Signed Robert Rigot		500	330.00	Unknown
Egyptian Falcon, 6 3/4 X 5 1/4 In.		100	400.00	Unknown
Owl, Signed Robert Rigot*		500	450.00	Unknown
Penguin, Signed Robert Rigot*		500	500.00	Unknown
Winged Bull, 5 1/4 X 1 3/8 In.		250	400.00	Unknown

Bing & Grondahl

Title	Issue Date	Number Issued	Issued Price	Current Price
Bald Eagle, Porcelain	1976	100	2500.00	2250.00 to 2500.00
Drummer Boy, Decorated	1976	100	2500.00	2250.00 to 2500.00
Drummer Boy, White	1976	750	500.00	500.00

Boehm porcelains were first made by Edward Marshall Boehm in Trenton, New Jersey, in 1950. The Malvern Boehm Studio of England was established after Mr. Boehm's death in 1969. Bone porcelain Boehm flowers and figurines are made at the English studio. Hard paste porcelains are still made in New Jersey and England. Lenox China has also issued a limited edition plate series featuring Boehm birds.

See listing for Boehm in Plate section

Boehm Porcelains

Title	Issue Date	Number Issued	Issued Price	Current Price
Adios	1969	130	1500.00	825.00 to 1500.00
African Elephant, Cow, Calf*	1977	50	9500.00	9500.00
American Cocker, Decorated	1951		7.50	375.00 to 575.00
American Cocker, White	1951		7.50	425.00 to 450.00
American Eagle, Large	1957	31	225.00	250.00 to 8500.00
American Eagle, Small	1957	76	150.00	6400.00
American Redstarts	1958	500	300.00	1600.00 to 2750.00
Arabian Stallions	1955	135	110.00	2900.00 to 3400.00
Barn Owl*	1972	350	3600.00	2900.00 to 5000.00
Basset Hound	1957	410	27.50	1300.00 to 1500.00
Beagle	1952	400	12.50	450.00 to 600.00
Bicentennial, Eagle Of Freedom I	1976	15	35000.00	35000.00

Baccarat, Penguin

Boehm, Colt, Emerald Eyes, 1978

Boehm, Barn Owl

Boehm, Black Grouse

Title	Issue Date	Number Issued	Issued Price	Current Price
Bicentennial, Young And Spirited Eaglets	1975	1121	950.00	950.00
Black Angus Bull	1950	200	20.00	650.00 to 1400.00
Blackbirds	1973	75	5400.00	5400.00
Black-Headed Grosbeak*	1969	750	900.00	1200.00 to 1500.00
Black Grouse*	1972	175	2800.00	1600.00 to 3400.00
Black-Tailed Bantams	1956	51	200.00	3000.00 to 7000.00
Black-Throated Blue Warbler	1958	500	400.00	400.00 to 1650.00
Blue Grosbeak And Oak Leaves	1967	750	500.00	425.00 to 1250.00
Blue Jays On Strawberries, 3	1962	250	2000.00	7250.00 to 7250.00
Blue Tits With Apple Blossoms	1973	300	2200.00	1400.00 to 2200.00
Bobcats	1971	200	1600.00	900.00 to 1800.00
Bobolink With Corn Stubble	1964	500	450.00	1100.00 to 1900.00
Bob White Quail	1953	750	200.00	1900.00 to 3400.00
Boxer, Large	1952	500	12.50	325.00 to 600.00
Boxer, Small	1952	400	6.00	250.00 to 500.00
Brahman Bull, Bisque White	1953	10	100.00	Unknown
Brahman Bull, Glazed Dapple	1953	50	100.00	Unknown
Brahman Bull, Glazed Red	1953	25	100.00	Unknown
Brown Pelican*	1972	100	9500.00	9500.00 to 10500.00
Brown Thrasher With Crocus	1973	400	1700.00	1700.00
Bunny Box With Carrot	1955	63	8.00	700.00 to 800.00
Bunny Female	1954	532	4.00	250.00 to 325.00
Bunny Milk Mug	1955	93	5.00	550.00 to 700.00
Cachette, French	1954	1766	12.50	450.00 to 550.00
Cactus Wren	1972	400	2400.00	1200.00 to 2800.00
California Quail	1957	500	300.00	1600.00 to 2600.00
Canada Warbler, Fledgling	1967	750	450.00	1500.00 to 2000.00
Canvasback Ducks	1951	74		750.00
Cape May Warbler	1977	500	750.00	750.00
Cardinals, Decorated, Pair	1955	500	450.00	2700.00 to 3800.00
Cardinals II**	1977	400	3200.00	3200.00
Carolina Wrens With Sugar Maple	1957	100	650.00	3250.00 to 5500.00
Cat With Kittens	1954	146	25.00	475.00 to 575.00
Catbird With Hyacinths*	1965	500	900.00	1050.00 to 2700.00
Cedar Waxwings	1956	100	600.00	3750.00 to 5250.00
Cerulean Warbler With Wild Roses	1957	100	750.00	2600.00 to 8000.00
Chaffinch	1974	200	1800.00	Unknown
Cheetah Head	1977	1000	275.00	275.00
Chick	1954	321	6.00	350.00 to 400.00
Chickadees And Holly Sculpture	1976	500	1150.00	1150.00
Child King*	1978	1000	975.00	975.00
Chipmunk Preening, Bisque Decorated	1959	317	35.00	Unknown
Chrysanthemum & Butterfly	1972	350	950.00	1200.00 to 1400.00
Cockatoo And Flowers, Painting On Porcelain	1971	50	4200.00	4200.00
Collie	1954	200	28.00	300.00 to 725.00
Colt, Emerald Eyes*	1978	400	650.00	650.00
Common Tern	1968	500	1400.00	3520.00 to 6000.00
Cottontail Bunny		25	5.00	850.00 to 950.00
Crested Flycatcher With Sweet Gum	1967	500	1650.00	1800.00 to 3400.00
Crested Tit	1974	500	850.00	Unknown
Cupid With Horn	1956	230	12.50	325.00 to 375.00
Dachshund	1953	235	2500.00	600.00 to 700.00
Daisies, Yellow	1971	350	600.00	Unknown
Debutante Camellia	1974	500	400.00	Unknown
Diana With Fawn	1953	42	35.00	375.00 to 650.00
Doberman Pinscher, Black Glazed	1951	200	12.50	Unknown
Doberman Pinscher, Red Glazed	1951	10	12.50	Unknown
Dogwood - Cornus Nuttali	1973	350	575.00	575.00
Double Peony, Pink	1974	400	550.00	Unknown
Downy Woodpeckers With Trumpet Vine	1957	500	400.00	1000.00 to 2300.00
Dutch Boy & Girl	1949	24	1.00	1500.00 to 2000.00
Eagle Of Freedom II	1976	300	5500.00	5500.00
Eastern Bluebirds With Rhododendron	1959	100	1800.00	5500.00 to 7200.00
Eastern Bluebird II, Wild Rose**	1977	400	2100.00	2100.00
Eastern Kingbird	1975	200	3200.00	Unknown
Edward Boehm Camellia	1978	500	400.00	450.00
Elephant Calf, Diamond Eyes	1977	400	850.00	850.00
Emmett Barnes II Camellia	1975	400	400.00	Unknown
English Bulldog	1957	46	25.00	1050.00 to 1900.00
Etrafon Head	1962	5000	5.00	100.00 to 150.00

Boehm, Black-Headed Grosbeak

Boehm, Green Jays

Boehm, Everglades Kite

Boehm, Foxes

Boehm, Goldcrest

Boehm, Catbird   Helen Boehm, Daylily, 1978

Boehm, African Elephant, Cow, Calf, 1977

Boehm, Mockingbirds, 1978

Boehm, Brown Pelican

Boehm, Orchard Oriole

Boehm, Hunter

Boehm, Child King, 1978

Boehm, Kestrels

Title	Issue Date	Number Issued	Issued Price	Current Price
European Goldfinch	1975	400	850.00	Unknown
Everglades Kites*	1973	50	5800.00	5800.00
Falcon Emblems, Pair*	1978	500	750.00	750.00
Falcon Head	1977	1000	300.00	300.00
Fawn	1954	50	10.00	700.00 to 850.00
Field Mouse With Vetch	1957	479	20.00	325.00 to 400.00
Fledgling Purple Finches, Bisque Decorated	1960	420	85.00	950.00
Flicker	1971	300	2200.00	2800.00 to 3000.00
Fluted Urn	1952	925	4.00	200.00 to 250.00
Fondo Marino	1970	25	2850.00	2850.00 to 3300.00
Foxes*	1971	200	1800.00	1800.00
Foxhound, Reclining	1952	225	22.50	425.00 to 1600.00
French Poodle, Standing	1952	150	40.00	425.00 to 800.00
Frog, Sapphire Eyes	1978	400	300.00	300.00
Gentians, Blue	1974	400	300.00	Unknown
German Shepherd	1957	25	25.00	1500.00 to 1800.00
Giant Panda	1975	100	3800.00	Unknown
God Anubis	1977	1000	375.00	375.00
Goddess Bastet	1977	1000	325.00	325.00
Goddess Selket	1977	1000	850.00	850.00
Gold Rose, Diamond Dew Drop	1978	400	450.00	450.00
Goldcrest With Larch*	1972	500	650.00	650.00 to 900.00
Golden-Crowned Kinglets With Oriental Poppie	1956	500	375.00	1300.00 to 2800.00
Golden Pheasant, Decorated	1954	7	350.00	6250.00
Golden Pheasant, White	1954	7	200.00	Unknown
Goldfinches With Scottish Thistle	1961	500	400.00	700.00 to 2100.00
Gorilla	1978	75	3500.00	3500.00
Great Dane, Reclining	1951	450	10.00	550.00 to 650.00
Great Horned Owl, Fledgling	1965	750	350.00	850.00 to 1500.00
Green Jays With Persimmons*	1966	400	185.00	2700.00 to 3400.00
Green-Winged Teal	1951	96		700.00
Green Woodpeckers	1973	50	4200.00	2600.00
Guardian Figures, Pair	1978	500	1700.00	1700.00
Helen Boehm, Daylily*	1978	500	750.00	750.00
Helen Boehm, Yellow Iris	1978	500	750.00	750.00
Hereford Bull	1950	196	30.00	900.00 to 2500.00
Hooded Mergansers	1968	500	1600.00	1600.00 to 2400.00
Hooded Warbler	1974	300	2400.00	Unknown
Horned Larks With Wild Grapes	1973	300	3800.00	3800.00
Hunter, Bay*	1952	250	125.00	650.00 to 1000.00
Hunter, Dapple Gray	1952	8	125.00	3750.00 to 4500.00
Hunter, White	1952	16		1200.00 to 1750.00
Kestrels*	1968	500	1800.00	1000.00 to 2800.00
Killdeer, Pair With Bluebells	1964	300	175.00	3080.00 to 6200.00
Kingfishers	1976	350	1200.00	Unknown
Lady Of Grace, Bisque White	1954	99	15.00	Unknown
Lady Of Grace, Glazed White	1954	20	15.00	Unknown
Lapwing	1973	100	2600.00	1450.00 to 2600.00
Lark Sparrow	1974	200	2100.00	2100.00
Lazuli Buntings With Wild Daisies	1973	400	1800.00	1000.00 to 2300.00
Lesser Prairie Chickens, Decorated, Pair	1962	300	1200.00	950.00 to 2000.00
Lion Cub	1954	125	15.00	450.00 to 1300.00
Little Owl, Malvern	1971	200	800.00	800.00 to 1200.00
Longtail Tit	1973	350	1450.00	3600.00
Madonna With Child, Della Robbia	1959	120	35.00	500.00 to 1200.00
Magnolia Grandiflora	1975	750	550.00	Unknown
Mallards, Pair	1952	500	180.00	500.00 to 1250.00
Mask Of Tutankhamun	1977	1000	2700.00	2700.00
Meadowlark With Dandelions And Mushrooms	1957	750	225.00	1300.00 to 3000.00
Mearns Quail, Pair, With Cactus	1963	350	950.00	1550.00 to 3500.00
Mercury	1953	100	28.00	425.00 to 600.00
Mergansers, Pair	1968	500	2000.00	Unknown
Mockingbirds*	1978	500	1600.00	1600.00
Mockingbirds, Pair With Bindweed	1961	500	650.00	2250.00 to 3800.00
Mountain Bluebirds With Magnolia	1963	300	1900.00	2860.00 to 5700.00
Mourning Doves	1958	500	250.00	725.00 to 1100.00
Mustangs, American	1976	100	3200.00	3200.00
Mute Swans*	1971	400	3400.00	3400.00 to 8000.00
Myrtle Warblers	1974	400	1500.00	1500.00
Neptune With Seahorse	1953	54	35.00	500.00 to 1200.00

Boehm, Peregrine Falcon

Boehm,
Verdins With Stewart Crucifixion-Thorn

Boehm, Otter, 1976

Boehm, Mute Swans (Bird Of Peace)

Boehm, Sacred Ibis, 1978

Boehm, Falcon Emblems, Pair, 1978

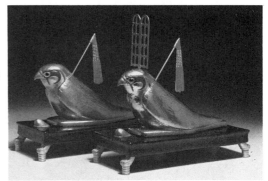

Boehm, Swan Centerpiece With Camellias, 1971

Boehm, Sugarbirds

Boehm, Yellowhammer On Hawthorn

Burgues, American Goldfinches
With Morning Glories

Burgues, Baltimore Oriole

Burgues, Young Burro

Burgues, Bighorn Sheep

Title	Issue Date	Number Issued	Issued Price	Current Price
Newborn Rabbits	1958	7		1250.00
Nonpareil Buntings	1958	750	175.00	800.00 to 1250.00
Northern Water Thrush	1967	500	800.00	950.00 to 2000.00
Nuthatch With Mushroom	1971	350	650.00	650.00 to 1000.00
Nuthatch With Mushroom, Signed	1971	350	650.00	450.00 to 1200.00
Nyala Antelope	1973	100	4700.00	4700.00
Obelisks, Pair	1978	500	650.00	650.00
Orchard Orioles*	1970	600	1200.00	1300.00 to 2000.00
Orchid Cactus	1976	500	600.00	600.00
Orchid Centerpiece**	1970	150	6200.00	8200.00 to 8500.00
Otter*	1976	100	950.00	950.00
Oven-Bird	1970	500	1050.00	1050.00 to 1800.00
Owl, Diamond Eyes	1978	400	500.00	500.00
Parula Warblers With Wild Morning Glories	1965	400	1500.00	1850.00 to 3200.00
Peace Rose, Supreme	1976	250	750.00	750.00
Pekin Robins	1975	100	6500.00	Unknown
Percheron Colt, Palomino	1952	100	10.00	1750.00 to 2250.00
Percheron Mare, Decorated	1950	50	25.00	2700.00 to 3000.00
Percheron Mare, White	1950	50	25.00	1300.00 to 1500.00
Percheron Stallion, Decorated	1950	200	30.00	1500.00 to 2750.00
Percheron Stallion, White	1950	50	30.00	3900.00 to 4000.00
Peregrine Falcon*	1973	350	3400.00	3400.00
Perfume Bottles	1978	1000	350.00	350.00
Pointer, Liver & White	1952	150	17.50	1700.00 to 1900.00
Polo Player	1957	100	850.00	3450.00 to 5000.00
Poodle, French, Reclining	1959	2300	8.50	195.00
Poodle, Ruby Eyes	1978	400	400.00	400.00
Pope Pius XII Bust	1958	50	400.00	500.00 to 1000.00
Ptarmigans	1962	350	800.00	1760.00
Pug Dog	1959	48	25.00	850.00 to 950.00
Puma	1975	50	5200.00	Unknown
Purple Martins	1974	50	6700.00	Unknown
Queen Of The Night Cactus	1976	500	600.00	600.00
Raccoons	1971	200	1600.00	1600.00 to 1800.00
Red-Billed Blue Magpie	1975	100	4200.00	420.00
Redbreasted Grosbeaks, Pair	1952	422	20.00	1000.00 to 3600.00
Red Squirrel	1954	94	4.00	Unknown
Red Squirrels With Oak	1972	100	2600.00	1400.00 to 2850.00
Red-Winged Blackbirds	1957	100	700.00	4250.0 to 7500.00
Ring-Necked Pheasants, Pair	1954	500	250.00	700.00 to 1800.00
Rivoli's Hummingbird	1976	500	650.00	Unknown
Roadrunner	1968	500	1700.00	2500.00 to 3700.00
Rose, Supreme Yellow	1976	250	750.00	750.00
Robin With Daffodils	1964	500	600.00	3500.00 to 4800.00
Robin II	1977	500	1300.00	1300.00
Ruby-Crowned Kinglets	1957	300	150.00	800.00 to 1500.00
Ruby-Throated Hummingbird	1974	300	1700.00	Unknown
Ruffed Grouse	1960	250	950.00	4000.00 to 5900.00
Ruffed Grouse II, With Chicks**	1977	200	3500.00	3500.00
Rufous Hummingbirds	1966	500	850.00	700.00 to 2000.00
Sacred Cow Head	1977	1000	325.00	325.00
Sacred Ibis*	1978	1000	325.00	325.00
Saint Francis Of Assisi	1958	264	75.00	1200.00 to 2000.00
Saint Maria Goretti	1952	233	10.00	175.00 to 600.00
Scarlet Tanager, With Oak	1977	400	1800.00	1800.00
Scissor-Tailed Flycatcher	1977	200	2400.00	2400.00
Scottish Terrier, Black	1954		600.00	550.00
Scottish Terrier, Grey	1951	210	6.00	1250.00 to 3000.00
Screech Owl	1973	500	850.00	800.00 to 1200.00
Shorthorn Bull, Glazed Red	1951	100	20.00	Unknown
Shorthorn Bull, Glazed Roan	1951	50	20.00	Unknown
Shorthorn Bull, Glazed White	1951	25	20.00	Unknown
Siamese Dancers	1949	200	1.00	Unknown
Slate-Colored Junco With Lyracantha	1970	600	1100.00	1200.00 to 1550.00
Snow Buntings	1972	400	1600.00	1600.00 to 2300.00
Snow Leopard	1978	75	3500.00	3500.00
Song Sparrows, Pair, With Tulips	1956	50	2000.00	8800.00 to 12500.00
Song Thrushes	1974	100	2800.00	Unknown
Stonechats	1974	150	2200.00	Unknown
Streptocalyx Peoppigii	1973	50	3400.00	Unknown

Burgues, King Penguins

Burgues, Red-Breasted Nuthatch

Burgues, Snow Bunting, Juvenile

Burgues, Magnolia

Burgues, Crab-Eater Seals

Burgues, Pink Lady Slipper Orchid

Burgues, Robin, Juvenile

Burgues, American Wild Goat, 1976

Burgues, Robin With Marsh Marigolds

Burgues, Red-Headed Woodpecker

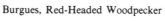

Burgues, Snowy Owl

Burgues,
Black-Tailed Prairie Dog

Burgues, Rhododendron

Burgues, Madonna

Title	Issue Date	Number Issued	Issued Price	Current Price
Sugarbirds*	1961	100	2500.00	6250.00 to 10000.00
Swallows	1974	350	3400.00	Unknown
Swan Centerpiece With Camellias*	1971	135	1950.00	3000.00
Swan Lake Camellia	1976	750	575.00	Unknown
Sweet Viburnum	1971	35	650.00	Unknown
Towhee	1963	500	350.00	1200.00 to 2400.00
Tree Creepers	1972	200	3200.00	1600.00 to 3700.00
Tropicana Rose	1978	500	450.00	450.00
Tufted Titmice	1965	500	500.00	900.00 to 1800.00
Turtle, Sapphire Eyes	1978	400	300.00	300.00
Varied Buntings	1965	300	2200.00	1600.00 to 4000.00
Varied Thrush	1974	400	1800.00	1800.00
Venus	1953	96	28.00	600.00 to 700.00
Verdins With Stewart Crucifixion-Thorn*	1969	600	800.00	900.00 to 1150.00
Waterlily, Blue	1974	750	350.00	350.00
Western Bluebirds With Azaleas	1969	400	4500.00	3300.00 to 5000.00
Western Meadowlark	1971	400	1100.00	1100.00 to 1200.00
Whippets	1954	248	50.00	3000.00 to 9000.00
White Mouse Preening	1957	469	15.00	250.00 to 350.00
Winter Robin With English Holly	1971	225	1150.00	650.00 to 1500.00
Wirehaired Fox Terrier	1951	150	12.50	400.00 to 500.00
Woodcock	1954	494	250.00	1050.00 to 2400.00
Wood Ducks, Pair	1952	201	30.00	1200.00 to 1400.00
Woodthrush	1966	400	3500.00	5000.00 to 8400.00
Woodthrush With Crabapple		2		750.00
Yellow-Bellied Sapsucker, Wild Appleblossom	1972	250	2700.00	1100.00 to 3750.00
Yellow-Billed Cuckoo	1974	200	2800.00	2800.00
Yellowhammer On Hawthorn*	1973	350	2800.00	2000.00 to 2800.00
Yellow-Headed Blackbird	1974	75	3200.00	3200.00
Young American Eagle	1969	850	700.00	800.00 to 1900.00
Young And Spirited 1976	1975	1121	950.00	Unknown

Borsato Porcelains have been made by Antonio Borsato of Milan, Italy, since 1937. Limited editions were first made in 1973.

See listing for Borsato in Plate section

Borsato Porcelains

Don Quixote				420.00
Fisherman, Head				510.00
Morsels Of Wisdom**	1974	100	2600.00	2600.00
St.George And The Dragon				1700.00

Dr. Irving Burgues, Austrian-born artist, is the designer of Burgues porcelains. His studio is located in Ocean County, New Jersey. Burgues porcelains are in the collections of many museums.

Burgues Porcelains

American Goldfinches With Morning Glories*		350	1250.00	1700.00
American Wild Goat*	1976	10		10000.00
Anemone		350	550.00	600.00
Anniversary Orchid	1976	200		75.00 to 75.00
Baltimore Oriole, Juvenile*		200	750.00	825.00
Barn Swallows, Pewter, American Express	1976	Year	100.00	150.00
Barrel Cactus	1977	500	200.00	225.00
Bay-Breasted Warbler		950	175.00	190.00
Belted Kingfisher Fledgling		750	350.00	500.00
Bighorn Sheep*		250	2750.00	3100.00
Bighorn Sheep, Glazed**		25	3000.00	3400.00
Black-Capped Chickadee	1976	950	145.00	160.00
Black-Tailed Prairie Dog*		950	195.00	1375.00
Burro, Young*		300	1250.00	1250.00
Canyon Wren		250	850.00	925.00
Cardinal, Juvenile		500	250.00	275.00
Carolina Wren With White Dogwood		350	750.00	825.00
Cassin's Kingbird		50	750.00	825.00
Cave Swallows, Male And Female		500	750.00	2800.00
Chanticleer**		100	1300.00	1850.00
Chestnut-Backed Chickadee		950		160.00
Chestnut-Sided Warbler		950		190.00
Chickadee On Dogwood		75	950.00	1100.00

Title	Issue Date	Number Issued	Issued Price	Current Price
Chipmunk With Acorn		750	150.00	350.00
Chipmunk With Fly Amanita		450	400.00	500.00
Clematis Sieboldi		500	175.00	190.00
Crab-Eater Seals*		200	1250.00	1375.00
Cymbidium Orchid		200		75.00
Daffodil Manco		250	450.00	500.00
Ecstasy, Paphiopedilum Orchid	1978	200		90.00
Golden-Crowned Kinglet		450	500.00	550.00
Golden-Winged Warbler In Nest		100	1100.00	1650.00
Great White Heron, Pewter, American Express	1976	Year	100.00	160.00
Heavenly Blue Morning Glory	1978	300	200.00	200.00
Hibiscus		200		85.00
Imperial Gold Lily		200		225.00
Junco On Snow		250	600.00	650.00
King Penguins*		350	850.00	925.00
Lilac Charm Rose	1973	75	700.00	775.00
Lily Harlequin**		250	575.00	635.00
Lucy's Warbler		950		190.00
Madonna*		30	125.00	2700.00
Magnolia, Oriental Strain*	1973	150	1600.00	1750.00
Magnolia Warbler	1976	950	145.00	160.00
Parula Warbler	1976	950	190.00	175.00 to 190.00
Perfection, Paphiopedilum Orchid	1978	200		90.00
Pileated Woodpecker	1976	350	225.00	225.00
Pink Glory Lily		200		225.00
Pink Lady Slipper Orchid		350	800.00	875.00
Polar Bear	1976	950	215.00	215.00
Polar Bear, Cubs	1976	950	185.00	185.00
Prickly Pear Cactus		250	900.00	995.00
Pygmy Owl, Pewter, American Express	1976	Year	100.00	100.00
Red-Breasted Nuthatch*		950	225.00	250.00
Redheaded Woodpecker*		350	1100.00	1200.00
Red Squirrel	1976	950	195.00	195.00
Rhododendron*		200	375.00	400.00
Robin, Juvenile**		950	150.00	175.00
Robin With Marsh Marigolds*		500	550.00	490.00 to 600.00
Ruby-Throated Hummingbird**		300	600.00	650.00
Rufous Hummingbird, Allamanda		350		300.00
Saw-Whet Owl		350		275.00
Snow Bunting, Juvenile*		950	165.00	185.00
Snow Bunting With Trumpet Honeysuckle		500	350.00	200.00 to 385.00
Snowy Owl*		500	450.00	260.00 to 495.00
Spirit Of Freedom, Equus Caballus, Color**	1976	50	1500.00	1500.00
Spirit Of Freedom, Equus Caballus, White	1976	50	1000.00	1000.00
Springtime, Paphiopedilum Orchid	1978	200		90.00
Sunny Glow, Paphiopedilum Orchid	1978	200		90.00
Veiltail Goldfish, Clear Glaze		150	875.00	1100.00
Veiltail Goldfish, Decorated		150	875.00	950.00
Water Lily		200	175.00	275.00
Water Lily Fire Crest		75	1250.00	1375.00
White-Breasted Nuthatches		75	3500.00	3850.00
White-Throated Sparrow	1973	250	800.00	800.00 to 875.00
Wild Rose		150	2500.00	2750.00
Wood Duckling		950		175.00
Wood Ducks, Pewter, American Express	1976	Year	100.00	100.00
Wood Thrush, Juvenile		500	225.00	265.00
Yellow-Billed Cuckoo		500	400.00	450.00
Yellow-Billed Cuckoo, Juvenile		950	175.00	190.00
Yellow Warbler		75	700.00	950.00
Young Burro*		300	1250.00	1375.00
Young Cottontail	1978	950	185.00	185.00
Young Saw-Whet Owl		350	500.00	550.00
Young Walrus	1976	950	225.00	225.00

Calhoun Collectors Society, metal

Title	Issue Date	Number Issued	Issued Price	Current Price
World Hall Of Presidents, 37	1977	2950	50.00	50.00
Eagles, Granget	1977	7490	300.00	300.00

Cappe Porcelain is made by the Royal Crown Porcelain Factory of Italy.

Title	Issue Date	Number Issued	Issued Price	Current Price
Cappe Porcelain				
American Wild Goat		10	10000.00	10000.00
The Battle, 15-3/4 In. X 18-1/2 In.		500	2250.00	2750.00
Sleeping Fisherman				450.00

C. E. Kloos, See Wildlife of the World Series.

The Coalport Studio at Stoke-on-Trent was founded in 1799 and is part of the Wedgwood Group.

Title	Issue Date	Number Issued	Issued Price	Current Price
Coalport Figurines				
Robin	1977	750	136.80	136.80

Colonial Mint has commissioned The Endangered Species sculpture collection. The artist creating these sculptures is T. M. O'Brien.

Title	Issue Date	Number Issued	Issued Price	Current Price
Colonial Mint Sculptures				
Endangered Species, Alligator, Pewter	1976	9500	65.00	65.00
Endangered Species, Alligator, Silver	1976	1000	195.00	195.00
Endangered Species, American Bald Eagle, Pewter	1976	9500	65.00	65.00
Endangered Species, American Bald Eagle, Silver	1976	1000	195.00	195.00
Endangered Species, Canadian Wood Bison, Pewter	1976	9500	65.00	65.00
Endangered Species, Canadian Wood Bison, Silver	1976	1000	195.00	195.00
Endangered Species, Eastern Cougar, Pewter	1976	9500	65.00	65.00
Endangered Species, Eastern Cougar, Silver	1976	1000	195.00	195.00
Endangered Species, Mexican Bear, Pewter	1976	9500	65.00	65.00
Endangered Species, Mexican Bear, Silver	1976	1000	195.00	195.00
Endangered Species, Pronghorn Sonoran, Pewter	1976	9500	65.00	65.00
Endangered Species, Pronghorn Sonoran, Silver	1976	1000	195.00	195.00
Endangered Species, Whooping Crane, Pewter	1976	9500	65.00	65.00
Endangered Species, Whooping Crane, Silver	1976	1000	195.00	195.00
Endangered Species, Red Wolf, Pewter	1976	9500	65.00	65.00
Endangered Species, Red Wolf, Silver	1976	1000	195.00	195.00
Crown Staffordshire				
Wild Fowl, Pintail	1974	250	175.00	175.00
Wild Fowl, Mallard	1975	2000	175.00	175.00
Wild Fowl, Wigeon	1976	250	175.00	175.00

The Cybis Porcelain firm of Trenton, New Jersey, was founded in 1942 by Boleslaw Cybis, an internationally known painter and sculptor. The studio has continued production since Mr. Cybis's death in 1957. Cybis porcelains are in the collections of many museums. The Cybis firm produces the work of American artists.

Title	Issue Date	Number Issued	Issued Price	Current Price
Cybis Limnettes				
Autumn	1973	100	125.00	Unknown
Country Fair	1973	100	125.00	Unknown
Easter Egg Hunt	1973	100	125.00	Unknown
Independence Celebrations	1973	100	125.00	Unknown
Merry Christmas	1973	100	125.00	Unknown
Sabbath Morning	1973	100	125.00	Unknown
Spring	1973	100	125.00	Unknown
The Pond	1973	100	125.00	Unknown
The Seashore	1973	100	125.00	Unknown
Windy Day	1973	100	125.00	Unknown
Winter	1973	100	125.00	Unknown
Cybis Porcelains				
Abigail Adams	1976	750	875.00	875.00
American Crested Iris With Bobwhite Chick		500	975.00	975.00
American White Buffalo		250	1250.00	1500.00
American White Turkey	1976	150	1450.00	1450.00
American Wild Turkey	1976	150	1950.00	1950.00
Apache, Chato		350	1950.00	1950.00
Apple Blossoms	1977	400	350.00	350.00
Autumn Dogwood With Chickadees**		500	1100.00	1100.00
Baby Bust		239	375.00	450.00 to 650.00
Beatrice		700	225.00	775.00 to 1100.00
Bicentennial, Colonial Flower Basket		100	2750.00	2750.00
Blackfeet, Beaverhead, Medicine Man		350	2000.00	2250.00
Blue-Gray Gnatcatchers, Pair		200	400.00	1450.00 to 1625.00

Cybis, Rapunzel

Cybis, Dakota, Laughing Water, Minnehaha

Cybis, Pegasus

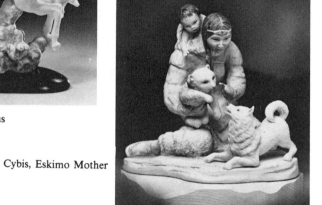

Cybis, Eskimo Mother

Cybis, Dutch Crocus

Cybis, Shoshone, Sacajawea

Cybis, Kwan Yin

Cybis, Iroquois, At The Council Fire

Cybis, Enchanted Prince Florimund
Cybis, Enchanted Princess Aurora

Cybis, Onondaga, Hiawatha

Title	Issue Date	Number Issued	Issued Price	Current Price
Blue-Headed Vireo With Lilac, Pair		275	1200.00	1800.00 to 2100.00
Bull		100	200.00	4000.00 to 4500.00
Calla Lily		500	700.00	800.00 to 1500.00
Carousel Goat		325	875.00	500.00 to 875.00
Carousel Horse		325	925.00	500.00 to 925.00
Carousel Horse, Ticonderoga		325	925.00	450.00 to 925.00
Carousel Lion		325	1025.00	1025.00
Carousel Tiger		325	925.00	925.00
Chipmunk With Bloodroot	1976	500	625.00	625.00
Christmas Rose		500	250.00	500.00 to 550.00
Clematis With House Wren**		350	1300.00	1300.00 to 1900.00
Colonial Basket, State Flowers	1976	100	2750.00	2750.00
Columbia, 1776 Through 1976		200	1000.00	2000.00 to 2900.00
Conductors' Hands		250	250.00	550.00 to 650.00
Court Jester**	1978	500	1450.00	1450.00
Cree Indian, Magic Boy		100	2500.00	3250.00
Crow Dancer**	1977	200	3875.00	3875.00
Cybele		500	675.00	350.00 to 675.00
Dahlia		350	450.00	1100.00 to 1800.00
Dahlia, Yellow		350	1250.00	1500.00
Dakota, Laughing Water, Minnehaha*		350	1500.00	1750.00
Dutch Crocus*		700	550.00	550.00 to 600.00
Eleanor Of Aquitaine		750	875.00	800.00 to 1500.00
Elephant		100	600.00	3900.00 to 6000.00
Enamoured Prince Florimund*		500	975.00	975.00
Enchanted Princess Aurora*			75.00	1125.00 to 1125.00
Eskimo Mother*		350	1875.00	1200.00 to 1875.00
Exodus		50	350.00	1500.00 to 3000.00
Flight Into Egypt		50	175.00	2750.00 to 3000.00
Folk Singer		283	300.00	252.00 to 775.00
Golden Clarion Lily		100	250.00	4000.00 to 4200.00
Gold-Winged Warbler, Andromeda		200	1075.00	1075.00
Good Queen Anne**	1978	750	975.00	975.00
Great Horned Owl, Kookooskoos, Colored		50	3250.00	3250.00
Great Horned Owl, Kookooskoos, White		150	1950.00	1950.00
Great Thunder	1977	200	3875.00	3875.00
Great White Heron		350	850.00	1600.00 to 2750.00
Guinevere		800	250.00	525.00 to 1250.00
Hamlet		500	350.00	975.00 to 1350.00
Hermit Thrush	1977	250	1450.00	1450.00
Holy Child Of Prague		10	1500.00	5000.00
Horse		100	150.00	1600.00 to 1800.00
Iris		250	500.00	3000.00 to 3200.00
Iroquois, At The Council Fire*		350	4250.00	2250.00 to 4250.00
Juliet		800	175.00	1750.00 to 2600.00
Kestrel**	1977	350	1875.00	1875.00
Kinglets On Pyracantha**	1978	500	900.00	900.00
Kwan Yin*		350	1250.00	1050.00 to 1450.00
Lady Macbeth		750	850.00	850.00
Little Blue Heron		500	425.00	1200.00 to 2000.00
Mary, Mary		750	475.00	475.00
Moses, The Great Lawgiver		750	250.00	1800.00 to 2500.00
Narcissus		500	350.00	400.00 to 600.00
Nashua		100	2000.00	2000.00
Noah	1976	500	975.00	975.00
Onondaga, Hiawatha*		350	1500.00	1750.00
Ophelia	1976	800	650.00	1075.00 to 1350.00
Pansies With Butterfly		1000	275.00	240.00 to 295.00
Pegasus*		500	1450.00	1350.00 to 1450.00
Poppy, The Performing Pony	1976	1000	325.00	325.00
Portia		750	825.00	825.00
Priscilla	1976	500	825.00	875.00
Prophet		50	250.00	1000.00 to 2000.00
Queen Esther		750	925.00	925.00
Queen Titania	1977	750	725.00	725.00
Rapunzel, Lilac**	1978	1000	525.00	525.00
Rapunzel, Pink*		1000	375.00	475.00
Ring-Necked Pheasant		150	750.00	175.00 to 2000.00
Scarlett		500	450.00	1200.00 to 1500.00
Sea King's Steed	1977	350	1250.00	1250.00

Cybis, Turtledoves

Title	Issue Date	Number Issued	Issued Price	Current Price
Shoshone, Sacajawea*		350	2250.00	2350.00
Skylarks, Pair		350	300.00	1000.00 to 1800.00
Solitary Sandpipers		400	500.00	1000.00 to 2000.00
Stallion		500	475.00	550.00 to 700.00
Thoroughbred		350	425.00	750.00 to 1100.00
Tranquility Base, Apollo 11 Moon Mission		111	1500.00	1600.00 to 1800.00
Turtle Doves*		500	350.00	4500.00 to 5000.00
Unicorn		500	1250.00	1050.00 to 1450.00
Unicorns, Gambol & Frolic	1977	1000	425.00	425.00
Wood Duck		500	325.00	450.00 to 495.00

Danbury Mint, crystal sculpture

Mother's Day, Mother & Child	1978	Year	15.00	15.00

Danbury Mint, pewter figurines

People Of Old West, Set Of 12, Each	1975	Year	55.00	55.00

Doris Lindner, see Royal Worcester

Edward J. Rohn porcelains, see Rohn

Juan Ferrandiz, Spanish artist, is designer of many Anri limited editions. These wood carvings are produced by Anri of Italy.

See listing for Ferrandiz in Plate section

Ferrandiz Figurines

Basket Of Joy	1978	1500	140.00	140.00
Cowboy	1976	2000	75.00	75.00
Harvest Girl	1976	2000	75.00	75.00
Leading The Way	1977	1500	100.00	100.00
Peace Pipe	1978	1500	140.00	140.00
The Tracker	1977	1500	100.00	100.00

Franklin Mint was organized in the early 1960s by Joseph Segel and Gilroy Roberts, chief sculptor engraver for the U.S.Mint. It is located in Franklin Center, Pennsylvania. Franklin Mint introduced the first sterling silver collector's plate in 1970. Franklin Mint Porcelain Figures are available only through Franklin Porcelain, a division of Franklin Mint. Medals have been made since the 1960s.

See listing for Franklin Mint in Paperweight and Plate Sections.

Franklin Mint Crystal Sculptures

Animals Of The Ark, Camels, Pair	1976	Year	90.00	90.00
Animals Of The Ark, Elephants, Pair	1976	Year	90.00	90.00
Animals Of The Ark, Giraffes, Pair	1976	Year	90.00	90.00
Animals Of The Ark, Hippopotamuses, Pair	1976	Year	90.00	90.00
Animals Of The Ark, Horses, Pair	1976	Year	90.00	90.00
Animals Of The Ark, Kangaroos, Pair	1976	Year	90.00	90.00
Animals Of The Ark, Lions, Pair	1976	Year	90.00	90.00
Animals Of The Ark, Polar Bears, Pair	1976	Year	90.00	90.00

Franklin Mint Figurines, porcelain

Baby Animal, Black Bear**	1977	Year	225.00	225.00
Baby Animal, Fawn**	1977	Year	225.00	225.00
Baby Animal, Lambs**	1977	Year	225.00	225.00
Baby Animal, Lion Cubs**	1977	Year	225.00	225.00
Joys Of Childhood, Coasting Along	1976	Year	120.00	120.00
Joys Of Childhood, Dressing Up	1976	Year	120.00	120.00
Joys Of Childhood, Fishing Hole	1976	Year	120.00	120.00
Joys Of Childhood, Hopscotch	1976	Year	120.00	120.00
Joys Of Childhood, Marble Champ	1976	Year	120.00	120.00
Joys Of Childhood, Ride 'em Cowboy	1976	Year	120.00	120.00
Joys Of Childhood, Stilt-Walker	1976	Year	120.00	120.00
Joys Of Childhood, The Nurse	1976	Year	120.00	120.00
Joys Of Childhood, Time Out	1976	Year	120.00	120.00
Joys Of Childhood, Trick Or Treat	1976	Year	120.00	120.00

Franklin Mint Figurines, metal

American Military Collection, 100 Each	1977	Year	19.50	19.50
American People, Astronaut	1975	15651	55.00	Unknown

Goebel, Standing Horse, Bisque

Goebel, Horned Owl

Title	Issue Date	Number Issued	Issued Price	Current Price
American People, Canal Boat Man	1974	15651	55.00	Unknown
American People, First Citizen	1974	15651	55.00	Unknown
American People, Gibson Girl	1974	15651	55.00	Unknown
American People, GI	1975	15651	55.00	Unknown
American People, Homesteader	1974	15651	55.00	Unknown
American People, Immigrant	1975	15651	55.00	Unknown
American People, Jazz Man	1975	15651	55.00	Unknown
American People, Pathfinder	1974	15651	55.00	Unknown
American People, Prospector	1974	15651	55.00	Unknown
America's Legendary Heroes, Johnny Appleseed	1976	Year	120.00	120.00
America's Legendary Heroes, Daniel Boone	1976	Year	120.00	120.00
America's Legendary Heroes, Casey Jones	1976	Year	120.00	120.00
America's Legendary Heroes, Charles Lindbergh	1976	Year	120.00	120.00
America's Legendary Heroes, Annie Oakley	1976	Year	120.00	120.00
America's Legendary Heroes, Will Rogers	1976	Year	120.00	120.00
America's Legendary Heroes, Betsy Ross	1976	Year	120.00	120.00
America's Legendary Heroes, Babe Ruth	1976	Year	120.00	120.00
America's Legendary Heroes, Mark Twain	1976	Year	120.00	120.00
America's Legendary Heroes, Alvin York	1976	Year	120.00	120.00
Bicentennial, Fighting Men, 13, Each	1976	Year	60.00	60.00
Bicentennial, Great American Eagle, Bronze	1976	2000	850.00	400.00 to 850.00
Bicentennial, Great American Eagle, Sterling	1976	200	2500.00	2500.00 to 4000.00
Boy With Dog, Bronze	1974	3420	300.00	150.00 to 300.00
Brahman Bull Ride	1977	Year	750.00	750.00
Bruno Lucchesi, Father And Son	1976		400.00	200.00 to 400.00
Bruno Lucchesi, Mother And Child, Bronze	1976		400.00	200.00 to 400.00
Chapel, Dreamer	1977	Year	225.00	225.00
Chapel, Reverie	1977	Year	225.00	225.00
Chess Set, Silver	1977	Year	1800.00	1800.00
Children Of The World, 12, Each	1977	Year	90.00	90.00
Circus, Silver, Set Of 6, Each	1976	Year	240.00	240.00
Colonial America, Butter Churner	1974	15216	50.00	Unknown
Colonial America, Candlemaker	1974	15216	50.00	Unknown
Colonial America, Innkeeper	1974	15216	50.00	Unknown
Colonial America, Planter	1974	15216	50.00	Unknown
Colonial America, Printer	1974	15216	50.00	Unknown
Colonial America, Schoolmaster	1974	15216	50.00	Unknown
Colonial America, Sea Captain	1974	15216	50.00	Unknown
Colonial America, Shoemaker	1974	15216	50.00	Unknown
Colonial America, Silversmith	1974	15216	50.00	Unknown
Colonial America, Trapper	1974	15216	50.00	Unknown
Cries Of Olde London, Chimney Sweep	1976		60.00	60.00
Cries Of Olde London, Fisherwoman	1976		60.00	60.00
Cries Of Olde London, Lavender Girl	1976		60.00	60.00
Cries Of Olde London, Newsman	1976		60.00	60.00
Cries Of Olde London, Strawberry Girl	1976		60.00	60.00
Flowers Of Season, Fall	1977	Year	195.00	195.00
Flowers Of Season, Spring	1977	Year	195.00	195.00
Flowers Of Season, Summer	1977	Year	195.00	195.00
Flowers Of Season, Winter	1977	Year	195.00	195.00
Girl With Cat	1974	2872	300.00	150.00 to 300.00
Great Cars Of America Collection, 4, Each	1976	Year	180.00	180.00
Indian Hunter, Bronze	1975	2129	600.00	300.00 to 600.00
Luxury Motor Cars, Rolls Royce	1977	Year	255.00	255.00
Main Street America, Barber Shop	1977	Year	165.00	165.00
Main Street America, General Store	1977	Year	165.00	165.00
Main Street America, Milliner's	1977	Year	165.00	165.00
Main Street America, Soda Fountain**	1977	Year	165.00	165.00
Mini Cars, 12, Each**	1977	Year	180.00	180.00
Pirates, Pewter	1976	Year	180.00	70.00 to 140.00
Western, Bronze, Set Of 8, Each	1976	1597	120.00	120.00
Wild Of Africa, Set Of 6, Each	1976	6157	120.00	10.00 to 30.00
Wildlife Of North America, Bighorn Sheep	1975	5980	60.00	10.00 to 20.00
Wildlife Of North America, Grizzly Bear	1975	5980	60.00	10.00 to 20.00
Wildlife Of North America, Mountain Lion	1975	5980	60.00	10.00 to 20.00
Wildlife Of North America, White-Tailed Deer	1975	5980	60.00	10.00 to 20.00

Frederick Gertner, see Royal Worcester

Goebel, Prancing Horse, Bisque

F.W. Goebel factory was founded in 1871 by Franz and William Goebel.
In 1934, under the tradename of Hummelwerk, the German factory, in

Title	Issue Date	Number Issued	Issued Price	Current Price

collaboration with Berta Hummel, produced the first Hummel figurines. Limited edition plates were introduced in 1971. A series of limited edition figurines commemorating the American Bicentennial was issued in 1974.

See listing for Goebel Hummel in Plate section

Goebel Figurines

Title	Issue Date	Number Issued	Issued Price	Current Price
Attacked By A Grizzly	1973	400	600.00	250.00 to 900.00
Bald Eagle	1977	200	5000.00	5000.00
Bicentennial, Eagle, Bisque	1976	5000	50.00	40.00 to 50.00
Bronco Buster	1975	400	900.00	900.00
Forging Westward	1973	400	600.00	250.00 to 900.00
George Washington	1973	400	600.00	250.00 to 900.00
Horned Owl*	1977	200	5000.00	5000.00
Mare With Colt, Bisque	1976	950	130.00	130.00
Owl	1976	950	40.00	37.50 to 40.00
Passing The Peace Pipe	1975	400	1200.00	1200.00
Paul Revere's Midnight Ride	1973	400	600.00	250.00 to 900.00
Plains Hunter	1975	400	1200.00	1200.00
Ploughing The Prairie	1975	400	900.00	900.00
Prancing Horse, Bisque*	1976	950	130.00	110.00 to 130.00
Signing The Declaration Of Independence	1973	400	600.00	250.00 to 900.00
Sophistication	1978	800		Unknown
Standing Horse, Bisque*	1976	950	130.00	110.00 to 130.00
Thunder	1977	500	500.00	500.00
Westward Bound	1973	400	600.00	250.00 to 900.00

Gorham, Rockwell,
Four Seasons, 1973, Set Of 4

Gorham Silver Co., of Providence, Rhode Island, was founded in 1831. Crystal and china were added in 1970. The first limited edition item, a silver Christmas ornament, was introduced in 1970. Limited edition porcelain plates were issued in 1971.

See also Vasari. See listing for Gorham in Plate section

Gorham Floral Arrangements

Title	Issue Date	Number Issued	Issued Price	Current Price
Fleurs Des Siecles, Fontainebleau	1975	500	600.00	600.00
Fleurs Des Siecles, Versailles	1975	500	1000.00	1000.00
Fleurs Des Siecles, Vincennes	1975	200	1200.00	1200.00

Gorham Figurines

Title	Issue Date	Number Issued	Issued Price	Current Price
Rockwell Four Seasons, Set Of 4**	1978	2500	400.00	400.00
Rockwell, Four Seasons, Boy & Dog, Set Of 4	1971	5000	200.00	175.00 to 200.00
Rockwell, Four Seasons, Grandpa & Me, Set Of 4	1974	2500	300.00	210.00 to 300.00
Rockwell, Four Seasons, Love Seasons, Set Of 4*	1973		300.00	225.00 to 300.00
Rockwell, Four Seasons, Me & My Pal, Set Of 4	1975	2500	300.00	225.00 to 300.00
Rockwell, Four Seasons, Young Love, Set Of 4	1972	5000	250.00	169.00 to 250.00
Tarter Cossack	1977	250	1200.00	1200.00

See listing for Granget in Plate section

Granget, Woodcarving, Lynx

Granget Crystal Sculptures

Title	Issue Date	Number Issued	Issued Price	Current Price
Long-Eared Owl, Asio Otus*	1973	350	2250.00	2250.00
Ruffed Grouse		150	1000.00	1000.00

Granget Porcelains

Title	Issue Date	Number Issued	Issued Price	Current Price
American Bald Eagle, Freedom In Flight	1976	200	3400.00	3400.00
American Robin, It's Spring Again	1976	150	1950.00	1950.00
Bluebirds, Reluctant Fledgling	1976	350	1750.00	1750.00
Blue Titmouse, Lively Fellow	1974	750	1295.00	1295.00
Bobwhite Quail, Off Season				2700.00 to 3300.00
California Sea Lions, Sea Frolic		500	1375.00	1375.00
Canadian Geese, Heading South		150	4650.00	4650.00
Cedar Waxwings, Anxious Moments		175	2675.00	2675.00
Chaffinch, Spring Melody	1974	750	1675.00	1675.00
Dolphin Group				1750.00 to 19000.00
Dolphins, Play Time, Decorated		100	9000.00	Unknown
Dolphins, Play Time, Undecorated		500	3500.00	3000.00 to 3500.00
Double Eagle, 24k Gold Vermeil On Pewter	1976	1200	250.00	250.00
Golden-Crested Wrens, Tiny Acrobats	1974	700	2060.00	2060.00
Goldfinch, Morning Hour	1974	750	1250.00	1250.00
Great Blue Herons, The Challenge		150		7400.00 to 9000.00
Great Titmouse Adults, Busy Activity	1974	750	2175.00	2175.00
Great Titmouse Babies, Fledged At Last	1974	650	2395.00	2395.00
Hairy Woodpecker With Nuthatches				1800.00 to 3000.00

Granget, Woodcarving, Fox

Granget, Woodcarving, Grouse

Granget, Woodcarving, Wild Boar

Granget, Woodcarving, Mallard

Granget Crystal Sculpture,
Long-Eared Owl,
Asio Otus, 1973

Gregory Higgins, Deer

Gregory Higgins, Partridge

Granget, Woodcarving, Partridge

Gregory Higgins, Cypress With Sterling Birds

Gregory Higgins, Butterfly Fish On Coral, Sterling

Gregory Higgins,
Hummingbird With Fuchsia

Gregory Higgins,
Peregrine Falcon & Sterling Jesses On Jade

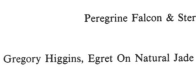

Gregory Higgins, Egret On Natural Jade

Gregory Higgins,
Sea Otter With
Sterling Abalone

Gregory Higgins,
Walrus On Cut Jade

Ispanky, Annabel Lee

Ispanky, Aaron

Ispanky, Abraham

Gregory Higgins,
Sea Bass With Vermeil Fish, Sterling

Gregory Higgins, Raccoon

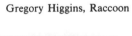

Gregory Higgins,
Trout With Sterling Hook On Cut Jade, Bronze

Gregory Higgins,
Pelican With Sterling Fish On Jade

Gregory Higgins,
Stilt With Cattails On Cut Jade

International Silver, Revolutionary Soldiers,
Chess Set

Ispanky, Dawn

Ispanky,
Ballet Dancers

Ispanky,
Eternal Love

Title	Issue Date	Number Issued	Issued Price	Current Price
Halla				1300.00 to 1400.00
Kingfisher, Detected Prey	1974	600	1975.00	1975.00
Mallard Family, First Lesson		175		2350.00 to 2850.00
Meadowlark, Spring Is Here		175	2450.00	2450.00
Mourning Doves, Engaged		250		1200.00 to 1750.00
Open Jumper, The Champion		500	1350.00	1350.00
Peregrine Falcon, Wood, 10 In.		2500	500.00	500.00
Peregrine Falcon, Wood, 12-1/2 In.		1500	700.00	700.00
Peregrine Falcon, Wood, 20 In.		250	2000.00	2000.00
Pintail Ducks, Safe At Home		350		4000.00
Red Deer Stag, The Royal Stag		150	4850.00	4850.00
Reluctant Fledgling	1977	350	1750.00	1750.00
Ring-Necked Pheasants, Take Cover		125		3800.00 to 6350.00
Robin, A Day Begins	1974	750	1795.00	1795.00
Ruffed Grouse		150	2000.00	2000.00
Screech Owl With Chickadees, Disdain		175		2200.00 to 3150.00
Secretary Bird, The Contest	1976	100	6000.00	6000.00
Springbok, The Sentinel		150	2000.00	2000.00
Stag				4000.00 to 4850.00
Woodcocks, A Family Affair		200		1000.00 to 1500.00

Granget Woodcarvings

Title	Issue Date	Number Issued	Issued Price	Current Price
Barn Owl, 10 In.		2500	600.00	600.00
Barn Owl, 12-1/2 In.		1500	700.00	700.00
Barn Owl, 20 In.		250	2000.00	2000.00
Black Grouse, Large*	1973	250	2800.00	3500.00
Black Grouse, Small	1973	1000	700.00	700.00
Fox, Large*	1973	200	2800.00	2800.00 to 3200.00
Fox, Small	1973	1000	650.00	650.00 to 750.00
Golden Eagle, Large	1973	250	2000.00	2250.00
Golden Eagle, Small	1973	1000	550.00	750.00
Lynx, Large*	1973	250	1600.00	2000.00
Lynx, Small	1973	1000	400.00	400.00
Mallard, Large*	1973	250	2000.00	2250.00
Mallard, Small	1973	1000	500.00	500.00
Partridge, Large*	1973	200	2400.00	2800.00
Partridge, Small	1973	1000	550.00	550.00
Peregrine Falcon, Large		250	2250.00	2250.00
Peregrine Falcon, Medium		1500	700.00	700.00
Peregrine Falcon, Small		1000	500.00	500.00
Ring-Necked Pheasant, Large			2250.00	2250.00
Ring-Necked Pheasant, Small			500.00	500.00
Rooster, Large	1973	250	2400.00	2800.00
Rooster, Small	1973	1000	600.00	650.00
Wild Boar, Large*	1973	200	2400.00	2400.00
Wild Boar, Small	1973	1000	275.00	275.00
Wild Sow With Young, Large		1000	2800.00	2800.00
Wild Sow With Young, Small		200	600.00	600.00

Gregory Higgins' sculptures are of manganese bronze, silver, and vermeil on a mineral rock base. Each piece is signed and numbered by the artist.

Gregory Higgins Sculptures

Title	Issue Date	Number Issued	Issued Price	Current Price
Angelfish On Cut Jade, Sterling		750	165.00	Unknown
Aquarium With Sterling Fish		500	285.00	Unknown
Avocet On Natural Jade		350	570.00	Unknown
Butterfly Fish On Coral, Sterling*		500	550.00	Unknown
Cypress With Sterling Birds*		500	240.00	Unknown
Deer*		500	240.00	Unknown
Egret On Natural Jade*		500	285.00	Unknown
Hummingbird With Fuchsia*		500	285.00	Unknown
Hummingbirds With Fuchsias		500	670.00	Unknown
Landlocked Salmon With Rapids Of Jade		500	450.00	Unknown
Marsh Wrens With Nest, Bronze		500	600.00	Unknown
Marsh Wrens With Nest, Sterling		500	700.00	Unknown
Owl		500	240.00	Unknown
Pelican With Sterling Fish On Jade*		500	285.00	Unknown
Peregrine Falcon & Sterling Jesses On Jade*		500	1200.00	Unknown
Raccoon*		500	240.00	Unknown
Sea Bass With Vermeil Fish, Sterling*		500	500.00	Unknown
Sea Otter With Sterling Abalone*		500	230.00	Unknown

Ispanky,
Second Base

Title	Issue Date	Number Issued	Issued Price	Current Price
Stilt With Cattails On Cut Jade*		750	175.00	Unknown
Swan		500	230.00	Unknown
Trout With Sterling Hook On Cut Jade, Bronze*		500	400.00	Unknown
Trout With Vermeil Hook And Fly, Sterling		500	450.00	Unknown
Walrus On Cut Jade*		500	240.00	Unknown
Warbler On Cut Jade, Bronze		750	175.00	Unknown
Warbler On Cut Jade, Sterling		750	260.00	Unknown
Warbler With Sterling Eggs, Bronze		500	600.00	Unknown
Warbler With Vermeil Eggs, Sterling		500	700.00	Unknown
Wren On Cut Jade, Bronze		750	165.00	Unknown
Wren On Cut Jade, Sterling		750	220.00	Unknown

Grossman Figurines

Title	Issue Date	Number Issued	Issued Price	Current Price
Grossman, Rockwell, Barbershop Quartet		1000		82.50
Rockwell, Dr.And Doll	1975	2000	249.00	250.00 to 300.00
Rockwell, No Swimming		1000		122.50 to 150.00
Rockwell, 100th Year Of Baseball		1000	125.00	102.50 to 125.00
Rockwell, See America First		1000		82.50 to 100.00

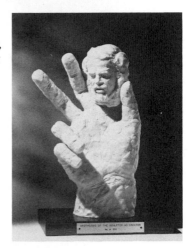

Ispanky,
Sculptor

Hamilton Mint Bronze figurines

See listing for Hamilton Mint in Plate section

Title	Issue Date	Number Issued	Issued Price	Current Price
Father's Day	1978	10000	27.50	27.50
Mother's Day	1978	10000	27.50	27.50

Higgins, Gregory, see Gregory Higgins

Holly Hobby started to make her cards for American Greeting Co. of Cleveland, Ohio, in 1966. Her designs became so popular the company added a line of figurines, plates, and other Holly Hobby items.

See listing for Holly Hobby in Plate section

Holly Hobby Figurines

Title	Issue Date	Number Issued	Issued Price	Current Price
Christmas, Girl With Wreath & Kitty	1975	2250	18.50	18.50
Christmas, Two Girls Wrapping Packages	1976	4500	17.50	17.50
Mother's Day, Girl With Rag Doll	1976	3000	7.50	7.50
Three Figures Marching	1975	2000	40.00	40.00

Hutschenreuther Porcelain Company of Selb, Germany, was established in 1856.

Hutschenreuther Figurines

Title	Issue Date	Number Issued	Issued Price	Current Price
Catherine The Great	1977	500	500.00	875.00
Helen Of Troy	1977	500	500.00	925.00
Jennie Churchill	1977	500	500.00	925.00
Queen Isabella	1977	500	500.00	925.00

Ispanky,
Great Spirit,
Decorated

International Silver

Title	Issue Date	Number Issued	Issued Price	Current Price
Revolutionary Soldiers, Chess Set*	1976	500	1400.00	1400.00
Safari Series, Pride Of Lions, Pewter	1975	2500	200.00	200.00

Ispanky porcelains are designed by Lazlo Ispanky at his studios in Pennington, New Jersey. Mr. Ispanky was born in Budapest in 1919, and moved to the U. S. in 1956. He works in wood, stone, and metal, as well as porcelain. The first limited edition pieces were The Hunt, Pioneer Scout, and Pack Horse. They were issued in 1966. Of the 500 Rosh Hashana pieces made, 498 have white beards and only 2 have gray beards.

See listing for Ispanky in Plate section

Ispanky Porcelains

Title	Issue Date	Number Issued	Issued Price	Current Price
Aaron*	1973	350	12000.0	1485.00
Abraham*	1973	500	600.00	360.00 to 600.00
Annabel Lee*	1972	500	750.00	375.00 to 750.00
Apotheosis Of The Sculptor*	1975	250	495.00	615.00
Artist Girl	1967	500	200.00	875.00 to 1000.00
Autumn Wind	1969	500	300.00	400.00 to 650.00
Ballerina	1967	500	350.00	190.00 to 500.00
Ballet Dancers*	1967	500	350.00	375.00 to 575.00
Banbury Cross	1974	350	550.00	550.00 to 710.00
Beauty And The Beast	1971	15	4500.00	4500.00
Belle Of The Ball	1974	500	550.00	550.00 to 710.00
Betsy Ross	1971	350	750.00	750.00 to 925.00

Ispanky,
Maid Of The Mist

Ispanky, King Arthur

Ispanky, Lorelei

Ispanky, Quest

Ispanky, Icarus

Title	Issue Date	Number Issued	Issued Price	Current Price
Bird Of Paradise	1967	250	1500.00	1500.00
Cavalry Scout, Decorated	1967	200	1000.00	1200.00
Cavalry Scout, White	1967	150	675.00	900.00
Celeste	1970	200	475.00	250.00 to 500.00
Christine	1971	300	350.00	550.00 to 700.00
Cinderella	1972	400	375.00	160.00 to 375.00
Daffodils	1969	250	950.00	450.00 to 950.00
Daisy	1977	1000	325.00	365.00
David	1971	400	450.00	270.00 to 450.00
Dawn*	1970	300	500.00	300.00 to 500.00
Day Dreams	1977	1000	300.00	335.00
Debutante	1971	500	350.00	225.00 to 430.00
Dianne	1974	500	500.00	300.00 to 600.00
Drummer Boy, Decorated*	1967	200	250.00	225.00 to 250.00
Drummer Boy, White	1967	600	150.00	175.00 to 185.00
Dutch Iris	1967	250	1400.00	1400.00 to 1500.00
Emerald Dragon	1973	100	2500.00	2500.00 to 2700.00
Eternal Love*	1971	300	400.00	400.00
Evening	1970	300	375.00	375.00 to 500.00
Excalibur*	1971	15	3500.00	3500.00
Exodus, Bronze		100	1500.00	1500.00
Felicia	1971	15	2500.00	2500.00
Forty-Niner, Decorated	1967	200	450.00	650.00
Forty-Niner, White	1967	350	250.00	250.00
Freedom	1971	250	300.00	500.00
Great Spirit, Decorated	1969	200	1500.00	1500.00 to 1850.00
Great Spirit, White*	1967	150	750.00	450.00 to 750.00
Hamlet And Ophelia	1974	350	1250.00	750.00 to 1250.00
Healing Hand, Decorated*	1975	600	750.00	750.00 to 925.00
Healing Hand, White	1975	600	650.00	800.00
Holy Family, Decorated	1974	450	900.00	900.00 to 1125.00
Holy Family, White	1974	450	750.00	700.00 to 925.00
Horse	1968	300	300.00	350.00 to 600.00
Horsepower	1970	100	1650.00	1650.00 to 2150.00
Hunt, Decorated	1967	200	2000.00	2200.00 to 2725.00
Hunt, White	1967	150	1200.00	1200.00 to 1485.00
Icarus*	1970	350	350.00	350.00 to 430.00
Isaiah	1969	300	475.00	415.00 to 600.00
Jessamy 1	1971	400	450.00	325.00 to 450.00
Joshua*	1975	350	750.00	750.00 to 925.00
King & Queen, Pair	1970	250	750.00	1200.00
King Arthur*	1967	500	300.00	125.00 to 400.00
King Lear & Cordelia	1974	250	1250.00	1250.00 to 1500.00
King Solomon**	1978	100	3000.00	3000.00
Little Mermaid	1978	800	350.00	350.00
Lorelei*	1973	500	550.00	330.00 to 550.00
Love	1967	300	375.00	160.00 to 375.00
Love Letters**	1973	450	750.00	750.00
Lydia	1976	400	450.00	450.00 to 560.00
Madame Butterfly*	1972	300	1500.00	825.00 to 1500.00
Madonna, The Blessed Saint, Decorated	1975	500	295.00	295.00
Madonna, The Blessed Saint, White	1975	500	195.00	195.00
Madonna, With Halo, Decorated	1975	500	350.00	350.00
Madonna, With Halo, White	1975	500	250.00	250.00
Maid Of The Mist*	1973	350	450.00	450.00 to 590.00
Maria	1969	350	750.00	750.00 to 1000.00
Meditation	1967	300	350.00	350.00 to 450.00
Memories**	1977	500	600.00	500.00 to 675.00
Mermaid Group, Decorated	1969	200	1000.00	1000.00 to 1800.00
Mermaid Group, White	1969	200	950.00	950.00
Messiah*	1973	750	450.00	450.00
Morning	1967	500	300.00	600.00 to 825.00
Morning Glory	1977	1000	325.00	325.00 to 365.00
Moses	1967	400	400.00	650.00 to 800.00
Mr.& Mrs.Otter	1971	500	250.00	195.00 to 350.00
My Name Is Iris	1978	700	500.00	500.00
Narcissus	1978	700	500.00	500.00
On The Trail, Decorated	1970	200	1700.00	1700.00 to 2100.00
On The Trail, White	1967	150	750.00	750.00 to 1125.00
Orchids	1976	250	1000.00	1400.00

Ispanky,
Madame Butterfly

Title	Issue Date	Number Issued	Issued Price	Current Price
Owl		300	750.00	750.00 to 825.00
Pack Horse, Decorated	1967	200	700.00	1250.00
Pack Horse, White	1967	150	500.00	350.00
Peace, Decorated	1970	100	375.00	350.00 to 600.00
Peace, White	1970	100	300.00	300.00 to 450.00
Peace Riders	1971	1	5000.00	35000.00
Pegasus, Decorated	1968	300	375.00	450.00 to 550.00
Pegasus, White	1968	300	300.00	300.00 to 400.00
Piano Girl	1976	800	300.00	435.00
Pilgrim Family, Decorated	1967	200	500.00	500.00 to 750.00
Pilgrim Family, White	1967	350	350.00	250.00 to 350.00
Pioneer Scout, Decorated	1967	200	1000.00	1000.00
Pioneer Scout, White	1967	200	675.00	405.00
Pioneer Woman, Decorated	1967	200	350.00	350.00 to 430.00
Pioneer Woman, White	1967	150	225.00	225.00 to 275.00
Poppy	1977	1000	325.00	365.00
Princess And The Frog	1972	500	675.00	675.00
Princess Of The Nile		500	275.00	275.00
Promises	1967	100	225.00	2000.00 to 2500.00
Queen Of Spring	1968	200	750.00	510.00 to 850.00
Quest*	1972	15	1500.00	1500.00
Rebekah	1973	300	400.00	400.00 to 495.00
Reverie	1970	200	200.00	500.00 to 850.00
Romance**	1978	500	800.00	800.00
Romeo & Juliet, Decorated*	1967	500	375.00	550.00 to 850.00
Rosh Hashana, Gray Beard**		2	275.00	10000.00
Rosh Hashana, White Beard		400	275.00	650.00 to 975.00
Second Base*	1974	500	650.00	375.00 to 650.00
Serene Highness	1977	100	2500.00	2500.00 to 2800.00
Snow Drop	1977	1000	325.00	365.00
Sophistication	1977	800	350.00	390.00
Spirit Of The Sea	1972	450	500.00	190.00 to 500.00
Spring Ballet	1972	400	450.00	300.00 to 450.00
Spring Bouquet	1972	50	3000.00	3000.00
Spring Fever**	1978	600	650.00	650.00
Storm	1969	500	400.00	350.00 to 500.00
Swanilda**	1976	1000	285.00	285.00 to 365.00
Swan Lake	1971	300	1000.00	600.00 to 1250.00
Tekieh*	1971	15	1800.00	1800.00
Ten Commandments, Decorated	1978	500	950.00	950.00
Ten Commandments, White**	1978	700	600.00	600.00
Texas Rangers	1973	400	1650.00	990.00 to 1650.00
Thrasher	1970	300	1000.00	1000.00
Thunder	1977	500	500.00	560.00
Tulips, Red	1967	50	1800.00	2000.00
Tulips, Yellow	1967	50	1800.00	725.00 to 2000.00
Water Lily	1977	1000	325.00	325.00 to 365.00

Ispanky, Messiah

Jean-Paul Loup, the editor of Art of Chicago, joined the Betournes Studio of Limoges, France, to issue their first limited edition plates in 1971. The plates and porcelain paintings are hand-applied enamel on copper. Each plate is signed by both Michel Betourne and Jean-Paul Loup.

See listing for Jean-Paul Loup in Plate section

Jean Paul Loup/Betournes Enamel on Copper Paintings

Four Seasons, Autumn**		200	250.00	Unknown
Four Seasons, Spring**		200	250.00	Unknown
Four Seasons, Summer**		200	250.00	Unknown
Four Seasons, Winter**		200	250.00	Unknown
Six Crafts, The Butcher		150	200.00	Unknown
Six Crafts, The Mower		150	200.00	Unknown
Six Crafts, The Plowman		150	200.00	Unknown
Six Crafts, The Reaper		150	200.00	Unknown
Six Crafts, The Sower		150	200.00	Unknown
Six Crafts, The Vinedresser		150	200.00	Unknown

Ispanky, Joshua

Kaiser Porcelain Manufactory was founded in 1872 by August Alboth in Coburg, Germany. The plant was moved to Staffelstein, Bavaria, in 1953. Their first limited edition plate was made in 1970. That year, the company's mark was changed from AK and a crown to 'Kaiser Porcelain.'

Ispanky,
Romeo & Juliet,
Decorated, 1967

Ispanky, Excalibur

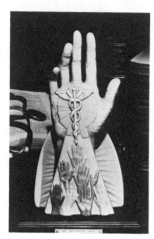

Ispanky,
Hippocratic Oath

Ispanky, Tekieh

See listing for Kaiser in Plate section

Kaiser Porcelains

Title	Issue Date	Number Issued	Issued Price	Current Price
American Eagle, 16 1/2 In.		800	1850.00	1850.00
American Eagle, 11 In.		1000		Unknown
American Eagle, 11 In., White*		4000	260.00	260.00
Arabian Stallion, Color**	1972	600	250.00	300.00 to 500.00
Arabian Stallion, 1 Leg Up, Color*	1977	500	600.00	600.00
Arabian Stallion, 1 Leg Up, White	1977	1500	250.00	250.00
Baby Titmice, Color	1974	800	400.00	500.00
Baby Titmice, White	1974	1200	200.00	200.00
Baltimore Oriole, Color	1970	2000	60.00	80.00 to 100.00
Baltimore Oriole	1977	1000	280.00	280.00
Bluebird, Color*	1973	2500	120.00	225.00
Blue Jay, Color**	1970	2000	60.00	85.00 to 100.00
Blue Jay With Wood Base	1974	1500	475.00	650.00
Canadian Geese	1977	1500	1500.00	1750.00
Cardinal, Color	1970	1500	60.00	350.00
Cardinal With Wood Base, Color	1971	1500	225.00	225.00
Eagle	1977	3000	450.00	500.00
Eagle, Color	1970	400	500.00	500.00 to 650.00
Eagle, White	1970	1200	250.00	200.00
Encroachment, Color*	1973	950	900.00	1100.00
Flushed, Color*	1973	950	1000.00	1150.00
Four Dolphins	1976	3000		Unknown
German Shepherd, White	1977	2000	185.00	185.00
German Shepherd, Color	1977	1000	250.00	290.00
Goshawk, Color*	1973	800	1200.00	2000.00
Goshawk, White*	1973	700	550.00	800.00
Hummingbirds With Wood Base	1974	1500	450.00	625.00
Irish Setter, White	1977	2000	185.00	185.00
Irish Setter, Color	1977	1000	290.00	290.00
Kingfisher, Color**	1972	1500	140.00	350.00
Kingfisher, White	1971	2000	45.00	55.00 to 60.00
Lady, Victorian, Dog	1977	2500	450.00	450.00
Lady, Victorian, Tennis	1977	2500	450.00	450.00
Lady, Victorian, Umbrella	1977	2500	450.00	450.00
Lipizzaner Horse, Color, Wood Base	1975	800	625.00	800.00
Lipizzaner Horse, White, Wood Base	1975	2200	275.00	350.00
Mare & Colt, Color, Wood Base	1975	1200	650.00	775.00
Mother Bear & Cub, Color, Wood Base	1976	800	400.00	550.00
Mother Bear & Cub, White, Wood Base	1976	1200	125.00	160.00
Owl, Color	1970	1500	150.00	350.00
Owl, Color, Wood Base	1975	800	850.00	1150.00
Owl, White	1972	2000	70.00	160.00
Owl, White, Wood Base	1975	1200	300.00	400.00
Owl, Horned		2000	650.00	650.00
Pelican	1977	1200	925.00	925.00
Peregrine Falcon, Color, Wood Base	1975	1500	850.00	1000.00
Pheasant	1977	1500	3200.00	3200.00
Pigeon Group, Color	1970	1500	150.00	350.00
Pigeon Group, White	1972	2000	60.00	140.00
Pony Group, Color**	1972	1000	150.00	350.00
Pony Group, White	1972	5000	50.00	150.00
Porpoises, Group Of 3, White*	1971	5000	85.00	375.00
Porpoises, Group Of 4, White, Wood Base	1975	3000	75.00	460.00
Porpoises, Group Of 5, White, Wood Base	1976	800	850.00	1100.00
Roadrunner, Color	1973	1000	350.00	500.00
Robin	1977	1500	340.00	375.00
Robin & Worm, Color	1970	2000	60.00	80.00 to 90.00
Robin With Wood Base	1974	1000	260.00	390.00
Scarlet Tanager, Color	1970	2000	60.00	80.00 to 90.00
Screech Owl, Color	1977	1000	175.00	175.00
Screech Owl, White	1977	2000	85.00	85.00
Seagull, Color	1973	800	850.00	1150.00
Seagull, White	1973	700	550.00	850.00
Seated Poodle	1977	1060	160.00	160.00
Sparrow, Color, Wood Base	1975	1500	300.00	350.00
Tay-Kaiser Eagle, Color	1973	800	1300.00	1300.00
Titmouse, Baby, Color		800		Unknown
Titmouse, Baby, White		1200	265.00	265.00

Kaiser, American Eagle, White

Kaiser, Goshawk, Color

Kaiser, Bluebird

Kaiser, Goshawk, White

Kaiser, Flushed, Color

Kaiser, Porpoises, Group Of 3, White, 1971

Kaiser, Waiting For Mother, Color

Kaiser, Encroachment, Color

Kazmar,
Pond Life

Kazmar,
American Avocet

Kazmar, Brown Pelican

Kazmar, Sea Lion Pup, Juvenile

Title	Issue Date	Number Issued	Issued Price	Current Price
Waiting For Mother, Color*	1973	950	550.00	650.00
Wild Ducks, Color**	1970	1500	150.00	500.00
Wild Ducks, White	1971	2000	75.00	175.00
Wood Ducks, Color, Wood Base	1975	800	1450.00	1675.00
Woodpeckers, Color, Wood Base	1975	800	900.00	1000.00
Kazmar Porcelain Figurines				
American Avocet*	1974	100	1575.00	1575.00
American Badger	1978	550	355.00	355.00
American Woodcock	1974	50	900.00	975.00
Baby Ducks, Pair	1976	700	180.00	180.00
Baby Llama		400	175.00	175.00
Beaver, Juvenile	1978	550	335.00	335.00
Blue-Footed Booby, Fledgling	1974	400	125.00	125.00
Brown Pelican*	1974	150	975.00	975.00
Ermine	1974	150	250.00	275.00
Golden Eagle, Fledgling	1976	700	190.00	190.00
Harp Seals	1977	600	275.00	275.00
Humboldt Penguin, Fledgling	1974	300	125.00	125.00
Ladder-Backed Woodpecker	1976	400	395.00	395.00
Llama, Juvenile	1974	400	175.00	175.00
Marsh Wrens**	1974	100	1275.00	1275.00
Pond Children, Baby White Ducks, Pair	1976	700	170.00	170.00
Pond Life*	1974	50	1750.00	1950.00
Red-Footed Booby	1978	550	165.00	165.00
Red Fox	1976	400	285.00	285.00
Saw-Whet Owl**	1974	200	775.00	795.00
Sea Lion Pup, Juvenile*	1974	400	165.00	165.00
Snowy Egret	1977	550	175.00	175.00
Weasel	1974	150	325.00	350.00
White Pelican	1974	150	975.00	975.00
Woodcock		100	900.00	900.00
Wood Ducks**	1978	100	1350.00	1450.00

King's Porcelain Factory is located in Italy. Their limited edition plates, introduced in 1973, are high bas relief and hand-painted. Limited edition figurines were first made in 1974.

See listing for King's Porcelain in Plate section

King's Porcelain Figurines

Blue Jay	1974	200	900.00	Unknown
European Roller	1974	350	500.00	Unknown
Hummingbird	1974	300	700.00	Unknown
Robins	1974	300	650.00	Unknown
Titmouse	1974	250	700.00	Unknown
Weasel	1974	200	325.00	Unknown
White Or Western Pelican	1974	100	975.00	Unknown
Woodcock	1974	100	900.00	Unknown
Wood Ducks, Pair	1974	100	1350.00	Unknown

Kirk limited editions are made by Samuel Kirk and Sons, Inc. The firm was started in Baltimore, Maryland, in 1815. The company is well known for both antique and modern silver wares.

See listing for Kirk in Plate section

Bicentennial Figures, Pewter, 12, Each	1975	3380	39.50	39.50
Bicentennial Figures, Silver, 12, Each	1975	294	275.00	275.00
Foxhounds, Silver Plate		500	150.00	Unknown
Mare & Foal, Silver Plate		250	200.00	Unknown
Pony & Girl, Silver Plate		250	150.00	Unknown

Kosta Glassworks of Sweden was founded in 1972 by King Charles II. The limited editions line, introduced in 1970, includes paperweights, plates and mugs.

See listing for Kosta in Paperweight and Plate Sections

Kosta Crystal Sculptures

Bald Eagle	1976	10000	68.00	68.00

Kramlik porcelains are made by Balint Kramlik, a native of Herend,

Title	Issue Date	Number Issued	Issued Price	Current Price

*Hungary, who now works in New Jersey. Mr. Kramlik worked with
Edward Marshall Boehm before producing his own limited editions.*

Kramlik, Balint, see listing in Plate section

Kramlik Figures

Title	Issue Date	Number Issued	Issued Price	Current Price
Boxer, Decorated		300	700.00	300.00
Fawn, Decorated		300	250.00	250.00
German Shepherd				250.00
Moses, White		100	350.00	350.00
New Year, White		100	500.00	500.00
Rabbit, Decorated		300	200.00	200.00
Wizard Of Oz Series, Cowardly Lion, Decorated		500	700.00	700.00
Wizard Of Oz Series, The Scarecrow, Decorated		500	600.00	600.00
Wizard Of Oz Series, Tin Woodsman, Decorated		500	700.00	700.00
Young Animal, Fawn	1975	300		250.00
Young Animal, Rabbit	1975	300		200.00

See listing for KpM, Royal Berlin in Plate section

See listing for Lalique Crystal in Plate section

Lalique Crystal Sculptures

Title	Issue Date	Number Issued	Issued Price	Current Price
Bicentennial, Eagle	1976		475.00	475.00
Eagle Head				115.00

Lichtenstein Sculptures

Title	Issue Date	Number Issued	Issued Price	Current Price
Airmail Plane, Chrome Plated		50	300.00	Unknown
Airmail Plane, Polished Bronze		50	275.00	Unknown
Airmail Plane, Silver		50	375.00	Unknown

*Lihs Lindner limited editions are designed by Mr. Helmut H. Lihs of
Long Beach, California, and manufactured by the Lindner Company
of Kueps Bavaria, Germany.*

See listing for Lihs Lindner in Plate section

Lihs Lindner Porcelains

Title	Issue Date	Number Issued	Issued Price	Current Price
Drummer Boy	1975	350	125.00	Unknown
Spirit Of America	1976	350	150.00	125.00

Lindner, Doris, see Royal Worcester

*The Lincoln Mint of Chicago, Illinois, entered the limited edition
field in 1971. Gold, silver, and vermeil plates are made.*

See listing for Lincoln Mint in Plate section

Lincoln Mint Figures

Title	Issue Date	Number Issued	Issued Price	Current Price
Builders Of America, Navigator, Sterling	1976	500	250.00	250.00
Builders Of America, Navigator, Pewter	1976	5000	55.00	55.00

*Lladro Porcelain factory of Tabernes Blanques, Spain, produces a
large line of limited and nonlimited porcelains.*

See listing for Lladro in Plate section

Lladro Porcelains

Title	Issue Date	Number Issued	Issued Price	Current Price
Allegory For Peace		150	550.00	550.00
Antique Automobile*		750	1100.00	1100.00
Eagle Owl		750	650.00	650.00
Eagles		750	900.00	900.00 to 1000.00
Eve At The Tree		600	450.00	600.00
The Forest		500	1500.00	1500.00
Girl With Guitar		750	650.00	850.00
Hamlet		750	350.00	350.00
Hansom Carriage		750	1250.00	1250.00
Hunting Scene		800	850.00	850.00
Judge		1200	325.00	325.00
Lyric Muse		400	750.00	750.00 to 800.00
Madonna With Child		300	450.00	450.00
Madonna With Child, Seated		300	400.00	400.00
Man From La Mancha		1500	800.00	800.00
Oriental Horse		350	1100.00	1200.00
Othello & Desdemona*		750	350.00	350.00
Peasant Woman		750	500.00	500.00
Seabirds With Nest		500	600.00	600.00
Soccer Players		750	2750.00	2750.00
Three Graces		500	950.00	1100.00

Lladro, Antique Automobile

Lladro, Othello & Desdemona

Medallic Art, Children Of Christmas,
Bronze

Moussalli,
American Redstart With Cherries

Moussalli, American Redstart With Flowers

Moussalli, Golden-Crowned Kinglet

Moussalli, Bay-Breasted Warbler

Moussalli, Golden Finch

Title	Issue Date	Number Issued	Issued Price	Current Price
Turkey Group		350	650.00	1300.00
Turtle Doves		750	675.00	675.00
Young Oriental Man		500	500.00	650.00

The Medallic Art Company of Danbury, Connecticut, was established by Henri and Felix Weil around the turn of the century. The name Medallic Art Company was first used in 1909.

Medallic Art Sculptures

Title	Issue Date	Number Issued	Issued Price	Current Price
Children Of Christmas, Bronze*	1975	100	275.00	Unknown
Children Of Christmas, Sterling Silver	1975	50	500.00	Unknown

Mico Kaufman Pewter Figures

Title	Issue Date	Number Issued	Issued Price	Current Price
Moby Dick Series, Ahab	1975	2000	50.00	Unknown
Moby Dick Series, Ishmael	1975	2000	50.00	Unknown
Moby Dick Series, Queequeg	1975	2000	50.00	Unknown
Moby Dick Series, Tashtego	1975	2000	50.00	Unknown

Morton Mevorach Sculptures

Title	Issue Date	Number Issued	Issued Price	Current Price
Birds Of Prey, Goshawk, Bronze	1975	500	400.00	Unknown
Birds Of Prey, Great Gray Owl, Bronze	1975	500	400.00	Unknown
Galaxy, Clear Plexiglas	1976	250	125.00	Unknown

Moussalli Porcelains

Title	Issue Date	Number Issued	Issued Price	Current Price
American Redstart With Cherries*		500	60.00	150.00
American Redstart With Flowers*	1972	500	600.00	600.00
Anna's Hummingbird			250.00	125.00 to 250.00
Baltimore Oriole		300	650.00	625.00
Baltimore Oriole With Snake				1200.00
Bay-Breasted Warbler*	1974	300	325.00	325.00
Black-Capped Chickadee	1969	250	550.00	700.00 to 1150.00
Bluebird On Crabapple Tree				1000.00
Canadian Warbler*		500	180.00	200.00 to 250.00
Cardinal		300	600.00	700.00 to 800.00
Eastern Bluebird On Rock	1969	500	250.00	350.00
Flycatcher	1974	300	360.00	360.00
Golden-Crowned Kinglet*	1974	400	225.00	225.00
Golden Finch*		150	550.00	275.00
House Wren*	1972	500	250.00	275.00 to 325.00
Hummingbird In Forsythia*		500	250.00	150.00 to 325.00
Hummingbird And Honeysuckle*		500	250.00	275.00 to 325.00
Indigo Bunting*	1972	150	650.00	325.00
Olive Warbler*		500	200.00	225.00 to 250.00
Redbreasted Grosbeak**	1971	300	435.00	435.00
Red-Faced Warbler*	1974	300	435.00	435.00
Redheaded Woodpecker*		200	450.00	525.00 to 575.00
Red-Winged Blackbird		300	700.00	625.00 to 1200.00
Say's Phoebe**	1974	300	360.00	360.00
Scarlet Tanager*		300	360.00	175.00
Slate-Colored Junco*		500	180.00	200.00 to 250.00
Snow Bunting**	1974	200	830.00	830.00
Tufted Titmouse*	1972	150	650.00	325.00
Wheatear*		300	350.00	400.00 to 450.00
Wren On Magnolia Branch*		300	600.00	725.00 to 775.00
Wren On A Rock*		500	170.00	300.00
Yellow-Throated Warbler	1969	500	120.00	180.00 to 450.00

Noritake marked porcelain was first made in Japan after 1904. Limited editions were introduced in 1971.

Noritake China Sculptures

Title	Issue Date	Number Issued	Issued Price	Current Price
Cat And Kitten	1976	Year		44.00 to 55.00
Deer And Fawn	1974	Year		24.95 to 50.00
Mare And Colt	1975	Year		39.50 to 50.00

Paramount Classics Silver Sculptures

Title	Issue Date	Number Issued	Issued Price	Current Price
Lindbergh's Spirit Of St.Louis	1977	650	1575.00	1575.00
Wright Brothers Flyer**	1976	1000	750.00	1100.00

Polland Pewter Sculptures

Title	Issue Date	Number Issued	Issued Price	Current Price
Buffalo Hunt	1976	2250	150.00	150.00
Cheyenne	1975		250.00	Unknown
Cold Saddles, Mean Horses	1975		200.00	Unknown

Moussalli, Wren On A Rock

Moussalli, Canadian Warbler

Moussalli, Olive Warbler

Moussalli, Hummingbird In Forsythia

Moussalli, Redheaded Woodpecker

Moussalli, Slate-Colored Junco

Hummingbird And Honeysuckle

Moussalli, Indigo Bunting

Moussalli, House Wren

Moussalli, Wren On Magnolia Branch

Moussalli, Scarlet Tanager

Moussalli, Red-Faced Warbler

Moussalli, Tufted Titmouse

Moussalli, Wheatear

Title	Issue Date	Number Issued	Issued Price	Current Price
Counting Coup	1975		225.00	Unknown
Crow Scout	1975		175.00	Unknown
Maverick Calf	1976		125.00	125.00
Monday Morning Wash	1976	2500	125.00	125.00
Outlaws	1975		250.00	250.00
Painting The Town	1976	2250	150.00	150.00
Rescue	1976	2500	137.50	137.50

The Poole Pottery of Poole, Dorset, England, has produced pottery since 1973. A limited edition porcelain line featuring game birds was introduced in 1973.

See listing for Poole in Plate section

Poole Porcelains

Title	Issue Date	Number Issued	Issued Price	Current Price
Canada Goose*	1973	500	350.00	Unknown
Grouse, Pair		1000		Unknown
Sandpipers, Pair		1000		Unknown

Reed & Barton Pewter Sculptures

Title	Issue Date	Number Issued	Issued Price	Current Price
Christmas Eve	1978	2500	45.00	45.00
Mother's Day, Passing Crisis	1978	1500	45.00	45.00

See listing for River Shore in Plate section

River Shore Porcelains

Title	Issue Date	Number Issued	Issued Price	Current Price
Lovable Animal, Akiku	1978	15000	37.50	37.50

Rohn porcelain sculptures are made by American artist Edward J. Rohn of Elmhurst, Illinois.

Rohn Porcelains

Title	Issue Date	Number Issued	Issued Price	Current Price
American G.I.	1971	100	600.00	600.00
Apache*	1973	125	900.00	900.00
Apprentice	1973	175	500.00	Unknown
Chosen One**	1976	125	850.00	850.00
Coolie*	1971	100	700.00	700.00
Cougar	1975	150	700.00	700.00
Crow Indian	1971	100	800.00	800.00
Gypsy	1972	125	1450.00	1450.00
Hunter	1974	100	1000.00	1000.00
Indian Woman	1976	200	850.00	850.00
Jazzman	1973	150	750.00	750.00
Jeanine*	1972	125	475.00	475.00
Longhorn	1975	25	975.00	975.00
Matador*	1973	90	2400.00	2400.00
Missy	1974	250	250.00	250.00
Monarch Butterflies	1975		850.00	850.00
Nostalgia, Casey**	1977	225	275.00	275.00
Nostalgia, Flapper**	1977	150	325.00	325.00
Nostalgia, Sou'wester**	1977	250	300.00	300.00
Nostalgia, Wally**	1977	125	250.00	250.00
Recruit	1974	250	250.00	250.00
Rhino	1974	300	600.00	600.00
Riverboat Captain*	1971	100	1000.00	1000.00
Sabbath	1978	70	1825.00	1825.00
Sherif*	1973	150	1500.00	1500.00
Small World Series, Big Brother	1974	250	90.00	Unknown
Small World Series, Burglars	1974	250	120.00	Unknown
Small World Series, Field Mushroom	1975	250	90.00	Unknown
Small World Series, Johnnies		1500	90.00	Unknown
Small World Series, Knee Deep	1974	500	60.00	Unknown
Small World Series, Oyster Mushroom	1975	250	140.00	Unknown
Small World Series, Quackers	1974	250	75.00	Unknown
Trailhand	1971	100	1200.00	1200.00
Truman, Harry	1976	75	2400.00	2400.00
Young Confederate Recruit	1974	500	250.00	250.00
White Rhino	1974	300	600.00	Unknown
Zaide	1977	70	1950.00	1950.00

Rohn woodcarvings are being interpreted in hand-carved wood by the master carvers of Anri of Italy.

Poole, Canada Goose

Title	Issue Date	Number Issued	Issued Price	Current Price
Rohn Woodcarvings				
Drifter, Bust			125.00	125.00
Indian, Bust, Kiowa			125.00	125.00
Pioneer Farmer	1978	1000	125.00	125.00
Pioneer Woman	1978	1000	125.00	125.00

Ronald Van Ruyckevelt, see Royal Worcester

See listing for Rosenthal in Plate section

Title	Issue Date	Number Issued	Issued Price	Current Price
Rosenthal Sculpture, porcelain				
Annual, Wirkkala	1971	3000	150.00	Unknown
Annual, Sapone	1972	3000	175.00	Unknown
Annual, Piene	1973	3000	250.00	Unknown
Annual, Fruhtrunk	1974	3000	300.00	Unknown
Annual, Narendra	1975	3000	375.00	Unknown
Annual, Dali	1976	3000	1250.00	Unknown
Rosenthal Sculpture, glass				
Annual, Clear	1974	1000	250.00	Unknown
Annual, Gold	1974	1000	450.00	Unknown
Annual, Silver	1974	1000	450.00	Unknown
Annual	1975	3000	200.00	Unknown

Rohn, Coolie

See listing for Rosenthal in Plate section

Title	Issue Date	Number Issued	Issued Price	Current Price
Royal Berlin, KpM, Figures				
Zodiac, Figurines, Decorated, Set Of 12			600.00	600.00
Zodiac Figurines, White, Sets Of 12			360.00	360.00

Royal Copenhagen Porcelain Manufactory, Ltd., of Copenhagen, Denmark, was established in 1755. In 1976, a new series of bronze figures sculpted by Sterett-Gittings Kelsey were introduced.

See listing for Royal Copenhagen in Plate section

Title	Issue Date	Number Issued	Issued Price	Current Price
Royal Copenhagen Bronzes				
Anita Price, Seated	1976	500	250.00	250.00
Anita Price, Standing	1976	500	300.00	300.00
Barbara Griffith, Seated	1976	500	250.00	250.00
Barbara Griffith, Standing	1976	500	300.00	300.00
Elise Gillet, Seated	1976	500	250.00	250.00
Elise Gillet, Standing	1976	500	300.00	300.00
Gitty Duncan, Seated	1976	500	250.00	250.00
Gitty Duncan, Standing	1976	500	300.00	300.00
Kitty Sanford, Seated	1976	500	250.00	250.00
Kitty Sanford, Standing	1976	500	300.00	300.00
Marian Kelsey, Seated	1976	500	250.00	250.00
Marian Kelsey, Standing	1976	500	300.00	300.00

Rohn, Jeanine, 1972

Royal Crown Derby of England was established as the Derby factory in 1750. The name Royal Crown Derby was used after 1890. Current limited editions were introduced in 1969.

See listing for Royal Crown Derby in Plate section

Title	Issue Date	Number Issued	Issued Price	Current Price
Royal Crown Derby Porcelains				
Welsh Dragon, Investiture Of Prince Of Wales*	1969	250	125.00	125.00

The Doulton Porcelain factory was founded in 1815. Royal Doulton is the name used on pottery made after 1902. A series of limited edition commemorative and special wares was made during the 1930s. Modern limited edition Christmas plates and mugs were first made in 1971. Royal Doulton also makes a line of limited edition porcelains.

See listing for Royal Doulton in Plate section

Title	Issue Date	Number Issued	Issued Price	Current Price
Royal Doulton Figurines				
Dancers, Flamenco	1977	750	400.00	400.00
Dancers, Indian Temple*	1977	750	400.00	400.00
Dancers, Philippine	1978	750	400.00	400.00
Dancers, Scottish	1978	750	400.00	400.00
Jefferson, Black-Throated Loon*	1974	150	1750.00	1750.00
Jefferson, Chipmunks	1974	75	1800.00	1800.00
Jefferson, Chipping Sparrow	1976	200	750.00	750.00
Jefferson, Crossbills, White-Winged	1974	250	1000.00	1000.00
Jefferson, Fledgling Bluebird	1976	250	450.00	450.00

Rohn, Riverboat Captain, 1971

Rohn, Apache

Royal Crown Derby, Welsh Dragon

Royal Doulton, Dancers, Indian Temple, 1977

Rohn, Matador

Rohn, The Sherif

Royal Doulton, Jefferson, Roseate Tern

Royal Doulton, Jefferson,
Snowy Owl, Male

Royal Doulton, Soldiers, Captain,
2nd New York Regiment, 1775

Royal Doulton, Jefferson, Black-Throated Loon

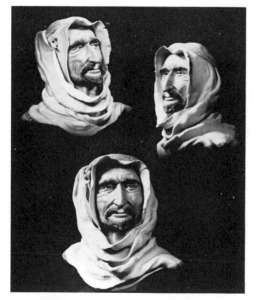

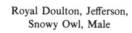

Title	Issue Date	Number Issued	Issued Price	Current Price
Jefferson, Harbor Seal	1975	75	1200.00	1200.00
Jefferson, King Eider Drake	1974	150	1400.00	1400.00
Jefferson, Puffins	1974	250	1200.00	1200.00
Jefferson, Roseate Tern*	1974	100	1850.00	2000.00
Jefferson, Snowshoe Hare	1975	75	2000.00	2000.00
Jefferson, Snowy Owl, Female	1974	150	1500.00	1500.00
Jefferson, Snowy Owl, Male*	1974	75	1800.00	1800.00
Lady Musicians, Cello**	1971	750	250.00	300.00
Lady Musicians, Chitarrone	1974	750	350.00	350.00
Lady Musicians, Cymbals	1974	750	325.00	325.00
Lady Musicians, Dulcimer	1975	750	375.00	375.00
Lady Musicians, Flute*	1973	750	250.00	300.00
Lady Musicians, French Horn	1976	750	400.00	400.00
Lady Musicians, Harp*	1973	750	275.00	300.00
Lady Musicians, Hurdy-Gurdy	1975	750	375.00	375.00
Lady Musicians, Lute*	1972	750	250.00	250.00
Lady Musicians, Viola D'amore	1976	750	400.00	400.00
Lady Musicians, Violin*	1972	750	250.00	250.00
Lady Musicians, Virginals**	1971	750	250.00	250.00
Prince Charles Bust**	1969	150	400.00	400.00
Queen Elizabeth & Duke Of Edinburgh Busts	1972	750	1000.00	500.00 to 1000.00
Soldiers, Captain, 2nd New York Regiment, 1775*	1976	350	750.00	750.00
Soldiers, Corporal, 1st N.Hampshire Reg., 1778	1975	350	750.00	750.00
Soldiers, General Washington At Prayer	1977	750	875.00	875.00
Soldiers, Indian Brave*	1967	500	2500.00	2500.00 to 3000.00
Soldiers, Major, 3rd New Jersey Regiment, 1776	1975	350	750.00	750.00
Soldiers, Private, Col.Craft's Mass.Regiment	1977	350	750.00	750.00
Soldiers, Private, Haslet's Delaware Regiment	1977	350	750.00	750.00
Soldiers, Private, Penn.Rifle Battalion	1978	350	750.00	750.00
Soldiers, Private, Rhode Island Regiment	1977	350	750.00	750.00
Soldiers, Private, 1st Georgia Regiment, 1777	1975	350	750.00	750.00
Soldiers, Private, 2nd S.Carolina Reg., 1781	1975	350	750.00	750.00
Soldiers, Private, 3rd N.Carolina Reg., 1778	1976	350	750.00	750.00
Soldiers, Private, 4th Conn.Regiment	1978	350	750.00	750.00
Soldiers, Sergeant, 1st Continental Dragoons	1978	350	750.00	750.00
Soldiers, Sergeant, 6th Maryland Regiment, 1777	1976	350	750.00	750.00
The Palio*	1971	500	2500.00	2500.00

The Royal Worcester Porcelain Factory, of Worcester, England, was founded under the name of Worcester in 1751. The name was changed to Royal Worcester in 1862. Limited edition porcelains have been made since the 1930s.

See listing for Royal Worcester in Plate section

Royal Worcester Pewter Figurines

Title	Issue Date	Number Issued	Issued Price	Current Price
Colonial Craftsmen, Blacksmith	1973	2500	225.00	Unknown
Colonial Craftsmen, Cabinetmaker	1973	2500	225.00	Unknown
Colonial Craftsmen, Clockmaker*		2500		Unknown
Colonial Craftsmen, Potter	1973	2500	195.00	Unknown

Dorothy Doughty, English artist, was born in San Remo, Italy, in 1892. She began modelling porcelain birds for Royal Worcester in the 1930s. The first model in the American bird series was issued in 1935. The British series was begun in 1964.

Royal Worcester, Dorothy Doughty Porcelains

Title	Issue Date	Number Issued	Issued Price	Current Price
American Redstarts And Hemlock	1935	66		5500.00
Apple Blossoms	1941	250	400.00	1400.00 to 3750.00
Audubon Warblers	1963	500	1350.00	2100.00 to 4200.00
Baltimore Orioles*	1938	250	350.00	880.00 to 5800.00
Bewick's Wrens & Yellow Jasmine	1956	500	600.00	2100.00 to 3800.00
Bluebirds	1936	350	500.00	8500.00 to 9000.00
Blue Tits & Pussy Willow	1964	500	250.00	3000.00
Bobwhite Quail*	1940	22	275.00	11000.00
Cactus Wrens*	1959	500	1250.00	1700.00 to 4500.00
Canyon Wrens	1960	500	750.00	2000.00 to 4000.00
Cardinals	1937	500	500.00	2000.00 to 9250.00
Carolina Paroquet, Color	1968	350	1200.00	1900.00 to 2200.00
Carolina Paroquet, White	1968	75	600.00	900.00 to 1100.00
Cerulean Warblers & Red Maple	1965	500	1350.00	1400.00 to 3000.00
Chickadees & Larch	1938	300	350.00	8500.00 to 8900.00

Royal Doulton, Indian Brave

Royal Doulton, The Palio

Royal Worcester, Dorothy Doughty,
Meadow Pipit, 1977

Royal Doulton,   Royal Doulton,
Lady Musicians, Harp   Lady Musicians, Flute

Royal Doulton,   Royal Doulton,
Lady Musicians, Violin Lady Musicians, Lute

Royal Worcester, Dorothy Doughty,
Nightingale And Honeysuckle

Royal Worcester, Dorothy Doughty, Cactus Wrens

Royal Worcester, Dorothy Doughty, Bobwhite Quail

Royal Worcester, Dorothy Doughty,
Baltimore Orioles

Royal Worcester, Dorothy Doughty,
Gnatcatchers

Royal Worcester, Dorothy Doughty,
Hooded Warblers

Title	Issue Date	Number Issued	Issued Price	Current Price
Chiffchaff	1965	500	1500.00	1300.00 to 2900.00
Crabapple Blossom Sprays And A Butterfly	1942	250		800.00
Crabapples	1940	250	400.00	3750.00 to 4250.00
Downy Woodpecker & Pecan, Color	1967	400	1500.00	1000.00 to 2400.00
Downy Woodpecker & Pecan, White	1967	75	1000.00	1900.00
Elf Owl	1959	500	875.00	850.00 to 2100.00
Gnatcatchers*	1955	500	600.00	2750.00 to 4900.00
Goldcrests, Pair	1972	500	4200.00	Unknown
Goldfinches & Thistle	1936	250	350.00	2000.00 to 7000.00
Gray Wagtail**	1968	500	600.00	700.00 to 1250.00
Hooded Warblers*	1961	500	950.00	4300.00
Hummingbirds And Fuchsia	1950	500		2800.00
Indigo Bunting And Plum Twig	1942	5000		
Indigo Buntings, Blackberry Sprays	1942	500	375.00	1700.00 to 3000.00
Kingfisher Cock & Autumn Beech	1965	500	1250.00	1900.00 to 2300.00
Kinglets & Noble Pine	1952	500	450.00	1300.00 to 4800.00
Lark Sparrow	1966	500	750.00	Unknown
Lazuli Buntings & Chokecherries, Color	1962	500	1350.00	3000.00 to 4500.00
Lazuli Buntings & Chokecherries, White	1962	100	1350.00	2600.00 to 3000.00
Lesser Whitethroats	1964	500	350.00	1200.00 to 4000.00
Magnolia Warbler	1950	150	1100.00	1900.00 to 3600.00
Meadow Pipit*	1977	500	1800.00	1800.00
Mexican Feijoa	1950	250	600.00	2600.00 to 4900.00
Mockingbirds	1940	500	450.00	7250.00 to 7750.00
Mockingbirds And Peach Blossom	1942	500		
Moorhen Chick	1964	500	1000.00	495.00 to 1250.00
Mountain Bluebirds	1964	500	950.00	1750.00 to 2300.00
Myrtle Warblers	1955	500	550.00	1300.00 to 4000.00
Nightingale & Honeysuckle*	1971	500	2500.00	1100.00 to 2750.00
Orange Blossoms & Butterfly	1947	250	500.00	4250.00 to 4500.00
Ovenbirds	1957	250	650.00	4500.00
Parula Warblers	1957	500	600.00	1700.00 to 3600.00
Phoebes On Flame Vine	1958	500	750.00	2250.00 to 5500.00
Red-Eyed Vireos	1952	500	450.00	2000.00
Redstarts & Gorse**	1968	500	1900.00	2300.00
Robin	1964	500	750.00	Unknown
Scarlet Tanagers*	1956	500	675.00	3000.00 to 4200.00
Scissor-Tailed Flycatcher, Color	1962	250	950.00	Unknown
Scissor-Tailed Flycatcher, White	1962	75	950.00	1300.00 to 1600.00
Vermilion Flycatchers*	1963	500	250.00	1100.00 to 3400.00
Wrens & Burnet Rose**	1964	500	650.00	1000.00
Yellow-Headed Blackbirds	1952	350	650.00	2000.00 to 2400.00
Yellowthroats On Water Hyacinth	1958	350	750.00	1700.00 to 4000.00

Royal Worcester,
Dorothy Doughty, Scarlet Tanagers

Royal Worcester, Frederick Gertner and Neal French Porcelains

Title	Issue Date	Number Issued	Issued Price	Current Price
Colonel Of The Noble Guard	1963	150	600.00	Unknown
Officer Of The Palatine Guard	1965	150	500.00	Unknown
Papal Gendarme	1967	150	450.00	Unknown
Privy Chamberlain Of The Sword & Cape	1959	150	500.00	Unknown
Trooper Of The Papal Swiss Guard	1956	150	500.00	Unknown

Royal Worcester, Dorothy Doughty,
Vermilion Flycatchers

Royal Worcester, Doris Lindner,
American Saddle Horse

Royal Worcester, James Alder Porcelain Sculptures

Title	Issue Date	Number Issued	Issued Price	Current Price
British Bird, Dipper	1977	500	1595.00	1595.00
British Bird, Wall Creeper	1977	500	995.00	995.00
English Bird, Bearded Reedling	1976	500	995.00	995.00
English Bird, Dartford Warbler	1976	500	995.00	995.00
English Bird, Hobby And Swallow	1976	250	6950.00	6950.00
English Bird, Shore Lark	1976	500	995.00	995.00
English Bird, Snow Bunting	1976	500	995.00	995.00
English Bird, Sparrow Hawk And Bullfinch	1976	250	6000.00	6000.00
English Bird, Sparrow Hawk And Bullfinch, Whit	1976	150	3500.00	3500.00
North American Bird, Carolina Wren	1978	150	995.00	995.00
North American Bird, Chestnut Collar Longspur	1978	150	1900.00	1900.00
North American Bird, Dickeissel**	1978	15	1500.00	1500.00
North American Bird, Red-Breasted Nuthatch	1978	150	1250.00	1250.00
North American Bird, Ruby-Crowned Kinglet	1978	150	1250.00	1250.00
North American Bird, Rufous Hummingbird**	1978	150	1500.00	1500.00

Doris Lindner began designing porcelain animal sculptures for Royal Worcester in 1931. Her limited edition Equestrian series was started in 1959.

Royal Worcester, Doris Lindner, Appaloosa

Royal Worcester, Doris Lindner,
Marion Coakes-Mould

Royal Worcester, Doris Lindner, New Born, Color

Royal Worcester, Doris Lindner,
Percheron Stallion

Title	Issue Date	Number Issued	Issued Price	Current Price
Royal Worcester, Doris Lindner Porcelains				
American Saddle Horse**	1973	750	1450.00	770.00 to 1675.00
Angus Bull	1961	500	350.00	Unknown
Appaloosa*	1969	750	550.00	1200.00 to 1500.00
Arab Stallion*	1963	500	450.00	Unknown
Arkle	1967	500	525.00	825.00
Brahman Bull	1968	500	400.00	440.00 to 8750.00
British Friesian Bull	1964	500	400.00	800.00 to 900.00
Bulldog	1968	500		Unknown
Charolais Bull**	1968	500	400.00	800.00 to 875.00
Clydesdale**	1977	500	1250.00	1250.00
Dairy Shorthorn Bull	1966	500	475.00	875.00 to 900.00
Duke Of Edinburgh*	1968	750	100.00	Unknown
Duke Of Marlborough	1976	350	5200.00	5200.00
Fox Hunter	1960	500	500.00	638.00 to 2450.00
Galloping Ponies, Colored	1975	500	3300.00	Unknown
Galloping, Classic	1975	250	2500.00	Unknown
Galloping In Winter	1976	250	3500.00	Unknown
Grundy	1977	500	1800.00	1800.00
Hackney	1976	500	1500.00	1500.00
Hereford Bull*	1959	1000	350.00	650.00 to 775.00
Highland Bull	1977	500	900.00	900.00
Hyperion	1965	500	525.00	850.00
Jersey Bull	1964	500	400.00	900.00 to 975.00
Jersey Cow	1961	500	300.00	550.00 to 600.00
Marion Coakes-Mould*	1970	750	750.00	1500.00
Merano	1963	500	500.00	1375.00
Mill Reef	1976	500	2000.00	2000.00
New Born, Color*	1976	500	1800.00	1800.00
New Born, White	1976	150	1250.00	1250.00
Nijinsky	1972	500	2000.00	2000.00
Officer Of Royal Horse Guards	1961	150	500.00	Unknown
Officer Of The Life Guards	1961	150	500.00	Unknown
Palomino**	1971	750	975.00	975.00 to 1275.00
Percheron Stallion*	1966	500	725.00	775.00 to 1400.00
Prince's Grace & Foal, Color**	1971	750	1500.00	1500.00 to 1700.00
Prince's Grace & Foal, White	1971	250	1400.00	1400.00 to 1600.00
Princess Anne On Doublet**	1973	750	4250.00	4250.00
Quarter Horse	1962	500	400.00	850.00 to 1100.00
Queen Elizabeth On Tommy	1947	100	275.00	13200.00
Red Rum	1976	250	2000.00	2000.00
Richard Meade	1976	500	2450.00	2450.00
Royal Canadian Mounty	1966	500	875.00	1450.00 to 1600.00
Santa Gertrudis Bull*	1961	500	350.00	675.00 to 700.00
Shire Stallion	1964	500	700.00	1300.00 to 1400.00
Suffolk Punch**	1969	500	650.00	975.00
Welsh Mountain Pony*	1966	500	3000.00	2500.00 to 3000.00

Norbert E. J. Roessler, American-born artist, makes bronzes, introduced by Royal Worcester in 1975.

Royal Worcester, Norbert E. J. Roessler, bronzes

Title	Issue Date	Number Issued	Issued Price	Current Price
Hummer, With Fuchsia	1976	500	225.00	225.00
Marlin	1976	500	250.00	250.00

Ronald and Ruth Van Ruyckevelt were designers at the Royal Worcester Porcelain Company in 1953. His first limited edition porcelain was made in 1956. Her Victorian Lady series started in 1958.

Royal Worcester, Van Ruyckevelt Porcelains

Title	Issue Date	Number Issued	Issued Price	Current Price
Alice		500	1875.00	1875.00
American Pintail, Pair	1970	500		3000.00
Argenteuil A-108	1969	338		Unknown
Beatrice	1960	500	125.00	Unknown
Blue Angel Fish	1958	500	375.00	900.00
Bluefin Tuna*	1967	500	500.00	950.00 to 1000.00
Blue Marlin	1965	500	500.00	1000.00

Royal Worcester, Doris Lindner,
Prince's Grace & Foal

Royal Worcester, Doris Lindner,
Arab Stallion

Royal Worcester, Doris Lindner,
Palomino

Royal Worcester, Doris Lindner,
Princess Anne On Doublet

Royal Worcester, Doris Lindner,
Duke Of Edinburgh

Royal Worcester, Doris Lindner,
Welsh Mountain Pony

Royal Worcester, Doris Lindner,
Hereford Bull

Royal Worcester,
Ronald Van Ruyckevelt,
Madelaine

Title	Issue Date	Number Issued	Issued Price	Current Price
Bobwhite Quail, Pair	1969	500		2000.00
Bridget	1969	500	300.00	600.00 to 700.00
Butterfly Fish	1957	500	375.00	1600.00
Caroline	1960	500	125.00	Unknown
Castelneau Pink	1969	429		825.00 to 875.00
Castelneau Yellow	1969	163		825.00 to 875.00
Cecilia		500	1875.00	1875.00
Charlotte & Jane**	1968	500	1000.00	1500.00 to 1650.00
Dolphin**	1968	500	500.00	900.00
Elaine**	1971	750	600.00	600.00 to 650.00
Elizabeth*	1967	500	300.00	750.00 to 800.00
Emily	1969	500	300.00	600.00
Esther	1978	500		Unknown
Felicity**	1971	750	600.00	600.00
Flying Fish	1962	300	400.00	450.00
Green-Winged Teal**	1971	500	1450.00	1450.00
Hibiscus	1962	500	300.00	350.00
Hogfish & Sergeant Major	1956	500	375.00	650.00
Honfleur A-105	1968	290		600.00
Honfleur A-106	1968	290		600.00
Languedoc**	1971	216		1150.00
Lisette	1959	500	100.00	Unknown
Louisa	1962	500	400.00	975.00
Madelaine*	1968	500	300.00	750.00 to 800.00
Mallards	1968	500		2000.00
Marion	1968	500	275.00	575.00 to 625.00
Melanie	1964	500	150.00	Unknown
Mennecy A-101	1968	338		675.00 to 725.00
Mennecy A-102	1968	334		675.00 to 725.00
Passionflower*	1961	500	300.00	400.00
Penelope	1959	500	100.00	Unknown
Picnic*	1976	250	2850.00	2850.00
Queen Elizabeth I	1976	250	3850.00	3850.00
Queen Elizabeth II**	1977	250		Unknown
Queen Mary I*	1976	250	4850.00	4850.00
Rainbow Parrot Fish**	1968	500	1500.00	1500.00
Red Hind	1958	500	375.00	900.00
Ring-Necked Pheasants	1968	500		3200.00 to 3400.00
Rock Beauty*	1964	500	425.00	850.00
Rosalind	1964	500	150.00	Unknown
Sailfish	1962	500	400.00	550.00
Saint Denis A-109	1969	500		925.00 to 950.00
Sister Of London Hospital	1963	500		475.00 to 500.00
Sister Of St.Thomas' Hospital	1963	500		475.00 to 500.00
Sister Of The Red Cross	1970	750		525.00 to 550.00
Sister Of University College Hospital	1966	500		475.00 to 500.00
Squirrelfish	1961	500	400.00	9000.00
Swordfish	1966	500	575.00	650.00
Tarpon	1964	500	500.00	975.00
Tea Party	1964	250	1000.00	2250.00 to 2400.00
White Doves	1972	25	3600.00	27850.00

Royal Worcester,
Ronald Van Ruyckevelt,
Elizabeth

Bernard Winskill, English sculptor, designed his first limited edition porcelain for Royal Worcester in 1969.

Royal Worcester, Bernard Winskill Porcelains

Title	Issue Date	Number Issued	Issued Price	Current Price
By A Short Head	1977	100	5000.00	5000.00
Duke Of Marlborough	1976	350	5200.00	Unknown
Duke Of Wellington**	1970	750	4500.00	Unknown
Exmoor Pony	1976	500	895.00	Unknown
George Washington, Bronze	1976	15	6000.00	Unknown
George Washington, Horseback**	1976	750	4000.00	Unknown
Napoleon Bonaparte*	1969	750	3500.00	3500.00
Shetland Pony	1976	500	795.00	795.00

Saari Metal Sculptures

Title	Issue Date	Number Issued	Issued Price	Current Price
Nixon, Stainless Steel	1972	5000	25.00	25.00 to 30.00

See listing for Silver Creations in Plate section

Sovereign Metalcasters Sculptures

Title	Issue Date	Number Issued	Issued Price	Current Price
President Kennedy, Sterling	1973	Year	150.00*	150.00

Royal Worcester,
Ronald Van Ruyckevelt,
Rainbow Parrot Fish

Royal Worcester, Pewter,
Colonial Craftsmen, Clockmaker

Royal Worcester, Van Ruyckevelt,
Queen Mary I

Royal Worcester,
Van Ruyckevelt, Picnic

Royal Worcester, Ronald Van Ruyckevelt,
Passionflower

Royal Worcester, Doris Lindner,
Santa Gertrudis Bull

Royal Worcester,
Ronald Van Ruyckevelt, Languedoc

Royal Worcester,
Ronald Van Ruyckevelt, Bluefin Tuna

Royal Worcester,
Ronald Van Ruyckevelt, Dolphin

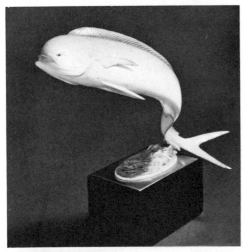

Royal Worcester,
Ronald Van Ruyckevelt, Rock Beauty

Royal Worcester, Ronald Van Ruyckevelt, Green-Winged Teal

Royal Worcester,
Ronald Van Ruyckevelt,
Elaine

Tay Porcelains are designed and modeled by Giuseppi Tagliariol in Monza, Italy.

Title	Issue Date	Number Issued	Issued Price	Current Price
Tay Porcelains				
American Woodcock 10 1/2 In.**	1974	500	625.00	700.00
Austrian Officer On Horseback	1973	100	1200.00	1200.00 to 1500.00
Bluebirds, Group Of Two, 9 1/4 In.	1976	500	500.00	550.00
Blue Jay, 13 In.	1970	500	375.00	675.00
Boreal Chickadee, 7 In.	1974	5000	275.00	360.00
Carolina Ducks, Group Of Two, 13 In.	1975	500	1350.00	1500.00
Custer On Horse, 13 X 14 1/2 In.	1976	500	1500.00	1500.00
Eagle, 12 In. X 15 In.**	1970	500	1000.00	1650.00
European Woodcock, 10 1/2 In.	1970	500	325.00	550.00
Falcon, 13 In.	1971	500	500.00	925.00
Gray Partridge, 11 1/2 In.	1972	500	800.00	1400.00
Great Crested Flycatcher, 9 In.	1974	1000	300.00	360.00
Gyrfalcon, 18 In.	1974	300	1250.00	1500.00
Indian On Horse, 13 X 14 1/2 In.	1976	500	1500.00	1500.00
Limpkin, 20 In.**	1970	500	600.00	1100.00
Mallard Duck, 13 1/2 In.	1974	500	900.00	1050.00
Mallard Duck, Flying, 15 In.	1974	500	550.00	675.00
Oriole, 9 1/2 In.	1975	1000	300.00	325.00
Owl, 10 1/2 In.	1974	500	350.00	450.00
Pheasant, 30 In.**	1971	500	1500.00	2000.00 to 2750.00
Quail Group, 10 In.	1971	500	400.00	725.00
Roadrunner, 10 X 19 In.**	1971	500	800.00	950.00 to 1400.00
Robin, 8 In.	1976	500	400.00	450.00
Smergos Ducks, Group Of Two, 10 In.	1975	500	1000.00	1100.00
Turtledoves On Roof Tile, 9 1/2 In.	1974	500	335.00	375.00
Turtledoves, Group Of Two, 10 In.		500		500.00
White-Throated Sparrow, 5 1/2 In.	1975	500	360.00	400.00

Royal Worcester,
Ronald Van Ruyckevelt,
Felicity

Towle Silversmiths of Newburyport, Massachusetts, was established by William Moulton in 1664. Towle limited editon ornaments were first issued in 1971. Plates followed in 1972.

See listing for Towle in Plate section

Title	Issue Date	Number Issued	Issued Price	Current Price
Towle Silver Figurines				
Goal Line Stand	1973	650	500.00	500.00
Mother & Child, Silver	1973		500.00	500.00

Van Ruyckevelt, see Royal Worcester

Title	Issue Date	Number Issued	Issued Price	Current Price
Vasari Figurines by Gorham				
Austrian Hussar	1973	250	300.00	300.00
Cellini	1973	200	400.00	400.00
Christ	1973	200	250.00	250.00
Creche	1973	200	500.00	500.00
D'Artagnan	1973	250	250.00	400.00
English Crusader	1973	250	250.00	250.00
French Crusader	1973	250	250.00	250.00
German Hussar	1973	250	250.00	250.00
German Mercenary	1973	250	250.00	250.00
Italian Crusader	1973	250	250.00	250.00
Leonardo Da Vinci	1973	200	250.00	250.00
Mercenary Warrior	1971	250	250.00	250.00
Michelangelo	1973	200	250.00	250.00
Ming Warrior	1971	250	200.00	200.00
Pirate	1973	250	200.00	200.00
Porthos	1973	250	250.00	250.00
Roman Centurion	1973	250	200.00	200.00
Spanish Grandee	1973	250	200.00	200.00
Swiss Warrior	1971	250	250.00	Unknown
The Cossack*	1973	250	250.00	250.00
Three Kings, Set Of 3	1973	200	750.00	750.00
Three Musketeers, Set Of 3*	1973	200	750.00	750.00
Venetian Nobleman	1973	250	200.00	200.00
Viking	1973	250	200.00	200.00
Wallace Silversmiths Pewter Figurines				
Jones, John Paul	1973	1000	350.00	350.00
Pitcher, Molly	1973	1000	400.00	400.00

Royal Worcester, Bernard Winskill,
Napoleon Bonaparte

Title	Issue Date	Number Issued	Issued Price	Current Price
Valley Forge	1973	1000	350.00	350.00
Washington Crossing The Delaware	1973	1000	400.00	400.00

Wedgwood was established in Etruria, England, by Josiah Wedgwood in 1759. The factory was moved to Barlaston in 1940. Wedgwood is famous for its Jasperware, Basalt, and Queensware, all produced in the eighteenth century. These wares are still used by Wedgwood for its limited editions, introduced in 1969.

See listing for Wedgwood in Paperweights and Plate sections

Wedgwood Busts

Title		Number Issued	Issued Price	Current Price
Eisenhower, Large, Black Basalt		521	200.00	200.00
Eisenhower, Small, Black Basalt		5000	75.00	75.00
Kennedy, Small, Black Basalt		2000	75.00	75.00
Lincoln, Large, Black Basalt		351	200.00	200.00
Lincoln, Small, Black Basalt		2000	75.00	75.00
Washington, Large, Black Basalt		10		12000.00
Washington, Small, Black Basalt		2000	75.00	75.00

William Turner

William Turner figurines are produced by Ispanky Studios

Title	Issue Date	Number Issued	Issued Price	Current Price
Barn Owl	1975	250	950.00	950.00

The Wildlife of the World Series offers limited edition numbered pieces cast in art bronze. They are being produced by C. E. Kloos of Arcadia, California.

Wildlife Figurines

Title	Issue Date	Number Issued	Issued Price	Current Price
Barbary Sheep	1976	250	295.00	295.00
Bighorn Sheep	1977	500	150.00	150.00
Bull Moose*	1975	100	1500.00	1500.00
Cougar Family*	1974	500	395.00	395.00
Elk	1977	500	195.00	195.00
Moose Rack, Monarch's Crown	1974	500	295.00	295.00
Mule Deer	1978	500	195.00	195.00
Osprey	1973	500	250.00	250.00
Pronghorn Antelope	1977	500	150.00	150.00
Rabbit, Doe With Young*	1973	500	95.00	95.00
Raccoon Family, Fishing Lesson	1973	500	295.00	295.00
Rocky Mountain Bighorn Sheep	1976	250	750.00	750.00
Rocky Mountain Goat*	1975	500	250.00	250.00
Rocky Mountain Goat, Head	1978	500	150.00	150.00
Siberian Argali	1976	500	295.00	295.00
Spring Move*	1976	50	3500.00	3500.00
Squirrel	1973	500	195.00	195.00
Summer Survival	1977	50	3500.00	3500.00
Timber Wolf	1974	500	395.00	395.00
Whitetail Deer	1977	500	195.00	195.00
Wild Boar	1973	500	175.00	175.00
Winter Meat*	1978	50	3500.00	3500.00

Winskill, see Royal Worcester

Royal Worcester, Bernard Winskill, Duke Of Wellington

Tay, Eagle

Vasari, The Cossack

Vasari, Three Musketeers

Wildlife Of The World Series, Rabbit,
Doe With Young

Wildlife Of The World Series,
Spring Move, 1976

Wildlife Of The World Series,
Cougar Family

Wildlife Of The World Series,
Winter Meat, 1978

Wildlife Of The World Series,
Rocky Mountain Goat

Wildlife Of The World Series,
Bull Moose

River Shore, Copper Plate, Rockwell, Lincoln,
No. 1, 1976

Pickard, Plate, Christmas, Alba Madonna, 1976

Royal Doulton, Plate, American Tapestries, Sleigh Bells, 1978

Boehm, Plate, Fancy Fowl, Pair, 1977

Wheaton, Presidential Plate, Lincoln

Pickard, Plate, Lockhart, Great Horned Owl, 1977

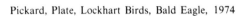

Pickard, Plate, Lockhart Birds, Bald Eagle, 1974

Pickard, Plate, Lockhart, American Panther, 1978

Pickard, Plate, Christmas, Nativity, 1977

Juharos, Plate, Omnibus Muralis, Life Of
Christ, 1977

Poole, Medieval Calendar Plate, April

Poole, Medieval Calendar Plate, March

Fenton, Craftsmen Plate, 1972, Blacksmith

Gorham, Plate, Rockwell, Four
Seasons, The Tender Years, 4,
1978

Fenton, Christmas Plate, 1972, Blue Satin

Fenton, Craftsmen Plate, 1974, Cooper

River Shore, Copper Plate, Rockwell, Peace Corps,
1978

River Shore, Copper Plate, Rockwell By Rockwell,
1977

Royal Doulton, Plate, Neiman, Punchinello, 1978

Royal Doulton, Plate, Log Of Dashing Wave,
Rounding The Horn, 1978

Royal Doulton, Plate, I Remember America,
Lovejoy Bridge, 1978

Kern Collectibles, Plate, Companion
Series, Mighty Sioux, 1978

J & E Specialties, Plate, Bicentennial,
Bunker Hill, 1976

Rosenthal, Plate, Burgues, June
Dream, 1978

Wedgwood, Christmas Plate, 1973

Wedgwood, Calendar Plate, 1973

Wedgwood, Child's Day Plate, 1972

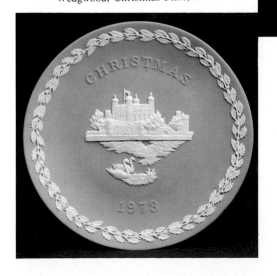

Wedgwood, Calendar Plate, 1974

Wedgwood, State Seal Compotier,
John Hancock & Massachusetts

Wedgwood, State Seal Compotier,
Philip Livingston & New York

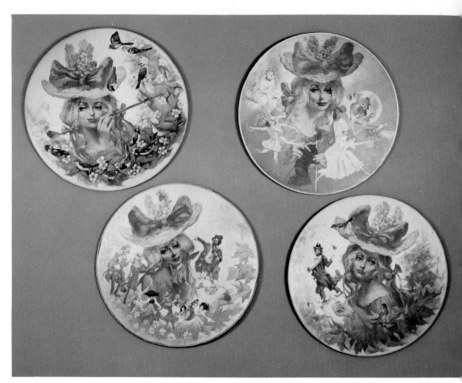

Gorham, Plate, Ritter, Four Seasons Series, To Love A Clown, 4, 1978

Wedgwood, Bicentennial Plate, 1973

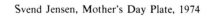

Svend Jensen, Mother's Day Plate, 1974

Svend Jensen, Plate, Christmas, Ugly
Duckling, 1975

Royal Crown Derby,
Derbyshire Landscape Dessert Plate,
Wolfscote Dale

Svend Jensen, Christmas Plate, 1974

Svend Jensen, Plate, Christmas, Snow
Queen, 1976

Pickard, Lockhart Bird Plate, 1971, Mallard

Pickard, Lockhart Bird Plate, 1972,
Mockingbird

Svend Jensen Plate, Christmas,
The Oak Tree, 1978

Royal Worcester, Doris Lindner, American Saddle Horse

Royal Worcester, Doris Lindner,
Princess Anne On Doublet

Royal Worcester, Doris Lindner, Palomino

Royal Worcester, Doris Lindner, Suffolk Punch

Royal Worcester, Bernard Winskill, Duke Of Wellington

Royal Worcester, Bernard Winskill, Napoleon Bonaparte

2. Paperweights

Title	Issue Date	Number Issued	Issued Price	Current Price

Baccarat limited editions are made in France by La Compagnie des Cristalleries de Baccarat, located near Paris. The factory was started in 1765. The firm went bankrupt and started operating again about 1822. Famous cane and millefiori paperweights were made there during the 1860-1880 period. In 1953, after a lapse of 80 years, sulphide paperweights were again introduced. A series of limited edition paperweights has been made each year since 1953.

See listing for Baccarat in Figurine section

Baccarat Paperweights

Baccarat, Gridel Elephant

Baccarat, Gridel Squirrel

Title	Issue Date	Number Issued	Issued Price	Current Price
Apples And Pears, Combined Edition	1974	200	250.00	250.00
Bergstrom, Evangeline	1974	500		50.00
Bicentennial, Mt. Rushmore, Double Overlay	1976	1000	500.00	459.50 to 500.00
Bonaparte, Memorial	1974	100		150.00
Bonaparte, Napoleon, Regular	1974	2000	60.00	60.00
Bonaparte, Overlay, Yellow	1974	400	175.00	129.50 to 175.00
Butterfly	1972	100	300.00	Unknown
Churchill, Winston, Overlay	1954	81	75.00	1500.00 to 2000.00
Churchill, Winston, Regular	1954	558	25.00	750.00 to 1000.00
Coronation, Overlay	1953	195	75.00	550.00 to 650.00
Coronation, Regular	1954	1492	20.00	300.00 to 350.00
Dahlia	1973	200	200.00	200.00 to 235.00
Eisenhower, Dwight D., Overlay, Poillerat	1953	178	75.00	600.00 to 700.00
Eisenhower, Dwight D., Regular, Poillerat	1953	1389	25.00	375.00 to 425.00
Flower Basket	1976	300	390.00	390.00
Flower Latticinio	1975	260	390.00	390.00
Flower With Lady Bug	1976	300	425.00	425.00
Franklin, Benjamin, Overlay	1955	180	75.00	650.00 to 750.00
Franklin, Benjamin, Regular	1955	414	25.00	400.00 to 500.00
Frog	1974	200	390.00	390.00
Grapes Cluster	1975	260	390.00	390.00
Gridel Elephant*	1973	250	150.00	150.00 to 165.00
Gridel Horse**	1973	250	150.00	150.00 to 165.00
Gridel Hunter	1975	250	150.00	150.00 to 175.00
Gridel Monkey, Black	1975	225	175.00	175.00
Gridel Pelican	1974	250	150.00	150.00
Gridel Pheasant	1976	250	175.00	175.00
Gridel Pigeons	1976		225.00	225.00
Gridel Red Devil	1977	250	250.00	250.00
Gridel Rooster*	1972	1200	150.00	150.00 to 165.00

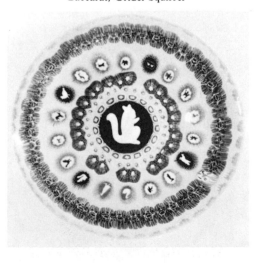

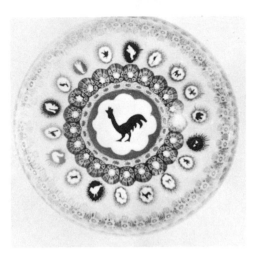

Baccarat, Gridel Rooster

Baccarat, Mushroom Overlay

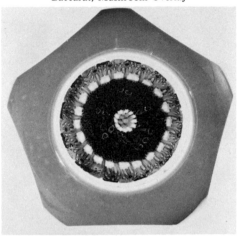

Baccarat, Pansy

Baccarat, Woodrow Wilson, Regular

Title	Issue Date	Number Issued	Issued Price	Current Price
Gridel Squirrel**	1972	1200	150.00	150.00 to 165.00
Gridel Stag	1976	250	225.00	225.00
Gridel Stork	1977	250	250.00	250.00
Gridel Swan	1974	250	150.00	150.00
Gridel White Monkey	1976	250	225.00	175.00 to 225.00
Henry, Patrick, Overlay	1977	400	275.00	245.00 to 275.00
Henry, Patrick, Regular	1977	1500	85.00	85.00
Hoover, Herbert, Overlay, Pale Blue	1971	400	155.00	175.00 to 187.50
Hoover, Herbert, Regular, Cobalt Blue	1970	2500	47.50	55.00 to 62.50
Jackson, Andrew, Overlay, Green	1972	400	155.00	175.00 to 250.00
Jackson, Andrew, Regular, Green	1972	2400	47.50	50.00 to 60.00
Jefferson, Thomas, Overlay	1954	156	75.00	550.00 to 650.00
Jefferson, Thomas, Regular	1954	594	25.00	325.00 to 375.00
Kennedy, John F. Memorial, Faceted	1964	314	65.00	250.00
Kennedy, John F., Overlay	1964	308	135.00	250.00 to 450.00
Kennedy, John F., Regular, Sulphide	1964	3572	35.00	175.00 to 250.00
King, Martin Luther, Sulphide		607	325.00	325.00
Lafayette, Marquis De, Overlay	1955	227	75.00	525.00 to 575.00
Lafayette, Marquis De, Regular	1955	744	25.00	300.00 to 325.00
Laval, Pierre, Memorial	1970	171		250.00
Laval, Pierre, Overlay	1970	113	155.00	155.00
Laval, Pierre, Regular	1970	31	47.50	47.50
Lee, Robert E., Overlay	1954	137	75.00	550.00 to 650.00
Lee, Robert E., Regular	1954	913	25.00	375.00
Lincoln, Abraham, Overlay	1954	197	75.00	475.00
Lincoln, Abraham, Regular	1954	1291	25.00	300.00 to 350.00
Luther, Martin, Overlay	1956	86	75.00	500.00 to 600.00
Luther, Martin, Regular	1956	607	25.00	200.00 to 225.00
Monroe, James, Overlay, Green Flash	1970	400	155.00	175.00 to 185.00
Monroe, James, Regular, Orange	1970	2500	47.50	50.00 to 55.00
Mushroom Overlay*	1973	200	180.00	200.00 to 225.00
Mushroom, Double Overlay, Millefiori Tuft	1976		250.00	250.00
Paine, Thomas, Overlay, Green	1976	400	225.00	225.00
Paine, Thomas, Regular, Blue Opaline	1976	2000	75.00	62.95 to 75.00
Pansy*	1974	200	250.00	250.00 to 290.00
Pope John XXIII, Overlay	1966	343	145.00	250.00 to 275.00
Pope John XXIII, Regular	1966	2157	37.50	125.00 to 165.00
Pope Pius XII, Overlay	1960	284	100.00	250.00 to 350.00
Pope Pius XII, Regular	1960	2157	30.00	125.00 to 150.00
Queen Elizabeth, Overlay	1954	200	75.00	450.00 to 550.00
Queen Elizabeth, Regular	1954	775	37.50	Unknown
Rayburn, Sam, Overlay	1961	93	100.00	450.00 to 550.00
Rayburn, Sam, Regular	1961	512	30.00	350.00
Rogers, Will, Overlay, Green Swirl	1968	389	150.00	250.00
Rogers, Will, Regular, Yellow	1968	2517	42.50	85.00 to 100.00
Roosevelt, Eleanor, Overlay, Amethyst	1971	420	155.00	175.00 to 250.00
Roosevelt, Eleanor, Regular, Amethyst	1971	2500	47.50	50.00 to 80.00
Roosevelt, Theodore, Overlay, Green	1967	381	150.00	150.00 to 250.00
Roosevelt, Theodore, Regular, Amethyst	1967	2359	42.50	65.00 to 100.00
Rose Latticinio	1976	150	475.00	475.00
Salamander**	1973	200	350.00	350.00
Seahorse, Crystal	1975		390.00	390.00
Snail	1977	300	490.00	490.00
Special Flower	1974	200	200.00	200.00 to 275.00
Spectacular Rose	1976	150	425.00	425.00
Snake**	1972	100	300.00	300.00
Stevenson, Adlai, Overlay, Amethyst Flash	1969	472	150.00	195.00
Stevenson, Adlai, Regular, Garnet Red	1969	2595	45.00	50.00 to 80.00
Strawberries	1974	200	390.00	390.00
Strawberries, Translucent Blue Ground	1974	200	390.00	390.00
Truman, Harry S, Overlay	1973	400	75.00	29.50 to 75.00
Truman, Harry S, Regular	1973	2250	55.00	55.00
Washington, George, Overlay	1954	200	75.00	375.00 to 550.00
Washington, George, Regular	1954	1182	25.00	250.00 to 300.00
Wilson, Woodrow, Overlay, Yellow	1972	400	160.00	235.00
Wilson, Woodrow, Regular, Turquoise*	1972	2400	50.00	52.50 to 55.00

Banford Paperweights, Ray and Bob

Title	Issue Date	Number Issued	Issued Price	Current Price
Bee Over Clematis Flower, Faceted			300.00	300.00 to 350.00
Blue And White Flowers, Jasper, Miniature			100.00	100.00

Title	Issue Date	Number Issued	Issued Price	Current Price
Bumble Bee On Flower, Miniature			250.00	250.00
Cherries, Faceted, Mini			200.00	200.00
Coiled Snake, Gold Bee Resting On Flower			250.00	250.00
Dragonfly Above Clematis Flower, Faceted			300.00	300.00
Green Snake, Jasper, Miniature			75.00	75.00
Iris	1976		250.00	250.00
Lavender Flower, Green Ground, Miniature			150.00	150.00
Roses, Three Pink, Two Red, Faceted, Mini			50.00	150.00
Roses, Two Pink, One Blue, Mini			125.00	125.00
Rosettes, Buds, Faceted, Miniature			200.00	200.00
Rosettes On Trellis, Faceted, Miniature			200.00	200.00
Single Red Rose, Jasper, Mini			100.00	100.00
Striped Snake, Jasper, Miniature			75.00	75.00
Striped Snake With Flower			150.00	150.00
Two Flowers Climbing A Trellis, Faceted			250.00	250.00 to 300.00

Bryden, Robert, Paperweights

Blue And White Ribbons On Rose Crown	1978	150	60.00	60.00
Millefiori Garden, Gem Faceted	1976	150	42.00	42.00
White Cape Cod Rose, Gem Faceted	1976	150	120.00	120.00

See also Spode Caithness Paperweights

Caption: Cristal D'Albret, Christopher Columbus, Overlay
Caption: Cristal D'Albret, Ernest Hemingway, Overlay

Caithness Paperweights

Arctic Fern		500	85.00	85.00
Comet	1977	3000	125.00	125.00
Dragonfly		1500	135.00	105.00
First Quarter	1977	1500	95.00	95.00
Four Elements, Earth, Air, Water, Fire			440.00	440.00
Four Planets, Set			300.00	300.00
May Dance			65.00	65.00
Moonflower			55.00	55.00
Plough, Star Formation	1977	3000	125.00	125.00
Sea Crabs	1977	1500	95.00	95.00
Sea Pearl	1977	500	150.00	150.00
Soda Crystal, Numbered			105.00	105.00
Zephyr	1977	400	150.00	150.00

John Choko and Pete Lewis are two Millville glass workers who share a workshop. Choko makes large weights, while Lewis works in miniature.

Choko, John, Paperweights

Lizard	1974		200.00	200.00
Pedestal Rose			200.00	200.00

Cristal d'Albret plates and paperweights are made at the glassworks of Vianne, France. Limited edition sulphide paperweights were first made in 1966.

See listing for Cristal d'Albret in Plate section

Caption: Cristal D'Albret, John James Audubon, Overlay
Caption: Cristal D'Albret, Paul Revere, Overlay

Cristal d'Albret Paperweights

American Eagle, Overlay	1976	400	250.00	250.00
Audubon, John James, Overlay*	1972	225	170.00	170.00
Audubon, John James, Regular	1972	1000	68.00	65.00 to 70.00
Ben Gurion, David, Regular	1973	750		Unknown
Ben Gurion, David, Overlay	1973	150		Unknown
Churchill, Winston, Pinchbeck, Gold	1975	1000	250.00	250.00
Churchill, Winston, Pinchbeck, Silver	1975	1000	250.00	250.00
Columbus, Christopher, Overlay*	1966	200	150.00	225.00 to 275.00
Columbus, Christopher, Regular	1966	1000	55.00	85.00 to 95.00
Da Vinci, Leonardo	1968	1000	70.00	70.00
Da Vinci, Leonardo, Overlay**	1968	200	160.00	160.00 to 180.00
Da Vinci, Leonardo, Regular	1968	1000	62.00	65.00 to 85.00
Gandhi, Sulphide, Poillerat	1976	500	100.00	89.50 to 100.00
Gustaf, King Of Sweden, Regular	1967	1000	55.00	55.00 to 65.00
Hemingway, Ernest, Overlay*	1969	225	160.00	160.00 to 180.00
Hemingway, Ernest, Regular	1969	1000	62.00	70.00 to 80.00
John Paul Jones, Overlay	1974	170	170.00	170.00
John Paul Jones, Regular	1974	430	68.00	68.00
Kennedy, John & Jackie, Overlay	1967	121	150.00	110.00
Kennedy, John & Jackie, Overlay	1969	300		Unknown
Kennedy, John & Jackie, Regular	1967	2000	55.00	68.00

Title	Issue Date	Number Issued	Issued Price	Current Price
King, Martin Luther, Sulphide, Poillerat	1976	500	120.00	107.50 to 120.00
Lind, Jenny, Overlay	1974	170	170.00	170.00
Lind, Jenny, Regular	1974	410	68.00	65.00 to 75.00
Lindbergh, Overlay, Poillerat	1976	200	180.00	180.00
Lindbergh, Regular, Poillerat	1976	415	70.00	70.00
MacArthur, Douglas, Overlay	1968	225	150.00	150.00 to 170.00
MacArthur, Douglas, Regular	1968	1000	55.00	62.00 to 90.00
Meir, Golda, Regular	1974	850		Unknown
Meir, Golda, Overlay	1974	150		Unknown
Moon Astronauts, Overlay	1971	200	160.00	160.00
Moon Astronauts, Regular	1971	1000	62.00	80.00
Prince Charles, Overlay	1970	200	150.00	150.00 to 170.00
Prince Charles, Regular	1970	1000	55.00	62.50 to 75.00
Revere, Paul, Overlay**	1969	200	160.00	160.00 to 180.00
Revere, Paul, Regular	1969	800	62.00	65.00 to 75.00
Roosevelt, Franklin D., Overlay	1967	300	150.00	150.00 to 185.00
Roosevelt, Franklin D., Regular	1967	2000	55.00	80.00
Schweitzer, Albert, Overlay	1969	200	160.00	160.00 to 185.00
Schweitzer, Albert, Regular	1969	1000	55.00	43.00 to 70.00
Sitting Bull, Terra Cotta, Poillerat	1976	1000	95.00	87.50 to 95.00
Sitting Bull, Tricolor Cameo, Poillerat	1976	500	120.00	107.50 to 120.00
Twain, Mark, Overlay	1969	225	150.00	150.00 to 200.00
Twain, Mark, Regular	1969	1000	55.00	62.00 to 80.00

See listing for Danbury Mint in Plate section

Danbury Mint Crystal Sculptures

Title	Issue Date	Number Issued	Issued Price	Current Price
Adams, John	1976	3500	90.00	90.00
Franklin, Benjamin	1976	3500	90.00	90.00
Hamilton, Alexander	1976	3500	90.00	90.00
Jefferson, Thomas	1976	3500	90.00	90.00
Madison, James	1976	3500	90.00	90.00
Washington, George	1976	3500	90.00	90.00

Edmund, Hugh Paperweights

Title	Issue Date	Number Issued	Issued Price	Current Price
Ballerina	1974	50	300.00	300.00
Bear, Copper Wheel Engraved	1976	50	230.00	230.00
Butterfly	1973	50	200.00	200.00
Cardinal	1974	50	250.00	250.00
Crane	1975	50	250.00	250.00
Elephant, Copper Wheel Engraved	1976	50	300.00	300.00
Hummingbirds	1973	50	300.00	300.00
Madonna And Child	1975	50	275.00	275.00
Puss 'n Boots	1973	50	250.00	250.00
Rainbow Trouts	1974	50	250.00	250.00
Rose, Copper Wheel Engraved	1976	50	300.00	250.00
Seal, Copper Wheel Engraved	1976	50	230.00	230.00
Squirrel	1975	50	250.00	250.00
Swan	1973	50	200.00	200.00
Thoroughbred	1974	50	300.00	300.00
Tiger Lily	1975	50	225.00	225.00

Erlacher Paperweights

Title	Issue Date	Number Issued	Issued Price	Current Price
Cinquefoil, Faceted			170.00	170.00
Grapes			150.00	150.00
Grapes, Faceted			170.00	170.00
Lily			150.00	150.00
Lily, Faceted			170.00	170.00
Virginia Cowslip			150.00	150.00
Virginia Cowslip, Faceted			170.00	170.00

Falchi Paperweights

Title	Issue Date	Number Issued	Issued Price	Current Price
Bicentennial, Eagle, Blue	1975	Year	10.00	10.00
Bicentennial, Eagle, Chocolate	1975	Year	11.00	11.00
Bicentennial, Eagle, Red	1975	Year	10.00	10.00
Bicentennial, Eagle, White	1975	Year	10.00	10.00
Key, Francis Scott	1975	800	500.00	500.00
Ross, Betsy	1975	800	500.00	500.00

Fischer Paperweights

Title	Issue Date	Number Issued	Issued Price	Current Price
Bicentennial, Spirit Of '76, Crystal	1975	10000	10.00	9.00 to 10.00
Star Of David, Crystal	1976	5000	10.00	10.00

Title	Issue Date	Number Issued	Issued Price	Current Price
See listing for Franklin Mint in Plate section				
Franklin Mint Paperweights				
Alice In Wonderland, Set Of 12	1977	Year	420.00	420.00
Bicentennial, John Adams	1974	6753	75.00	Unknown
Bicentennial, Benjamin Franklin	1974	6753	75.00	Unknown
Bicentennial, Admiral Comte De Grasse	1974	6753	75.00	Unknown
Bicentennial, Thomas Jefferson	1974	6753	75.00	Unknown
Bicentennial, John Paul Jones	1974	6753	75.00	Unknown
Bicentennial, Marquis De Lafayette	1974	6753	75.00	Unknown
Bicentennial, King Louis XVI	1974	6753	75.00	Unknown
Bicentennial, Montesquieu	1974	6753	75.00	Unknown
Bicentennial, Jean-Jacques Rousseau	1974	6753	75.00	Unknown
Bicentennial, George Washington	1974	6753	75.00	Unknown
Carter Inaugural**	1977	Year	95.00	95.00
Great Leaders, Alexander The Great	1976	Year	90.00	Unknown
Great Leaders, Simon Bolivar	1976	Year	90.00	Unknown
Great Leaders, Napoleon Bonaparte	1976	Year	90.00	Unknown
Great Leaders, Julius Caesar	1976	Year	90.00	Unknown
Great Leaders, Charlemagne	1976	Year	90.00	Unknown
Great Leaders, Winston Churchill	1976	Year	90.00	Unknown
Great Leaders, Elizabeth I	1976	Year	90.00	Unknown
Great Leaders, Joan Of Arc	1976	Year	90.00	Unknown
Great Leaders, Abraham Lincoln	1976	Year	90.00	Unknown
Great Leaders, Louis XIV	1976	Year	90.00	Unknown
Great Leaders, Peter The Great	1976	Year	90.00	Unknown
Great Leaders, George Washington	1976	Year	90.00	Unknown
Royal Family, Prince Andrew	1972	1741	35.00	Unknown
Royal Family, Prince Charles	1972	1741	35.00	Unknown
Royal Family, Prince Edward	1972	1741	35.00	Unknown
Royal Family, Prince Philip	1972	1741	35.00	Unknown
Royal Family, Princess Anne	1972	1741	35.00	Unknown
Royal Family, Queen Elizabeth II	1972	1741	35.00	Unknown
Gentile Glass Paperweights				
Apollo 11, Moon Landing And Astronaut, Set	1969	1800	25.00	25.00
Apollo 15		1000	15.00	15.00
Apollo 17	1972	1000	15.00	15.00
Beetle Family		50	250.00	250.00
Bicentennial Bell, Two-Color	1976	2600	10.00	10.00
Bicentennial Cannon, Two-Color	1976	2600	10.00	10.00
Bicentennial, First Battle	1976	2600	10.00	10.00
Bicentennial Flag, Faceted	1976	250	75.00	75.00
Bicentennial Flag, Plain	1976	250	60.00	60.00
Bicentennial Flag, Two-Color	1976	2600	10.00	10.00
Bicentennial, Martinsburg	1976	500	10.00	10.00
Bicentennial, Millefiore	1976	300	12.00	12.00
Bicentennial, Monongalia County	1976	500	10.00	10.00
Bicentennial, Rice Landing	1976	300	10.00	10.00
Bicentennial, Star City	1976	500	10.00	10.00
Bicentennial, Telephone	1976	500	10.00	10.00
Bicentennial, 200 Years Of Progress	1976	2600	10.00	10.00
Caterpillar On Ground		50	185.00	185.00
Caterpillar On 3 Leaves		50	250.00	250.00
Center Beetle		50	125.00	125.00
Devil's Fire		1800	28.00	28.00
God Bless America, Peace	1973	1800	7.50	7.50
Grape Crystal Faceted, Star Bottom		200	250.00	250.00
Grape With Leaf, Plain		200	200.00	200.00
Green Lizard With Beetle		50	225.00	225.00
Green Lizard, Plain		50	200.00	200.00
Kennedy, John F., Faceted		900	25.00	25.00
Kennedy, John F., Plain		3600	15.00	15.00
Millefiore, Broken Heart, Faceted		100	50.00	50.00
Millefiore, Broken Heart, Plain		500	35.00	35.00
Millefiore Heart, Faceted		100	50.00	50.00
Millefiore Heart, Plain		500	35.00	35.00
Old Glory, Faceted		1000	75.00	75.00
Old Glory, Plain		1000	50.00	50.00
Pearl Harbor		1000	12.00	12.00
Salamander, Circled		200	130.00	130.00

Kosta,
Annual Paperweight,
1973

Pairpoint,
Amethyst Snake Pedestal,
1972

Pairpoint, Faceted Red Rose

Pairpoint, Red Pedestal Rose, 1972

Title	Issue Date	Number Issued	Issued Price	Current Price
Salamander, Circled With Baby In Shell		100	250.00	250.00
Salamander, Circled With Beetle		200	135.00	135.00
Salamander, Circled With Worm		50	135.00	135.00
Salamander, Crawling		200	125.00	125.00
Salamander, On Two Leaves Attacking Beetles		50	225.00	225.00
Snake, Crawling		200	75.00	75.00
Snake, Cross-Over		100	85.00	85.00
Snake Family		50	185.00	185.00
Snake, Figure 8		200	85.00	85.00
Snake, Figure 8 With Beetle			100.00	130.00
Spiral Wig Stand		500	30.00	30.00
Strawberry With Blossom And Leaves, Faceted	1976	100	250.00	250.00
Strawberry With Blossom And Leaves, Plain	1976	100	200.00	200.00
Three Cherry Crystal Faceted, Star Bottom		100	250.00	250.00
Three Cherry With Leaf, Plain		200	200.00	200.00
Washington, George, Faceted		500	25.00	25.00
Washington, George, Plain		1000	15.00	15.00
Washington, Martha, Faceted		500	25.00	25.00
Washington, Martha, Plain		1000	15.00	15.00

Gorham Paperweights

Egg**	1978	2500	85.00	85.00

Hacker, Harold Paperweights

Flower With Buds			200.00	200.00
Salamander			300.00	300.00
Swans In Pond			200.00	200.00
Turtle			75.00	75.00
Two Mice			75.00	75.00

Hummel Paperweights

Sister Berta	1978	4000	150.00	150.00

Kaziun, Charles, Paperweights

Blue Convolvulus Flower On Opaque Pink				400.00
Clichy Rose, Millefiori			460.00	460.00
Miniature Small Red Rose On White Lace				525.00
Pansy, Lavender And Blue On Apricot Jasper			460.00	480.00
Poinsettia, Tawny Red On White Ground			550.00	550.00
Red And White Swirl, K Center, Ring Of Hearts			275.00	275.00
Spider Lily, Pedestal On Red And White Jasper			180.00	180.00
White Swirl With K Center, Ring Of Hearts			275.00	275.00

Kosta Glassworks of Sweden was founded in 1742 by King Charles II. The limited edition line, introduced in 1970, includes paperweights, plates, and mugs.

See listing for Kosta in Plate section

Kosta Paperweights

Annual, Mom	1970	Year	24.50	12.00 to 20.00
Annual, Dad	1971	Year	26.50	12.00 to 20.00
Annual, Twins, Pair	1972	Year	30.00	11.00 to 30.00
Annual, Miss Kosta*	1973	Year	30.00	30.00
Annual, Aunt Rosie	1974	Year	40.00	40.00
Annual, Grandfather	1975	Year	40.00	40.00
Annual	1976	Year		Unknown
Annual	1977	Year		Unknown

Pete Lewis and John Choko are two Millville glass workers who share a workshop. Choko makes large weights, while Lewis works in miniature.

Lewis, Pete, Miniature Paperweights

Pansy			150.00	150.00
Stylized Flower			150.00	150.00

Lotton, Charles, Paperweights

Multi-Flora, Amber			100.00	100.00
Multi-Flora, Translucent Blue			100.00	100.00

Lundberg Studios Paperweights

Fish, Seaweed, Jellyfish, Millefiori	1974	250	150.00	150.00
Tropical Fish	1976	250	75.00	69.50 to 75.00
Things That Go Bump In The Night, Bat	1976	300	75.00	75.00

Title	Issue Date	Number Issued	Issued Price	Current Price
Things That Go Bump In The Night, Scarab	1976	300	85.00	85.00

Max Erlacher, see Erlacher

Metropolitan Museum of Art

Blue And White Ribbons With Rose Crown	1976		60.00	60.00
Millefiori Garden, Gem Faceted	1976	150	42.00	42.00
White Cape Cod Rose, Gem Faceted	1976	150	120.00	120.00

Old South Jersey Paperweights

Bicentennial, American Flag	1976	3000	25.00	25.00
Bicentennial, Independence Hall	1976	3000	25.00	25.00
Bicentennial, Liberty Bell	1976	3000	25.00	25.00
Bicentennial, Minute Man	1976	3000	25.00	25.00
Bicentennial, Paul Revere	1976	3000	25.00	25.00
Bicentennial, Spirit Of '76	1976	3000	25.00	25.00

Pairpoint limited editions are made by the Pairpoint Glass Company of Sagamore, Massachusetts. Artisans in Glass, Inc., of New York is the distributor of Pairpoint limited editions.

See listing for Pairpoint in Plate section

Pairpoint Paperweights

Amethyst Pedestal Rose, Engraved	1974	146	165.00	95.00 to 165.00
Amethyst Pedestal Rose, Plain Base	1974	60	85.00	85.00 to 165.00
Amethyst Snake Pedestal*	1972	75	125.00	125.00
Faceted Red Rose**	1974	300	200.00	125.00 to 200.00
French Blue Snake Pedestal, Blue Snake	1974	100	95.00	95.00
French Blue Snake Pedestal, Green Snake	1974	100	95.00	95.00
Lace And Twist Crown, 5 Colors	1974	100	45.00	45.00
Opal Snake Pedestal, Emerald Green Snakes	1973	34	95.00	95.00
Opal Snake Pedestal, French Blue Snakes	1973	33	95.00	95.00
Opal Snake Pedestal, Peachblow Pink Snakes	1973	63	85.00	85.00
Opal Snake Pedestal, Varicolored Snakes	1973	25		Unknown
Red Pedestal Rose*	1972	300	200.00	250.00 to 335.00
Red Pedestal Rose, Engraved	1972	300	200.00	200.00
Red Pedestal Rose, Plain Base	1972	60	85.00	85.00
Red, White, And Blue Crown**	1974	500	80.00	45.00 to 80.00
Yellow Rose Of Texas, Pedestal, Plain Base	1973	79	85.00	85.00

The Perthshire Company, founded in 1968, is located in Crieff, Scotland. Limited edition paperweights were first made in 1969.

Perthshire Paperweights

Amethyst, Double Overlay**	1974	300	295.00	350.00
Amethyst Overlay Bottle	1971	300	200.00	350.00 to 400.00
Butterfly	1975	450	195.00	250.00
Carpet Ground, 6 Silhouette Canes	1977	400	220.00	220.00
Christmas, Holly And Berries**	1971	250	100.00	200.00 to 300.00
Christmas, Mistletoe**	1972	300	100.00	250.00 to 300.00
Christmas, Poinsettia	1976	350	200.00	200.00
Christmas Robin*	1974	325	130.00	150.00 to 200.00
Christmas Rose*	1975	350	150.00	150.00 to 175.00
Circle	1977	450	50.00	50.00
Close Millefiori**	1973	400	140.00	130.00 to 140.00
Cushion Weight**	1971	250	80.00	95.00 to 120.00
Cushion Weight, 6 Clusters	1975	400	100.00	Unknown
Dahlia**	1972	200	250.00	400.00 to 500.00
Damson Plum	1977	500	220.00	200.00 to 220.00
Dragonfly**	1970	500	75.00	300.00 to 350.00
Dragonfly On Bouquet, Faceted**	1974	300	350.00	600.00
Faceted Bouquet	1974	300	350.00	350.00
Faceted Carpet Ground	1972	300	130.00	Unknown
Faceted Cushion Ground**	1972	300	130.00	130.00 to 150.00
Faceted Flower**	1974	600	.90	Unknown
Faceted Millefiori	1973	250	52.50	52.50
Flower And Bud**	1974	350	130.00	Unknown
Flower In Basket	1973	300	75.00	90.00
Flower On Latticinio	1973	300	125.00	150.00
Forget-Me-Not	1976	400	180.00	180.00
Garland On Cushion	1974	350	130.00	150.00
Magnum Cushion	1976	300	450.00	450.00

Pairpoint, Red, White, And Blue Crown

Perthshire, Paperweight, Christmas Rose

Perthshire, Dragonfly, 1970

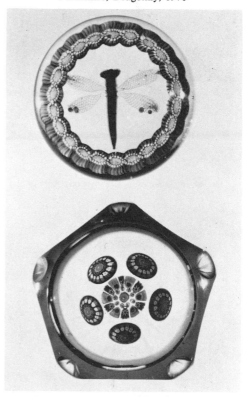

Perthshire, Translucent Overlay, Various Colors, 1970

Perthshire, Dahlia, 1972

Perthshire, Faceted Cushion Ground, 1972

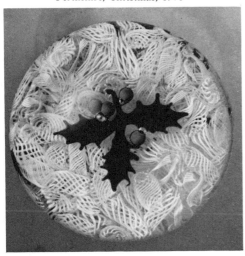

Perthshire, Christmas, 1971

Perthshire, Paperweight, Christmas Robin

Title	Issue Date	Number Issued	Issued Price	Current Price
Millefiori, Canes, Translucent Ground	1977	400	160.00	160.00
Miniature Faceted Blue And White Flower	1976	400	150.00	150.00
Miniature Flower In Basket	1972	1000	75.00	150.00
Miniature Overlay Butterfly	1976	500	200.00	Unknown
Moss Ground	1976	300	250.00	250.00
New Cushion Ground	1975	400	100.00	100.00
Nosegay, Latticinio	1977	400	200.00	200.00
Pansy, Faceted	1971	350	125.00	200.00 to 250.00
Penguin, Ice Blue Overlay, Faceted**	1976	350	350.00	400.00
Patterned Millefiori On Cobalt Ground	1972	300	55.00	55.00 to 70.00
Patterned Millefiori On Maroon Ground	1972	300	55.00	55.00 to 70.00
Primrose, Triple Overlay	1977	400	400.00	400.00
Red, White, And Blue Crown*	1969	350	125.00	150.00
Ribbon, Small Rose Florette**	1971	150	80.00	100.00 to 125.00
Robin Redbreast	1975	325	125.00	125.00
Rooster	1977	300	320.00	320.00
Scattered Millifiori On Blue Ground**	1974	500	95.00	95.00
Star	1977	300	50.00	50.00
Swan In A Pond**	1973	250	195.00	300.00
Translucent Overlay, Various Colors**	1970	150	300.00	300.00 to 350.00
Tudor Rose	1975	400	160.00	Unknown

See listing for Royale Germania Crystal in Plate section

Royale Germania Crystal Paperweights

Title	Issue Date	Number Issued	Issued Price	Current Price
Annual, Capitol, Blue	1970	350	180.00	125.00 to 390.00
Annual, Independence Hall, Red	1971	350	200.00	170.00 to 340.00
Annual, Washington's Inauguration, Green	1972	350	270.00	155.00 to 310.00
Annual, Constitution, Lilac*	1973	300	270.00	180.00 to 360.00
Annual, Gold Rush, Smoky Topaz*	1974	250	425.00	316.65 to 425.00
Annual, Lincoln*	1975	250	570.00	575.00

St. Clair Paperweights

Title	Issue Date	Number Issued	Issued Price	Current Price
Lincoln			20.00	20.00
McGovern	1972	2000	25.00	25.00
Nixon	1972	2000	25.00	25.00
Pink Rose				85.00 to 100.00
Plain Rose			100.00	100.00
Red Rose, Three Facets			75.00	75.00
Red Rose, Four Facets			125.00	125.00

The original St. Louis glasshouse was established in 1767 at St. Louis, France. The name became Compagnie des Cristalleries de St. Louis in 1829. The first paperweights were made during the 1840s. Modern paperweights were started again in 1952.

St. Louis Paperweights

Title	Issue Date	Number Issued	Issued Price	Current Price
American Eagle, Overlay, Poillerat	1976	400	250.00	250.00
Bicentennial, Gold Washington Medal, Crystal	1976	250	310.00	310.00
Bicentennial, Gold Washington Medal, Overlay	1976	400	450.00	450.00
Blue Camomile	1975	250	250.00	250.00
Blue And White Carpet Ground**	1972	250	175.00	Unknown
Carpet Ground**	1972	250	180.00	250.00
Carter, Jimmy	1978	200	90.00	90.00
Carter, Jimmy, Overlay	1978	10	195.00	195.00
Cherries, Latticinio Basket, Faceted	1953	250	280.00	500.00
Clematis, Green	1970	150		Unknown
Clematis, Red	1970	150		Unknown
Clichy Rose, Millefiori Canes, Pedestal	1976	250	520.00	520.00
Clichy Roses, Yellow, Opaque Blue, Crystal	1976	250	330.00	330.00
Corrugated White Canes, White Carpet Ground	1973	250	180.00	130.00 to 180.00
Dahlia, Blue	1970	150		Unknown
Dahlia, Green	1970	150		Unknown
Dahlia, Red	1970	150		Unknown
Dahlia On Latticinio	1973	250	140.00	140.00 to 170.00
De Gaulle, General	1978	500	90.00	90.00 to 150.00
De Gaulle, General, Overlay	1978	250	195.00	195.00
Doily, Millefiori**	1972	250		250.00
Double Overlay, Two Flower Bouquet	1975	250	350.00	350.00
Flat Bouquet On Opaque White Ground**	1972	250	150.00	150.00 to 160.00
Flower On Opaque Orange Underlay*	1973	250	190.00	190.00
Fuchsia On Latticinio	1976	250	350.00	350.00

Perthshire, Ribbon,
Small Rose Florette, 1971

Royale Germania,
Annual Paperweight, 1973

Royale Germania,
Paperweight, Annual,
Gold Rush, Smoky Topaz

Royale Germania, Paperweight,
Annual, Lincoln

Smith, Double White Clematis

Smith, Red Desert Flower

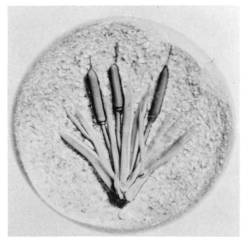

Smith, Six-Petal Purple Flower

Smith, Cattail

Smith, Double Yellow Clematis

Smith, Double Red Pointed Petal Clematis

Title	Issue Date	Number Issued	Issued Price	Current Price
Handcooler, Bicentennial Colors	1976		200.00	200.00
Honeycomb, Red	1974	250	230.00	230.00
Ingold, Francois	1967	9		Unknown
King Of France Commemorative	1967	2000	210.00	225.00 to 240.00
Lafayette Sulphide	1967	250	200.00	300.00 to 350.00
Marbrie, Blue Yellow & White**	1971	250	210.00	200.00 to 225.00
Millefiori Cluster	1972	250	140.00	160.00 to 180.00
Millefiori Garland*	1973	250	210.00	210.00
Millefiori, Hawaiian Pattern	1975	250	200.00	200.00
Millefiori, Latticinio Ribbon**	1972	250	160.00	170.00 to 200.00
Mushroom, Blue Overlay	1970	100	220.00	220.00
Mushroom, Green Overlay	1970	100	220.00	175.00
Mushroom, White Overlay	1970		220.00	210.00 to 220.00
Newel Post	1974	250	360.00	360.00
Patterned Millefiori	1972	250	120.00	150.00 to 170.00
Penholder	1973	125	325.00	325.00
Piedouche*	1972	250	250.00	300.00 to 520.00
Pinwheel, Blue & White Swirl**	1971	250	140.00	140.00
Pinwheel, 5-Color Swirl		250	160.00	140.00 to 170.00
Pompon	1975	250		Unknown
Queen Elizabeth, Sulphide		2000	325.00	325.00
Red Flower Faceted**	1973	250	140.00	140.00
Roses On Snow Ground, Crystal	1976		330.00	330.00
Scattered Canes And Lace Tubes	1972	250	160.00	170.00 to 200.00
Schumann, Robert, Commemorative	1969	300	225.00	300.00 to 350.00
Star-Shape Millefiore	1971	250	140.00	170.00
Stylized Flower On Opaque Absinthe Ground*	1974		190.00	190.00
Three-Color Crown Weight*	1974	250	180.00	180.00
White Dahlia, Mauve Ground	1974	250	190.00	190.00
Yellow Flower, Faceted		250	140.00	140.00

St. Louis Seals

Title	Issue Date	Number Issued	Issued Price	Current Price
Blue	1974	1000	50.00	50.00
Red	1974	1000	50.00	50.00

Smith paperweights are made by Hugh and Carolyn Smith of Millville, New Jersey.

Smith Paperweights

Title	Issue Date	Number Issued	Issued Price	Current Price
Blue Flower, Gray Jasper, H.S.			130.00	130.00
Cattail, H.S.*		200	125.00	130.00
Cattails, Faceted, H.S.			150.00	150.00
Closed Gentian, H.S.			230.00	230.00
Closed Gentian, Faceted, H.S.			280.00	280.00
Closed Morning Glory, H.S.			130.00	130.00
Closed Morning Glory, Faceted, H.S.			150.00	150.00
Columbine, C.S.			150.00	150.00
Columbine, Faceted, C.S.			170.00	170.00
Dark Blue Stylized Flower, Gold Jasper, H.S.			130.00	130.00
Double White Clematis, H.S.*		200	125.00	130.00
Double White Clematis, Faceted, H.S.			150.00	150.00
Double Red Pointed Petal Clematis*		200	125.00	125.00
Double Yellow Clematis*		200	125.00	125.00
Fire-Orange Heart Flower, C.S.			130.00	130.00
Fire-Orange Heart Flower, Faceted, C.S.			150.00	150.00
Five-Petal Blue Mountain Flower*		200	125.00	125.00
Green Holly On White Jasper, H.S.			150.00	150.00
Grapes			150.00	150.00
Grapes, Faceted			170.00	170.00
Ground Pink	1974	25	170.00	170.00
Holly & Berry, H.S.			230.00	230.00
Holly & Berry, Faceted, H.S.			280.00	280.00
Lily			150.00	150.00
Lily, Faceted			170.00	170.00
Madonna Lily, C.S.	1978	35	275.00	275.00
Nemesia, H.S.	1978	35	275.00	275.00
Off-Red Flower On Green, White Jasper, C.S.			130.00	130.00
Orchid			230.00	230.00
Orchid, Faceted			280.00	280.00
Periwinkle, H.S.			230.00	230.00
Periwinkle, Faceted, H.S.			280.00	280.00

Smith, White Trillium

Smith, Five-Petal Blue Mountain Flower

Title	Issue Date	Number Issued	Issued Price	Current Price
Pink Dogwood			230.00	230.00
Pink Dogwood, Faceted			280.00	280.00
Pleated Clematis			230.00	230.00
Pleated Clematis, Faceted			280.00	280.00
Pleated Clematis, C.S.	1978	35	275.00	275.00
Pokeberry, H.S.	1978	35	275.00	275.00
Purple Flower On Brown, White Jasper, H.S.			130.00	130.00
Purple Trillium, H.S.			230.00	230.00
Purple Trillium, Faceted, H.S.			280.00	280.00
Red Desert Flower*		200	125.00	125.00
Red Heart Flower				230.00
Red Heart Flower, Faceted			280.00	280.00
Red Maids, C.S.	1978	35	275.00	275.00
Red Passion Flower			230.00	230.00
Red Passion Flower, Faceted			280.00	280.00
Red Poinsettia	1974	25	170.00	170.00
Red Poinsettia, H.S.	1978	150	275.00	275.00
Scarlet Cress, C.S.	1978	35	275.00	275.00
Shaded Orange Clematis			230.00	230.00
Shaded Orange Clematis, Faceted			280.00	280.00
Six-Petal Purple Flower*		200	125.00	125.00
Spider Lily, H.S.	1978	35	275.00	275.00
Springtime, H.S.	1978		360.00	360.00
Springtime, Faceted, H.S.	1978		400.00	400.00
Stylized Blue Flower, Gray Jasper, H.S.			130.00	130.00
Stylized Pink Flower, White Jasper, H.S.			130.00	130.00
Stylized Red Flower On Blue, White Jasper, H.S			150.00	150.00
Stylized Red Flower, Green Jasper, C.S.			130.00	130.00
Stylized Red Flower On White Jasper, C.S.			130.00	130.00
Stylized Tulip, C.S.			130.00	130.00
Stylized Tulip, Faceted, C.S.			140.00	140.00
Stylized White Flower On Gold Jasper, C.S.			130.00	130.00
Stylized White Flower On Red Jasper, C.S.			130.00	130.00
Stylized Yellow Flower, Blue Jasper, H.S.			150.00	150.00
Stylized Yellow Flower, Jasper, Faceted, H.S.			150.00	150.00
Virginia Cowslip, H.S.			230.00	230.00
Virginia Cowslip, Faceted, H.S.			280.00	280.00
White Dogwood, C.S.			130.00	130.00
White Dogwood, Faceted, C.S.			150.00	150.00
White Trillium*		200	125.00	125.00
Wild Black Cherries, H.S.	1978	35	275.00	275.00

Spode, Caithness Paperweights

Title	Issue Date	Number Issued	Issued Price	Current Price
Spode, Caithness, Earth	1971	500	20.00	25.00
Spode, Caithness, Jupiter	1971	500	20.00	25.00
Spode, Caithness, Neptune	1971	500	20.00	25.00
Spode, Caithness, Saturn	1971	500	20.00	25.00
Spode, Caithness, Uranus	1971	500	20.00	25.00

Stankard, Paul, Paperweights

Title	Issue Date	Number Issued	Issued Price	Current Price
Anthony's Fire, Single Flower			250.00	250.00
Anthony's Fire, Single Flower, Faceted			300.00	300.00
Anthony's Fire, Clear, Double Flower			300.00	300.00
Anthony's Fire, Clear, Double Flower, Faceted			350.00	350.00
Anthony's Fire, Triple Flower			350.00	350.00
Anthony's Fire, Triple Flower, Faceted			400.00	400.00
Bell Wort		75	250.00	250.00
Bicentennial, Trilaflora			600.00	600.00
Blackberry		50	400.00	400.00
Bouquet			600.00	600.00 to 800.00
Cayenne Pepper	1975	50	250.00	250.00
Chokeberry	1975	75	400.00	300.00 to 400.00
Cinquefoil				200.00
Circaflora	1976		500.00	500.00
Compound Blackberry				400.00
Compound Blueberry			400.00	400.00
Compound Strawberry		50	400.00	400.00
Daylily	1976	75	200.00	200.00 to 250.00
Dogwood		75		200.00
Flaming Glory				200.00
Flax, Green	1977		300.00	300.00

St. Louis, Flower On Opaque
Orange Ground, 1973

St. Louis, Stylized Flower On Opaque
Absinthe Ground, 1974

St. Louis, Millefiore Garland, 1973

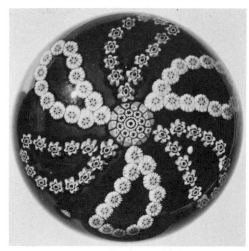

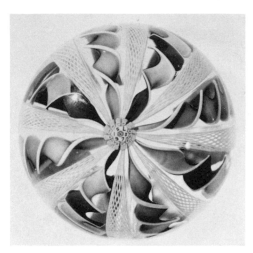

St. Louis, Three-Color Crown, 1974

St. Louis, Piedouche

Title	Issue Date	Number Issued	Issued Price	Current Price
Flower On Twisted Stem				200.00
Forget-Me-Not			200.00	200.00
Goat's Rue	1975	50	250.00	250.00
Lady Slipper		50		200.00
Meadowreath			250.00	300.00
Medicinal Herb, Cinquefoil			200.00	200.00
Merrybell		75		200.00
Orchid, Cattleya		75	300.00	300.00
Orchid, Lady Slipper		75	300.00	300.00
Orchid, Spider	1977	75	350.00	350.00
Painted Trillium			250.00	200.00 to 250.00
Pink Meadowreath			250.00	250.00
Poinsettia		50		200.00
Red Plantain		50	250.00	250.00
Spiderwort	1975	75	250.00	250.00
Spring Beauty		50		200.00
Strawberries	1977		400.00	400.00
Summer Field Arrangement	1978	25	800.00	800.00
Touch-Me-Not	1976	50	250.00	250.00
Trilaflora		6	600.00	600.00
White Marsh Gentian		75		Unknown
Wildflowers, Faceted			250.00	250.00
Wildflowers, Unfaceted				200.00
Wild Marsh Gentian		75	250.00	250.00
Wild Rose, Single Flower			250.00	250.00
Wild Rose, Single Flower, Faceted			300.00	300.00
Wild Rose, Double Flower			300.00	300.00
Wild Rose, Double Flower, Faceted			350.00	350.00
Wild Rose, Triple Flower			350.00	350.00
Wild Rose, Triple Flower, Faceted			400.00	400.00
Wintergreen		50	400.00	400.00
Yellow Meadowreath, Single Flower			250.00	250.00
Yellow Meadowreath, Single Flower, Faceted			300.00	300.00
Yellow Meadowreath, Double Flower			300.00	300.00
Yellow Meadowreath, Double Flower, Faceted			350.00	350.00
Yellow Meadowreath, Triple Flower			350.00	350.00
Yellow Meadowreath, Triple Flower, Faceted			400.00	400.00

Van Son Paperweights

Title	Issue Date	Number Issued	Issued Price	Current Price
Commemorative, Black & Yellow*	1972	1500	25.00	Unknown

Wedgwood was established in Etruria, England, by Josiah Wedgwood in 1759. The factory was moved to Barlaston in 1940. Wedgwood is famous for its Jasperware, Basalt, and Queensware, all produced in the eighteenth century. These wares are still used by Wedgwood for its limited editions, introduced in 1969.

See listing for Wedgwood in Figurines and Plate sections

Wedgwood Paperweights

Title	Issue Date	Number Issued	Issued Price	Current Price
Bicentennial, G.Washington, Jasperware Cameo	1976	340	125.00	125.00
Caduceus	1975	1500	35.00	35.00
Christmas, Angel	1975		60.00	60.00
Eisenhower, Black Jasper				100.00
Liberty Bell	1975	2500	35.00	35.00
Libra, Black Jasper	1975	1500	35.00	35.00

See listing for Wheaton in Plate section

Wheaton Village 1888 Glass Factory offers paperweights created by Blaire Hardenburg.

Title	Issue Date	Number Issued	Issued Price	Current Price
Bicentennial Floral, Clear**	1976	13	325.00	450.00
Bicentennial Floral, Blue**	1976	13	325.00	450.00
Christmas, Star Of Bethlehem	1975	500	15.00	40.00
Christmas, Fireplace	1976	385	30.00	30.00
Christmas, Snowman	1977	400	40.00	40.00
Christmas, Special	1977	100	50.00	75.00
Wheaton Village, Red, Blue, Green Or Lavender		50	80.00	80.00

Whitefriars paperweights are made by Whitefriars Glass Ltd. of Wealdstone, Middlesex, England. The original Whitefriars glasshouse was established in 1680. Paperweights were first made in 1848. They were

Van Son, Commemorative Paperweight

Title	Issue Date	Number Issued	Issued Price	Current Price

discontinued for many years until modern paperweights were again made in the 1960s. Until recently the company was known as James Powell & Sons (Whitefriars, Ltd.).

Whitefriars Paperweights

Title	Issue Date	Number Issued	Issued Price	Current Price
Ball Cut Cylinder, No.9755	1974		90.00	90.00 to 110.00
Bicentennial	1975	750	200.00	200.00
Bicentennial, Liberty Bell	1975	600	200.00	200.00
Christmas	1975	1000	300.00	300.00
Diamond Cut, Red, White And Blue, No.9781	1974		85.00	85.00 to 95.00
Dome Shape, No.9748	1974		85.00	85.00 to 95.00
Flag				450.00
Large Facets				110.00
Liberty Bell	1976	600	200.00	200.00
Millefiori, Butterfly Center	1976		200.00	200.00
Mitre Cut				110.00
Olympics	1972	500		65.00 to 75.00
Queen's Anniversary	1972	500		65.00 to 75.00
Square Facets				110.00
Two Calla Lilies, Blue Ground				350.00
United States Patriotic	1977	500	300.00	300.00
White				
Window Cut, Regular, No.9736	1974		75.00	75.00 to 90.00
Window Cut, Small, No.9746	1974		75.00	70.00 to 80.00

Whittemore paperweights are made by Francis Dyer Whittemore, Jr. of Landsdale, Pennsylvania. His first paperweights were made in 1964. Each weight is marked with a 'w' within a cane.

Whittemore Paperweights

Title	Issue Date	Number Issued	Issued Price	Current Price
Bleeding Heart		100	350.00	350.00
Blue Anemone, Yellow Torsade				300.00
Bouquet On Blue Ground				300.00
Calla Lily On Pink Ground				300.00
Cherries On Pink Ground				100.00
Cherry Spray On Leaves				350.00
Christmas	1977	1000	300.00	300.00
Christmas, Candles & Holly	1971	100	350.00	300.00 to 375.00
Christmas, Stocking & Candy Canes	1972	100	350.00	325.00 to 375.00
Christmas, Wise Men	1976	1000	300.00	300.00
Colorado Flower, Columbine	1976	75		350.00
Colorado Flower, Columbine, Faceted	1976	25		400.00
Connecticut Flower, Mountain Laurel	1976	100	350.00	350.00
Delaware Flower, Peach Blossom	1976	100	350.00	350.00
Diamond Cut, Color Vary, No.9737	1974		85.00	85.00
Dome With Bleeding Heart, Emerald		100		350.00
Dome With Calla Lily Blossoms				275.00
Dome With Pink Rose, Cobalt Ground				275.00
Dome With Purple And Yellow Pansies, Cobalt				275.00
Fuschia, Overlay	1975	25		400.00
Fuschia, Regular	1975	75		350.00
Georgia Flower, Cherokee Rose	1976	100	350.00	350.00
Holly On Blue Ground	1972		300.00	300.00
Iowa State Flower, Iowa Rose	1976	100		325.00 to 375.00
Long Stem Rose With Bud				400.00
Maryland Flower, Black-Eyed Susan	1976	100	350.00	350.00
Massachusetts Flower, Mayflower	1976	100	350.00	350.00
Millefiori, Owl Center	1977		200.00	200.00
Minnesota Flower, Lady Slipper	1976	100		350.00
Modernistic Mushrooms				300.00
Modernistic Mushrooms, Faceted				350.00
Monument Valley, Marigold Carnival	1972	Year	20.00	15.00 to 20.00
New Hampshire Flower, Purple Lilac	1976	100	350.00	350.00
New Jersey Flower, Violet	1976	100	350.00	350.00
New York Flower, Rose	1976	100	350.00	350.00
North Carolina & Virginia Flower, Dogwood	1976	75	350.00	350.00
North Carolina & Virginia Flower, Dogwood, Fct	1976	25	400.00	400.00
North Dakota Flower, Prairie Rose	1976	75	350.00	350.00
North Dakota Flower, Prairie Rose, Faceted	1976	25	400.00	400.00
Nosegay On Foot		250	250.00	250.00
Partridge In Pear Tree				300.00

Title	Issue Date	Number Issued	Issued Price	Current Price
Oklahoma Flower, Mistletoe	1976			350.00
Oklahoma Flower, Mistletoe, Faceted	1976			400.00
Olympics	1976	1000		Unknown
Parrot On A Branch			350.00	350.00
Pedestal, 4 Canes, 5 Leaves	1976	250	200.00	200.00
Pennsylvania Flower, Mountain Laurel	1976		350.00	350.00
Rhode Island Flower, Violet	1976	100	350.00	350.00
Shaded Blue Rose, Pedestal	1976			165.00
Silver Jubilee	1977		150.00	150.00
South Carolina Flower, Jessamine	1976	75	350.00	350.00
South Carolina Flower, Jessamine, Faceted	1976	25		400.00
Spring Bouquet				300.00
Striped Yellow Dahlia				400.00
Tennessee Flower, Iris	1976	100	350.00	350.00
Three Flower Bouquet				300.00
Three Flower Bouquet, Faceted				350.00
Virginia Flower, Dogwood	1976	100	350.00	350.00
Window Cut, Additional Windows, No.9780	1974		85.00	85.00
Yellow Crimped Rose, Pedestal				125.00

Ysart, Paul, Paperweights

Title	Issue Date	Number Issued	Issued Price	Current Price
Bicentennial, Bouquet			250.00	190.00 to 250.00
Butterfly			250.00	190.00 to 250.00
Double Fish				280.00 to 350.00
Dragonfly			250.00	300.00
Flowers On Lace Cushion			250.00	250.00
Hart, Jasper Ground			250.00	250.00
Poinsettia On Blue Ground				190.00 to 250.00
Reptile				450.00
Single Flower			250.00	190.00 to 250.00
Tri-Color Bouquet In White Basket			250.00	250.00

3. Plates, Plaques, and Miscellaneous

Title	Issue Date	Number Issued	Issued Price	Current Price
A. Michelsen, see Michelsen				
A. Y. Jackson, see Wellings Mint				
Agazzi, see Count Agazzi				
Air Force plate, see Quality Systems				
Alice in Wonderland plate, see Collector Creations				
American Academy of Arts				
Zolan's Children, Erik And Dandelion	1978	Year	19.00	19.00
America the Beautiful Plates				
U.S.Capitol, Red Carnival	1969	500	17.50	17.50 to 45.00
U.S.Capitol, Red Satin	1969	500	17.50	30.00 to 50.00
Mount Rushmore, Green Carnival	1970	500	17.50	20.00 to 45.00
Statue Of Liberty, Amber Carnival	1971	500	17.50	17.50 to 20.00
Monument Valley, Arizona, Rubigold Carnival	1972	500	17.50	17.50 to 20.00
Liberty Bell, Clear, Iridized Carnival	1973	500	17.50	17.50 to 20.00
Golden Gate Bridge, Amethyst Carnival	1974	500	19.95	19.95
Mount Vernon, Yellow Carnival	1975	500	19.95	19.95

American Archives, see International Silver

American Commemorative Council, in conjunction with The National Historical Society, has issued a series of plates to commemorate the bicentennial. The plates are made by Gorham China Company. The first plate was issued in 1972.

Title	Issue Date	Number Issued	Issued Price	Current Price
American Commemorative Council Plates				
Southern Landmark, Monticello	1973	9800	35.00	70.00
Southern Landmark, Williamsburg	1973	9800	40.00	40.00 to 70.00
Southern Landmark, Beauvoir	1974	9800	40.00	70.00
Southern Landmark, Cabildo	1974	9800	40.00	50.00
Southern Landmark, Hermitage	1975	9800	40.00	50.00 to 70.00
Southern Landmark, Oak Hill	1975	9800	40.00	45.00
Southern Landmark, Governor Tryon's Palace	1976	9800	40.00	70.00
Southern Landmark, Montpelier	1976	9800	40.00	40.00
Southern Landmark, Elmscourt	1977	9800	40.00	45.00
Southern Landmark, Ashland	1977	9800	40.00	40.00
Southern Landmark, Mt.Vernon	1978	9800	40.00	40.00
American Crystal Plates				
Astronaut	1969			20.00 to 50.00
Christmas	1970			5.00 to 50.00

American Historical, Natural History Plate, Painted Lady

Andrew Wyeth, Kuerner Farm Plate

Anri, Christmas Plate, 1971

Anri, Christmas Plate, 1972

Anri, Father's Day, 1972

Title	Issue Date	Number Issued	Issued Price	Current Price
Christmas	1971		25.00	5.00 to 30.00
Christmas	1972			30.00
Christmas	1973		20.00	20.00
Mother's Day	1971			5.00 to 15.00
Mother's Day	1972	2000	5.00	5.00 to 45.00
Mother's Day	1973			5.00 to 25.00
Vanishing Wildlife, Falcon	1971			6.00 to 20.00

America House Plates

Title	Issue Date	Number Issued	Issued Price	Current Price
Landing Of Columbus, Bronze	1972	1500	100.00	100.00
Landing Of Columbus, Silver	1972	1000	200.00	200.00 to 400.00

American Historical Plates, Ltd., of Mineola, New York, introduced limited editions in 1972. Their plates are produced by Castleton (Shenango) China.

American Historical Plates

Title	Issue Date	Number Issued	Issued Price	Current Price
Aviation, Amelia Earhart	1972	3500	40.00	30.00
Aviation, Charles Lindbergh	1972	3500	40.00	40.00
Bicentennial, A New Dawn**	1972	7600	60.00	30.00 to 60.00
Bicentennial, One Nation	1974	7600	60.00	30.00
Bicentennial, Silent Foe	1973	7600	60.00	30.00 to 60.00
Bicentennial, The Declaration	1973	7600	60.00	30.00 to 60.00
Bicentennial, The Star-Spangled Banner	1973	7600	60.00	30.00 to 60.00
Bicentennial, Turning Point	1972	7600	60.00	30.00 to 60.00
Bicentennial, USS Constitution	1973	7600	60.00	30.00 to 60.00
Bicentennial, Westward Ho**	1974	7600	60.00	30.00
General Douglas MacArthur	1976	1000	30.00	30.00 to 32.50
Natural History, Painted Lady*	1973	1500	40.00	40.00
Natural History, Roseate Spoonbill	1973	1500	40.00	40.00

American Horticulture Society Boxes

Title	Issue Date	Number Issued	Issued Price	Current Price
Old Garden Roses, Set Of 5	1976	5000	500.00	500.00

Andrew Wyeth Plates

Title	Issue Date	Number Issued	Issued Price	Current Price
The Hunter	1974		35.00	20.00 to 50.00
Kuerner Farm, Signed*	1971	275	350.00	Unknown
Kuerner Farm, Unsigned	1971	2500	50.00	Unknown

Anheuser Busch Plates

Title	Issue Date	Number Issued	Issued Price	Current Price
Americana, The Brew House, Silver	1974	5000	15.00	Unknown
Americana, Clydesdale Horses, Silver	1973	1000	15.00	Unknown

Anna Perenna, see Rosenthal

Anri, an Italian manufacturer of hand-carved wooden limited edition plates, was founded by Anton Riffeser, Sr. in 1916. Anri entered the limited edition market with a Christmas plate in 1971. Mother's Day and Father's Day plates were added in 1972.

Anri, see also Ferrandiz

Anri Bells

Title	Issue Date	Number Issued	Issued Price	Current Price
Christmas, First Edition	1976	Year	6.00	4.95 to 6.00
Christmas, Angel	1977	Year	7.00	7.00

Anri Ornaments

Title	Issue Date	Number Issued	Issued Price	Current Price
Christmas, Hanging Angels, Set Of 6	1975	Year		27.95 to 31.50

Anri Plates

Title	Issue Date	Number Issued	Issued Price	Current Price
Christmas, Jakob In Groden*	1971	10000	45.00	20.00 to 55.00
Christmas, Pipers At Alberobello*	1972	10000	45.00	25.00 to 105.00
Christmas, Alpine Horn	1973	10000	45.00	60.00 to 130.00
Christmas, Young Man And Girl	1974	10000	50.00	20.00 to 50.00
Christmas, Christmas In Ireland	1975	10000	60.00	25.00 to 60.00
Christmas, Alpine Christmas	1976	10000	65.00	34.99 to 65.00
Christmas, Legend Of Heiligenblut	1977	10000	65.00	65.00
Father's Day, Alpine Father & Children*	1972	2000	35.00	17.00 to 40.00
Father's Day, Father Playing Fiddle*	1973	5000	45.00	15.00 to 45.00
Father's Day, Cliff Gazing	1974	5000	50.00	27.00 to 50.00
Father's Day, Sailing	1975	5000	60.00	50.00 to 60.00
Mother's Day, Alpine Mother And Children*	1972	5000	35.00	17.00 to 39.00
Mother's Day, Alpine Mother And Children*	1973	5000	45.00	14.50 to 50.00
Mother's Day, Alpine Mother And Children	1974	5000	50.00	27.00 to 50.00
Mother's Day, Alpine Mother And Children	1975	5000	60.00	39.50 to 60.00

Anri, Father's Day, 1973

Anri, Mother's Day, 1972

Anri, Mother's Day, 1973

Bareuther, Christmas Plate, 1972

Bareuther, Christmas Plate, 1969

Bareuther, Christmas Plate, 1967   Bareuther, Christmas Plate, 1968

Bareuther, Christmas Plate, 1970

Bareuther, Christmas Plate, 1971

Bareuther,
Christmas Bell, 1973

Title	Issue Date	Number Issued	Issued Price	Current Price
Mother's Day, Knitting	1976	5000	60.00	47.50 to 60.00
Mother's Day	1977	5000	60.00	57.50
Mother's Day	1978	5000	60.00	57.50

Antique Trader Weekly, a Dubuque, Iowa, publication, introduced its line of limited edition plates in 1971. Artist Ralph Anderson of Schiller Park, Illinois, designed the first set of holiday plates. The plates are manufactured by Taylor, Smith, and Taylor of East Liverpool, Ohio.

Antique Trader Plates

Title	Issue Date	Number Issued	Issued Price	Current Price
Bible, David & Goliath	1973	2000	10.75	10.75
Bible, Moses And The Golden Idol	1973	2000	10.75	10.75
Bible, Noah's Ark	1973	2000	10.75	10.75
Bible, Samson	1973	2000	10.75	10.75
Christmas, Christ Child	1971	1500	11.95	15.00
Christmas, Flight Into Egypt	1972	1000	11.95	15.00
Currier & Ives, Baseball		2000	10.00	10.00
Currier & Ives, Franklin Experiment		2000	10.00	10.00
Currier & Ives, Haying Time		2000	10.00	10.00
Currier & Ives, The Road-Winter		2000	10.00	10.00
Currier & Ives, Winter In The Country		2000	10.00	10.00
Easter, Child And Lamb	1971	1500	11.95	15.00
Easter, Shepherd With Lamb	1972	1000	11.95	15.00
Father's Day, Pilgrim Father	1971	1500	11.95	15.00
Father's Day, Deer Family	1972	1000	11.95	15.00
Mother's Day, Madonna And Child	1971	1500	11.95	15.00 to 29.95
Mother's Day, Mother Cat And Kittens	1972	1000	11.95	15.00 to 24.95
Mother's Day	1974			16.95
Mother's Day	1975			16.95
Russell, A Bad One		2000	11.95	18.50
Russell, Discovery Of Last Chance Gulch**		2000	11.95	18.50
Russell, Doubtful Visitor		2000	11.95	18.00
Russell, Innocent Allies		2000	11.95	18.00
Russell, Medicine Man		2000	11.95	50.00 to 85.00
Thanksgiving, First Thanksgiving	1972	1000	11.95	15.00
Thanksgiving, Pilgrims	1971	1500	11.95	15.00

Arabia Co. of Finland Plates

Title	Issue Date	Number Issued	Issued Price	Current Price
Christmas, Annual	1974		20.00	20.00
Christmas, Annual	1975	3000	20.00	20.00

Arizona Artisan Plates

Title	Issue Date	Number Issued	Issued Price	Current Price
Mexican Christmas	1974		20.00	20.00
Navajo Christmas	1975		20.00	20.00
Navajo Thanksgiving Feast	1975		15.00	15.00

Arlington Mint Plates

Title	Issue Date	Number Issued	Issued Price	Current Price
Hands In Prayer, Sterling	1972		125.00	45.00 to 125.00

Armetale Plates

Title	Issue Date	Number Issued	Issued Price	Current Price
Charles Lindbergh, 50th Anniversary	1976	10000	18.50	18.50

The Armstrong Bicentennial series was commissioned by David Armstrong and David Downs of Pomona, California. The bronze plates are made by the cire perdue (lost wax) method.

Armstrong Plates

Title	Issue Date	Number Issued	Issued Price	Current Price
Bicentennial, Calm Before The Storm	1971	250	250.00	300.00
Bicentennial, Gaspee Incident	1972	175	250.00	Unknown

Arta Enamel Factory, located in Austria, introduced limited edition plates in 1973. The plates are hand-painted on white enamel.

Arta Enamel Plates

Title	Issue Date	Number Issued	Issued Price	Current Price
Christmas, Nativity	1973	300	50.00	20.00
Mother's Day, Mother & Children	1973	220	50.00	20.00

Audubon Crystal Ltd., of 180 Hills Point Road, Westport, Conn. is issuing the Audubon Collection of handmade crystal plates dealing with endangered species of birds.

Audubon Crystal Plates

Title	Issue Date	Number Issued	Issued Price	Current Price
American Eagle	1976	5000	195.00	195.00

Bareuther, Father's Day Plate, 1970

Bareuther, Christmas Plate, 1973

Bareuther, Father's Day Plate, 1972

Title	Issue Date	Number Issued	Issued Price	Current Price
Peregrine Falcon	1977	5000	200.00	200.00
Kirtland's Warbler	1976	5000	195.00	195.00

Arthur King, see King

Asta Stromberg, see Stromberg

Atelier D'Art Faure, see Poillerat

Audubon Bird plates, see Franklin Mint, Reed & Barton,

Audubon Crystal

Avondale Plates

Melissa	1978	30000	65.00	65.00

*Aynsley pottery has been made in the Staffordshire district since 1775.
Fine decorated earthenware was produced in the early years. Bone china was
introduced by founder John Aynsley's grandson in the mid-1800s.*

Aynsley Plates

1000th Year Of English Monarchy	1973	1000	30.00	25.00
Pilgrim Fathers	1970			40.00 to 75.00
Prince Of Wales	1969			50.00

Ball Christmas Ornaments are made of acrylic

Ball Ornaments

Christmas, Angel	1976	Year	7.50	6.50 to 7.50
Christmas, Nativity Scene, Black Base	1976	20000	25.00	19.95 to 25.00

*Bareuther & Co., a German porcelain factory, was founded in 1867 by the
Ries family. In 1884, the factory was sold to Oskar Bareuther.
The first limited edition Bareuther Christmas plate was issued in 1967 in
honor of the factory's 100th Anniversary. Mother's Day and Father's
Day plates followed in 1969.*

Bareuther Bells

Christmas, Angels*	1973	2500	15.00	4.50 to 18.00
Christmas, Candles	1974	2500	17.00	11.35 to 17.00
Christmas, Santas	1975	2500	19.00	12.65 to 19.00
Christmas, Bells	1976	2500	21.00	21.00
Christmas, Ornaments	1977	2500	22.50	22.50
Christmas, Candles And Pine Cones	1978	2500	25.00	25.00

Bareuther Eggs

Easter	1974	Year	13.50	17.50

Bareuther Plates

Christmas, Stifskirche*	1967	10000	10.00	50.00 to 100.00
Christmas, Kappelkirche*	1968	10000	10.00	10.00 to 40.00
Christmas, Christkindlemarkt*	1969	10000	10.00	7.00 to 22.00
Christmas, Chapel In Oberndorf*	1970	10000	12.50	16.00
Christmas, Toys For Sale*	1971	10000	14.50	8.00 to 25.00
Christmas, Christmas In Munich*	1972	10000	14.50	30.00 to 45.00
Christmas, Snow Scene*	1973	10000	15.00	8.00 to 27.00
Christmas, Church In The Black Forest	1974	10000	19.00	10.50 to 30.00
Christmas, Snowman	1975	10000	21.50	10.50 to 21.50
Christmas, Chapel In The Hills	1976	10000	23.50	11.76 to 23.50
Christmas, Mother Reading Christmas Story	1977	2500	24.50	24.50
Christmas, Mittenwald	1978	2500	27.50	27.50
Father's Day, Castle Neuschwanstein*	1969	2500	10.00	25.00 to 75.00
Father's Day, Castle Pfalz*	1970	2500	12.50	2.50 to 20.00
Father's Day, Castle Heidelberg*	1971	2500	12.50	8.00 to 22.00
Father's Day, Castle Hohenschwangau*	1972	2500	14.50	12.00 to 19.00
Father's Day, Castle Katz*	1973	2500	15.00	12.00 to 18.00
Father's Day, Wurzburg Castle	1974	2500	19.00	12.65 to 27.00
Father's Day, Castle Lichtenstein	1975	2500	21.50	14.35 to 21.50
Father's Day, Castle Hohenzollern	1976	2500	21.50	11.75 to 23.50
Father's Day, Castle Eltz	1977	2500	24.50	24.50
Father's Day, Castle Falkenstein	1978	2500	27.50	27.50
Jubilee	1977	5000	35.00	35.00
Mother's Day, Mother And Children*	1969	5000	10.00	17.50 to 75.00
Mother's Day, Mother And Children*	1970	5000	12.50	4.00 to 17.00
Mother's Day, Mother And Children*	1971	5000	12.50	7.00 to 25.00
Mother's Day, Mother And Children*	1972	5000	14.50	12.00 to 19.00
Mother's Day, Mother And Children*	1973	5000	15.00	12.00 to 18.00

Bareuther, Mother's Day Plate, 1969

Bareuther, Father's Day Plate, 1969

Bareuther, Mother's Day Plate, 1970

Bareuther, Father's Day Plate, 1973

Bareuther, Father's Day Plate, 1971

Bareuther, Mother's Day Plate, 1972

Bareuther, Mother's Day Plate, 1973

Bareuther, Mother's Day Plate, 1971

Title	Issue Date	Number Issued	Issued Price	Current Price
Mother's Day, Musical Children	1974	5000	19.00	10.00 to 23.00
Mother's Day, Spring Outing	1975	5000	21.50	13.00 to 36.50
Mother's Day, Rocking The Cradle	1976	5000	32.00	11.75 to 23.50
Mother's Day, Victorian Mother & Children	1977	5000	24.50	24.50
Mother's Day, Blindman's Bluff	1978	5000	27.50	27.50
Thanksgiving, First Thanksgiving*	1971	2500	12.50	8.00 to 28.00
Thanksgiving, Harvest*	1972	2500	14.50	10.00 to 19.00
Thanksgiving, Country Road In Autumn*	1973	2500	15.00	10.00 to 25.00
Thanksgiving, Old Mill	1974	2500	19.00	12.00 to 20.00
Thanksgiving, Wild Deer In Forest	1975	2500	21.50	16.50 to 21.50
Thanksgiving, Thanksgiving On The Farm	1976	2500	23.50	23.50
Thanksgiving, Horses	1977	2500	24.50	24.50
Thanksgiving, Apple Harvest	1978	2500	27.50	27.50

Barrymore, Lionel, see Gorham

Baxter Sperry Mugs

Title	Issue Date	Number Issued	Issued Price	Current Price
Herald Garden Club	1976	134	3.00	3.00
Liberty School	1976	99	3.00	3.00
Odd Fellows Hall	1976	120	3.00	3.00
St.Christopher's	1976	88	3.00	3.00
St.Luke's Church	1976	127	3.00	3.00

Baxter Sperry Plates

Title	Issue Date	Number Issued	Issued Price	Current Price
Herald Garden Club	1976	58	3.00	3.00
Liberty School	1976	91	3.00	3.00
Odd Fellows Hall	1976	52	3.00	3.00
St.Christopher's	1976	77	3.00	3.00
St. Luke's Church	1976	128	3.00	3.00

Bayel Crystal has been made in France since 1666. Limited edition crystal plates were first made in 1972.

Bayel Plates

Title	Issue Date	Number Issued	Issued Price	Current Price
Rose*	1972	300	50.00	50.00
Lilies	1973	300	50.00	50.00
Orchid	1973	300	50.00	50.00
Eagle Head	1974	300	50.00	50.00 to 60.00
Eagle In Flight	1974	300	50.00	50.00
Bicentennial, Liberty Bell	1974	500	50.00	50.00
Bicentennial, Independence Hall	1975	500	60.00	60.00 to 65.00
Bicentennial, Spread Eagle	1976	500		70.00 to 70.00

Belleek Eggs

Title	Issue Date	Number Issued	Issued Price	Current Price
Easter	1972		25.00	15.00 to 30.00

Belleek Plates

Title	Issue Date	Number Issued	Issued Price	Current Price
Bicentennial, George Washington	1976	990	60.00	60.00
Christmas, Castle Caldwell	1970	5000	25.00	65.00 to 130.00
Christmas, Celtic Cross	1971	5000	35.00	15.00 to 30.00
Christmas, Flight Of The Earls	1972	7500	35.00	22.50 to 30.00
Christmas, Tribute To W.B. Yeats	1973	7500	38.50	22.50 to 40.00
Christmas, Devenish Island	1974	7500	45.00	39.00 to 125.00
Christmas, Celtic Cross	1975	7500	49.00	40.00 to 59.00
Christmas, Dove Of Peace	1976	7500	55.00	Unknown
Christmas, Wren	1977	7500	55.00	Unknown

Belleek Vase, see Lenox

The Bengough Collection of Canadiana was founded by Bomac Batten Ltd. of Canada. Its limited edition line is silver and gold.

Bengough Plates

Title	Issue Date	Number Issued	Issued Price	Current Price
Christmas, Charles Dickens' Christmas Carol*	1972	490	125.00	Unknown
Northwest Mounted Police, 1898 Dress Uniform	1972	1000	140.00	Unknown
Northwest Mounted Police, First Uniform	1972	1000	140.00	Unknown
Royal Canadian Police, Review Order Dress	1972	1000	140.00	Unknown

Berlin Design limited edition plates and mugs were first made in 1970 by the Kaiser Alboth Factory of Germany. The items are made exclusively for distribution by Schmid Brothers of Randolph, Massachusetts.

Berlin Bells

Title	Issue Date	Number Issued	Issued Price	Current Price
Christmas, Angel, White	1972	5000	10.00	6.99 to 12.00

Title	Issue Date	Number Issued	Issued Price	Current Price
Christmas, Angels*	1973	Year	15.00	12.00 to 15.00
Christmas, Deer	1974	Year		6.50 to 23.95
Christmas, Candles	1975	Year		16.65 to 25.00
Christmas, Birds	1976	Year		19.95 to 25.00
Berlin Goblets				
Composer, Beethoven	1972	3000	37.50	Unknown
Composer, Mozart	1972	3000	37.50	Unknown
Berlin Mugs				
Christmas, Callenberg Castle	1971	700	40.00	4.50 to 25.95
Christmas, Heidelberg Castle*	1972	700	40.00	25.00 to 50.00
Christmas, Marienberg Castle*	1973	700	50.00	35.00 to 50.00
Christmas, Kaub On Rhine	1974	Year	35.00	6.50 to 25.00
Berlin Plates				
Christmas, Christmas In Bernkastel	1970	4000	14.50	29.95 to 150.00
Christmas, Christmas In Rothenburg*	1971	20000	14.50	5.00 to 25.95
Christmas, Christmas In Michelstadt	1972	Year	15.00	10.00 to 25.00
Christmas, Christmas At Wendelstein*	1973	Year	20.00	14.00 to 32.00
Christmas, Christmas In Bremen	1974	Year	25.00	8.00 to 25.00
Christmas, Christmas In Dortland	1975	Year	30.00	14.00 to 30.00
Christmas, Christmas Eve In Augsburg	1976	Year	32.00	27.50 to 32.00
Christmas, Christmas Eve In Hamburg	1977	Year	32.00	32.00
Commemorative, Olympic, Montreal	1976		32.00	25.50 to 32.00
Commemorative, Olympic, Munich	1972			15.00
Father's Day, Brooklyn Bridge On Opening Day	1971	2000	14.50	3.00 to 20.00
Father's Day, Continent Spanned*	1972	3000	15.00	7.50 to 20.00
Father's Day, Landing Of Columbus*	1973	2000	18.00	12.00 to 45.00
Father's Day, Balloon	1974		22.50	12.00 to 45.00
Historical, Crossing The Delaware	1975		30.00	18.75 to 30.00
Historical, Early Train, Nurnberg	1976		32.00	25.00 to 32.00
Historical, Zeppelin 124-1908	1977			Unknown
Mother's Day, Gray Poodles	1971	20000	14.50	7.50 to 24.00
Mother's Day, Fledglings*	1972	10000	15.00	7.95 to 25.00
Mother's Day, Ducks*	1973	5000	16.50	15.00 to 40.00
Mother's Day, Squirrels	1974		22.50	14.00 to 44.50
Mother's Day, Cats	1975		30.00	11.50 to 39.00
Mother's Day, Doe And Fawn	1976		32.00	12.50 to 32.00
Mother's Day Stork Family	1977	Year	32.00	32.00
Vermeer, The Geographer*	1973	3000	100.00	100.00
Vermeer, Girl With Letter	1973	3000	120.00	120.00
Vermeer, The Milkmaid	1973	3000	120.00	120.00
Berlin Stein				
First Edition	1975			Unknown
Nurnberg	1976			80.00
Lenbeck Water Castle	1977			88.00

Berta Hummel, see Hummel Schmid

Betournes, see Jean Paul Loup

Title	Issue Date	Number Issued	Issued Price	Current Price
Bethlehem Plates				
First Christmas Eve	1977	Year	29.95	29.95
Bethlehem Bell				
First Christmas Eve	1977	Year	23.00	23.00

Bareuther, Thanksgiving Plate, 1971

Bareuther, Thanksgiving Plate, 1972

Bareuther, Thanksgiving Plate, 1973

Bengough, Christmas Plate, 1972

Bing & Grondahl, Danish pioneer in the field of limited edition Christmas plates, was founded in 1853. The firm's famous cobalt underglaze technique was introduced at the Paris World Exhibition in 1889. Bing & Grondahl's first limited edition Christmas plate, issued in 1895, was inspired by the Danish tradition of exchanging plates of cookies at Christmastime. The Easter plaque was made between 1910 and 1935 only. In 1915, the company introduced its first 5-year Jubilee plate. Mother's Day plates were introduced in 1969. Each mold is destroyed at the end of the year.

Title	Issue Date	Number Issued	Issued Price	Current Price
Bing & Grondahl Bells				
Annual, Roskilde Cathedral	1974	Year	50.00	67.50 to 200.00
Annual, St.Peter's Church	1975	Year	60.00	50.00 to 75.00
Annual, Old North Church	1976	Year	67.50	50.00 to 67.50
Annual, Notre Dame Cathedral	1978	Year	69.50	69.50

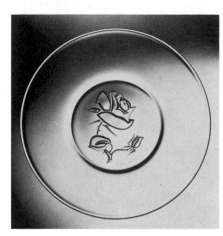

Bayel, Rose Plate, 1972

Berlin, Christmas Bell, 1973

Berlin, Christmas Mug, 1972

Title	Issue Date	Number Issued	Issued Price	Current Price
Annual, St.Paul's Cathedral	1977	Year	67.50	67.50
Annual, Notre Dame Cathedral	1978	Year	69.50	69.50
Bing & Grondahl Mugs				
Explorer Series, Santa Maria	1978	Year	50.00	50.00
Bing & Grondahl Plaques				
Easter	1910	Year		50.00
Easter	1911	Year		50.00
Easter	1912	Year		60.00
Easter	1913	Year		50.00
Easter	1914	Year		50.00
Easter	1915	Year		50.00
Easter	1916	Year		35.00 to 55.00
Easter	1917	Year		50.00 to 60.00
Easter	1918	Year		50.00 to 55.00
Easter	1919	Year		50.00
Easter	1920	Year		50.00 to 55.00
Easter	1921	Year		50.00 to 55.00
Easter	1922	Year		50.00 to 65.00
Easter	1923	Year		50.00 to 55.00
Easter	1924	Year		50.00 to 55.00
Easter	1925	Year		50.00 to 55.00
Easter	1926	Year		50.00 to 75.00
Easter	1927	Year		65.00 to 75.00
Easter	1928	Year		80.00 to 95.00
Easter	1929	Year		110.00
Easter	1930	Year		125.00 to 140.00
Easter	1931	Year		200.00
Easter	1932	Year		125.00 to 140.00
Easter	1933	Year		125.00 to 200.00
Easter	1934	Year		375.00 to 400.00
Easter	1935	Year		700.00
Bing & Grondahl Plates				
Bicentennial*	1976		50.00	22.50 to 50.00
Christmas, Behind The Frozen Window*	1895	Year	.50	1900.00 to 3000.00
Christmas, New Moon Over Snow-Covered Trees*	1896	Year	.50	1185.00 to 1950.00
Christmas, Christmas Meal Of The Sparrows*	1897	Year	.75	600.00 to 1050.00
Christmas, Roses And Christmas Star*	1898	Year	.75	300.00 to 750.00
Christmas, Crows Enjoying Christmas*	1899	Year	.75	400.00 to 1050.00
Christmas, Church Bells Chiming In Christmas*	1900	Year	.75	425.00 to 750.00
Christmas, Three Wise Men From The East*	1901	Year	1.00	200.00 to 327.00
Christmas, Interior Of A Gothic Church*	1902	Year	1.00	147.00 to 360.00
Christmas, Happy Expectation Of Children*	1903	Year	1.00	119.00 to 270.00
Christmas, View From Frederiksberg Hill*	1904	Year	1.00	74.00 to 150.00
Christmas, Anxiety Of The Coming Christmas*	1905	Year	1.00	74.00 to 120.00
Christmas, Sleighing On Christmas Eve*	1906	Year	1.00	60.00 to 105.00
Christmas, The Little Match Girl*	1907	Year	1.00	80.00 to 132.00
Christmas, St.Petri Church Of Copenhagen*	1908	Year	1.00	49.00 to 62.00
Christmas, Happiness Over The Yule Tree*	1909	Year	.50	55.00 to 96.00
Christmas, The Old Organist*	1910	Year	1.50	56.00 to 81.00
Christmas, Sung By Angels To Shepherds*	1911	Year	1.50	56.00 to 81.00
Christmas, Going To Church On Christmas Eve*	1912	Year	1.50	56.00 to 80.00
Christmas, Bringing Home The Yule Tree*	1913	Year	.50	56.00 to 80.00
Christmas, Castle Of Amalienborg, Copenhagen*	1914	Year	1.50	45.00 to 72.00
Christmas, Dog Getting Double Meal*	1915	Year	1.50	68.00 to 108.00
Christmas, Prayer Of The Sparrows*	1916	Year	1.50	50.00 to 75.00
Christmas, Arrival Of The Christmas Boat*	1917	Year	1.50	46.00 to 75.00
Christmas, Fishing Boat Returning Home*	1918	Year	1.50	50.00 to 75.00
Christmas, Outside The Lighted Window*	1919	Year	2.00	45.00 to 84.00
Christmas, Hare In The Snow*	1920	Year	2.00	44.00 to 75.00
Christmas, Pigeons In The Castle Court*	1921	Year	2.00	43.00 to 60.00
Christmas, Star Of Bethlehem*	1922	Year	2.00	45.00 to 75.00
Christmas, Royal Hunting Castle*	1923	Year	2.00	45.00 to 75.00
Christmas, Lighthouse In Danish Waters*	1924	Year	2.50	45.00 to 67.50
Christmas, The Child's Christmas*	1925	Year	2.50	45.00 to 67.50
Christmas, Churchgoers On Christmas Day*	1926	Year	2.50	52.00 to 60.00
Christmas, Skating Couple*	1927	Year	2.50	47.00 to 84.00
Christmas, Eskimos Looking At Village Church*	1928	Year	2.50	45.00 to 60.00
Christmas, Fox Outside Farm On Christmas Eve*	1929	Year	2.50	48.00 to 75.00

Berlin, Christmas Plate, 1973

Berlin, Christmas Plate, 1971

Berlin, Christmas Mug, 1973

Berlin, Mother's Day Plate, 1972

Berlin, Father's Day Plate, 1972

Berlin, Plate, Father's Day, 1973

Berlin, Mother's Day, 1973

Berlin, Vermeer Plate, The Geographer

Bing & Grondahl, Christmas Plate, 1895

Bing & Grondahl, Christmas Plate, 1896

Bing & Grondahl, Christmas Plate, 1897

Bing & Grondahl, Christmas Plate, 1898

Bing & Grondahl, Christmas Plate, 1899

Bing & Grondahl, Christmas Plate, 1900

Title	Issue Date	Number Issued	Issued Price	Current Price
Christmas, Yule Tree In Town Hall Square*	1930	Year	2.50	57.00 to 96.00
Christmas, Arrival Of The Christmas Train*	1931	Year	2.50	49.00 to 84.00
Christmas, Lifeboat At Work*	1932	Year	2.50	50.00 to 78.00
Christmas, The Korsor Nyborg Ferry*	1933	Year	2.50	45.00 to 66.00
Christmas, Church Bell In Tower*	1934	Year	3.00	45.00 to 75.00
Christmas, Lillebelt Bridge*	1935	Year	3.00	40.00 to 85.00
Christmas, Royal Guard, Amalienborg Castle*	1936	Year	3.00	46.00 to 75.00
Christmas, Arrival Of Christmas Guests*	1937	Year	3.00	46.00 to 75.00
Christmas, Lighting The Candles*	1938	Year	3.00	72.00 to 108.00
Christmas, Old Lock-Eye, The Sandman*	1939	Year	3.00	66.00 to 143.00
Christmas, Delivering Christmas Letters*	1940	Year	4.00	87.00 to 139.00
Christmas, Horses Enjoying Christmas Meal*	1941	Year	4.00	151.00 to 300.00
Christmas, Danish Farm On Christmas Night*	1942	Year	4.00	89.00 to 165.00
Christmas, The Ribe Cathedral*	1943	Year	5.00	89.00 to 150.00
Christmas, Sorgenfri Castle*	1944	Year	5.00	59.00 to 105.00
Christmas, Old Water Mill*	1945	Year	5.00	71.00 to 135.00
Christmas, Commemoration Cross*	1946	Year	5.00	45.00 to 75.00
Christmas, Dybbol Mill*	1947	Year	5.00	45.00 to 81.00
Christmas, Watchman, Sculpture Of Town Hall*	1948	Year	5.50	45.00 to 75.00
Christmas, 19th Century Danish Soldier*	1949	Year	5.50	59.00 to 135.00
Christmas, Kronborg Castle At Elsinore*	1950	Year	5.50	50.00 to 90.00
Christmas, Jens Bang, New Passenger Boat*	1951	Year	6.00	50.00 to 90.00
Christmas, Copenhagen Canals At Wintertime*	1952	Year	6.00	43.00 to 60.00
Christmas, King's Boat In Greenland Waters*	1953	Year	7.00	45.00 to 81.00
Christmas, Birthplace Of H.C.Andersen*	1954	Year	7.50	58.00 to 96.00
Christmas, Kalundborg Church*	1955	Year	8.00	56.00 to 75.00
Christmas, Christmas In Copenhagen*	1956	Year	8.50	67.00 to 135.00
Christmas, Christmas Candles*	1957	Year	9.00	67.00 to 137.50
Christmas, Santa Claus*	1958	Year	9.50	63.00 to 112.50
Christmas, Christmas Eve*	1959	Year	10.00	75.00 to 149.00
Christmas, Danish Village Church*	1960	Year	10.00	87.00 to 240.00
Christmas, Winter Harmony*	1961	Year	10.50	60.00 to 135.00
Christmas, Winter Night*	1962	Year	11.00	37.00 to 90.00
Christmas, Christmas Elf*	1963	Year	11.00	68.00 to 139.00
Christmas, Fir Tree And Hare*	1964	Year	11.50	30.00 to 59.95
Christmas, Bringing Home The Christmas Tree*	1965	Year	12.00	33.00 to 69.95
Christmas, Home For Christmas*	1966	Year	12.00	28.00 to 49.95
Christmas, Sharing The Joy Of Christmas*	1967	Year	13.00	22.00 to 49.95
Christmas, Christmas In Church*	1968	Year	14.00	20.00 to 45.50
Christmas, Guests' Arrival*	1969	Year	14.00	12.00 to 25.00
Christmas, Pheasants In Snow*	1970	Year	14.50	9.00 to 22.50
Christmas, Girl At Piano*	1971	Year	15.00	7.50 to 21.95
Christmas, Dogsled*	1972	Year	16.50	8.50 to 21.95
Christmas, Family Reunion*	1973	Year	19.50	7.50 to 27.50
Christmas, Christmas In The Village	1974	Year	22.00	7.50 to 22.00
Christmas, The Old Water Mill*	1975	Year	27.50	11.00 to 32.00
Christmas, Christmas Welcome*	1976	Year	27.50	27.50
Christmas, Little Nisse	1977	Year	29.50	29.50
Christmas, A Christmas Tale*	1978	Year	32.00	32.00
Commemorative, May 4				20.00
Commemorative, Liberation	1970			30.00
Commemorative, 800th Birthday	1972			12.00 to 21.00
Commemorative, Greenland	1972			12.50
Commemorative, King Frederik	1972		75.00	15.00 to 80.00
Commemorative Olympic	1972			9.00 to 20.00
Commemorative, Queen Margarethe	1972			16.00 to 80.00
Commemorative, Olympic Games, Montreal*	1976		29.50	18.50 to 29.50
Commemorative, King Carl Gustav XVI	1977		75.00	75.00
Commemorative, Anniversary*	1978	Year	45.00	37.50 to 45.00
Heritage, Norseman	1976	Year	30.00	30.00
Heritage, Navigators	1977	Year	30.00	30.00
Jubilee, Behind The Frozen Window	1915	Year	3.00	85.00 to 145.00
Jubilee, The Crows Enjoying Christmas	1920	Year	4.00	85.00 to 105.00
Jubilee, Chained Dog	1925	Year	5.00	85.00 to 125.00
Jubilee, The Old Organist	1930	Year	5.00	145.00 to 165.00
Jubilee, The Little Match Girl	1935	Year	6.00	450.00 to 700.00
Jubilee, The Three Wise Men	1940	Year	10.00	1400.00 to 1650.00
Jubilee, Amalienborg Castle	1945	Year	10.00	165.00 to 325.00
Jubilee, Village Church In Greenland	1950	Year	15.00	100.00 to 185.00
Jubilee, Dybbol Mill	1955	Year	20.00	100.00 to 175.00

Bing & Grondahl, Christmas Plate, 1901

Bing & Grondahl, Christmas Plate, 1905

Bing & Grondahl, Christmas Plate, 1907

Bing & Grondahl, Christmas Plate, 1902

Bing & Grondahl, Christmas Plate, 1908

Bing & Grondahl, Christmas Plate, 1903

Bing & Grondahl, Christmas Plate, 1906

Bing & Grondahl, Christmas Plate, 1909

Bing & Grondahl, Christmas Plate, 1904

Bing & Grondahl, Christmas Plate, 1910

Bing & Grondahl, Christmas Plate, 1911

Bing & Grondahl, Christmas Plate, 1915

Bing & Grondahl, Christmas Plate, 1917

Bing & Grondahl, Christmas Plate, 1912

Bing & Grondahl, Christmas Plate, 1918

Bing & Grondahl, Christmas Plate, 1916

Bing & Grondahl, Christmas Plate, 1913

Bing & Grondahl, Christmas Plate, 1914

Bing & Grondahl, Christmas Plate, 1919

Bing & Grondahl, Christmas Plate, 1920

Bing & Grondahl, Christmas Plate, 1921

Bing & Grondahl, Christmas Plate, 1925

Bing & Grondahl, Christmas Plate, 1927

Bing & Grondahl, Christmas Plate, 1922

Bing & Grondahl, Christmas Plate, 1928

Bing & Grondahl, Christmas Plate, 1923

Bing & Grondahl, Christmas Plate, 1924

Bing & Grondahl, Christmas Plate, 1926

Bing & Grondahl, Christmas Plate, 1929

Bing & Grondahl, Christmas Plate, 1930

Bing & Grondahl, Christmas Plate, 1931

Bing & Grondahl, Christmas Plate, 1935

Bing & Grondahl, Christmas Plate, 1939

Bing & Grondahl, Christmas Plate, 1932

Bing & Grondahl, Christmas Plate, 1936

Bing & Grondahl, Christmas Plate, 1940

Bing & Grondahl, Christmas Plate, 1933

Bing & Grondahl, Christmas Plate, 1934

Bing & Grondahl, Christmas Plate, 1937

Bing & Grondahl, Christmas Plate, 1938

Bing & Grondahl, Christmas Plate, 1941

Bing & Grondahl, Christmas Plate, 1942

Bing & Grondahl, Christmas Plate, 1943

Bing & Grondahl, Christmas Plate, 1947

Bing & Grondahl, Christmas Plate, 1951

Bing & Grondahl, Christmas Plate, 1944

Bing & Grondahl, Christmas Plate, 1948

Bing & Grondahl, Christmas Plate, 1952

Bing & Grondahl, Christmas Plate, 1945

Bing & Grondahl, Christmas Plate, 1949

Bing & Grondahl, Christmas Plate, 1953

Bing & Grondahl, Christmas Plate, 1946

Bing & Grondahl, Christmas Plate, 1950

Bing & Grondahl, Christmas Plate, 1954

Bing & Grondahl, Christmas Plate, 1955

Bing & Grondahl, Christmas Plate, 1961

Bing & Grondahl, Christmas Plate, 1959

Bing & Grondahl, Christmas Plate, 1956

Bing & Grondahl, Christmas Plate, 1962

Bing & Grondahl, Christmas Plate, 1957

Bing & Grondahl, Christmas Plate, 1958

Bing & Grondahl, Christmas Plate, 1960

Bing & Grondahl, Christmas Plate, 1963

Bing & Grondahl, Christmas Plate, 1964

Bing & Grondahl, Christmas Plate, 1965

Bing & Grondahl, Christmas Plate, 1969

Bing & Grondahl, Christmas Plate, 1970

Bing & Grondahl, Christmas Plate, 1966

Bing & Grondahl, Christmas Plate, 1971

Bing & Grondahl, Christmas Plate, 1967

Bing & Grondahl, Mother's Day Plate, 1974

Bing & Grondahl, Christmas Plate, 1972

Bing & Grondahl, Christmas Plate, 1968

Bing & Grondahl, Christmas Plate, 1973

Bing & Grondahl, Plate, Commemorative,
Olympic Games, Montreal

Bing & Grondahl, Plate,
Mother's Day, Heron

Bing & Grondahl, Plate, Christmas,
The Old Water Mill

Bing & Grondahl, Plate, Jubilee,
Horses Enjoying Meal

Bing & Grondahl, Plate,
Christmas, A Christmas Tale

Bing & Grondahl, Plate,
Commemorative, 125th Anniversary

Bing & Grondahl, Plate,
Mother's Day, Doe And Fawn

Bing & Grondahl, Plate, Christmas,
Christmas Welcome

Bing & Grondahl, Plate,
Bicentennial, 1976

Bing & Grondahl, Plate,
Mother's Day, Swan Family

Title	Issue Date	Number Issued	Issued Price	Current Price
Jubilee, Kronborg Castle At Elsinore	1960	Year	25.00	95.00 to 135.00
Jubilee, Churchgoers On Christmas Day	1965	Year	25.00	60.00 to 85.00
Jubilee, Royal Castle Of Amalienborg	1970	Year	30.00	7.95 to 40.00
Jubilee, Horses Enjoying Meal*	1975	Year	40.00	20.00 to 40.00
Madonna	1977	10000	45.00	37.50 to 45.00
Mother's Day, Dogs	1969	5000	8.00	135.00 to 450.00
Mother's Day, Bird & Chicks	1970	Year	9.00	8.50 to 39.00
Mother's Day, Cat & Kittens	1971	Year	10.00	5.00 to 15.00
Mother's Day, Mare & Foal	1972	Year	10.00	6.00 to 16.50
Mother's Day, Duck & Ducklings	1973	Year	13.00	7.50 to 19.50
Mother's Day, Polar Bears*	1974	Year	13.00	7.00 to 25.00
Mother's Day, Doe And Fawn*	1975	Year	19.50	9.00 to 25.00
Mother's Day, Swan Family*	1976	Year	22.50	15.75 to 22.50
Mother's Day, Squirrel And Young	1977	Year	22.50	16.95 to 23.50
Mother's Day, Heron*	1978	Year	24.50	24.50
Sneslev Molle	1977	250	37.50	37.50
The Kitchen, 4 Plates	1977	7500		150.00

Bing & Grondahl Thimbles

Annual	1978	Year	19.50	19.50

Blue Delft, Christmas Plate, 1973

Blue Delft, Mother's Day Plate, 1973

Blue Delft Co., whose Dutch name is Schoonhaven, issued its first Christmas tile in 1967. Matching plates and spoons were added in 1970. Mother's Day and Father's Day plates and spoons followed in 1971.

Blue Delft, see also Crown Delft, Royal Delft, Zenith

Blue Delft Mugs

Father's Day, Francesco Lana's Airship	1971	Year	10.00	Unknown
Father's Day, Dr.Jonathan's Balloon	1972	Year	10.00	Unknown

Blue Delft Plates

Christmas, Drawbridge Near Binnenhof	1970	Year	12.00	6.00 to 18.00
Christmas, St.Laurens Church	1971	Year	2.00	5.00
Christmas, Church At Bierkade Of Amsterdam	1972	Year	2.00	5.00 to 25.00
Christmas, St.Jan's Church*	1973	Year	2.00	5.00 to 25.00
Christmas, Dongeradeel	1974	Year	13.00	15.00
Christmas, Maassluis	1975	Year	15.00	15.00 to 16.50
Christmas, Montelbaanstower	1976	Year	15.00	15.00 to 15.95
Christmas, Harbour Tower Of Hoorn	1977	Year	19.50	19.50
Christmas, Binnenpoort Gate	1978	Year	21.00	21.00
Father's Day, Francesco Lana's Airship	1971	Year	12.00	6.00 to 9.00
Father's Day, Dr.Jonathan's Balloon	1972	Year	12.00	9.00 to 12.00
Mother's Day, Mother & Daughter Of 1600s	1971	Year	12.00	6.00 to 12.00
Mother's Day, Mother & Daughter, Isle Of Urk	1972	Year	12.00	6.00 to 12.00
Mother's Day, Rembrandt's Mother*	1973	Year	12.00	6.00 to 12.00
Mother's Day	1974			13.00

Boehm, Bird Of Peace Plate

Boehm, Eaglet Plate

Blue Delft Spoons

Christmas, Drawbridge Near Binnenhof	1970	Year	7.00	7.50
Christmas, St.Laurens Church	1971	Year	7.00	7.00 to 10.00
Christmas, Church At Bierkade Of Amsterdam	1972	Year	7.00	7.00 to 9.00
Christmas, St.Jan's Church	1973	Year		8.25
Christmas, Dongeradeel	1974	Year	8.75	8.75
Christmas, Maassluis	1975	Year		4.00 to 9.50
Christmas, Montebaanstower	1976	Year	9.00	9.00
Christmas, Harbour Tower Of Hoorn	1977	Year	10.00	10.00
Christmas, Binnenpoort Gate	1978	Year	10.00	10.00

Blue Delft Tiles

Bicentennial, Declaration Of Independence	1976	Year	6.50	6.50
Bicentennial, Washington Crossing Delaware	1976	Year	6.50	6.50
Christmas, Winter Scene	1967	Year	5.00	15.00 to 25.00
Christmas, Admiring The Tree	1968	Year	5.00	12.50 to 20.00
Christmas, Windmill	1969	Year	5.00	5.00
Christmas, Drawbridge Near Binnenhof	1970	Year	5.00	5.00 to 7.50
Christmas, St.Laurens Church	1971	Year	5.00	5.00 to 6.50
Christmas, Church At Bierkade	1972	Year	5.00	5.00 to 6.00
Christmas, St.Jan's Church	1973	Year	5.00	5.00
Christmas, Dongeradeel	1974	Year	6.00	6.00
Christmas, Maassluis	1975	Year	6.00	6.00
Christmas, Montebaanstower	1976	Year	6.00	6.00
Christmas, Harbour Tower Of Hoorn	1977	Year	7.00	7.00

Borsato, Tender Musings Plaque

Buffalo Pottery, Christmas Plate, 1950

Buffalo Pottery, Christmas Plate, 1952

Title	Issue Date	Number Issued	Issued Price	Current Price
Christmas, Binnenpoort Gate	1978	Year	7.50	7.50
Happiness Is, Mother's	1977	Year	6.50	6.50

Boehm porcelains were first made by Edward Marshall Boehm in Trenton, New Jersey, in 1950. The Malvern Boehm studio of London was established after Mr. Boehm's death in 1969. Bone china Boehm figurines are made at the English factory. Hard paste porcelains are still made in New Jersey. Lenox China has also issued a limited edition plate series featuring Boehm birds.

See listing for Boehm in Figurine section

Boehm Plaques

Title	Issue Date	Number Issued	Issued Price	Current Price
African Elephant	1977	10	3000.00	3000.00
Autumn Repast	1976	25	3800.00	3800.00
Bay Lynx	1976	10	3000.00	Unknown
Cedar Throne Bas Relief	1978	250	1500.00	1500.00
Coach & Four	1971	50	2800.00	Unknown
Cockatoo & Flowers	1971	50	4200.00	Unknown
Drummer	1971	12	2400.00	Unknown
Eastern Bluebirds, Pair	1970	120	2700.00	Unknown
Finches In Harmony	1975	25	3800.00	Unknown
Floral, Enam.Crane Vase	1974	25	4600.00	Unknown
Freedom	1976	11	3800.00	Unknown
Fruit, Pair	1974	8	10000.00	Unknown
George Washington	1976	5	4200.00	Unknown
Glories Of Spring	1973	100	3600.00	Unknown
Golden Throne Bas Relief	1977	250	1500.00	1500.00
Ivory Chest Bas Relief	1977	250	1500.00	1500.00
Leopard	1976	10	3000.00	Unknown
Lion	1977	10	3000.00	3000.00
Meadowlarks, Pair	1970	110	2700.00	Unknown
Mockingbirds, Pair	1970	150	2700.00	Unknown
Nature's Bounty	1972	50	42.00	Unknown
Nightingales	1973	25	3600.00	Unknown
Ram	1976	10	3000.00	3000.00
Royal Horse Guards	1975	15	3800.00	Unknown
Song Sparrows	1970	130	1500.00	Unknown
Spring Awakening	1976	25	3800.00	3800.00
Summer's Beauty	1976	25	3800.00	3800.00
Twentieth Century Floral	1972	50	4200.00	Unknown
Venus	1975	10	4200.00	Unknown
Votive Shield Bas Relief	1978	250	1500.00	1500.00
Washington Crossing The Delaware	1976	5	4500.00	Unknown
Winter's Treasure	1976	25	3800.00	3800.00

Boehm Bird plates, see also Lenox

Boehm Plates

Title	Issue Date	Number Issued	Issued Price	Current Price
African Butterflies	1976	100	450.00	Unknown
Apples	1976	100	450.00	Unknown
Azure-Winged Magpies	1975	100	400.00	400.00
Bird Of Peace*	1971	5000	150.00	200.00 to 550.00
Birds Of World, Set Of 8	1973	4500	400.00	400.00
Blue-Backed Fairy Bluebirds	1975	100	400.00	400.00
Blue Mountain Swallowtails	1975	100	450.00	450.00
Cherries	1975	100	450.00	450.00
Chiragra Spider Conch	1976	100	450.00	Unknown
Clematis	1978	5000	62.00	62.00
Comma With Loops	1976	100	450.00	Unknown
Double Clematis	1976	100	450.00	Unknown
Eaglet, Companion, Young America 1776*	1972	6000	175.00	100.00 to 295.00
Fancy Fowl, Pair**	1977	100	1500.00	1500.00
Golden-Fronted Leafbird	1976	100	400.00	Unknown
Golden-Throated Barbet	1976	100	400.00	Unknown
Grapes	1976	100	450.00	Unknown
Honor America, American Bald Eagle	1974	11033	85.00	85.00
Jezebels	1975	100	450.00	450.00
Lilies	1975	100	450.00	450.00
Loganberries	1975	100	450.00	450.00
Monarch Butterfly	1978	5000	62.00	62.00
Orange Spider Conch	1976	100	450.00	Unknown
Passion Flowers	1975	100	450.00	450.00

Title	Issue Date	Number Issued	Issued Price	Current Price
Peaches	1976	100	450.00	Unknown
Pears	1975	100	450.00	450.00
Plums	1975	100	450.00	450.00
Red Admiral	1978	5000	62.00	62.00
Rhododendrons, Azaleas	1978	5000	62.00	62.00
Rooster Conch	1975	100	450.00	450.00
Solandras Maxima	1976	100	450.00	Unknown
Strawberries	1976	100	450.00	Unknown
Tutankhamun Commemorative, 10 1/2 In.	1977	5000	125.00	125.00
Tutankhamun Commemorative, 12 1/2 In.	1977	250	750.00	750.00
Violet Spider Conch	1975	100	450.00	450.00

Buffalo Pottery, Christmas Plate, 1953

Bohemian Plates are manufactured by Hippolyt Freiherr V. Poschinger

Bohemian Plates

Annual	1974	500	130.00	130.00 to 140.00
Annual	1975	500	140.00	140.00
Annual	1976	500	150.00	150.00

Bonita limited edition plates are made by the Bonita Silver Company of Mexico. They were first issued in 1972.

Bonita Plates

Mother's Day, Mother And Baby, Silver	1972	4000	125.00	25.00 to 100.00

Borsato Porcelains have been made by Antonio Borsato of Milan, Italy, since 1937. Limited editions were first made in 1973.

See listing for Borsato in Figurine section

Borsato Plaques

Golden Years, 13 1/2 In.Diameter	1973	700	1450.00	1450.00
Tender Musings, 13 1/2 In.Diameter*	1974	250	1650.00	1650.00

Borsato Plates

Serenity	1978		75.00	75.00

Buffalo Pottery, Christmas Plate, 1958

Paul Briant & Sons Silversmiths of Washington state entered the limited edition market in 1971. The plates are made of 24K gold plate over copper.

Briant Plates

Christmas, Fruits Of The Spirit	1971	350	125.00	Unknown
Christmas, Labour Of Love, Gold Over Copper	1972	700	100.00	Unknown
Christmas, Annunciation, Silver	1973		100.00	Unknown
Easter, Last Sacrifice	1972	500		Unknown
Easter, The Last Sacrifice, Gold Over Copper	1972	500	85.00	Unknown

Buffalo Pottery was made in Buffalo, New York, after 1902. The company was established by the Larkin Company, famous manufacturers of soap. Limited edition Christmas plates were made between 1950 and 1962.

Buffalo Pottery Plates

Christmas*	1950	1800		35.00 to 45.00
Christmas	1951	1800		35.00 to 40.00
Christmas*	1952	1800		35.00 to 40.00
Christmas*	1953	1800		35.00 to 40.00
Christmas	1954	1800		30.00 to 35.00
Christmas	1955	1800		30.00 to 35.00
Christmas	1956	1800		25.00 to 30.00
Christmas	1957	1800		25.00 to 30.00
Christmas*	1958	1800		25.00 to 30.00
Christmas	1959	1800		25.00 to 30.00
Christmas	1960	1800		25.00 to 30.00
Christmas, Edged In Gold*	1962	900		125.00 to 150.00

Buffalo Pottery, Christmas Plate, 1962

Bygdo was organized in 1939 by Mr. Svend Knudsen. Christmas plates & mugs, first issued in 1969, are based on the fairy tales of Hans Christian Andersen. A number of other commemorative series have been introduced since 1970.

Bygdo Mugs

Christmas, Shepherdess & Chimney Sweep*	1969	1000	10.00	5.00 to 10.00
Christmas, Clumsy Hans	1970	1000	10.00	5.00 to 10.00

Bygdo, Christmas Plate, 1970

Bygdo, Christmas Plate, 1973

Bygdo, Christmas Mug, 1969, Side View

Title	Issue Date	Number Issued	Issued Price	Current Price
Christmas, The Flying Trunk	1971	1000	10.00	5.00 to 10.00
Christmas, Chinese Nightingale	1972	1000	10.00	5.00 to 10.00
Bygdo Plates				
Apollo 11, First Moon Landing	1969		10.00	7.50 to 10.00
Christmas, The Shepherdess & Chimney Sweep	1969	5000	10.00	10.00 to 11.00
Christmas, Clumsy Hans*	1970	5000	10.00	9.00
Christmas, The Flying Trunk	1971	5000	10.00	6.00 to 10.00
Christmas, Chinese Nightingale	1972	5000	10.00	6.00 to 10.00
Christmas*	1973	5000	10.00	10.00
Church, Artemarks Kurka	1973	5000	10.00	10.00
Commemorative, King Frederik IX		40000	10.00	7.50 to 10.00
Commemorative, Mormon	1974	10000		Unknown

Calhoun Collector Society, see also Royal Cornwall, Mingolla

Calhoun Collector Society Plates

Title	Issue Date	Number Issued	Issued Price	Current Price
Christmas, Bethlehem	1977	Year		Unknown
Koutsis, Adam's Rib	1978	19500	45.00	45.00
Koutsis, In The Beginning	1977	19500	37.50	Unknown
Koutsis, Banished From Eden	1978	19500	45.00	45.00
Koutsis, In His Image	1977	19500	37.50	37.50
Mingolla, Picking Flowers	1978	Year	65.00	65.00

Calhoun Collector Society Bells

Title	Issue Date	Number Issued	Issued Price	Current Price
Christmas, Bethlehem	1977	Year	23.00	23.00
Queen Elizabeth I	1978	3000	39.50	39.50
Queen Mary I	1977	3000	39.50	39.50

Capo di Monte limited editions are made in Italy. Christmas plates were first made in 1972. Mother's Day plates followed in 1973.

Capo di Monte Bells

Title	Issue Date	Number Issued	Issued Price	Current Price
Christmas	1973	350	17.50	13.00 to 16.95
Christmas	1974			13.00 to 17.95
Christmas	1975	1000		16.50 to 20.00
Christmas	1976	500	21.50	17.50 to 21.50

Capo di Monte Plates

Title	Issue Date	Number Issued	Issued Price	Current Price
Christmas, Bells And Holly	1973	500	55.00	28.00 to 75.00
Christmas, Cherubs*	1972	500	55.00	40.00 to 110.00
Christmas	1974	1000		40.00 to 65.00
Christmas	1975	1000		40.00 to 65.00
Christmas	1976	250	65.00	54.95 to 65.00
Mother's Day	1973	500	55.00	28.00 to 54.00
Mother's Day	1974	500		28.00 to 60.00
Mother's Day	1975	500		40.00 to 65.00
Mother's Day	1976	500	65.00	65.00

The Caritas, or charity, plate was commissioned by Rose Kennedy for a charitable cause.

Caritas Plate

Title	Issue Date	Number Issued	Issued Price	Current Price
Rose Kennedy	1973		20.00	11.00 to 23.00

Carlo Monti limited edition plates are of enamel on copper. 1973 is the first year they were made.

Carlo Monti Plates

Title	Issue Date	Number Issued	Issued Price	Current Price
Mother's Day, Madonna & Child	1973	2000	35.00	9.00 to 35.00

Carte a Jouer plates, see Puiforcat

The Cartier Plate series is a collection of porcelain plates reproducing famous stained glass in French cathedrals. The plates are made in Limoges, France.

Cartier Plates

Title	Issue Date	Number Issued	Issued Price	Current Price
Chartres Cathedral	1972	12500	50.00	14.00 to 40.00
Chartres Cathedral, Millous	1974	500	130.00	120.00 to 130.00

Certified Rarities are issuing a set of Railroad Ballad Art Plates engraved by the Master Engravers of America. These plates are available in solid sterling silver plate inlaid with 24 Kt. gold, crafted by

Title	Issue Date	Number Issued	Issued Price	Current Price
Towle Silversmiths, or in solid brass by Kent Silversmiths of Sheffield, England.				

Railroad Ballad Art Plates

Title	Issue Date	Number Issued	Issued Price	Current Price
America's First Family	1977		40.00	40.00
Ballad Of Casey Jones, Brass	1976	5000	36.00	36.00
Ballad Of Casey Jones, Silver And Gold	1976	1500	100.00	100.00
Ballad Of Casey Jones, Silver And Gold, 10 In.	1976	1500	250.00	250.00
Ballad Of John Henry, Brass	1976	5000	36.00	36.00
Ballad Of John Henry, Silver And Gold	1976	1500	100.00	100.00
Ballad Of John Henry, Silver And Gold, 10 In.	1976	1500	250.00	250.00
Big Rock Candy Mountains, Brass	1977	5000	36.00	36.00
Big Rock Candy Mountains, Silver And Gold	1977	1500	100.00	100.00
Big Rock Candy Mountains, Silver & Gold, 10 In	1977	1500	250.00	250.00
A Railroader For Me, Brass	1977	5000	36.00	36.00
A Railroader For Me, Silver And Gold	1977	1500	100.00	100.00
A Railroader For Me, Silver And Gold, 10 In.	1977	500	250.00	250.00
Wabash Cannonball, Brass	1977	5000	36.00	36.00
Wabash Cannonball, Silver And Gold	1977	1500	100.00	100.00
Wabash Cannonball, Silver And Gold, 10 In.	1977	1500	250.00	250.00
Wreck Of The Old 97, Brass	1976	5000	36.00	36.00
Wreck Of The Old 97, Silver And Gold	1976	1500	100.00	100.00
Wreck Of The Old 97, Silver And Gold, 10 In.	1976	1500	250.00	250.00

Capo di Monte, Christmas Plate, 1972

The Chagall plate is part of a series issued by Georg Jensen of New York City.

Chagall Plate

Title	Issue Date	Number Issued	Issued Price	Current Price
The Lovers*	1972	12500	50.00	25.00 to 35.00

Chaim Gross, see Judaic Heritage Society

Charles Russell, see Antique Trader

Chateau, Inc., of Indianapolis, Indiana, entered the limited edition field in 1972. The plates are produced in Denmark by the Kesa factory.

Chateau Plates

Title	Issue Date	Number Issued	Issued Price	Current Price
Apollo 16	1973	1000	20.00	Unknown
Auto, 1915 Model T Ford		1000	20.00	Unknown
Auto, 1913 Rolls-Royce		1000	20.00	Unknown
Bicentennial, First		2500	20.00	Unknown
Bicentennial, Second		2500	20.00	Unknown
Christmas	1974	3000	4.95	Unknown
Christmas	1975			Unknown
City, Boston	1972	1000	15.00	Unknown
City, Chicago	1972	1000	15.00	Unknown
City, Indianapolis	1972	2000	15.00	Unknown
City, New Orleans	1972	275	15.00	Unknown
City, San Francisco	1972	1500	15.00	Unknown
City, Washington, D.C.	1972	275	15.00	Unknown
Dixie		2500	20.00	Unknown
Famous American, Eisenhower, Crystal		2500	20.00	Unknown
State, Alabama	1972	750	15.00	Unknown
State, Alaska	1972	250	15.00	Unknown
State, Arizona	1972	450	15.00	Unknown
State, Arkansas	1972	450	15.00	Unknown
State, California	1972	775	15.00	Unknown
State, Colorado	1972	250	15.00	Unknown
State, Connecticut	1972	250	15.00	Unknown
State, Delaware	1972	250	15.00	Unknown
State, Florida	1972	1000	15.00	Unknown
State, Georgia	1972	1000	15.00	Unknown
State, Hawaii	1972	500	15.00	Unknown
State, Idaho	1972	250	15.00	Unknown
State, Illinois	1972	1500	15.00	Unknown
State, Indiana	1972	1500	15.00	Unknown
State, Iowa	1972	1500	15.00	Unknown
State, Kansas	1972	450	15.00	Unknown
State, Kentucky	1972	1000	15.00	Unknown
State, Louisiana	1972	650	15.00	Unknown
State, Maine	1972	500	15.00	Unknown
State, Maryland	1972	500	15.00	Unknown

Chagall, The Lovers Plate

Title	Issue Date	Number Issued	Issued Price	Current Price
State, Massachusetts	1972	500	15.00	Unknown
State, Michigan	1972	700	15.00	Unknown
State, Minnesota	1972	1500	15.00	Unknown
State, Mississippi	1972	400	15.00	Unknown
State, Missouri	1972	1500	15.00	Unknown
State, Montana	1972	225	15.00	Unknown
State, Nebraska	1972	500	15.00	Unknown
State, Nevada	1972	250	15.00	Unknown
State, New Hampshire	1972	250	15.00	Unknown
State, New Jersey	1972	500	15.00	Unknown
State, New Mexico	1972	500	15.00	Unknown
State, New York	1972	525	15.00	Unknown
State, North Carolina	1972	750	15.00	Unknown
State, North Dakota	1972	325	15.00	Unknown
State, Ohio	1972	1425	15.00	Unknown
State, Oklahoma	1972	1150	15.00	Unknown
State, Oregon	1972	775	15.00	Unknown
State, Pennsylvania	1972	500	15.00	Unknown
State, Rhode Island	1972	250	15.00	Unknown
State, South Carolina	1972	750	15.00	Unknown
State, South Dakota	1972	250	15.00	Unknown
State, Tennessee	1972	750	15.00	Unknown
State, Texas	1972	2000	15.00	Unknown
State, Utah	1972	250	15.00	Unknown
State, Vermont	1972	340	15.00	Unknown
State, Virginia	1972	525	15.00	Unknown
State, Washington	1972	475	15.00	Unknown
State, West Virginia	1972	525	15.00	Unknown
State, Wisconsin	1972	825	15.00	Unknown
State, Wyoming	1972	250	15.00	Unknown
State, Alabama	1973	1500	15.00	Unknown
State, Alaska	1973	250	15.00	Unknown
State, Arizona	1973	500	15.00	Unknown
State, Arkansas	1973	500	15.00	Unknown
State, California	1973	2000	15.00	Unknown
State, Colorado	1973	250	15.00	Unknown
State, Connecticut	1973	500	15.00	Unknown
State, Delaware	1973	250	15.00	Unknown
State, Florida	1973	1000	15.00	Unknown
State, Georgia	1973	1000	15.00	Unknown
State, Hawaii	1973	500	15.00	Unknown
State, Idaho	1973	250	15.00	Unknown
State, Illinois	1973	2000	15.00	Unknown
State, Indiana	1973	1500	15.00	Unknown
State, Iowa	1973	1500	15.00	Unknown
State, Kansas	1973	1000	15.00	Unknown
State, Kentucky	1973	1000	15.00	Unknown
State, Louisiana	1973	750	15.00	Unknown
State, Maine	1973	500	15.00	Unknown
State, Maryland	1973	500	15.00	Unknown
State, Massachusetts	1973	1000	15.00	Unknown
State, Michigan	1973	1000	15.00	Unknown
State, Minnesota	1973	1500	15.00	Unknown
State, Mississippi	1973	500	15.00	Unknown
State, Missouri	1973	1500	15.00	Unknown
State, Montana	1973	250	15.00	Unknown
State, Nebraska	1973	1000	15.00	Unknown
State, Nevada	1973	250	15.00	Unknown
State, New Hampshire	1973	250	15.00	Unknown
State, New Jersey	1973	1000	15.00	Unknown
State, New Mexico	1973	500	15.00	Unknown
State, New York	1973	2000	15.00	Unknown
State, North Carolina	1973	750	15.00	Unknown
State, North Dakota	1973	500	15.00	Unknown
State, Ohio	1973	1500	15.00	Unknown
State, Oklahoma	1973	1500	15.00	Unknown
State, Oregon	1973	775	15.00	Unknown
State, Pennsylvania	1973	1500	15.00	Unknown
State, Rhode Island	1973	500	15.00	Unknown
State, South Carolina	1973	750	15.00	Unknown

Title	Issue Date	Number Issued	Issued Price	Current Price
State, South Dakota	1973	250	15.00	Unknown
State, Tennessee	1973	1000	15.00	Unknown
State, Texas	1973	2000	15.00	Unknown
State, Utah	1973	500	15.00	Unknown
State, Vermont	1973	350	15.00	Unknown
State, Virginia	1973	750	15.00	Unknown
State, Washington	1973	500	15.00	Unknown
State, West Virginia	1973	525	15.00	Unknown
State, Wisconsin	1973	1000	15.00	Unknown
State, Wyoming	1973	250	15.00	Unknown

Chief Wapello plate, see Wapello County

Church plate, see Danish Church

Churchill Mint Plaques

Mother's Day, Horse And Foal, Silver	1973	500	75.00	Unknown

Churchill Mint Plates

Christmas, Mockingbird On Holly	1972	2000	150.00	Unknown
Christmas, Scissor-Tailed Flycatcher	1973	2000	150.00	Unknown

Churchill plate, see Silver Creations

Coalport Bell

Bicentennial	1976		25.00	25.00

Cleveland Mint, Churchill plate, see Silver Creations

Coalport Goblets

Silver Jubilee, Porcelain	1977	2000	41.00	41.00

Coalport Plates

Christmas	1976			40.00
Indy 500	1972	2000	49.95	50.00
Mayflower, 350th Anniversary				125.00

Coalport Christmas Ornaments

Angel	1973			5.00
Christmas Tree	1973			5.00
Drummer Boy	1973			5.00
Kings	1973			5.00
Santa	1973			5.00

Coalport Vases

Ram's Head	1977	200	342.00	342.00

Collector Creations Plates

Alice In Wonderland, Damascene	1973	750	100.00	Unknown
Christmas, Christmas By Thomas Nast, Damascene	1973	750	100.00	Unknown

Cowboy Artists, Plate, Charles Dye
and John Hampton, Pair, 1976

Cowboy Artists, Plate,
Joe Beeler and George Phippen, Pair, 1977

Collector's Weekly, an antiques publication published in Kermit, Texas, introduced limited edition plates in 1971. The cobalt glass plates are made by the Big Pine Key Glass Works of Florida.

Collector's Weekly Plates

American, Eagle, Carnival	1973	900	9.75	Unknown
American, Miss Liberty, Carnival	1971	500	12.50	Unknown
American, Miss Liberty, Carnival	1972	900	12.50	Unknown
Mother's Day, Vase	1975	250		85.00
Remington, Apache	1972			22.50

Continental Mint issued the Norman Rockwell plates starting in 1976.

Continental Mint Plates

Rockwell, Painting The Place	1977	5000		24.50
Rockwell, Taking His Medicine	1976	5000		24.50

Cowboy Artists of America plates perpetuate the memory and culture of the Old West. Charlie Dye, John Hampton, George Phippen and Joe Beeler founded the association. Pickard China is producing the plates.

Cowboy Artists Plates

Charles Dye And John Hampton, Pair*	1976	3000	130.00	130.00
Joe Beeler And George Phippen, Pair*	1977	3000	130.00	130.00

Title	Issue Date	Number Issued	Issued Price	Current Price
Count Agazzi Plates				
Apollo 11	1969	1000	17.00	18.00 to 25.00
Children's Hour, Owl	1970	2000	12.50	10.00 to 12.50
Children's Hour, Cat	1971	2000	12.50	10.00 to 12.50
Children's Hour, Pony	1972	2000	12.50	15.00
Children's Hour, Panda	1973	2000	12.50	15.00
Christmas	1973	1000	19.50	15.00
Easter, Playing The Violin	1971	600	12.50	15.00
Easter, At Prayer	1972	600	12.50	15.00
Easter, Winged Cherub	1973	600	12.50	15.00
Famous Personalities	1968	600	8.00	25.00 to 35.00
Famous Personalities	1970	1000	12.50	12.50
Famous Personalities	1973	600	15.00	15.00
Father's Day	1972	144	35.00	40.00
Father's Day	1973	288	19.50	19.50
Mother's Day	1972	144	35.00	30.00 to 45.00
Mother's Day	1973	720	19.50	19.50
Peace	1973	720		10.00 to 15.00
Cowles, Fleur				
Wildlife Collection, Tiger Bouquet	1978	6000	50.00	50.00

Creative World, Pearl Buck plate, see Pearl Buck

Creative World, see also Veneto Flair

Title	Issue Date	Number Issued	Issued Price	Current Price
Creative World Plates				
Brown, Looking Out To Sea, 8 In.	1978	15000	50.00	50.00
Brown, Village Smithy, 8 In.	1978		50.00	50.00
Brown, Yankee Doodle, Copper, 8 In.	1978		50.00	50.00
Stained Glass, Madonna	1973	1500	90.00	Unknown

Cristal d'Albret plates and paperweights are made at the glassworks of Vianne, France. Limited edition sulphide paperweights were first made in 1966. Limited edition crystal plates were introduced in 1972.

See listing for Cristal d'Albret in Paperweight section

Title	Issue Date	Number Issued	Issued Price	Current Price
Cristal d'Albret Plates				
Bird Of Peace	1972	3700	64.00	32.00 to 68.00
Four Seasons, Autumn*	1973	648	75.00	39.95 to 75.00
Four Seasons, Spring*	1973	312	75.00	85.00 to 159.00
Four Seasons, Summer	1972	1000	75.00	21.00 to 125.00
Four Seasons, Winter	1974		88.00	55.00 to 88.00

Crown and Rose Pewter

Title	Issue Date	Number Issued	Issued Price	Current Price
Crown and Rose Bells				
Bicentennial, Pewter	1975	5500	55.00	55.00 to 65.00
Bicentennial, Pewter	1976	5000	55.00	55.00
Crown Delft Plates				
Christmas, Man By The Fire	1969		10.00	17.00 to 20.00
Christmas, Two Sleigh Riders	1970		10.00	12.00 to 18.00
Christmas, Christmas Tree On Market Square	1971		10.00	12.00 to 15.00
Christmas, Baking For Christmas	1972		10.00	12.00
Christmas	1973	1000		12.00
Father's Day	1970		10.00	7.50 to 10.00
Father's Day	1971		10.00	12.00
Father's Day	1972	1000		12.00
Father's Day	1973	1000		12.00
Mother's Day, Sheep	1970		10.00	13.00
Mother's Day, Stork	1971		10.00	12.00
Mother's Day, Ducks	1972		10.00	12.00
Mother's Day	1973	1000		12.00
Crown Delft Tiles				
Christmas, Man By The Fire	1969		4.50	7.50 to 10.00
Christmas, Two Sleigh Riders	1970		4.50	5.00 to 9.00
Christmas, Christmas Tree On Market Square	1971		4.50	4.50 to 6.50
Christmas, Baking For Christmas	1972		4.50	4.50
Christmas	1973		5.00	5.00
Father's Day	1970		4.50	5.00 to 7.50
Father's Day	1971		4.50	4.50 to 6.00
Mother's Day, Sheep	1970		4.50	5.00 to 7.50

Cristal d'Albret, Four Seasons Plate, Autumn

Cristal d'Albret, Four Seasons Plate, Spring

Title	Issue Date	Number Issued	Issued Price	Current Price
Mother's Day, Stork	1971		4.50	4.50

Crown Staffordshire Plates

Title	Issue Date	Number Issued	Issued Price	Current Price
Christmas, Poinsettia	1972	4000	25.00	18.00 to 30.00
Christmas, Rose	1973	4000	7.50	13.99 to 30.00
Christmas, Parisian Couple	1974	4000		19.50 to 35.00
Christmas, Embracing Couple	1975	4000		19.50 to 35.00
Christmas, Two Bells With Holly	1976	4000	35.00	35.00
Christmas, Cock O'the North	1977	4000	35.00	35.00
Mother's Day, Peace Rose	1973	4000	27.50	17.50 to 45.00
Mother's Day, Americana Rose	1974	4000		17.50 to 45.00
Mother's Day, Floral Bouquet	1975	4000		35.00
Mother's Day, Floral Bouquet	1976	4000	35.00	35.00
Mother's Day, Spring Flowers	1977	Year	35.00	35.00
Mother's Day, Love In A Mist	1978	Year	35.00	35.00
St.Patrick's Day, Castle On The Blarney Stone	1978	2000	30.00	30.00
Wild Fowl, Pintail	1974	2000		175.00
Wild Fowl, Wigeon	1976	2000		175.00

Currier & Ives plates, see Antique Trader, Danbury Mint, Reed & Barton

Bill Curry Productions of Chesapeake, Ohio, first made limited edition tile plaques in 1972. The tiles are produced by Screencraft, U.S.A. of Massachusetts.

Curry Plaques

Title	Issue Date	Number Issued	Issued Price	Current Price
Christmas, Baby Santa Claus	1972	1000	12.00	Unknown
Christmas, Mistletoe Bird	1973	1000	12.00	Unknown
Indian, Cheyenne Chief	1973	1000	10.00	Unknown
Indian, Cheyenne Chief, Proof	1973	50	25.00	Unknown
Indian, Chief Crazy Horse	1973	1000	10.00	Unknown
Indian, Chief Crazy Horse, Proof	1973	50	25.00	Unknown
Indian, Chief Gall, Sioux	1973	1000	10.00	Unknown
Indian, Chief Gall, Sioux, Proof	1973	50	25.00	Unknown
Indian, Chief Rain-In-The-Face, Sioux	1973	1000	10.00	Unknown
Indian, Chief Rain-In-The-Face, Sioux, Proof	1973	50	25.00	Unknown
Indian, Chief Red Fox, Sioux	1973	1000	10.00	Unknown
Indian, Chief Red Fox, Sioux, Proof	1973	50	25.00	Unknown
Indian, Chief Sitting Bull, Sioux	1973	1000	10.00	Unknown
Indian, Chief Sitting Bull, Sioux, Proof	1973	50	25.00	Unknown
Indian, Chief Yellow Hand, Cheyenne	1973	1000	10.00	Unknown
Indian, Chief Yellow Hand, Cheyenne, Proof	1973	50	25.00	Unknown
Indian, Comanche Chief	1973	1000	10.00	Unknown
Indian, Comanche Chief, Proof	1973	50	25.00	Unknown
Indian, Nez Perce Chief	1973	1000	10.00	Unknown
Indian, Nez Perce Chief, Proof	1973	50	25.00	Unknown
Indian, Shoshone Chief	1973	1000	10.00	Unknown
Indian, Shoshone Chief, Proof	1973	50	25.00	Unknown
Indian, Sioux Chief	1973	1000	10.00	Unknown
Indian, Sioux Chief, Proof	1973	50	25.00	Unknown
Indian, Yuma Chief	1973	1000	10.00	Unknown
Indian, Yuma Chief, Proof	1973	50	25.00	Unknown

Cybis, See listing in Figurine section

Cybis, Boxes

Title	Issue Date	Number Issued	Issued Price	Current Price
Lidded Heart Box	1976	100	1000.00	1000.00

d'Albret, see Cristal d'Albret

D'Arceau Limoges porcelains are being crafted by Henri D'Arceau et Fils of Limoges, France. The Christmas Series was inspired by the stained-glass windows of Chartres Cathedral. The plates are being distributed by Bradford Galleries.

D'Arceau Limoges Porcelain Plates

Title	Issue Date	Number Issued	Issued Price	Current Price
Christmas, Flight Into Egypt*	1975	Year	24.00	21.95 to 30.00
Christmas, Dans La Creche	1976	Year	24.00	24.00
Christmas, Le Refus D'hebergement	1977	Year	24.00	24.00
Four Seasons, Summer Girl	1978	Year		Unknown
Ganeau's Women, Scarlet	1976	Year	15.00	25.00
Ganeau's Women, Sarah*	1976	Year	20.00	25.00
Ganeau's Women, Colette	1976	Year	20.00	27.00

D'arceau Limoges, Plate, Ganeau's Women, Sarah, 1976

D'arceau Limoges, Plate, Christmas, Flight Into Egypt, 1975

D'arceau Limoges, Plate, Lafayette Series, Battle Of Brandywine, 1974

Danbury Mint, Bicentennial, 1973,
The Boston Tea Party

Danbury Mint, Christmas Plate, 1972,
Currier & Ives

Danbury Mint, The Pieta Plate

Danbury Mint, Plate, Great American
Sailing Ship, America, 1977

Title	Issue Date	Number Issued	Issued Price	Current Price
Ganeau's Women, Lea	1976	Year	20.00	27.00
Lafayette Series, The Secret Contract	1973	Year	12.00	32.00 to 45.00
Lafayette Series, Landing At North Island	1973	Year	17.00	42.50 to 57.00
Lafayette Series, Meeting At City Tavern	1974	Year	17.00	34.95 to 37.50
Lafayette Series, Battle Of Brandywine*	1974	Year	17.00	32.50 to 47.50
Lafayette Series, Messages To Franklin	1975	Year	66.00	66.00
Lafayette Series, Siege At Yorktown	1975	Year	17.00	35.00 to 54.00
Women Of The Century, Scarlet En Crinoline	1976	Year	14.80	14.80
Women Of The Century, Sarah En Tournure	1976	Year	19.87	19.87

Da Vinci Last Supper plate, see Cleveland Mint

Dali, see Daum, Lincoln Mint, Puiforcat

Damron Hand-Blown Glass Bells are hand-engraved by R. K. Damron. The Damron Family has been engraving glass for over one hundred years. The bells are made by Damron's Glass Engraving of West Palm Beach, Florida.

Damron Bells

Title	Issue Date	Number Issued	Issued Price	Current Price
Bicentennial, Blue	1976	5000	25.00	25.00
Mother's Day, Ruby Love Birds	1975	3000	19.50	19.50

Danbury Mint, a division of Glendinning Companies, Inc., creates and markets art medals and limited edition plates. All limited editions are struck for the Danbury Mint by other organizations. Limited edition plates were first introduced in 1972.

Danbury Mint Metal Plates

Title	Issue Date	Number Issued	Issued Price	Current Price
Bicentennial, Boston Tea Party, Gold & Silver*	1973	7500	125.00	125.00 to 150.00
Bicentennial, 1st Continental Congress, Silver	1974	7500	125.00	125.00 to 150.00
Christmas, Currier & Ives, Road, Winter, Silver*	1972	7500	125.00	55.00 to 225.00
Christmas, Currier & Ives, Central Park, Silver	1973	7500	125.00	100.00 to 160.00
Christmas, Currier & Ives, Grist Mill, Sterling	1974	7500	125.00	150.00
Creation Of Adam, Sterling	1972	7500	150.00	125.00 to 175.00
The Pieta, Sterling*	1973	7500	150.00	150.00 to 200.00

Danbury Mint Bells

Title	Issue Date	Number Issued	Issued Price	Current Price
Bicentennial, Bunker Hill	1975	Year	25.00	25.00
Bicentennial, Paul Revere	1975		25.00	25.00
Christmas, Michelangelo Angel, Silver	1975	Year	29.95	29.95
Christmas, Girl With Candle, Silver Plate	1977	Year	29.50	29.50
Mother's Day, Silver	1975	Year	23.50	23.50
Rockwell, Dr.And Doll		Year	27.50	27.50

Danbury Mint Ornaments

Title	Issue Date	Number Issued	Issued Price	Current Price
Gold	1976	Year	12.50	12.50
Trumpeting Angels	1977	Year	13.50	13.50

Danbury Mint Porcelain plates

Title	Issue Date	Number Issued	Issued Price	Current Price
Abraham Lincoln	1978		30.00	30.00
Christmas, Silent Night	1975	Year	24.50	24.50
Christmas, Joy To The World	1976	Year	27.50	27.50
Christmas, The Nativity	1977	Year	27.50	27.50
Great American Sailing Ship, America*	1977	Year	35.00	35.00
Great American Sailing Ship, Bon Homme	1977	Year	35.00	35.00
Great American Sailing Ship, Columbia	1977	Year	35.00	35.00
Great American Sailing Ship, Flying Cloud	1977	Year	35.00	35.00
Great American Sailing Ship, Sea Witch	1977	Year	35.00	35.00
Great American Sailing Ship, USS Constitution	1977	Year	35.00	35.00
White House China, John Adams	1978	Year	30.00	30.00
White House China, Lincoln	1978	Year	30.00	30.00
White House China, Washington	1978	Year	30.00	30.00

Danbury Mint Porcelain bowl

Title	Issue Date	Number Issued	Issued Price	Current Price
Bicentennial, Rockwell, B. Franklin, Signing	1976	Year	65.00	65.00

Danish Church Plates

Title	Issue Date	Number Issued	Issued Price	Current Price
Christmas, Roskilde Cathedral	1968		12.00	10.00 to 25.00
Christmas, Ribe Cathedral	1969		13.00	9.00 to 13.00
Christmas, Marmor Kirken	1970		13.00	6.00 to 11.00
Christmas, Ejby Kirken	1971		13.00	10.00 to 18.00
Christmas, Kalundborg Kirken	1972		13.00	11.00 to 18.00
Christmas, Grundtvig Kirken	1973		15.00	11.00 to 19.00
Christmas, Broager Kirken	1974		15.00	9.50 to 22.00

Title	Issue Date	Number Issued	Issued Price	Current Price
Christmas, Sct. Knuds Kirken	1975		18.00	24.00
Christmas, Osterlas Church	1976		22.00	22.00
Christmas	1977		23.00	23.00

De Grazia Los Ninos, Children Of The World, Plate, White Dove, Signed, 1976

Daum, the French firm noted for Daum Nancy cameo glass, was founded in 1875 by Auguste and Antonin Daum. Crystal, a new medium for the company, was introduced following World War II. The first limited edition Four Seasons plate series was made by the pate de verre process in 1969. Daum also produces limited edition plates in crystal.

Daum Plates

Title	Issue Date	Number Issued	Issued Price	Current Price
Composer, Bach	1970	2000	60.00	12.00 to 60.00
Composer, Beethoven	1970	2000	60.00	20.00 to 60.00
Composer, Debussy	1972	2000	60.00	45.00 to 60.00
Composer, Gershwin	1972	2000	60.00	45.00 to 60.00
Composer, Mozart	1971	2000	60.00	60.00
Composer, Wagner	1971	2000	60.00	45.00 to 60.00
Composer, Wagner	1971	2000	60.00	45.00 to 60.00
Dali, Pair	1971	2000	60.00	70.00 to 400.00
Four Seasons, Set Of 4	1970	2000	600.00	80.00 to 600.00
Peacock				80.00 to 100.00

Davis plates are sponsored by Mr. & Mrs. Vernon Davis of Hagerstown, Maryland. They feature famous photographs taken by Mr. Davis during his career as a journalist.

Davis Plates

Title	Issue Date	Number Issued	Issued Price	Current Price
Camp David	1972	250	12.00	12.00
Last Trolley	1973	250	12.00	12.00

Dresden, Plate, Christmas, Rothenberg Scene, 1975

De Grazia Commemorative Dishes are being reproduced by Jodi Kirk, who paints them and fires them.

De Grazia Plates

Title	Issue Date	Number Issued	Issued Price	Current Price
Beautiful Burden	1972	200	75.00	100.00
Bell Of Hope	1972	200	75.00	100.00
End Of A Long Day	1974	200	75.00	Unknown
Fiesta Flowers	1974	200	75.00	Unknown
Heavenly Blessing	1972	200	75.00	100.00
Pima Indian Drummer Boy	1973	200	75.00	100.00
Lord's Candle	1975	200	75.00	Unknown
White Dove	1975	200	75.00	Unknown
Yumas Waiting For Train		25	250.00	250.00

Dresden, Plate, Christmas, Bavarian Village, 1976

De Grazia Los Ninos, Children Of The World Plates are being made by Gorham and Fairmont China.

De Grazia Plates

Title	Issue Date	Number Issued	Issued Price	Current Price
Bell Of Hope	1977		45.00	45.00
Festival Of Lights	1976	9500	45.00	45.00
Festival Of Lights, Signed	1976	500	100.00	100.00
Los Ninos, Signed	1976	500	100.00	133.00 to 189.00
Los Ninos, Unsigned	1976	4500	35.00	35.00
White Dove, Signed*	1976	500	100.00	100.00
White Dove, Unsigned	1976	9500	40.00	40.00

Delft, see Blue Delft, Crown Delft, Royal Delft, Zenith

Dresden, Plate, Christmas, Old Mill In Black Forest, 1977

Dennis the Menace Plates

Title	Issue Date	Number Issued	Issued Price	Current Price
Christmas	1976		12.00	12.00

Detlefsen Plates

Title	Issue Date	Number Issued	Issued Price	Current Price
Americana, Coming Around The Mountain	1974	4000	40.00	40.00 to 50.00
Americana, Covered Bridge	1975	4000	40.00	26.65 to 40.00
Americana, Happy Days	1976	4000	40.00	40.00
Americana, Memories	1973	4000	40.00	40.00 to 65.00

Devlin, Stuart, see Reco

Di Volteradici, see Volteradici

Dorothy Doughty, see Royal Worcester

Downs Collectors Showcase Plates

Title	Issue Date	Number Issued	Issued Price	Current Price
American Song Bird	1978	7500	25.00	25.00

Dresden, Mother's Day Plate, 1973

Dresden, Mother's Day Plate, 1974

Dresden, Plate, Mother's Day,
Dachshund Family, 1975

Dresden, Plate, Mother's Day,
Mother Owl And Young, 1976

Title	Issue Date	Number Issued	Issued Price	Current Price
Dresden Plates				
Christmas, Shepherd Scene	1971	3500	15.00	20.00 to 150.00
Christmas, Niklas Church	1972	8500	15.00	7.00 to 25.00
Christmas, Mountain Church	1973	6000	18.00	18.00 to 40.00
Christmas, Village Scene	1974	5000	20.00	10.00 to 30.00
Christmas, Rothenberg Scene*	1975	5000	24.00	16.00 to 24.00
Christmas, Bavarian Village*	1976	5000	26.00	26.00
Christmas, Old Mill In Black Forest*	1977	5000	28.00	28.00
Mother's Day, Doe & Fawn	1972	8000	15.00	9.00 to 42.00
Mother's Day, Mare & Foal*	1973	8000	16.00	13.00 to 40.00
Mother's Day, Tiger & Cub*	1974	8000	20.00	12.00 to 24.00
Mother's Day, Dachshund Family*	1975	8000	24.00	16.00 to 24.50
Mother's Day, Mother Owl And Young*	1976	5000	26.00	19.95 to 26.00
Mother's Day, Chamois*	1977	5000	28.00	28.00
Edward Warren Sawyer, see George Washington Mint				
Egermann Bells				
Ruby	1975		20.00	20.00
Ruby	1976		21.50	21.50
Egermann Decanters				
Thanksgiving, Turkey & Basket	1970	50	35.00	75.00 to 95.00
Thanksgiving, Turkey & Basket	1971	360	35.00	35.00 to 55.00
Thanksgiving, Turkey & Cornucopia	1972	500	45.00	37.50 to 45.00
Thanksgiving, Vintage	1973	500	45.00	45.00
Egermann Plates				
Christmas	1972	500	55.00	20.00 to 55.00
Christmas*	1973	1000	55.00	30.00 to 55.00
Eschenbach Plates				
Christmas, Nuremberg	1971		13.00	7.00 to 15.00
Christmas, Church Maria Gern	1972		13.00	9.00 to 16.50
Christmas	1973			14.00 to 16.50
Christmas	1974			10.00 to 17.50
Ewings, see Scottish				
Fairfield Collection Boxes				
Founding Fathers, Set Of 4, Silver	1976	2000	950.00	950.00
Founding Fathers, Set Of 4, Gold Vermeil	1976	500	1150.00	1150.00
Faure, see Poillerat				
Fairmont China Plates				
Carousel Horses, Joyce, Pair	1977	3000	80.00	80.00
Mallards, Whistling In	1977	5000	45.00	45.00
Owen, Root Canal	1977	5000	45.00	45.00
Red Skelton, Freddie The Freeloader	1976	10000	55.00	55.00 to 100.00
Red Skelton, W.C.Fields	1977	10000	55.00	55.00
Red Skelton, Happy	1978	10000	55.00	55.00
Ruffin, Navajo Lullaby	1976	7500	40.00	40.00 to 49.00
Ruffin, Statesman	1977		65.00	65.00
Ruffin, Through The Years	1977	5000	45.00	45.00
Ruffin, Pueblo Child	1978			Unknown
Serenity	1978	10000	47.50	47.50
Spencer, Hug Me	1978	10000	55.00	75.00 to 100.00
Spencer, I Love You	1978	550	285.00	285.00
Spencer, Patient Ones, Signed	1977	500	100.00	100.00
Spencer, Patient Ones, Unsigned	1977	9500	45.00	45.00 to 65.00
Spencer, Yesterday, Today, Tomorrow	1978	10000	47.50	47.50
Thorpe, Tenderness	1978	5000	45.00	45.00

Fenton Art Glass Company, founded in 1905 in Martins Ferry, Ohio, by Frank L. Fenton, is now located in Williamstown, West Virginia. It is noted for early carnival glass, produced between 1907 and 1920. Fenton is still using carnival glass, as well as blue and white satin glass, for its limited edition commemorative plates, introduced in 1970. The company trademark is an early glassworker. Editions are limited to a six-month production period. The molds are destroyed at the end of that period.

Title	Issue Date	Number Issued	Issued Price	Current Price
Fenton Bells				
Bicentennial, Blue	1974	Year	10.00	7.50 to 18.00
Bicentennial, Red Slag	1975	Year	10.00	9.75 to 10.00

Title	Issue Date	Number Issued	Issued Price	Current Price
Bicentennial, Chocolate	1976	Year	11.00	11.00
Bicentennial, White	1976	Year	10.00	10.00
Fenton Comports				
Bicentennial, Jefferson, Blue	1974	3600	75.00	60.00 to 150.00
Bicentennial, Jefferson, Chocolate	1976	3600	75.00	75.00
Bicentennial, Jefferson, Red	1975	3600	75.00	75.00 to 150.00
Bicentennial, Jefferson, White	1976	3600	60.00	60.00
Fenton Plates				
Bicentennial Eagle, Blue	1974	Year	15.00	8.95 to 20.00
Bicentennial Eagle, Chocolate	1976	Year	17.50	17.50
Bicentennial Eagle, Red	1975	Year	15.00	15.00
Bicentennial Eagle, White	1976	Year	15.00	15.00
Christmas, Little Brown Church, Blue Satin	1970	Year	12.50	25.00
Christmas, Little Brown Church, Carnival*	1970	Year	12.50	25.00
Christmas, Little Brown Church, Brown	1970	Year	17.50	150.00
Christmas, Old Brick Church, Blue Satin	1971	Year	12.50	10.00 to 25.00
Christmas, Old Brick Church, Brown	1971	Year	17.50	75.00
Christmas, Old Brick Church, Carnival*	1971	Year	12.50	9.00 to 13.00
Christmas, Old Brick Church, White Satin	1971	Year	12.50	12.00 to 30.00
Christmas, Two-Horned Church, Blue Satin**	1972	Year	12.50	8.00 to 40.00
Christmas, Two-Horned Church, Brown	1972	Year	17.50	17.50
Christmas, Two-Horned Church, Carnival	1972	Year	12.50	12.00 to 17.95
Christmas, Two-Horned Church, White Satin	1972	Year	12.50	10.00 to 12.50
Christmas, St.Mary's, Blue Satin	1973	Year	12.50	12.50
Christmas, St.Mary's, Carnival	1973	Year	12.50	12.00 to 35.00
Christmas, St.Mary's, White Satin	1973	Year	12.50	12.50 to 35.00
Christmas, St.Mary's, Brown	1973	Year	17.50	50.00
Christmas, The Nation's Church, Blue Satin	1974	Year	13.50	13.50
Christmas, The Nation's Church, Carnival	1974	Year	13.50	6.50 to 13.95
Christmas, The Nation's Church, White Satin	1974	Year	13.50	13.50
Christmas, The Nation's Church, Brown	1974	Year	18.50	18.50
Christmas, Birthplace Of Liberty, Blue Satin	1975	Year	13.50	13.50 to 25.00
Christmas, Birthplace Of Liberty, Carnival	1975	Year	13.50	13.50 to 25.00
Christmas, Birthplace Of Liberty, White Satin	1975	Year	13.50	13.50
Christmas, Birthplace Of Liberty, Brown	1975	Year	20.00	20.00
Christmas, Old North Church, Blue Satin	1976	Year	15.00	15.00
Christmas, Old North Church, Carnival	1976	Year	15.00	15.00
Christmas, Old North Church, White Satin	1976	Year	15.00	15.00
Christmas, Old North Church, Brown	1976	Year	25.00	35.00
Christmas, San Carlos, Blue Satin	1977	Year	15.00	15.00
Christmas, San Carlos, Carnival	1977	Year	15.00	15.00
Christmas, San Carlos, White Satin	1977	Year	15.00	15.00
Craftsmen, Glassblower, Carnival	1970	Year	10.00	5.00 to 15.00
Craftsmen, Printer, Carnival*	1971	Year	10.00	10.00 to 12.50
Craftsmen, Blacksmith, Carnival**	1972	Year	10.00	9.00 to 20.00
Craftsmen, Shoemaker, Carnival*	1973	Year	10.00	10.00 to 12.50
Craftsmen, Cooper, Carnival**	1974	Year	11.00	8.25 to 12.50
Craftsmen, Silversmith	1975	Year	13.50	13.50
Craftsmen, Gunsmith	1976	Year	13.50	12.95 to 13.50
Craftsmen, Potter, Carnival	1977	Year	15.00	15.00
Craftsmen, Wheelwright	1978	Year	15.00	15.00
Lafayette And Washington, Blue	1975	Year	15.00	15.00
Lafayette And Washington, Red	1975	Year	17.50	15.00 to 17.50
Lafayette And Washington, White	1975	Year	15.00	15.00
Lafayette And Washington, Blue	1976	Year	15.00	15.00
Lafayette And Washington, Chocolate	1976	Year	17.50	17.50
Lafayette And Washington, White	1976	Year	15.00	15.00
Mother's Day, Madonna, Child, Blue Satin	1971	Year	12.50	8.35 to 13.00
Mother's Day, Madonna, Child, Carnival	1971	Year	12.50	8.35 to 13.00
Mother's Day, Madonna Of Goldfinch, Blue Satin	1972	Year	12.50	8.50 to 13.00
Mother's Day, Madonna Of Goldfinch, Carnival	1972	Year	12.50	7.00 to 12.00
Mother's Day, Madonna Of Goldfinch, White	1972	Year	12.50	8.35 to 13.00
Mother's Day, Cowper Madonna, Blue Satin	1973	Year	12.50	13.00
Mother's Day, Cowper Madonna, Carnival	1973	Year	12.50	10.00 to 14.50
Mother's Day, Cowper Madonna, White Satin	1973	Year	12.50	12.50
Mother's Day, Madonna Of Grotto, Blue Satin	1974	Year	12.50	14.00
Mother's Day, Madonna Of Grotto, Carnival	1974	Year	12.50	9.00 to 13.50
Mother's Day, Madonna Of Grotto, White Satin	1974	Year	12.50	14.00
Mother's Day, Taddei Madonna, Blue Satin	1975	Year	13.50	13.50

Dresden, Plate, Mother's Day,
Chamois, 1977

Egermann, Christmas Plate, 1973

Fenton, Christmas Plate, 1970, Carnival

Fenton, Christmas Plate, 1971, Carnival

Title	Issue Date	Number Issued	Issued Price	Current Price
Mother's Day, Taddei Madonna, Carnival	1975	Year	13.50	9.00 to 13.50
Mother's Day, Taddei Madonna, White Satin	1975	Year	13.50	13.00 to 13.50
Mother's Day, Holy Night, Blue Satin	1976	Year	13.50	13.50
Mother's Day, Holy Night, Carnival	1976	Year	13.50	13.50
Mother's Day, Holy Night, White Satin	1976	Year	13.50	13.50
Mother's Day, Madonna & Child, Blue	1977	Year	15.00	15.00
Mother's Day, Madonna & Child, Carnival	1977	Year	25.00	15.00
Mother's Day, Madonna & Child, White Satin	1977	Year	15.00	15.00
Mother's Day, Madonnina, White Satin	1978	Year	15.00	15.00
Mother's Day, Madonnina, Blue Satin	1978	Year	15.00	15.00
Mother's Day, Madonnina, Carnival	1978	Year	15.00	15.00
Valentine's Day, Romeo & Juliet, Blue Satin	1972	Year	15.00	12.00 to 20.00
Valentine's Day, Romeo & Juliet, Carnival	1972	Year	15.00	12.00 to 20.00

Fenton Steins

Title	Issue Date	Number Issued	Issued Price	Current Price
Patriot Red	1975	Year	17.50	17.50
Valley Forge White	1975	Year	15.00	15.00
Chocolate	1976	Year	17.50	17.50
Independence Blue	1976	Year	15.00	15.00
Valley Forge White	1976	Year	15.00	10.00 to 15.00

Fenton Vase

Title	Issue Date	Number Issued	Issued Price	Current Price
Bittersweet, Heart Pattern	1975	750	115.00	115.00
Blue, Feather	1975	1000	85.00	85.00
Cascade, Blue & White	1975	700	100.00	100.00
Changing Heart	1975	600	125.00	125.00
Hanging Heart	1975	600	125.00	125.00
Hyacinth, Feather	1975	450	175.00	175.00
Labyrinth, Amethyst	1975	700	85.00	85.00
Labyrinth, Blue	1975	700	85.00	85.00
Summer Tapestry	1975	550	200.00	200.00
Turquoise, Iridescent, Heart Pattern	1975	600	135.00	135.00

Juan Ferrandiz, Spanish artist, is designer of many Anri limited editions. In 1972, he introduced his own series of wood and porcelain limited edition plates. The wooden plates are manufactured by Anri of Italy, and Hutschenreuther of West Germany produces the porcelain plates.

Ferrandiz Bells

Title	Issue Date	Number Issued	Issued Price	Current Price
Christmas, Adeste Fidelis	1976		25.00	25.00
Christmas, Oh Tannenbaum	1977		25.00	25.00

Ferrandiz Christmas Ornaments

Title	Issue Date	Number Issued	Issued Price	Current Price
Annual, Flying Angel, *1, Set	1974			30.00 to 36.00
Annual, Flying Angel, *2, Set	1975			25.00 to 39.00
Annual, Set Of Six Angels, Each	1976		8.00	8.00

Ferrandiz Plates

Title	Issue Date	Number Issued	Issued Price	Current Price
Birthday, Boy	1972			10.00 to 20.00
Birthday, Girl	1972			10.00 to 20.00
Birthday, Boy	1973			20.00
Birthday, Girl	1973			20.00
Birthday, Girl	1974			16.65 to 25.00
Birthday, Girl	1975			23.35 to 35.00
Christmas, Away In The Manger, Porcelain*	1972	5000	30.00	19.00 to 35.00
Christmas, Finishing The Cradle, Wood	1972	2500	35.00	27.50 to 60.00
Christmas, Boy With Lamb, Wood	1973	1500	40.00	75.00 to 100.00
Christmas, Porcelain	1973	3000	30.00	15.00 to 28.00
Christmas, Nativity, Wood	1974			75.00
Christmas, Flight Into Egypt, Wood	1975			60.00
Christmas, Mary & Joseph Pray, Wood	1976	1500	40.00	75.00 to 85.00
Christmas, Girl With Tree, Wood	1977	4000		58.00 to 65.00
Mother's Day, Mother Sewing, Wood*	1972	2500	35.00	20.00 to 45.00
Mother's Day, Mother And Child, Wood	1973	1500	40.00	45.00
Mother's Day, Mother And Child, Wood	1974			45.00 to 60.00
Mother's Day, Mother Holding Dove, Wood	1975			55.00 to 60.00
Mother's Day, Mother And Child, Wood	1976		60.00	60.00
Mother's Day, Girl With Flowers, Wood	1977		65.00	65.00
Mother's Day, Beginning, Wood	1978	3000	77.50	77.50
Mother's Day, Orchard Mother, Porcelain	1977	10000	65.00	65.00
Mother's Day, Pastoral Mother, Porcelain	1978	10000	75.00	75.00

Fenton, Craftsmen Plate, 1974, Cooper

Fenton, Craftsmen Plate, 1971, Printer

Fenton, Craftsmen Plate, 1973, Shoemaker

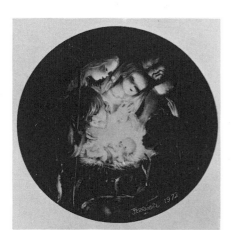

Ferrandiz, Christmas Plate, 1972, Porcelain

Fontana, Christmas Plate, 1973

Ferrandiz, Mother's Day Plate, 1972

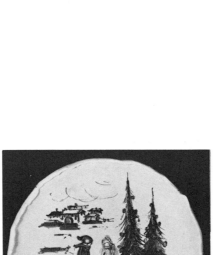

Fontana, Christmas Plate, 1972

Fontana, Mother's Day Plate, 1973

Fostoria, History Plate, 1972

Fostoria, History Plate, 1973

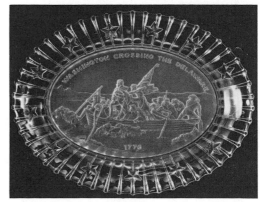

Franklin Mint, American West Plate,
Horizon's West, Silver

Franklin Mint, American West Plate,
Mountain Man, Silver

Franklin Mint, Audubon Bird Plate, Eagle

Franklin Mint, Christmas Plate, 1970

Title	Issue Date	Number Issued	Issued Price	Current Price
Spring Dance, Wood	1978	2500	500.00	500.00
Wedding	1972			60.00 to 75.00
Wedding	1973			20.00 to 60.00
Wedding	1974			25.00 to 60.00
Wedding	1975			40.00 to 60.00
Wedding	1976		60.00	60.00
Fischer Bells				
Annual, Cameo, Crystal	1976	2500	50.00	50.00
Bicentennial, Spirit Of '76	1975	2000		15.95
Bicentennial	1976	1776	20.00	16.50 to 20.00
Christmas, Star, Crystal	1972	6025	10.00	6.00 to 12.50
Christmas, Tree, Crystal	1973	10000	12.00	8.00 to 12.00
Christmas, Angel, Crystal	1974			8.00 to 12.00
Christmas, Candle, Crystal	1975	5000	15.00	9.00 to 15.00
Christmas, Wreath, Crystal	1976	5000	20.00	20.00
Mother's Day, A Bell For Mother	1975	5000	15.00	13.95 to 15.00
Mother's Day, Silhouette	1976	5000	20.00	20.00
Mother's Day, Crystal	1977	5000	20.00	20.00
Star Of David	1976	5000	20.00	20.00
Fontana Plates				
Christmas, Couple & Dog*	1972	2000	35.00	5.00 to 35.00
Christmas, Sleighing*	1973	1000	35.00	10.00 to 37.00
Christmas	1974	1000		33.00
Mother's Day, Mother And Child*	1973	2000	35.00	5.00 to 35.00

*Fostoria Glass Company was founded in Fostoria, Ohio, in 1887, and
moved to its present location in Moundsville, West Virginia in 1891.
The firm has made all types of glassware, tableware, bottles, and decorative
glass through the years. Limited edition plates were introduced in 1971.*

Title	Issue Date	Number Issued	Issued Price	Current Price
Fostoria Bells				
Mother's Day	1978	10000	20.00	20.00
Fostoria Plates				
History, Betsy Ross	1971	5000	12.50	5.00 to 25.00
History, Francis Scott Key*	1972	8000	12.50	5.00 to 16.00
History, Washington Crossing Delaware*	1973		12.50	9.00 to 16.00
History, Spirit Of '76	1974		13.00	13.00 to 16.00
Mount Rushmore	1975		16.00	15.00 to 16.00
State, California	1971	6000	12.50	7.00 to 13.00
State, Florida	1972		12.50	7.00 to 13.00
State, Hawaii	1972		12.50	7.00 to 13.00
State, Massachusetts	1972		12.50	7.00 to 13.00
State, Michigan				7.00 to 13.00
State, New York	1971	2000	12.50	7.00 to 14.00
State, Ohio	1971	3000	12.50	7.00 to 13.00
State, Pennsylvania	1972		12.50	7.00 to 13.00
State, Texas				7.00 to 13.00

Four Seasons, Rockwell, see Gorham

*Franklin Mint was organized in the early 1960s by Joseph Segel and
Gilroy Roberts, chief sculptor engraver for the U.S. Mint. It
is located in Franklin Center, Pennsylvania. Franklin Mint
introduced the first sterling silver collector's plate on the market in 1970.*

Title	Issue Date	Number Issued	Issued Price	Current Price
Franklin Mint Crystal Bells				
Crystal, Child At Prayer	1977	Year	75.00	75.00
Crystal, Dove	1976	11569	60.00	60.00 to 85.00
Franklin Mint Bowls				
Bicentennial	1976	750	3000.00	Unknown
Wyeth	1973	7659	375.00	425.00 to 525.00
Franklin Mint Boxes				
Mother's Day	1977	Year	85.00	85.00
Franklin Mint Christmas Ornaments				
12 Days Of Christmas, Silver	1966	1000	150.00	100.00 to 200.00
12 Days Of Christmas, Bronze	1966	6000	35.00	35.00
12 Days Of Christmas, Nickel Silver	1966	2764	15.00	15.00
Annual, Silent Night, Sterling	1971	14683	30.00	45.00 to 60.00

Title	Issue Date	Number Issued	Issued Price	Current Price
Annual, First Noel, Sterling	1972	15436	30.00	22.00 to 42.50
Annual, O Come All Ye Faithful, Sterling	1973	14816	30.00	20.00 to 42.50
Annual, Hark The Herald Angels Sing, Sterling	1974	12229	40.00	35.00 to 45.00
Annual, It Came Upon A Midnight Clear	1976	Year	47.50	47.50
Annual, Little Town Of Bethlehem, Sterling	1975	7626	47.50	47.50

Franklin Mint Plaques

Title	Issue Date	Number Issued	Issued Price	Current Price
Airplane Scenes, Set Of 4, Sterling, Each	1976		90.00	Unknown
America, Bronze On Ebony	1970	400	250.00	Unknown
America, Sterling Silver	1970	150	750.00	Unknown
Children At Play, Parks, Silver	1969	200	375.00	475.00
Danaides, Paul Vincze, Silver	1967	75	1250.00	125.00 to 200.00
Horses, Roberts, Silver	1968	250	350.00	125.00 to 250.00
John F.Kennedy Memorial, Silver	1967	50	7.50	3500.00 to 28750.00
Kikabdanu, Sierra-Franco, Silver	1969	375	150.00	125.00 to 250.00
Lords Of Serengeti, 5, Each	1978	Year	150.00	150.00
Mayan Paradise, Sierra-Franco, Silver	1969	125	225.00	225.00 to 500.00
Moore's Woman Knitting	1975	1000	280.00	Unknown
Mother & Child, Hromych, Silver	1968	200	175.00	125.00 to 250.00
Nature's Four Seasons, Set Of 4, Porcelain	1977	Year	75.00	75.00
Picasso, The Hunter	1976	2602	375.00	150.00 to 300.00
Toreador & Bull, Romano, Silver	1969	225	250.00	125.00 to 250.00
Westerners, Phillips	1976	5163	120.00	Unknown
Wild Geese, Roberts, Silver	1969	50	750.00	Unknown
World Map	1976	Year	375.00	375.00
Zodiac, Set Of 12, Bronze, Each	1970	300	125.00	Unknown
Zodiac, Set Of 12, Silver, Each	1970	100	375.00	125.00 to 250.00
Yacht America, Bronze	1970	400	250.00	Unknown
Yacht America, Silver	1970	150	750.00	125.00 to 250.00

Franklin Mint Crystal Plates

Title	Issue Date	Number Issued	Issued Price	Current Price
Annual, Snowflake	1977	Year	185.00	185.00
Gilroy Roberts, The Liberty Tree	1976	Year	120.00	30.00 to 60.00
James Wyeth, Seven Seas, The Arctic	1976	Year	120.00	120.00
James Wyeth, Seven Seas, The Atlantic	1976	Year	120.00	120.00
James Wyeth, Seven Seas, The Caribbean	1976	Year	120.00	120.00
James Wyeth, Seven Seas, The Indian Ocean	1976	Year	120.00	120.00
James Wyeth, Seven Seas, The Mediterranean	1976	Year	120.00	120.00
James Wyeth, Seven Seas, The Pacific	1976	Year	120.00	120.00
James Wyeth, Seven Seas, The South China Sea	1976	Year	120.00	120.00

Franklin Mint Plates, metal

Title	Issue Date	Number Issued	Issued Price	Current Price
Am.Revolution Bicentennial, Boston Tea Party	1976	3596	75.00	75.00
Am.Revolution Bicentennial, Concord Bridge	1976	3596	75.00	75.00
Am.Revolution Bicentennial, Fort Ticonderoga	1976	3596	75.00	75.00
Am.Revolution Bicentennial, Patrick Henry	1976	3596	75.00	75.00
Am.Revolution Bicentennial, Paul Revere's Rid	1976	3596	75.00	75.00
American West, Horizon's West, Gold	1972	67	2200.00	Unknown
American West, Horizon's West, Silver*	1972	5860	150.00	45.00 to 90.00
American West, Mountain Man, Gold	1973	67	2200.00	Unknown
American West, Mountain Man, Silver*	1973	5860	150.00	45.00 to 150.00
American West, Plains Hunter, Gold	1973	67	2200.00	1500.00
American West, Plains Hunter, Silver	1973	5860	150.00	45.00 to 90.00
American West, Prospector, Gold	1973	67	2200.00	Unknown
American West, Prospector, Silver	1973	5860	150.00	45.00 to 90.00
Annual, Tribute To Arts, Vermeil Silver	1976	Year	280.00	280.00
Audubon Society Bird, Goldfinch*	1972	10193	125.00	25.00 to 50.00
Audubon Society Bird, Cardinal	1972	10193	125.00	25.00 to 50.00
Audubon Society Bird, Ruffed Grouse	1972	10193	125.00	25.00 to 50.00
Audubon Society Bird, Wood Duck	1972	10193	125.00	25.00 to 50.00
John James Audubon Bird, Bald Eagle*	1973	3040	150.00	25.00 to 50.00
John James Audubon Bird, Night Heron	1973	3005	150.00	25.00 to 50.00
John James Audubon Bird, Warbler	1973	3034	150.00	25.00 to 50.00
John James Audubon Bird, Wood Thrush	1973	5273	150.00	25.00 to 50.00
Bernard Buffet, Gazelle	1973	570	150.00	27.50 to 55.00
Bernard Buffet, Giraffe	1975	333	150.00	27.50 to 55.00
Bernard Buffet, Lion	1976	263	150.00	27.50 to 55.00
Bernard Buffet, Panda*	1974	408	150.00	27.50 to 55.00
Bicentennial Council, Jefferson*	1973	8556	175.00	50.00 to 100.00
Bicentennial Council, John Adams	1974	8442	175.00	50.00 to 100.00
Bicentennial Council, Caesar Rodney	1975	8319	175.00	50.00 to 100.00

Franklin Mint, Easter Plate, 1973

Franklin Mint, Christmas Plate, 1972

Franklin Mint, James Wyeth Plate, 1972

Franklin Mint, Plate, James Wyeth,
Skating On Brandywine, 1975

Franklin Mint, Mother's Day Plate, 1973

Franklin Mint, President Plate,
George Washington

Franklin Mint, Plate,
Butterflies Of World, 1977

Franklin Mint, Plate, Mother's Day, 1975

Plates, Plaques, and Miscellaneous

Title	Issue Date	Number Issued	Issued Price	Current Price
Bicentennial Council, John Hancock	1976	10166	175.00	50.00 to 100.00
Butterflies Of World, 6, Each*	1977	Year	240.00	240.00
Christmas, Rockwell, Bringing Home The Tree*	1970	18321	100.00	100.00 to 350.00
Christmas, Rockwell, Under The Mistletoe	1971	24792	100.00	40.00 to 100.00
Christmas, Rockwell, The Carolers	1972	29074	125.00	40.00 to 100.00
Christmas, Rockwell, Trimming The Tree	1973	18010	125.00	40.00 to 100.00
Christmas, Rockwell, Hanging The Wreath	1974	12822	175.00	40.00 to 100.00
Christmas, Rockwell, Home For Christmas*	1975	11059	180.00	40.00 to 100.00
Easter, Resurrection, Silver	1973	7116	175.00	50.00 to 100.00
Easter, He Is Risen	1974	3719	185.00	50.00 to 100.00
Easter, The Last Supper*	1975	2004	200.00	50.00 to 100.00
Four Seasons, Autumn Garland	1975	2648	240.00	45.00 to 90.00
Four Seasons, Spring Blossoms, Sterling	1975	2648	240.00	45.00 to 90.00
Four Seasons, Summer Bouquet, Sterling	1975	2648	240.00	45.00 to 90.00
Four Seasons, Winter Spray*	1975	2648	240.00	45.00 to 90.00
Inaugural, Nixon, Agnew, Sterling	1973	10483	50.00	60.00 to 120.00
Inaugural, Gerald R.Ford, Gold	1974	11	3500.00	Unknown
Inaugural, Gerald R.Ford, Sterling	1974	1141	200.00	60.00 to 120.00
James Wyeth, Brandywine*	1972	19670	125.00	35.00 to 70.00
James Wyeth, Winter Fox	1973	10394	125.00	40.00 to 80.00
James Wyeth, Riding To The Hunt, Sterling	1974	10751	150.00	40.00 to 80.00
James Wyeth, Skating On Brandywine*	1975	8058	175.00	40.00 to 80.00
James Wyeth, Brandywine Battlefield	1976	6968	125.00	40.00 to 80.00
Judaic Heritage Society, Chanukah, Sterling	1973	2000	150.00	50.00 to 100.00
Judaic Heritage Society, Chanukah, Gold	1973	100	1900.00	Unknown
Judaic Heritage Society, Pesach, Sterling	1972	5000	150.00	50.00 to 100.00
Judaic Heritage Society, Pesach, Gold	1972	100	1900.00	Unknown
Judaic Heritage Society, Purim, Sterling	1974	1000	150.00	55.00 to 110.00
Mother's Day, Mother & Child	1972	21987	125.00	27.00 to 50.00
Mother's Day*	1973	6154	125.00	32.50 to 75.00
Mother's Day	1974	5116	12.50	69.50 to 135.00
Mother's Day*	1975	2704	175.00	32.50 to 75.00
Mother's Day	1976	1858	180.00	50.00 to 100.00
Mother's Day	1977	Year	195.00	Unknown
President, Adams, John Quincy	1973	2501	150.00	42.50 to 150.00
President, Adams, John	1972	4859	150.00	42.50 to 110.00
President, Arthur, Chester	1976	1604	150.00	42.50 to 105.00
President, Buchanan, James	1973	1841	150.00	42.50 to 110.00
President, Cleveland, Grover	1976	1644	150.00	42.50 to 110.00
President, Fillmore, Millard	1974	1967	150.00	42.50 to 105.00
President, Garfield, James	1976	1675	150.00	42.50 to 110.00
President, Grant, U.S.	1973	1754	150.00	42.50 to 110.00
President, Harrison, Benjamin	1975	2955	150.00	42.50 to 110.00
President, Harrison, William	1974	2182	150.00	42.50 to 110.00
President, Hayes, Rutherford	1975	1705	150.00	42.50 to 110.00
President, Jackson, Andrew	1973	2408	150.00	42.50 to 110.00
President, Jefferson, Thomas	1972	4933	150.00	42.50 to 110.00
President, Lincoln, Abraham	1975	2955	150.00	42.50 to 110.00
President, Madison, James	1973	3058	150.00	42.50 to 110.00
President, McKinley, William	1976	1571	150.00	42.50 to 110.00
President, Monroe, James	1973	2722	150.00	42.50 to 110.00
President, Pierce, Franklin	1974	1907	150.00	42.50 to 110.00
President, Polk, James	1974	2083	150.00	42.50 to 100.00
President, Roosevelt, Theodore	1976	1555	150.00	42.50 to 110.00
President, Taft, William H.	1976	Year	150.00	42.50 to 110.00
President, Taylor, Zachary	1974	2023	150.00	42.50 to 100.00
President, Tyler, John	1974	2144	150.00	42.50 to 110.00
President, Van Buren, Martin	1973	2291	150.00	42.50 to 110.00
President, Washington, George*	1972	10304	150.00	42.50 to 265.00
Thanksgiving, First Thanksgiving*	1972	10142	125.00	35.00 to 70.00
Thanksgiving, Wild Turkey*	1973	3547	125.00	35.00 to 70.00
Thanksgiving Prayer	1974	5150	150.00	35.00 to 70.00
Thanksgiving, Family Thanksgiving*	1975	3025	175.00	35.00 to 70.00
Thanksgiving, Home From The Hunt	1976	3474	175.00	35.00 to 70.00
Younger Bird, American Bald Eagle	1972	13939	125.00	69.50 to 145.00
Younger Bird, Bobwhite	1972	13939	125.00	69.50 to 145.00
Younger Bird, Cardinal	1972	13939	125.00	47.00 to 150.00
Younger Bird, Mallards	1972	13939	125.00	55.00 to 115.00

Franklin Mint University, Alumni, Fraternity Plates, Sterling

Title	Issue Date	Number Issued	Issued Price	Current Price
University Of Texas	1972	422	150.00	Unknown

Title	Issue Date	Number Issued	Issued Price	Current Price
University Of Virginia	1972	475	150.00	Unknown
University Of Minnesota	1972	82	150.00	Unknown
University Of Pennsylvania	1972	647	150.00	Unknown
University Of Wisconsin	1972	93	150.00	Unknown
University Of Pittsburgh	1972	215	150.00	Unknown
Case Institute Of Technology	1972	61	150.00	Unknown
University Of Nebraska, Seal	1972	115	150.00	Unknown
University Of Mississippi	1972	482	150.00	Unknown
University Of Nebraska, Columns	1972	92	150.00	Unknown
Tufts University, Seal	1972	168	150.00	Unknown
Louisiana State, Seal	1972	122	150.00	Unknown
Tufts University, Ballou Hall	1972	86	150.00	Unknown
Louisiana State, Memorial Tower	1972	174	150.00	Unknown
University Of North Carolina, Seal	1972	168	150.00	Unknown
University Of North Carolina, Well	1972	269	150.00	Unknown
University Of Oklahoma, Seal	1972	150	150.00	Unknown
University Of Oklahoma, Library	1972	112	150.00	Unknown
University Of California	1972	777	150.00	Unknown
Kansas State University	1972	474	150.00	Unknown
University Of Kansas	1972	555	150.00	Unknown
College Of William And Mary	1972	663	150.00	Unknown
Northeastern University	1972	398	150.00	Unknown
Auburn University, Seal	1972	279	150.00	Unknown
Auburn University, Sanford Hall	1972	388	150.00	Unknown
University Of Louisville, Seal	1972	118	150.00	Unknown
Oklahoma State University, Seal	1972	119	150.00	Unknown
University Of Louisville, Administration Blg.	1972	93	150.00	Unknown
Oklahoma State University, Library	1972	223	150.00	Unknown
Brown University	1972	447	150.00	Unknown
University Of South Carolina	1972	272	150.00	Unknown
Baylor University	1972	485	150.00	Unknown
University Of Wyoming	1972	447	150.00	Unknown
University Of Colorado	1972	577	175.00	Unknown
Duke University	1972	709	175.00	Unknown
University Of Idaho	1972	329	175.00	Unknown
University Of Illinois	1972	1007	175.00	Unknown
University Of Kentucky	1972	543	175.00	Unknown
Newcomb University	1972	112	175.00	Unknown
Ohio University	1972	221	175.00	Unknown
Luland University	1972	428	175.00	Unknown
University Of Arizona	1972	467	175.00	Unknown
Virginia Tech University	1972	473	175.00	Unknown
Southern Methodist University	1972	299	175.00	Unknown
Temple University	1972	599	175.00	Unknown
Colorado State University	1972	160	175.00	Unknown
Delta Upsilon Fraternity	1972	166	175.00	Unknown
Georgetown University	1972	660	175.00	Unknown
Indiana University	1972	482	175.00	Unknown
Mississippi State University	1972	280	175.00	Unknown
University Of Rochester	1972	273	175.00	Unknown
University Of Virginia	1972	580	175.00	Unknown
Bowling Green State University	1972	149	175.00	Unknown
University Of Houston	1972	229	175.00	Unknown
Michigan State University	1972	705	175.00	Unknown
University Of Pittsburgh	1972	290	175.00	Unknown
University Of Toledo	1972	121	175.00	Unknown
University Of South Carolina	1972	194	200.00	Unknown
University Of Miami	1972	274	200.00	Unknown
Vanderbilt University	1972	419	200.00	Unknown
Brown University	1972	260	200.00	Unknown
University Of Georgia	1972	321	200.00	Unknown
University Of Mississippi	1972	120	200.00	Unknown
Allegheny College	1974	141	175.00	Unknown
Baylor University	1974	184	175.00	Unknown
Boston University	1974	201	175.00	Unknown
Bucknell University	1974	239	175.00	Unknown
California State Polytechnic Univ., Pomona	1974	85	175.00	Unknown
Carnegie-Mellon University	1974		175.00	Unknown
Catholic University Of America	1974	139	175.00	Unknown
Chi Phi Fraternity	1974		175.00	Unknown

Franklin Mint, Plate, Four Seasons,
Winter Spray, 1975

Franklin Mint, Plate, Easter,
The Last Supper, 1975

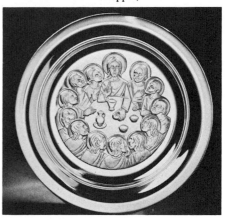

Franklin Mint, Plate, Bernard Buffet,
Panda, 1974

Franklin Mint, Plate,
Audubon Society Bird, Goldfinch, 1972

Franklin Mint, Plate, Christmas, Rockwell,
Home For Christmas, 1975

Franklin Mint, Plate, Thanksgiving,
Family Thanksgiving, 1975

Franklin Mint, Plate, Thanksgiving,
First Thanksgiving, 1972

Franklin Mint, Plate,
Thanksgiving, Wild Turkey, 1973

Title	Issue Date	Number Issued	Issued Price	Current Price
Citadel	1974		175.00	Unknown
Colgate University	1974	216	175.00	Unknown
Fairleigh Dickinson University	1974		175.00	Unknown
Florida State University	1974	278	175.00	Unknown
Furman University	1974	292	175.00	Unknown
Georgia Institute Of Technology	1974	497	175.00	Unknown
Kappa Alpha Order	1974		175.00	Unknown
Kent State University	1974	176	150.00	Unknown
Lambda Chi Alpha Fraternity	1974	431	150.00	Unknown
Middlebury College	1974	191	175.00	Unknown
Muskingum College	1974	97	175.00	Unknown
Northwestern University	1974	681	175.00	Unknown
Ohio Wesleyan University	1974	174	175.00	Unknown
Oregon State University	1974	361	175.00	Unknown
Phi Delta Theta Fraternity	1974	480	150.00	Unknown
Pi Kappa Alpha Fraternity	1974	222	175.00	Unknown
Purdue University	1974	477	175.00	Unknown
Randolph-Macon Woman's College	1974	192	175.00	Unknown
St.Lawrence University	1974	169	175.00	Unknown
St. Louis University	1974	354	175.00	Unknown
San Diego State University	1974		175.00	Unknown
Sigma Alpha Epsilon Fraternity	1974	485	175.00	Unknown
State University Of New York, Albany	1974		175.00	Unknown
Texas Tech University	1974	199	150.00	Unknown
The Citadel	1974	570	150.00	Unknown
Union College	1974	166	175.00	Unknown
U.S.Air Force Academy	1974		175.00	Unknown
U.S.Marine Corps.	1974		175.00	Unknown
U.S.Merchant Marine Academy	1974	310	175.00	Unknown
U.S.Military Academy	1974	1520	175.00	Unknown
U.S.Naval Academy	1974	2249	175.00	Unknown
University Of Dayton	1974	267	175.00	Unknown
University Of Delaware	1974		175.00	Unknown
University Of Delaware	1974	412	150.00	Unknown
University Of Massachusetts	1974	238	175.00	Unknown
University Of Michigan	1974	517	175.00	Unknown
University Of Oregon	1974	441	175.00	Unknown
University Of Richmond	1974		175.00	Unknown
University Of Santa Clara	1974	326	175.00	Unknown
University Of The Pacific	1974	188	175.00	Unknown
University Of Utah	1974	244	150.00	Unknown
University Of Virginia	1974	410	175.00	Unknown
University Of Washington	1974	178	175.00	Unknown
University Of Wyoming	1974		175.00	Unknown
Utah State University	1974	143	150.00	Unknown
Villanova University	1974	412	150.00	Unknown
Virginia Military Institute	1974	654	150.00	Unknown
Virginia Military Institute	1974	506	175.00	Unknown
Wake Forest University	1974	167	150.00	Unknown
Washington And Lee University	1974		175.00	Unknown
West Virginia University	1974	470	175.00	Unknown
Western Michigan	1974	194	150.00	Unknown

Franklin Mint Porcelain Plates

Title	Issue Date	Number Issued	Issued Price	Current Price
Christmas, Andersen Plates, Set Of 12	1975	16875	456.00	240.00 to 456.00
Christmas, Silent Night	1976	Year	65.00	65.00
Grimm Brothers, Set Of 12	1976	Year	504.00	504.00
Mother's Day, Mother's Love**	1977	Year	65.00	65.00

Franklin Mint Stained-Glass Plates

Title	Issue Date	Number Issued	Issued Price	Current Price
Christmas, Partridge	1976	Year	150.00	150.00
Easter, The Crucifixion	1976	3904	250.00	75.00 to 150.00

Franklin Mint Spoons

Title	Issue Date	Number Issued	Issued Price	Current Price
Apostle, Set Of 12	1973	9749	227.50	200.00 to 230.00
American Colonies, Set Of 13	1975	38825	182.00	182.00
Bicentennial, Set Of 13	1976	19078	195.00	195.00
Christmas, 12 Days, Set, Gold	1972	1018	195.00	195.00
Christmas, 12 Days, Set, Silver*	1972	3306	145.00	120.00 to 145.00
Christmas, Charles Dickens, Set Of 12, Pewter	1976	Year	234.00	234.00
Love, Set Of 8, Gold	1976	Year	2800.00	Unknown

Title	Issue Date	Number Issued	Issued Price	Current Price
Love, Set Of 8, Sterling	1976	Year	236.00	Unknown
Royal Horticulture, Set Of 12	1976	2550	360.00	360.00
Zodiac, Set Of 12, Gold	1972	1229	189.00	Unknown
Zodiac, Set Of 12, Silver	1972	5386	135.00	Unknown

Franklin Mint Vase

Noble Orchid	1977	Year	50.00	50.00

Franklin Mint, Plate, Bicentennial Council, Jefferson, 1973

Frankoma Pottery was the first U.S. firm to introduce Christmas plates in 1965. It was originally known as The Frank Potteries when John F. Frank opened shop in 1933. The factory is now located in Sapulpa, Oklahoma. Their limited edition plates are of a semitranslucent 'Della Robbia' white glaze over a colored body.

Frankoma Mugs

Title	Issue Date	Number Issued	Issued Price	Current Price
Democratic, Yellow	1975	Year	3.00	3.00 to 3.75
Democratic, Red	1976	Year	3.00	3.00
Democratic, Beige*	1977	Year	3.00	3.00
GOP, White	1968	Year	3.00	25.00 to 33.00
GOP, Red	1969	Year	3.00	11.00 to 13.00
GOP, Blue	1970	Year	3.00	8.00 to 9.00
GOP, Black	1971	Year	3.00	9.00 to 12.00
GOP, Green And White	1972	Year	3.00	8.00 to 9.00
GOP, Gold	1973	Year	3.00	4.00 to 9.00
GOP, Brown	1974	Year	3.00	4.50 to 5.00
GOP, Yellow	1975	Year	3.00	3.00 to 4.00
GOP, Red	1976	Year	3.00	3.00
GOP, Dusty Pink	1977	Year	3.00	3.00
GOP, Woodland Moss	1978	Year	3.00	3.00

Frankoma Plates

Title	Issue Date	Number Issued	Issued Price	Current Price
Bicentennial, Provocations	1972	Year	6.00	4.50 to 10.00
Bicentennial, Patriots And Leaders	1973	Year	6.00	7.00 to 8.00
Bicentennial, Battles For Independence	1974	Year	6.00	6.00 to 10.00
Bicentennial, Victories For Independence	1975	Year	6.00	5.50 to 6.00
Bicentennial, Symbols Of Freedom*	1976	Year	6.00	6.00 to 7.00
Christmas, Good Will Towards Men*	1965	Year	5.00	150.00 to 195.00
Christmas, Bethlehem Shepherds	1966	Year	5.00	70.00 to 85.00
Christmas, Gifts For The Christ Child*	1967	Year	5.00	48.00 to 65.00
Christmas, Flight Into Egypt	1968	Year	5.00	7.00 to 16.00
Christmas, Laid In A Manger*	1969	Year	5.00	4.50 to 10.00
Christmas, King Of Kings	1970	Year	5.00	4.00 to 10.00
Christmas, No Room In The Inn*	1971	Year	5.00	2.50 to 10.00
Christmas, Seeking The Christ Child	1972	Year	5.00	2.50 to 10.00
Christmas, The Annunciation*	1973	Year	5.00	7.50 to 10.00
Christmas, She Loved And Cared	1974	Year	5.00	5.00 to 10.00
Christmas, Peace On Earth*	1975	Year	5.00	5.00
Christmas, Gift Of Love	1976	Year	6.00	6.00
Christmas, Birth Of Eternal Life	1977	Year	6.00	6.00
Christmas, All Nature Rejoices	1978	Year	6.00	6.00
Grace Madonna*	1977	Year	12.50	12.50
Teenagers Of The Bible, Jesus The Carpenter*	1973	Year	5.00	7.50
Teenagers Of The Bible, David The Musician	1974	Year	5.00	6.00
Teenagers Of The Bible, Jonathan The Archer	1975	Year	5.00	5.50
Teenagers Of The Bible, Dorcas, Seamstress	1976	Year	5.00	5.00
Teenagers Of The Bible, Peter The Fisherman	1977	Year	5.00	5.00
Teenagers Of The Bible, All Nature Rejoices	1978	Year	5.00	5.00

Frankoma Vases

Title	Issue Date	Number Issued	Issued Price	Current Price
Colored, Coffee	1978	3000	15.00	15.00
Colored, Blue	1978	3000	15.00	15.00
Stars And Stripes*	1976	3500	10.00	10.00

Frederick Remington, see George Washington Mint, Gorham

Fujihara Plates

Title	Issue Date	Number Issued	Issued Price	Current Price
Chinese Lunar Calendar, Year Of The Rat	1972	1710	20.00	20.00
Chinese Lunar Calendar, Year Of The Ox	1973	1710	20.00	20.00

Fukagawa Plates

Title	Issue Date	Number Issued	Issued Price	Current Price
Under The Plum Branch	1977		38.00	38.00
Child Of Straw	1978		42.00	42.00

Franklin Mint, Christmas Spoon, 1972, Twelve Days Of Christmas

Frankoma, Christmas Plate, 1965

Frankoma, Christmas Plate, 1967

Frankoma, Christmas Plate, 1969

Frankoma, Christmas Plate, 1971

Frankoma, Christmas Plate, 1973

Frankoma, Plate, Christmas,
Peace On Earth, 1975

Frankoma, Plate, Grace Madonna, 1977

Frankoma, Plate, Teenagers Of The Bible,
Jesus The Carpenter, 1973

Frankoma, Plate, Bicentennial,
Symbols Of Freedom, 1976

Frankoma, Mug,
Democratic, Beige, 1977

Frankoma, Vase,
Stars And Stripes, 1976

Title	Issue Date	Number Issued	Issued Price	Current Price

Furstenberg Porcelain Factory, the oldest in the German Federal Republic, was founded in 1747 by King Carl I. Limited editions, introduced in 1971, include plates and Christmas ornaments. The company mark is a blue F surmounted by a crown. All series were closed in 1976.

Furstenberg Ornaments

Title	Issue Date	Number Issued	Issued Price	Current Price
Christmas, Angel	1973	2000	25.00	8.00 to 18.50

Furstenberg Eggs

Title	Issue Date	Number Issued	Issued Price	Current Price
Maypole*	1973	3000	15.00	13.00 to 30.00
Bouquet*	1974	2000	18.50	10.00 to 19.00
Blue Cornflowers	1975	2000	20.00	12.00 to 24.00

Furstenberg Plates

Title	Issue Date	Number Issued	Issued Price	Current Price
Christmas, Rabbits	1971	7500	14.00	8.00 to 28.00
Christmas, Snow-Laden Village	1972	6000	15.00	8.00 to 27.50
Christmas, Church On Christmas Eve*	1973	3000	18.00	12.00 to 24.00
Christmas, Tranquil Winter Scene, Birds*	1974	4000	20.00	15.00 to 30.00
Christmas, Winter Landscape	1975	4000	24.00	11.00 to 24.00
Christmas, Winter Birds	1976	4000	25.00	25.00
Deluxe Christmas, Wise Men	1971	1500	45.00	12.00 to 60.00
Deluxe Christmas, Holy Family	1972	2000	45.00	12.00 to 52.00
Deluxe Christmas, European Village*	1973	2000	60.00	29.50 to 60.00
Easter, Sheep	1971	3500	15.00	24.00 to 150.00
Easter, Chicks	1972	4000	15.00	7.50 to 26.00
Easter, Bunnies*	1973	4000	6.00	10.00 to 80.00
Easter, Pussywillow*	1974	4000	20.00	5.00 to 32.00
Easter, Village Church	1975	4000	24.00	16.00 to 42.00
Easter, Country Watermill	1976	4000	25.00	20.50 to 25.00
Mother's Day, Humming Bird	1972	5000	15.00	5.00 to 26.00
Mother's Day, Hedgehogs*	1973	5000	16.00	10.00 to 20.00
Mother's Day, Deer*	1974	4000	20.00	10.00 to 24.00
Mother's Day, Mother Swan	1975	4000	24.00	11.00 to 24.00
Mother's Day, Koala Bear*	1976	4000	25.00	25.00
Olympics	1972	5000	20.00	40.00 to 80.00
Olympics*	1976	5000	37.50	37.50

Furstenberg Steins

Title	Issue Date	Number Issued	Issued Price	Current Price
Christmas	1976	4000	25.00	25.00

Gainsborough, see Gorham

Georg Jensen of Denmark, the famous Danish silver company, entered the limited edition market in 1971 with the introduction of an annual Christmas spoon. The spoons are made of gold-plated silver. Each spoon is made until October 1 of the year, when the mold is destroyed. Limited edition plates, which include the Andrew Wyeth, Cartier, and Chagall plates, were first made in 1971.

Georg Jensen, see also Andrew Wyeth, Cartier, Chagall

Georg Jensen Plates

Title	Issue Date	Number Issued	Issued Price	Current Price
Christmas, Doves	1972	Year	15.00	5.00 to 25.00
Christmas, Christmas Eve*	1973	Year	15.00	9.00 to 55.00
Christmas, Christmas Story	1974	Year	17.50	20.95 to 24.00
Christmas, Winter Scene	1975	Year	22.50	15.00 to 22.50
Christmas, Hall, Timber House	1976	Year	35.00	35.00
Mother's Day, Mother & Child*	1973	10000	15.00	7.50 to 45.00
Mother's Day, Sweet Dreams	1974	Year	15.00	8.00 to 17.50
Mother's Day, Mother's World	1975	Year	22.50	15.00 to 22.50

Georg Jensen Spoons

Title	Issue Date	Number Issued	Issued Price	Current Price
Christmas, Cherry Blossom**	1971	Year	25.00	45.00 to 55.00
Christmas, Cornflower**	1972	Year	25.00	35.00 to 400.00
Christmas, Corn Marigold**	1973	Year	25.00	25.00 to 30.00
Christmas, Corn Cockle*	1974	Year	25.00	25.00
Christmas, Woodruff	1975	Year		Unknown
Christmas, Sweetbriar**	1976	Year	55.00	55.00
Christmas, Sweet Violet**	1977	Year	55.00	55.00
Christmas, Globe Flower**	1978	Year	55.00	55.00
Bicentennial*	1976	3000	76.00	76.00

George Washington Mint of New York City was founded in 1971. Limited edition gold, silver, and proof plates were introduced in 1972.

Furstenberg, Christmas Plate, 1973

Furstenberg, Plate, Christmas,
Tranquil Winter Scene, Birds, 1974

Furstenberg, Plate, Mother's Day,
Koala Bear, 1976

Furstenberg, Plate, Olympics, 1976

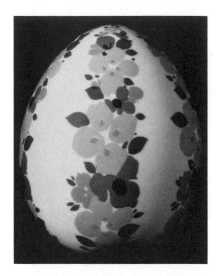

Furstenberg, Easter Egg, 1973

Fuerstenberg, Easter Egg, 1974

Furstenberg, Deluxe Christmas Plate, 1973

Fuerstenberg, Easter Plate, 1974

Furstenberg, Easter Plate, 1973

Furstenberg, Mother's Day Plate, 1973

Fuerstenberg, Mother's Day Plate, 1974

Georg Jensen, Christmas Spoon, 1972

Georg Jensen, Christmas Spoon, 1971

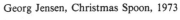

Georg Jensen, Christmas Spoon, 1973

Title	Issue Date	Number Issued	Issued Price	Current Price
The plates are made by the Medallic Art Company. George Washington Mint went out of business in 1973. The Picasso, Remington, and Mother's Day series were continued by the Medallic Art Company.				

George Washington Mint Plates

Title	Issue Date	Number Issued	Issued Price	Current Price
Israel Anniversary, The Struggle	1973	10000	300.00	Unknown
Mother's Day, Whistler's Mother, Gold	1972	100	2000.00	Unknown
Mother's Day, Whistler's Mother, Proof	1972	100	1000.00	Unknown
Mother's Day, Whistler's Mother, Sterling	1972	9800	150.00	37.00 to 150.00
Mother's Day, Motherhood, Sterling	1974	2500	175.00	175.00
N.C.Wyeth, Massed Flags, Gold	1973	100	2000.00	2000.00
N.C.Wyeth, Massed Flags, Proof	1973	100	1000.00	1000.00
N.C.Wyeth, Massed Flags, Sterling	1973	2300	150.00	100.00 to 150.00
N.C.Wyeth, Uncle Sam's America, Gold	1972	100	2000.00	Unknown
N.C.Wyeth, Uncle Sam's America, Proof	1972	100	1000.00	Unknown
N.C.Wyeth, Uncle Sam's America, Sterling	1972	9800	150.00	36.00 to 175.00
Picasso, Don Quixote De La Mancha, Gold	1972		2000.00	Unknown
Picasso, Don Quixote De La Mancha, Proof	1972	100	1000.00	Unknown
Picasso, Don Quixote De La Mancha, Sterling	1972	9800	125.00	49.00 to 125.00
Picasso, The Rites Of Spring, Sterling	1974	9800	125.00	Unknown
Remington, The Rattlesnake, Gold	1972	100	1000.00	195.00
Remington, The Rattlesnake, Proof	1972	100	1000.00	Unknown
Remington, Coming Through The Rye, Sterling	1974	2500	300.00	150.00 to 225.00
Remington, The Rattlesnake, Sterling	1972	800	250.00	175.00 to 285.00
Sawyer, American Indian, Curley, Gold	1972	100	2000.00	Unknown
Sawyer, American Indian, Curley, Proof	1972	100	1000.00	Unknown
Sawyer, American Indian, Curley, Sterling	1972	7300	150.00	75.00 to 150.00
Sawyer, American Indian, Two Moons, Gold	1973	100	2000.00	Unknown
Sawyer, American Indian, Two Moons, Proof	1973	100	1000.00	Unknown
Sawyer, American Indian, Two Moons, Sterling	1973	7300	150.00	100.00 to 150.00

Ghent Collection, see Halbert's, Gorham, Fairmont

Gibson Girl Plates

Title	Issue Date	Number Issued	Issued Price	Current Price
Gibson Girl, Set Of 24	1971	100	150.00	Unknown

Gilbert Poillerat, see Cristal d'Albret, Poillerat

Hummel limited edition plates, made by W.Goebel Porzellanfabrik of Oeslau, Germany, are based on the sketches of Berta Hummel. The F.W.Goebel factory was founded in 1871 by Franz and William Goebel. In 1934, under the trade name of Hummelwerk, the Germany factory, in collaboration with Berta Hummel, produced the first Hummel figurines. Limited edition plates were introduced in 1971. A series of limited edition figurines commemorating the American Bicentennial was issued in 1974. Ispanky joined with Goebel in 1977.

See listing for Goebel in Figurine section

Goebel Glass Bells

Title	Issue Date	Number Issued	Issued Price	Current Price
Annual, Girl Praying	1978	Year	25.00	25.00

Goebel Porcelain Bells

Title	Issue Date	Number Issued	Issued Price	Current Price
Annual, Let's Sing	1978	Year	50.00	Unknown

Goebel Eggs

Title	Issue Date	Number Issued	Issued Price	Current Price
Easter	1978	Year	8.00	10.00
Easter, Duckling	1979		9.00	9.00

Goebel Ornaments

Title	Issue Date	Number Issued	Issued Price	Current Price
Christmas, Angel	1976	Year	15.00	15.00
Christmas, Santa	1978		15.00	15.00

Goebel Crystal Plates

Title	Issue Date	Number Issued	Issued Price	Current Price
Annual	1978	Year	45.00	45.00

Goebel Hummel Porcelain Plates

Title	Issue Date	Number Issued	Issued Price	Current Price
Anniversary, Stormy Weather	1975	Year	100.00	75.00 to 100.00
Annual, Heavenly Angel	1971	Year	25.00	925.00 to 1000.00
Annual, Hear Ye, Hear Ye*	1972	Year	30.00	100.00 to 120.00
Annual, Globetrotter*	1973	Year	32.50	200.00 to 225.00
Annual, Goosegirl	1974	Year	40.00	75.00 to 115.00
Annual, Ride Into Christmas	1975	Year	50.00	50.00 to 85.00
Annual, Apple Tree Girl*	1976	Year	50.00	50.00 to 80.00
Annual, Apple Tree Boy	1977	Year	52.50	195.00 to 235.00
Annual, Happy Pastime	1978	Year	65.00	Unknown

Georg Jensen,
Christmas Spoon, 1974

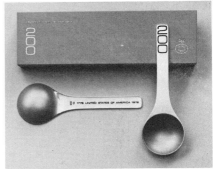

Georg Jensen, Spoon, Bicentennial, 1976

Georg Jensen, Christmas Plate, 1973

Georg Jensen, Mother's Day Plate, 1973

Goebel, Plate, Mother's Day, Cats, 1976

Title	Issue Date	Number Issued	Issued Price	Current Price
Goebel Plates				
Christmas, Charlot Byj	1973	Year	16.50	13.50 to 18.00
Christmas, Charlot Byj	1974	Year	22.00	25.00
Christmas, Charlot Byj	1975	Year	25.00	25.00
Christmas, Charlot Byj	1976	Year	25.00	25.00
Christmas, Robeson, Flight To Egypt, Porcelain	1975	Year	50.00	50.00
Christmas, Robeson, Flight To Egypt, Pewter	1975	Year	45.00	
Mother's Day, Rabbits	1975	Year	45.00	45.00
Mother's Day, Cats*	1976	Year	45.00	45.00
Mother's Day, Panda	1977	Year	45.00	45.00
Mother's Day, Doe & Fawn	1978	Year	50.00	50.00
Twelve Tribes, Ispanky	1978	10000	125.00	125.00
Wildlife, Robin	1974	Year	45.00	45.00
Wildlife, Blue Titmouse	1975	Year	50.00	29.50 to 50.00
Wildlife, Barn Owl	1976	Year	50.00	33.50 to 50.00
Wildlife, Bullfinch	1977	Year	50.00	45.00
Wildlife, Sea Gull	1978	Year	55.00	55.00
Golf Digest Plates				
Second Hole, Dorado Beach Club	1973	2000	45.00	45.00
Twelfth Hole, Spyglass Hill	1973	2000	45.00	45.00

Gorham, See American Commemorative Council, De Grazia, Juhacos

Gorham Silver Co., of Providence, Rhode Island, was founded in 1831. Crystal and China were added in 1970. The first limited edition item, a silver Christmas ornament, was introduced in 1970. Limited edition porcelain plates were issued in 1971.

See listing for Gorham in Figurine section

See also De Grazia

Gorham, Bell, Rockwell, Christmas, Gay Blades, 1978

Title	Issue Date	Number Issued	Issued Price	Current Price
Gorham Bells				
Catherine The Great	1977	5000	75.00	75.00
Elizabeth I	1977	5000	75.00	75.00
Isabella I	1977	5000	75.00	75.00
Marie Antoinette	1977	5000	75.00	75.00
Marie De Medicio	1977	5000	75.00	75.00
Mary, Queen Of Scots	1977	5000	75.00	75.00
Bicentennial, Freedom, Bronze	1976	9800	50.00	50.00
Bicentennial, Freedom, Ameralloy	1976		19.50	19.50
Bicentennial, Rockwell, Tavern Sign Painter	1976	18500	19.50	12.75 to 19.50
Currier And Ives, Winter Scene	1976	Year	9.95	9.95
Currier And Ives, American Homestead	1977	Year	9.95	9.95
Currier & Ives, Yule Logs**	1978	Year	12.95	12.95
Love's Harmony, No.1	1975	Year	19.50	19.50
Love's Harmony, No.2	1976	Year	19.50	19.50
Love's Harmony, No.3, Fondly Do We Remember	1977	Year	19.50	19.50
Love's Harmony, No.4	1978	Year	22.50	22.50
Rockwell, Christmas, Santa's Helper	1975	Year	19.50	18.00 to 19.50
Rockwell, Christmas, Snow Sculpture	1976	Year	19.50	19.50
Rockwell, Christmas, Chilling Chore	1977	Year	19.50	19.50
Rockwell, Christmas, Gay Blades*	1978	Year	22.50	22.50
Gorham Bowl				
Rockwell, Bicentennial, Yankee Doodle*	1976	9800	50.00	35.00 to 50.00
Sons Of Liberty, Paul Revere, Sterling	1972	250	1250.00	1250.00
Gorham Ornaments				
Christmas, Christmas Caroling, Parian	1976	Year	9.95	9.95
Christmas, Evening Prayer, Parian	1977	Year	9.95	9.95
Christmas, Crystal	1975	Year	19.50	16.50 to 32.50
Christmas, Crystal	1976	Year	19.50	19.50
Christmas, Crystal Tree	1977	Year	19.95	19.95
Christmas, Snowflake, Sterling	1970	Year	10.00	35.00 to 77.50
Christmas, Snowflake, Sterling	1971	Year	10.00	7.75 to 40.00
Christmas, Snowflake, Sterling	1972	Year	10.00	27.50
Christmas, Snowflake, Sterling	1973	Year	10.95	7.75 to 25.00
Christmas, Snowflake, Sterling	1974	Year	17.50	11.65 to 17.50
Christmas, Snowflake, Sterling	1975	Year	17.50	17.50 to 20.00
Christmas, Snowflake, Sterling	1976	Year	17.50	17.50
Christmas, Snowflake, Sterling	1977	Year	19.95	19.95
Christmas, Snowflake, Sterling	1978	Year	19.95	19.95

Gorham, Bowl, China Crystal, Christmas, Michael Kamm, 1978

Gorham, Bowl, Rockwell, Bicentennial,
Yankee Doodle, 1976

Title	Issue Date	Number Issued	Issued Price	Current Price
Gorham China Floral Bowls				
Fontainebleau		250	600.00	600.00
Versailles		500	1000.00	1000.00
Vincennes		200	1200.00	1200.00
Gorham China Crystal Bowls				
Christmas, Michael Kamm*	1978	1000	100.00	100.00
Gorham Plates				
America's Cup Plates, Set Of 5		1000	200.00	200.00
American Rose Society, America	1976	9800	39.00	39.00
American Rose Society, Cathedral	1976	9800	39.00	39.00
American Rose Society, Seashell	1976	9800	39.00	39.00
American Rose Society, Yankee Doodle	1976	9800	29.00	29.00
Anniversary Of Israel, Silver		2000	200.00	200.00
Apache Girl	1977		25.00	25.00
Apache Mother And Child	1976	9800	25.00	25.00
Audubon, House Mouse	1977	2500	90.00	90.00
Audubon, Royal Louisiana Heron	1977	2500	90.00	90.00
Audubon, Showy Owl	1977	2500	90.00	90.00
Audubon, Virginia Deer	1977	2500	90.00	90.00
Barrymore, Quiet Waters, Porcelain*	1971	15000	25.00	20.00 to 25.00
Barrymore, San Pedro, Porcelain*	1972	15000	25.00	Unknown
Barrymore, Little Boatyard, Silver	1972	1000	100.00	Unknown
Barrymore, Nantucket, Silver	1973	1000	100.00	Unknown
Bicentennial, 1776, China	1972		17.50	17.50
Bicentennial, 1776, Silver*	1972	500	500.00	300.00 to 500.00
Bicentennial, 1776, Vermeil	1972	250	750.00	750.00
Bicentennial, Boston Tea Party, Pewter	1973	5000	35.00	17.50 to 35.00
Bicentennial, Boston Tea Party, Silver	1973	750	550.00	500.00 to 550.00
Bicentennial, Burning Of Gaspee, Pewter	1972	5000	35.00	35.00
Bicentennial, Burning Of Gaspee, Silver	1972	750	550.00	550.00
Bicentennial, Rockwell, Ben Franklin	1976	18500	19.50	19.50
Bicentennial, Washington On Charger	1975	9000		90.00
Black Regiment	1976	7500	25.00	25.00
Black Regiment	1977	7500	25.00	25.00
Catesby, Bird, Cardinal	1976	9900		39.00
Currier & Ives, Noel	1976	Year	10.50	10.50
First Lady, Amy And Rosalynn	1977	Year	24.95	24.95
Gainsborough, The Honorable Mrs.Graham*	1973	7500	50.00	20.00 to 50.00
Hampton, Cherokee Princess	1977	3000	48.00	175.00
Jansen, Anniversary	1976	7500	40.00	40.00
Jansen, Prince Tatters, Johnny And Duke	1977	7500	40.00	40.00
Jansen, Prince Tatters, Randy & Rex	1978	7500	42.50	42.50
Jansen, Sugar & Spice, Dana And Debbie	1976	7500	40.00	40.00
Jansen, Sugar & Spice, Becky & Baby	1977	7500	42.50	42.50
Kentucky Derby, The Big Three, Rockwell	1974	10000	17.50	17.50
Moppets, Anniversary		20000	13.00	13.00
Moppets, Christmas, Christmas March	1973	20000	12.50	Unknown
Moppets, Christmas, Trimming The Tree	1974	18500		8.00 to 13.50
Moppets, Christmas, Carrying The Tree*	1975	20000	13.00	8.00 to 13.00
Moppets, Christmas, Asleep Under The Tree	1976	18500	13.00	13.00
Moppets, Christmas, Star For Treetop	1977		13.00	13.00
Moppets, Mother's Day, Flowers For Mother	1973	20000	12.50	20.00
Moppets, Mother's Day, Mother's Hat	1974	20000		13.00
Moppets, Mother's Day, In Mother's Clothes*	1975	20000	13.00	6.00 to 13.00
Moppets, Mother's Day, Flowers	1976	20000	13.00	13.00
Moppets, Mother's Day, Gift For Mother	1977	20000	13.00	13.00
President, Eisenhower	1977	9800	30.00	30.00
President, Kennedy	1977	9800	30.00	30.00
Rembrandt, Man In Gilt Helmet, Porcelain*	1971	10000	50.00	27.00 to 50.00
Rembrandt, Self-Portrait With Saskia	1972	10000	50.00	20.00 to 50.00
Remington, Aiding A Comrade	1973	Year	25.00	20.00 to 25.00
Remington, A New Year On The Cimarron*	1973	Year	25.00	20.00 to 25.00
Remington, Cavalry Officer	1975	5000	37.50	37.50
Remington, Old Ramond And A Breed, Set*	1974	5000	40.00	27.00 to 40.00
Remington, The Fight For The Waterhole*	1973	Year	25.00	20.00 to 25.00
Remington, The Flight	1973	Year	25.00	20.00 to 25.00
Remington, Trapper	1975	5000	37.50	37.50
Ritter, Four Seasons Series, Falling In Love, 4	1977	5000	100.00	100.00
Ritter, Four Seasons Series, Love A Clown, 4**	1978	5000	120.00	120.00

Gorham, Barrymore Plate, Quiet Waters

Gorham, Plate, Barrymore, San Pedro,
Porcelain, 1972

Gorham, Bicentennial Plate, 1776, Silver

Gorham, Plate, Jansen, Sugar & Spice,
Dana And Debbie, 1976

Title	Issue Date	Number Issued	Issued Price	Current Price
Rockwell, April Fool	1978	10000	27.50	27.50
Rockwell, Benjamin Franklin	1975	18500	19.50	Unknown
Rockwell, Boy Scout, A Scout Is Loyal	1976	18500	19.50	19.50
Rockwell, Boy Scout, Our Heritage	1976	18500	19.50	19.50
Rockwell, Boy Scout, A Good Sign	1977	18500	19.50	19.50
Rockwell, Christmas, Tiny Tim	1974	Year	12.50	9.50 to 22.50
Rockwell, Christmas, Good Deeds*	1975	Year	17.50	12.50 to 25.00
Rockwell, Christmas, Christmas Trio	1976	Year	19.50	19.50
Rockwell, Christmas, Yuletide Reckoning	1977	Year	19.50	19.50
Rockwell, Christmas, Plan Christmas Visits**	1978	Year	24.50	24.50
Rockwell, Family Tree, American Heritage	1975			38.00 to 110.00
Rockwell, Four Freedoms, Freedom Of Speech	1976	Year	37.50	37.50
Rockwell, Four Freedoms, Freedom To Worship	1976	Year	37.50	37.50
Rockwell, Four Freedoms, Freedom From Want	1976	Year	37:50	37.50
Rockwell, Four Freedoms, Freedom From Fear	1976	Year	37.50	37.50
Rockwell, Four Seasons, Boy & Dog, 4	1971	Year	60.00	200.00 to 350.00
Rockwell, Four Seasons, Young Love, 4	1972	Year	60.00	90.00 to 205.00
Rockwell, Four Seasons, Seasons Of Love, 4*	1973	Year	60.00	53.50 to 140.00
Rockwell, Four Seasons, Grandpa & Me, 4	1974	Year	60.00	32.00 to 100.00
Rockwell, Four Seasons, Grand Pals, 4	1976	Year	70.00	51.00 to 70.00
Rockwell, Four Seasons, The Tender Years, 4**	1978	Year	100.00	100.00
Rockwell, Four Seasons, Going On Sixteen, 4	1977	Year	75.00	75.00
Santa Fe, Bead Maker	1978	7500	37.50	37.50
Santa Fe, Navajo Silversmith	1977	7500	37.50	37.50
Spencer, Dear Child	1975	10000	37.50	65.00 to 150.00
Spencer, Hug Me	1978	10000	55.00	55.00
Spencer, Promises To Keep	1976	10000	40.00	40.00 to 75.00
Valentine, Fluttering Heart	1978	9800	24.50	24.50

Gorham Spoons

Title	Issue Date	Number Issued	Issued Price	Current Price
Apostle Spoon Collection, Christ, Sterling		2750	100.00	100.00
Christmas, Star Of Bethlehem	1971	Year	10.00	10.00 to 30.00
Christmas, Musical Instruments	1972	Year	10.00	20.00 to 25.00
Christmas, Bells*	1973	Year	10.95	10.95 to 16.95
Christmas, Musician	1974	Year	14.50	12.00 to 18.50
Christmas, Santa	1975	Year	17.50	17.50
Christmas	1976	Year	19.75	19.75
Christmas, Dove And Wreath	1977	Year	19.75	19.75

Gorham Steins

Title	Issue Date	Number Issued	Issued Price	Current Price
Rockwell, A Boy Meets His Dog	1977	9800	25.00	25.00
Rockwell, Pride Of Parenthood	1976	9800	25.00	25.00

Gorham Tea Caddy

Title	Issue Date	Number Issued	Issued Price	Current Price
Bicentennial, Boston Tea Party	1973	10000	17.76	13.00 to 25.00

Gourinat, Dolan Co. Plates

Title	Issue Date	Number Issued	Issued Price	Current Price
Doves Of Peace	1978	3000	60.00	60.00

Grafburg Plates are made by the Grafburg Factory of Grafburg, Bavaria.

Grafburg Plates

Title	Issue Date	Number Issued	Issued Price	Current Price
Christmas, Black-Capped Chickadee	1975	5000	20.00	10.00 to 20.00
Christmas, Squirrels	1976	5000	22.00	22.00

Grafburg Pyramid

Title	Issue Date	Number Issued	Issued Price	Current Price
Christmas, Pyramid	1976	5000	25.00	25.00

Grande Copenhagen Plates

Title	Issue Date	Number Issued	Issued Price	Current Price
Bicentennial	1976	Year		18.50 to 24.50
Christmas, Alone Together	1975	Year	24.50	15.00 to 50.00
Christmas, Christmas Eve	1976	Year	24.50	24.50

Grandma Moses plates were produced in the 1950s by Syracuse China Co. There is some confusion about the plates, however, because Atlas China Co. purchased some of the Syracuse blanks and decorated them. The Atlas plates were less expensive and did not have the same titles.

See also Ridgewood, Grandma Moses

Grandma Moses Plates

Title	Issue Date	Number Issued	Issued Price	Current Price
First Set Of 4			80.00	80.00 to 120.00
Second Set Of 4			80.00	80.00 to 120.00

Gorham, Plate, Moppets, Christmas,
Carrying The Tree, 1975

Gorham, Plate, Moppets, Mother's Day,
In Mother's Clothes, 1975

Gorham, Gainsborough Plate,
The Honorable Mrs. Graham

Gorham, Plate, Rembrandt,
Man In Gilt Helmet, Porcelain, 1971

Gorham, Rockwell Plate, Four Seasons,
1973, Set Of 4

Gorham, Remington Plate,
A New Year On The Cimarron

Gorham, Plate, Rockwell, Christmas,
Good Deeds, 1975

Gorham, Remington Plate,
The Fight For The Waterhole

Gorham, Christmas Demispoon, 1973

Gorham, Plate, Remington,
Old Ramond And A Breed,
Set, 1974

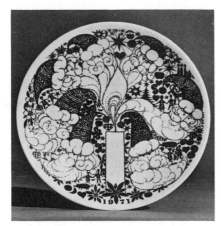

Gustavsberg, Christmas Plate, 1971

Gustavsberg, Christmas Plate, 1972

Gustavsberg, Christmas Plate, 1973

Title	Issue Date	Number Issued	Issued Price	Current Price
See listing for Granget in Figurine section				
See Royal Cornwall				
Granget Plates				
Bicentennial, Freedom In Flight	1976	5000	100.00	100.00
Bicentennial, Freedom In Flight, Gold Edition	1976	200	200.00	200.00
Cottontails, American	1975	2500	85.00	49.00 to 85.00
Cottontails, European	1975	5000	85.00	30.00
Foxes, Spring Journey	1978	1500	125.00	125.00
Kildeer, American	1973	5000	75.00	69.00 to 75.00
Partridge, American	1974	5000	75.00	50.00 to 110.00
Partridge, European	1974	5000	75.00	33.50 to 62.50
Polar Bear	1977	2500	100.00	100.00
Squirrels, American	1973	5000	75.00	12.99 to 75.00
Squirrels, European	1973	5000	45.00	15.00 to 33.00
Sparrows, American	1972	5000	50.00	50.00 to 150.00
Sparrows, European	1972	5000	35.00	15.00 to 28.00
Wrens, American	1976	2500	90.00	89.50 to 90.00
Wrens, European	1976	5000	65.00	62.50 to 65.00
Greenaway, see Kate Greenaway				

Greentree Pottery of Audubon, Iowa, was established in 1968 by Judy Sutcliffe. The pottery produces many privately commissioned plates. All plates are handmade.

Title	Issue Date	Number Issued	Issued Price	Current Price
Greentree Plates				
Grant Wood's Studio	1971	2000	10.00	Unknown
Grant Wood's Antioch School	1972	2000	10.00	12.00
Grant Wood At Stone City	1973	2000	10.00	Unknown
Grant Wood's Adolescence	1974	2000	10.00	Unknown
Grant Wood's Birthplace	1975	2000	10.00	Unknown
Grant Wood's American Gothic	1976	2000	10.00	Unknown
Kennedy, Center For The Performing Arts	1972	2000	20.00	Unknown
Kennedy, Birthplace, Brookline, Mass.	1973	2000	12.00	Unknown
Mississippi River, Delta Queen	1973	2000	10.00	Unknown
Mississippi River, Tri-Centennial	1973	2000	10.00	Unknown
Motorcar, 1929 Packard Dietrich Convertible	1972	2000	20.00	Unknown
Motorcar, Model A Ford	1973	2000	20.00	Unknown
Gregory, Mary, see Mary Gregory				
Gross, Chaim, see Judaic Heritage Society				
Grossman Bells				
Bicentennial	1976			8.99 to 13.50
Grossman Plates				
Looney Tunes, Mother's Day, Bugs Bunny	1976	10000	13.00	13.00
Looney Tunes, Christmas	1977	10000	13.00	13.00
My Kitty	1977		13.00	13.00
Rockwell, First Smoke	1977	10000	24.00	11.50 to 12.00
Rockwell, Take Your Medicine	1977	10000	24.00	24.00
Gunther Granget, see Granget				

Gustavsberg limited editions were first introduced into the United States in 1971. The plates are made at the Gustavsberg factory in Stockholm, Sweden.

Title	Issue Date	Number Issued	Issued Price	Current Price
Gustavsberg Plates				
Accession, Karl Gustaf XVI	1973	Year	9.00	Unknown
Christmas, Candle*	1971	Year	12.50	Unknown
Christmas, Birds*	1972	Year	12.50	Unknown
Christmas, Angels*	1973	Year	12.50	Unknown
Christmas, Straw Deer	1975	Year	12.50	Unknown
Christmas, Candles	1976	Year	12.50	Unknown
Congratulations	1972	Year	12.50	Unknown
Congratulations	1973	Year	12.50	Unknown
Endangered Species, Hedgehog		Year	24.00	Unknown
Endangered Species, Owl		Year	24.00	Unknown
90th Anniversary, Gustaf Adolf VI	1972	Year	9.00	Unknown
United Nations	1972	Year	12.50	Unknown
Christmas	1974	Year	12.50	Unknown

Title	Issue Date	Number Issued	Issued Price	Current Price

Halbert Plates are part of the Ghent Collection and are being sold by Halbert's Collector's Division, Bath, Ohio.

Halbert Plates

Title	Issue Date	Number Issued	Issued Price	Current Price
America's First Family, Copper	1977	9500	40.00	40.00
Bicentennial Wildlife, American Bald Eagle	1976	2500	95.00	95.00
Bicentennial Wildlife, American Bison	1976	2500	95.00	95.00
Bicentennial Wildlife, American Wild Turkey	1976	2500	95.00	95.00
Bicentennial Wildlife, White-Tailed Deer	1976	2500	95.00	95.00
Christmas, Cardinals In The Snow	1974	10135	20.00	14.95 to 27.00
Christmas, Three Kings	1975	12750	29.00	21.00 to 29.00
Christmas, Partridges	1976	12750	32.00	32.00
Christmas, Fox And Evergreen	1977	12750	32.00	32.00
Making Of A Nation	1978	1978	80.00	80.00
Mother's Day, Cottontails	1975	12750	22.00	14.95 to 27.00
Mother's Day, Mallards	1976	12750		21.50 to 29.00
Mother's Day, Chipmunks	1977	12750	32.00	32.00
Mother's Day, Racoon Family	1978	12750	32.00	32.00

Hallmark Plates

Title	Issue Date	Number Issued	Issued Price	Current Price
Christmas, Madonna And Child, Pewter	1977	7500	75.00	75.00

Hamilton Mint of Arlington Heights, Illinois, is a private mint. Limited edition gold and silver plates were introduced in 1972. Editions are serially numbered on the back. When an edition is completed, the die is destroyed.

See listing for Hamilton Mint in Figurine section

Hamilton Mint Plates

Title	Issue Date	Number Issued	Issued Price	Current Price
Bicentennial, Boston Tea Party, Pewter	1975	Year	30.00	30.00 to 41.50
Bicentennial, Bunker Hill, Pewter	1976	Year	30.00	30.00 to 41.50
Bicentennial, Molly Pitcher, Pewter	1976	Year	30.00	30.00 to 41.50
Christmas, Spirit And Joy Of Christmas, Silver	1974	Year	125.00	125.00
Christmas, Tannenbaum, Silver	1975	Year	150.00	150.00
Easter, Triptych, Pewter**	1975		40.00	30.00 to 45.00
Easter, Gospel St.Luke	1977	10000	40.00	40.00
Easter, Entry Into Jerusalem	1978	10000	40.00	40.00
John F.Kennedy Memorial, Gold On Pewter	1974	Year	40.00	Unknown
John F.Kennedy Memorial, Pewter	1974	Year	25.00	22.00 to 23.50
Mother's Day, Generations Of Love, Gold	1973	25	1750.00	Unknown
Mother's Day, Generations Of Love, Sterling	1973	1000	125.00	Unknown
Mother's Day, Devotion, Golden Pewter	1975			30.00 to 40.00
Mother's Day, Love's Circle, Pewter	1976	Year	35.00	35.00
Mother's Day, Love's Circle, Gold On Pewter	1976	Year	40.00	40.00
Picasso, Le Gourmet, Sterling	1972	5000	25.00	75.00 to 125.00
Picasso, Tragedy	1972	5000	25.00	50.00 to 125.00
Picasso, The Lovers, Sterling	1973	5000	25.00	95.00 to 150.00
St.Patrick's Day, Silver	1973	Year	75.00	120.00
Thanksgiving, Pewter	1975	Year	40.00	40.00

Hammersley, see Spode

Harm Bird plates, see Spode

Haviland & Co. was founded in Limoges, France in 1893 by David Haviland, an American. Limited editions were introduced in 1970.

Haviland Cup and Saucer

Title	Issue Date	Number Issued	Issued Price	Current Price
Presidential, Lincoln	1972	2500	80.00	55.00 to 80.00

Haviland Ornaments

Title	Issue Date	Number Issued	Issued Price	Current Price
Birds Of Peace & Love	1973	5000	17.50	17.50
Christmas, Dancing Angels*	1971	30000	8.95	6.00 to 11.00
Christmas, Horse	1972	30000	9.95	5.00 to 11.00
Christmas, Ringing Bells	1973	30000	9.95	4.00 to 11.00
Christmas, Caroling Angels	1974	30000	10.95	6.00 to 11.00
Christmas, Littlest Angel	1975	20000	11.50	7.65 to 12.00
Christmas, Sleepy Angels	1976	20000	12.50	9.75 to 12.50
Christmas, Bountiful Angel	1977	20000	13.50	13.50
Christmas, Sledding Angels	1978	20000	16.00	16.00

Haviland Plates

Title	Issue Date	Number Issued	Issued Price	Current Price
Bicentennial, Burning Of The Gaspee	1972	10000	39.95	6.50 to 50.00
Bicentennial, Boston Tea Party*	1973	10000	39.95	17.00 to 40.00

Haviland, Plate, Bicentennial, Signing Declaration, 1976

Haviland, Plate, Christmas, Nine Ladies Dancing, 1978

Haviland, Christmas Ornament, 1971

Haviland, Plate, Mother's Day, Evening At Home, 1978

Haviland, Bicentennial Plate, 1973

Haviland, Christmas Plate, 1972

Haviland, Christmas Plate, 1971

Haviland, Presidential Plate, Lincoln

Haviland, Christmas Plate, 1970

Haviland, Presidential Plate, Hayes

Haviland, Christmas Plate, 1973

Haviland, Presidential Plate, Grant

Haviland, Presidential Plate, Washington

Haviland & Parlon, Plate, Zodiac,
Astrological Man, 1977

Cybis, Unicorn

Royal Worcester, Doris Lindner,
Prince's Grace & Foal

Royal Worcester, Dorothy Doughty, Redstarts & Gorse

Royal Worcester, Dorothy Doughty, Wrens & Burnet Rose

Royal Worcester, Dorothy Doughty, Gray Wagtail

Royal Worcester, Ronald Van Ruyckevelt,
Rainbow Parrot Fish

Royal Worcester,
Ronald Van Ruyckevelt, Felicity

Royal Worcester,
Ronald Van Ruyckevelt, Elaine

Royal Worcester, Ronald Van Ruyckevelt,
Green-Winged Teal

Royal Worcester, Ronald Van Ruyckevelt.
Charlotte & Jane

Royal Worcester, Doris Lindner, Charolais Bull

Royal Worcester, Ronald Van Ruyckevelt, Dolphin

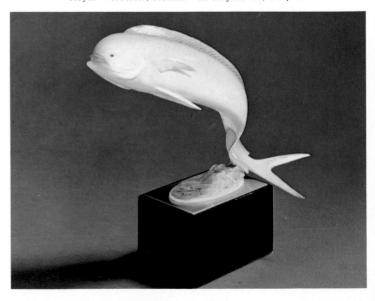

Moussalli, Tufted Titmouse

Moussalli, Indigo Bunting

Moussalli, Redbreasted Grosbeak

Moussalli, Say's Phoebe

Moussalli, Snow Bunting

Royal Worcester, Ronald Van Ruyckevelt, Languedoc

Moussalli, Black-Capped Chickadee

Burgues, White-Breasted Nuthatches, Male & Female

Burgues, Veiltail Goldfish

Burgues, King Penguins

Burgues, Bighorn Sheep

Burgues, Daffodil Manco

Burgues, Ruby-Throated Hummingbird

Burgues, Chipmunk With Fly Amanita

Cybis, Shoshone, Sacajawea

Cybis, Blackfeet, Beaverhead, Medicine Man

Cybis, Autumn Dogwood With Chickadees

Cybis, Clematis With House Wren

Cybis, Carousel Horse

Royal Doulton, Christmas Plate, 1973

Royal Doulton, Prince Charles Bust

Granget, Woodcarving, Eagle

Royal Doulton, Cello   Royal Doulton, Virginals   St.Louis, Red Flower Faceted

St.Louis, Pinwheel, Blue & White Swirl   St.Louis, Pinwheel, 5-Color Swirl

St.Louis, Marbrie, Blue, Yellow, & White   St.Louis, Flat Bouquet On Opaque White Ground

Cristal d'Albret, Paul Revere, Overlay   Cristal d'Albret, Leonardo da Vinci, Overlay

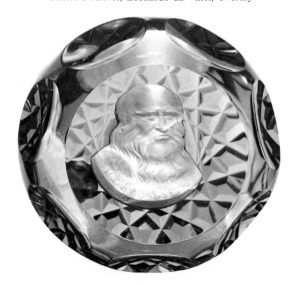

Burgues, Lily Harlequin

Ispanky, Romance, 1978

Boehm, Eastern Bluebird II, Wild Rose

Burgues, Ruby-Throated Hummingbird

Boehm, Ruffed Grouse II, With Chicks

Boehm, Cardinals II, 1977

Title	Issue Date	Number Issued	Issued Price	Current Price
Bicentennial, First Continental Congress	1974	10000	39.95	20.00 to 39.95
Bicentennial, Paul Revere's Ride	1975	10000	40.00	20.00 to 41.00
Bicentennial, Signing Declaration*	1976	10000	48.00	48.00
Christmas, Partridge In A Pear Tree*	1970	30000	25.00	150.00 to 225.00
Christmas, Two Turtle Doves*	1971	30000	25.00	18.75 to 67.50
Christmas, Three French Hens*	1972	30000	27.50	12.00 to 40.00
Christmas, Four Colly Birds*	1973	30000	28.50	17.50 to 35.00
Christmas, Five Golden Rings	1974	30000	30.00	16.00 to 32.00
Christmas, Six Geese A-Laying	1975	30000	32.00	15.00 to 32.00
Christmas, Seven Swans	1976	30000	30.00	24.00 to 38.00
Christmas, Eight Maids A'milking	1977	30000	40.00	32.00 to 40.00
Christmas, Nine Ladies Dancing*	1978	30000	45.00	45.00
Mother's Day, Breakfast	1973	10000	29.95	6.00 to 29.00
Mother's Day, The Wash	1974	10000	29.95	10.00 to 30.00
Mother's Day, Walk In Park	1975	10000	29.95	16.25 to 30.00
Mother's Day, Market	1976	10000	38.00	23.50 to 38.00
Mother's Day, Wash Before Dinner	1977	10000	38.00	38.00
Mother's Day, Evening At Home*	1978	10000	40.00	40.00
Presidential, Grant*	1970	3000	100.00	25.00 to 110.00
Presidential, Hayes*	1972	2500	110.00	25.00 to 110.00
Presidential, Lincoln*	1969	2500	100.00	42.50 to 130.00
Presidential, Washington*	1968	2500	35.00	26.00 to 125.00
Presidential, Martha Washington	1968	2500	35.00	17.50 to 45.00

Haviland & Parlon,
Unicorn Tapestry Plate, 1971

Robert Haviland purchased the company now known as Robert Haviland and C.Parlon in 1942. The firm is in Limoges, France.

Haviland & Parlon Plates

Title	Issue Date	Number Issued	Issued Price	Current Price
Christmas, Madonna, Raphael	1972	5000	35.00	98.00 to 200.00
Christmas, Madonna, Feruzzi	1973	5000	35.00	27.50 to 200.00
Christmas, Madonna, Raphael	1974	5000	42.50	27.50 to 200.00
Christmas, Madonna, Murillo	1975	5000	42.50	19.75 to 200.00
Christmas, Madonna, Botticelli	1976	5000	42.00	Unknown
Mother's Day, Carlsen, Mother & Child	1975	15000	37.50	65.00 to 200.00
Mother's Day, Carlsen, Pinky And Baby	1976	15000	42.50	28.75 to 42.50
Lady And Unicorn	1977	20000	50.00	50.00
Lady And Unicorn, Sight	1978	20000	48.00	48.00
Scarab Plate	1977	2500	80.00	100.00 to 100.00
Unicorn Tapestry, Captivity*	1971	12000	35.00	95.00 to 240.00
Unicorn Tapestry, Start Of The Hunt*	1972	12000	35.00	30.00 to 118.00
Unicorn Tapestry, Fountain*	1973	12000	35.00	46.50 to 120.00
Unicorn Tapestry, End Of The Hunt	1974	12000	37.50	40.00 to 75.00
Unicorn Tapestry, Defends	1975	12000	40.00	26.65 to 75.00
Unicorn Tapestry, Captured*	1976	12000	42.50	42.50
Zodiac, Astrological Man*	1977	5000	50.00	50.00

Henry Ford Museum Plates

Title	Issue Date	Number Issued	Issued Price	Current Price
Bicentennial, Museum Tower	1976	900	14.95	14.95

Haviland & Parlon,
Unicorn Tapestry Plate, 1972

Hibel, see also Royal Doulton, Rosenthal

Edna Hibel is a contemporary American artist whose paintings appear on many plates.

Hibel Plates

Title	Issue Date	Number Issued	Issued Price	Current Price
Yasuko	1976	2000	275.00	900.00
Flower Girl Of Provence	1977	12750	175.00	175.00
Mr.Obata	1977	2000	275.00	500.00
Nobility Of Children, La Contessa Isabella	1976	12750	120.00	120.00
Nobility Of Children, Le Marquis M.Pierre	1978		120.00	120.00

Haviland & Parlon,
Unicorn Tapestry Plate, 1973

Haviland & Parlon, Plate,
Unicorn Tapestry, Captured, 1976

The Historic Plate Company is a division of Jerald Sulky Co. of Waterloo, Iowa. The limited edition series, featuring great harness racing horses, was introduced in 1972.

Historic Plates

Title	Issue Date	Number Issued	Issued Price	Current Price
Hambletonian 10*	1972	2000	20.00	Unknown
Hambletonian 10, The Maid	1974	2000		Unknown

Hudson Pewter Bells

Title	Issue Date	Number Issued	Issued Price	Current Price
Bicentennial, Adams	1976			22.50 to 27.50
Bicentennial, Franklin	1976			22.50 to 27.50
Bicentennial, Jefferson	1976			22.50

Historic, Plate, Hambletonian 10, 1972

Title	Issue Date	Number Issued	Issued Price	Current Price
Bicentennial, Madison	1976			22.50 to 27.50
Bicentennial, Washington	1976			22.50 to 27.50
Christmas, Drummer Boy	1976			21.50 to 27.50
Hudson Pewter Plaques				
Christmas, Santa Claus	1977	6000	30.00	30.00
Old Glory	1977	5000	30.00	30.00
Hudson Pewter Plates				
Americana	1973			40.00
Americana	1974		30.00	45.00
Americana	1975			30.00 to 45.00
Bicentennial, Spirit Of '76	1975	10000		45.00 to 55.00
Bicentennial, Declaration Of Independence	1976			29.99
Christmas, Life Of Christ, Nativity	1977	5000	65.00	65.00
Christmas, Night Before Christmas	1976			51.95 to 75.00
Charles Lindbergh	1977	5000		Unknown
God Bless America	1977	10000	65.00	65.00

Hummel, see Goebel Hummel and Schmid Hummel

Hutschenreuther Porcelain Company of Selb, Germany, was established in 1814. Limited edition plates were first made in 1970.

Hutschenreuther, see also Granget

Hutschenreuther Plates

Title	Issue Date	Number Issued	Issued Price	Current Price
Birthday	1978	10000	165.00	165.00
Floral Heirlooms, Zinnias, Sugar Bowl	1977	5000	65.00	65.00
Friendship	1978	Year	80.00	80.00
Mother & Child	1978	Year	55.00	55.00
Plate Of Month, Set Of 12	1977	5000	780.00	780.00
Princess Snowflake	1978	10000	50.00	50.00
Ruthven Birds, Bluebird & Goldfinch*	1972	5000	100.00	34.95 to 150.00
Ruthven Birds, Mockingbird & Robin*	1973	5000	100.00	79.50 to 150.00
Ruthven Birds	1974	5000		Unknown
Ruthven Birds, Screech Owls	1977	5000		37.50
Wedding	1978	10000	210.00	210.00
Zodiac Set	1977	1500	1500.00	1500.00

Imperial Glass Corporation was founded in Bellaire, Ohio, in 1901. In 1940, Imperial bought out Central Glass Works of Wheeling, West Virginia. In 1958, they purchased all the molds, trademarks, etc., of the Heisey Co. of Newark, Ohio. The production facilities of Cambridge Glass Company were acquired in 1960. Imperial's limited editions were introduced in 1970 and are available in crystal or carnival.

Imperial Plates

Title	Issue Date	Number Issued	Issued Price	Current Price
Christmas, Partridge, Blue Carnival*	1970	Year	12.00	5.00 to 27.50
Christmas, Partridge, Frosted	1970	Year	15.00	8.00 to 22.75
Christmas, Two Turtle Doves, Green Carnival	1971	Year	12.00	5.00 to 17.75
Christmas, Two Turtle Doves, Frosted*	1971	Year	16.50	11.00 to 17.00
Christmas, Three French Hens, Amber Carnival	1972	Year	12.00	12.00 to 20.00
Christmas, Three French Hens, Frosted	1972	Year	16.50	10.00 to 26.00
Christmas, Four Colly Birds, White Carnival	1973	Year	12.00	14.00 to 24.95
Christmas, Four Colly Birds, Frosted	1973	Year	16.50	7.00 to 16.50
Christmas, Five Golden Rings, Green Carnival	1974	Year	12.00	8.35 to 15.00
Christmas, Five Golden Rings, Frosted	1974	Year	16.50	11.00 to 20.50
Christmas, Six Geese A-Laying, Yellow Carnival	1975	Year	14.00	9.35 to 14.00
Christmas, Six Geese A-Laying, Frosted	1975	Year	19.00	12.95 to 19.00
Christmas, Seven Swans, Ultra Blue Carnival	1976	Year	16.00	12.95 to 21.00
Christmas, Seven Swans, Frosted	1976	Year	21.00	21.00
Christmas, Eight Maids A-Milking, Carnival	1977	Year	18.00	18.00
Christmas, Eight Maids A-Milking, Frosted	1977	Year	23.00	23.00
Christmas, Nine Drummers, Pink Carnival	1978	Year	20.00	20.00
Christmas, Nine Drummers Drumming, Frosted	1978	Year	25.00	25.00
Coin, 1964 Kennedy Half Dollar*	1971	Year	15.00	7.50 to 20.00
Coin, Eisenhower*	1972	Year	15.00	4.00 to 17.50
Coin, Bicentennial, Crystal*	1976	Year	20.00	20.00

Incolay Plates

Title	Issue Date	Number Issued	Issued Price	Current Price
Romantic Poets, She Walks In Beauty	1977		60.00	60.00
Romantic Poets, A Thing Of Beauty	1978		60.00	60.00

Hummel Goebel, Annual Plate, 1973

Hummel Goebel, Annual Plate, 1972

Hummel Schmid, Mother's Day Plate, 1972

Hummel Schmid,
Christmas Bell, 1973

Hummel Schmid, Christmas Plate, 1973

Hummel Schmid, Christmas Plate, 1972

Goebel Hummel,
Plate, Annual,
Apple Tree Girl, 1976

Hutschenreuther, Ruthven Bird Plates, 1972

Hutschenreuther, Ruthven Bird Plates, 1973

Imperial, Christmas Plate, 1970, Carnival

Imperial, Christmas Plate, 1971, Crystal

Imperial, Plate, Coin,
1964 Kennedy Half Dollar, 1971

Imperial, Plate, Coin, Eisenhower, 1972

Title	Issue Date	Number Issued	Issued Price	Current Price
Indian Art Eggs				
Easter	1972	5000	12.00	15.00 to 20.00
Easter, Egg	1973	5000	12.00	12.95 to 16.50
Easter, Egg	1976	3000	19.50	19.50

International Silver Company of Meriden, Connecticut, was incorporated by a group of New England silversmiths in 1898. The company makes a large variety of silver and silver-plated wares. Limited edition pewter and silver plates were first made in 1972.

Title	Issue Date	Number Issued	Issued Price	Current Price
Chess Set				
American Revolution, Pewter	1976	500	1400.00	1400.00
International Silver Plates				
Christmas, Christmas Rose, Gold & Silver*	1972	2500	100.00	50.00 to 75.00
Christmas, Tiny Tim, Pewter*	1974	7500	75.00	50.00 to 75.00
Christmas, Caught, Pewter	1975	7500	75.00	59.95 to 75.00
Christmas, Bringing Home The Tree, Pewter*	1976	7000	75.00	75.00
Christmas, Fezziwig's Christmas Ball	1977	7500		75.00
Presidential Series, Washington, Pewter	1975	7500	75.00	50.00 to 75.00
Presidential Series, Jefferson, Pewter*	1976	7500	75.00	64.50 to 75.00
Presidential Series, Lincoln, Pewter*	1976	7500	75.00	64.50 to 75.00
Presidential Series, F.Roosevelt, Pewter	1976	7500	75.00	75.00
Presidential Series, Eisenhower, Pewter	1977	7500	75.00	75.00
Presidential Series, Kennedy, Pewter	1977	7500	75.00	75.00
Seasons, American Past, Autumn, Pewter	1976	7500	60.00	65.00
Seasons, American Past, Spring, Pewter	1976	7500	60.00	65.00
Seasons, American Past, Summer, Pewter	1976	7500	60.00	65.00
Seasons, American Past, Winter, Pewter	1976	7500	60.00	65.00
We Are One, Declaration, Pewter*	1972	7500	40.00	175.00 to 275.00
We Are One, Ride Of Paul Revere, Pewter*	1973	7500	40.00	100.00 to 140.00
We Are One, Crossing The Delaware, Pewter	1974	7500	50.00	50.00 to 60.00
We Are One, Stand At Concord Bridge, Pewter	1973	7500	40.00	50.00 to 110.00
We Are One, Surrender Of Cornwallis	1974	7500	50.00	50.00 to 60.00
We Are One, Surrender At Yorktown, Pewter	1975	7500	50.00	50.00 to 60.00
We Are One, Valley Forge, Pewter	1975	7500	50.00	42.50 to 60.00

The Ispanky plate was designed by Lazlo Ispanky, noted porcelain sculptor. Medallic Art Company of Danbury, Connecticut, produced the plate.

See listing for Ispanky in Figurine section

See Goebel, Hummel

Title	Issue Date	Number Issued	Issued Price	Current Price
Ispanky Plaques				
Bald Eagle	1972	200		130.00
Ispanky Plates				
Panda, Sterling*	1973	3500	150.00	150.00 to 2000.00
Ispanky Vases				
Vase, Romeo And Juliet	1976	5000	75.00	75.00

Israel Creations, Inc. commissioned the Naaman Works of Israel to produce the first Passover plate in the 1960s. In 1967, the Annual Israel Commemorative plate series was started.

Title	Issue Date	Number Issued	Issued Price	Current Price
Israel Creations Plates				
Tower Of David	1967	5000	7.50	7.50 to 12.50
Wailing Wall	1967	5000	7.50	12.50 to 20.00
Masada	1968	5000	7.50	7.50 to 12.00
Rachel's Tomb	1969	5000	7.50	7.50 to 10.00
Tiberias	1970	5000	8.00	7.00 to 12.00
Nazareth	1971	5000	8.00	7.00 to 11.00
Beersheba	1972	5000	9.00	7.00 to 9.00
Aire	1973	5000	9.00	9.00
J & E Specialties Plates				
Bicentennial, Betsy Ross	1976	1000	22.50	22.50
Bicentennial, Bunker Hill**	1976	1000	22.50	22.50
Bicentennial, Declaration Of Independence	1976	1000	22.50	22.50
Bicentennial, Liberty And Justice	1976	10000	12.95	12.95
Bicentennial, Spirit Of '76	1976	1000	22.50	22.50

Imperial, Plate, Coin,
Bicentennial, Crystal, 1976

International Silver, Plate, Christmas,
Bringing Home The Tree, Pewter, 1976

International Silver, Bicentennial Plate,
1972, We Are One

International Silver, Plate,
Presidential Series, Lincoln, Pewter, 1976

International Silver, Bicentennial Plate,
1974, Crossing The Delaware

International Silver,
Christmas Plate, 1972

International Silver, Plate,
Christmas, Tiny Tim, Pewter, 1974

International Silver, Plate,
Presidential Series, Jefferson, Pewter, 1976

Ispanky, Panda Plate, 1973

Jean-Paul Loup, Christmas Plate, 1971

Title	Issue Date	Number Issued	Issued Price	Current Price
Bicentennial, Surrender Of Cornwallis	1976	1000	22.50	22.50
Bicentennial, Washington Crossing Delaware	1976	1000	22.50	22.50

Jackson, A. Y., see Wellings Mint

Jansen, Leo, see Gorham

Jean-Paul Loup, the editor of Art of Chicago, joined the Betournes Studio of Limoges, France, to issue their first limited edition plates in 1971. The plates and porcelain paintings are hand-applied enamel on copper. Each plate is signed by both Michel Betourne and Jean-Paul Loup.

See listing for Jean-Paul Loup in Figurine section

Jean-Paul Loup, Betournes Plates

Title	Issue Date	Number Issued	Issued Price	Current Price
Christmas*	1971	300	125.00	250.00 to 800.00
Christmas	1972	300	150.00	280.00 to 500.00
Christmas	1973	300	175.00	175.00 to 250.00
Christmas	1974	400	200.00	200.00
Christmas	1975	250	250.00	250.00
Mother's Day, Champleve	1974	500	250.00	700.00
Mother's Day, Enamel	1975	400	285.00	285.00

Jensen, Georg, see Georg Jensen

Jensen, Svend, see Svend Jensen

Josair Plates

Title	Issue Date	Number Issued	Issued Price	Current Price
Bicentennial, American Eagle, Crystal	1972	400	250.00	Unknown
Bicentennial, American Flag, Crystal	1973	400	250.00	Unknown
Bicentennial, Abraham Lincoln	1974	400	250.00	Unknown
Bicentennial, George Washington	1975	400	250.00	Unknown
Bicentennial, Declaration Of Independence	1976	400	250.00	Unknown

The Judaic Heritage Society first made medals commemorating Jewish traditions in 1969. Limited edition plates were introduced in 1972.

Judaic Heritage Society Cups

Title	Issue Date	Number Issued	Issued Price	Current Price
Cup Of Fulfillment, Gold	1973	25	3000.00	3000.00
Cup Of Fulfillment, Silver	1973	999	325.00	325.00

Judaic Heritage Society Plates

Title	Issue Date	Number Issued	Issued Price	Current Price
Chanukah, Gold	1972	100	1900.00	1900.00
Chanukah, Silver	1972	2000	150.00	150.00
Pesach, Silver	1972	5000	150.00	150.00
Purim, Silver	1974	1000	175.00	175.00

Stephen Juharos Omnibus Muralis Series, made by Gorham China Company, is offered by Kern Collectibles.

Juharos Plates

Title	Issue Date	Number Issued	Issued Price	Current Price
Omnibus Muralis, 200 Years With Old Glory*	1976		60.00	60.00
Omnibus Muralis, Life Of Christ**	1977		65.00	65.00

Kaiser Porcelain Manufactory was founded in 1872 by August Alboth in Coburg, Germany. The plant was moved to Staffelstein, Bavaria, in 1953. Their first limited edition plate was made in 1970. That year, the company's mark was changed from AK and a crown to 'Kaiser Porcelain.'

See listing for Kaiser in Figurine section

Kaiser Bowls

Title	Issue Date	Number Issued	Issued Price	Current Price
Bicentennial	1976	5000	250.00	300.00

Kaiser Plaques

Title	Issue Date	Number Issued	Issued Price	Current Price
Birds, Cardinal & Blue Titmouse, Pair	1973	2000	200.00	200.00

Kaiser Plates

Title	Issue Date	Number Issued	Issued Price	Current Price
Anniversary, Love Birds	1972	12000	16.50	22.00 to 30.00
Anniversary, Couple In The Park	1973	7000	18.00	12.00 to 24.00
Anniversary, Couple Canoeing	1974	7000	22.00	16.95 to 27.50
Anniversary, Tender Moments	1975	7000	25.00	16.65 to 27.50
Anniversary, Serenade To Lovers	1976		25.00	19.95 to 25.00
Anniversary, A Simple Gift	1977		25.00	25.00
Anniversary, A Viking Toast	1978		30.00	30.00
Bicentennial, Declaration Of Independence	1976	1000	75.00	55.95 to 75.00
Christmas, Waiting For Santa	1970	Year	12.50	20.00 to 48.00

Juharos, Plate, Omnibus Muralis,
200 Years With Old Glory, 1976

Title	Issue Date	Number Issued	Issued Price	Current Price
Christmas, Silent Night	1971	Year	13.50	22.50 to 48.00
Christmas, Coming Home For Christmas	1972	10000	16.50	21.00 to 42.00
Christmas, Holy Night	1973	8000	18.00	20.00 to 39.00
Christmas, Christmas Carolers	1974	8000	22.00	19.95 to 30.00
Christmas, Bringing Home The Christmas Tree	1975	8000	25.00	16.65 to 27.50
Christmas, Christ, The Saviour, Is Born	1976		25.00	16.50 to 30.00
Christmas, Three Wise Men	1977		25.00	25.00
Golden Mask Of Tutankhamun	1977	15000	65.00	65.00
Little Critters, Set Of 6	1973	5000	100.00	66.50 to 120.00
Loates, Blue Jays	1978	10000	70.00	70.00
Midnight Sun, Northern Lullaby	1978	15000	65.00	65.00
Mother's Day, Mare & Foal	1971	Year	13.00	19.00 to 39.00
Mother's Day, Flowers For Mother	1972	8000	16.50	10.00 to 35.00
Mother's Day, Mother Cat And Kittens	1973	7000	17.00	10.00 to 22.00
Mother's Day, Fox & Cubs	1974	7000	22.00	9.00 to 26.00
Mother's Day, German Shepherd And Pups	1975	7000	25.00	10.00 to 26.00
Mother's Day, Swan And Cygnets	1976		25.00	16.50 to 25.00
Mother's Day, Rabbits	1977		25.00	25.00
Passion Play	1970			15.00 to 23.75
Toronto Horse Show	1973	1000	29.00	30.00 to 60.00
Trester, Yesterday's World	1978	5000	70.00	70.00
Yacht, Cetonia	1972	1000	50.00	25.00 to 27.50
Yacht, Westward	1972	1000	50.00	25.00 to 27.50

Kate Greenaway, who was a famous illustrator of children's books, drew pictures of children in high-waisted empire dresses. She lived from 1846 to 1901. The current limited edition Kate Greenaway plates are made by Meakin pottery of England.

Kate Greenaway Plates

Title	Issue Date	Issued Price	Current Price
Mother's Day	1971	14.95	34.00
Mother's Day	1972	14.95	21.00 to 26.00
Mother's Day	1973	16.95	21.00
Mother's Day	1974	16.95	21.00

Kay Mallek, see Mallek

Keane Plates

Title	Issue Date	Issued Price	Current Price
Balloon Girl	1976	24.50	24.50
My Kitty	1977		24.00

Keller & George, jewelers from Charlottesville, Virginia, commissioned Reed & Barton to produce a series of Bicentennial plates in damascene. The series was begun in 1972.

Keller & George Plates

Title	Issue Date	Number Issued	Issued Price	Current Price
Bicentennial, Monticello, Damascene	1972	1000	75.00	Unknown
Bicentennial, Monticello, Silver Plate	1972	200	200.00	Unknown
Bicentennial, Mt. Vernon, Damascene	1973		75.00	Unknown

Kera Mugs

Title	Issue Date	Number Issued	Issued Price	Current Price
Christmas, Kobenhavn	1967	Year	6.00	Unknown
Christmas, Forste	1968	Year	6.00	Unknown
Christmas, Andersen's House	1969	Year	6.00	Unknown
Christmas, PA Langelinie	1970	Year	6.00	Unknown
Christmas, Lille Peter	1971	Year	6.00	Unknown

Kera Plates

Title	Issue Date	Number Issued	Issued Price	Current Price
Christmas, Kobenhavn	1967	Year	6.00	12.00 to Unknown
Christmas, Forste	1968	Year	6.00	10.00 to Unknown
Christmas, Andersen's House	1969	Year	6.00	5.00 to Unknown
Christmas, PA Langelinie	1970	Year	6.00	6.00 to Unknown
Christmas, Lille Peter	1971	Year	6.00	6.00 to Unknown
Moon, Apollo 11	1969		6.00	6.00 to Unknown
Moon, Apollo 13	1970		6.00	6.00 to Unknown
Mother's Day	1970	Year	6.00	6.00 to Unknown
Mother's Day	1971	Year	6.00	6.00 to Unknown

Kern Collectibles Plates

Title	Issue Date	Number Issued	Issued Price	Current Price
Companion Series, Cubs	1977	5000	40.00	40.00
Companion Series, Mighty Sioux**	1978	5000	40.00	40.00
Linda's Lovables, The Blessing	1977	7500	30.00	30.00

King's Porcelain, Christmas Plate, 1973

King's Porcelain,
Flowers Of America Plate, 1973

King's Porcelain, Mother's Day Plate, 1973

King's Porcelain, Mother's Day Plate, 1974

Kosta, Annual Plate, 1973

KPM,
Easter Egg,
1973

KPM,
Easter Egg,
1974

Lalique, Annual Plate, 1967

Title	Issue Date	Number Issued	Issued Price	Current Price
Kilkelly Plates				
Pipe And Shamrock	1975		20.00	20.00
Third Look In Logan	1976		20.00	20.00

Arthur King, New York City jeweler, designs and creates his own series of limited edition plates. The hammered style silver plates are 4 inches in diameter.

Title	Issue Date	Number Issued	Issued Price	Current Price
King Plates				
Christmas	1972	750	325.00	Unknown
Gold Reserve Act	1973	750	400.00	Unknown

King's Porcelain Factory is located in Italy. Their limited edition plates, introduced in 1973, are high bas relief and hand-painted. Limited edition figurines were first made in 1974.

See listing for King's Porcelain in Figurine section

Title	Issue Date	Number Issued	Issued Price	Current Price
King's Porcelain Plates				
Christmas, Nativity*	1973	1500	150.00	75.00 to 180.00
Christmas, Madonna And Child	1974	1500	150.00	75.00 to 180.00
Christmas, Christmas Choir	1975	1000	160.00	100.00 to 160.00
Christmas, Peeking At The Tree	1976	1500	200.00	200.00
Flowers Of America, Carnation*	1973	1000	85.00	50.00 to 100.00
Flowers Of America, Roses	1974	1000	100.00	66.65 to 100.00
Flowers Of America, Yellow Dahlia	1975	1000	110.00	73.35 to 100.00
Flowers Of America, Bluebells	1976	1000	130.00	13.00
Flowers Of America, Anemones	1977	1000	13.00	30.00
Mother's Day, The Dancing Girl*	1973	1500	100.00	75.00 to 150.00
Mother's Day, The Dancing Boy*	1974	1500	115.00	76.65 to 115.00
Mother's Day, Cameo, Mother And Child	1975	1500	140.00	93.35 to 140.00
Mother's Day, Maiden With Sheep And Lamb	1976	1500	180.00	144.50 to 180.00

Kingsbridge crystal limited editions are made in Bavaria, West Germany. Each piece is hand engraved, numbered, and signed.

Title	Issue Date	Number Issued	Issued Price	Current Price
Kingsbridge Decanters				
Wild Ducks, 1/2 Liter	1974	300	50.00	55.00 to 65.00
Wild Ducks, 2/3 Liter	1974	300	60.00	65.00 to 70.00
Wild Ducks, 3/4 Liter	1974	300	70.00	70.00
Eagle, Cylinder, 3/4 Liter	1975	300	75.00	75.00
Eagle, Square, 3/4 Liter	1975	300	90.00	90.00
Kingsbridge Plates				
Wild Ducks		300	100.00	100.00 to 115.00
Kingsbridge Vases				
Wild Ducks, Ball		300	50.00	55.00 to 60.00
Wild Ducks, Footed		300	60.00	55.00 to 65.00

Kirk limited editions are made by Samuel Kirk and Sons, Inc. The firm was started in Baltimore, Maryland, in 1815. The company is well known for both antique and modern silver wares. Limited edition plates and spoons were first made in 1972.

See listing for Kirk in Figurine section

Title	Issue Date	Number Issued	Issued Price	Current Price
Kirk Plates				
Bicentennial, Washington, Silver	1972	5000	75.00	25.00 to 75.00
Christmas, Flight Into Egypt, Silver	1972	3500	150.00	60.00 to 150.00
Mother's Day, Mother & Child, Silver	1972	3500	75.00	37.50 to 100.00
Mother's Day, Silver	1973	2500	80.00	40.00 to 80.00
Thanksgiving, Thanksgiving Ways And Means	1972	3500	150.00	30.00 to 150.00
U.S.S. Constellation	1972	825	75.00	75.00
Kirk Spoons				
Christmas, Snowflake, Gold	1972	81	125.00	95.00 to 145.00
Christmas, Snowflake, Silver	1972	6000	12.50	12.50 to 15.0

Edwin Knowles China Company of Newell, West Virginia, made its first limited edition plates in 1977.

Title	Issue Date	Number Issued	Issued Price	Current Price
Knowles Plates				
Wizard Of Oz, Over The Rainbow	1977	Year	19.00	19.00
Wizard Of Oz, If I Had A Brain	1978	Year	19.00	19.00

Title	Issue Date	Number Issued	Issued Price	Current Price
Kobycia Bells				
Christmas, Wooden	1974			16.00 to 35.00
Christmas, Wooden	1975	1000		22.95 to 29.00
Kobycia Eggs				
Easter	1974			55.00 to 86.00
Easter	1975	2000		11.00 to 17.50
Easter, Deluxe	1976	500	50.00	50.00

Lalique, Plate, Annual, Jayling, 1973

Kosta Glassworks of Sweden was founded in 1742 by King Charles II. The limited edition line, introduced in 1970, includes paperweights, plates, and mugs.

See listing for Kosta in Paperweight section

Title	Issue Date	Number Issued	Issued Price	Current Price
Kosta Mugs				
Annual, Heraldic Lion	1971	Year		25.00 to 40.00
Annual, Owl	1972	Year		25.00 to 35.00
Annual, Eagle	1973	Year	40.00	27.50 to 40.00
Kosta Plates				
Annual, Madonna & Child	1971	Year	30.00	10.00 to 30.00
Annual, St.George & The Dragon	1972	Year	30.00	17.50 to 25.00
Annual, Ship*	1973	Year	40.00	25.00 to 40.00
Annual	1974	Year	40.00	29.50 to 40.00

KPM, see Royal Berlin

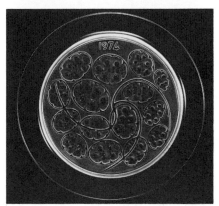
Lalique, Plate, Annual, Silver Pennies, 1974

Kramlik limited edition porcelain paintings are made in New Jersey, by Balint Kramlik. Kramlik, a native of Herend, Hungary, worked with Edward Marshall Boehm before producing his own limited edition porcelain paintings. Each painting is 9 x 12 inches unframed.

Title	Issue Date	Number Issued	Issued Price	Current Price
Kramlik Eggs				
Christmas, First Edition	1974	950	35.00	21.99 to 39.50
Christmas	1975	1000	35.00	21.99 to 35.00
Easter	1975	1000	35.00	21.99 to 35.00
Easter, Bicentennial	1976	1000	35.00	27.95 to 35.00
Balint Kramlik Porcelain Paintings				
Bald Eagle		200	400.00	Unknown
Black-Capped Chickadee On Cherry Blossom		100	400.00	Unknown
Blue Jay, Female		200	400.00	Unknown
Blue Jay, Male		200	400.00	Unknown
Blue-Winged Warbler On Mountain Bay Rose		100	400.00	Unknown
Brown Thrasher		200		Unknown
Brown Thrasher On Carolina Rose		100	400.00	Unknown
Cardinal		200		Unknown
Cuckoo		200		Unknown
Flemish Floral		200		Unknown
Flower Market With Mockingbird				Unknown
Green Woodpecker		200		Unknown
Marguerite, French Daisy		200	400.00	Unknown
Marguerite, French Daisy, Blue		200	400.00	Unknown
Marguerite, Yellow Flowers		200	400.00	Unknown
Medicinal Herb, Digitalis Purpurea	1973	50	150.00	Unknown
Medicinal Herb, Gentiana Asclepiadea	1973	50	150.00	Unknown
Medicinal Herb, Papaver Somniforum	1973	50	150.00	Unknown
Medicinal Herb, Passiflora Exoniensis	1973	50	150.00	Unknown
Spotted-Breasted Oriole On Clematis		100	400.00	Unknown
Summer Flowers With Bluebird		200		Unknown
Kurz Bells				
Christmas	1973	500	50.00	50.00
Christmas	1974			65.00
Christmas	1975			75.00
Kurz Plates				
Christmas	1972	500	60.00	55.00 to 80.00
Christmas	1973	500	70.00	70.00
Christmas	1974	250		70.00
Mother's Day	1973	500	65.00	60.00 to 65.00
Kurz Tankards				
Bicentennial, Series Of Four, Each	1976			33.00

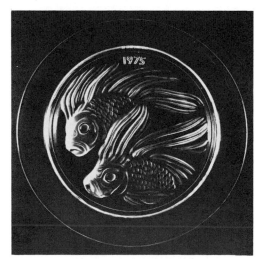
Lalique, Plate, Annual, Fish Duet, 1975

Lalique, Plate, Annual, American Eagle, 1976

Title	Issue Date	Number Issued	Issued Price	Current Price
Christmas	1973	500	55.00	55.00
Christmas	1974			70.00 to 80.00
Christmas	1975			80.00 to 90.00

La Scala, see Voteradici

Lake Shore Prints issues plates made by Gorham and Ridgewood. The Rockwell series started in 1973.

Lake Shore Plates

Butter Girl	1973	9433	14.95	55.00 to 95.00
Truth About Santa	1974	15141	19.50	24.00
Home From The Fields	1975	8500	24.50	15.00 to 25.00
A President's Wife	1976	2500	70.00	85.00

Lalique & Cie was established in 1909 by Rene Lalique in Paris. The glass was famous internationally. The present factory, located in Alsace, was opened in 1920. Limited edition annual plates were first issued in 1965. The production of the plates has been increased each year, with a range between 2,000 in 1965 to 7,500 in 1973.

Lalique Plates

Annual, Two Birds	1965	2000	25.00	1025.00 to 1750.00
Annual, Dreamrose	1966	5000	25.00	125.00 to 300.00
Annual, Fish*	1967	5000	30.00	100.00 to 250.00
Annual, Antelope*	1968	6000	30.00	50.00 to 150.00
Annual, Butterfly*	1969	6000	30.00	50.00 to 110.00
Annual, Peacock*	1970	6000	35.00	40.00 to 85.00
Annual, Owl*	1971	7000	35.00	35.00 to 77.50
Annual, Shell*	1972	7000	40.00	40.00 to 75.00
Annual, Jayling*	1973	7500	42.50	35.00 to 60.00
Annual, Silver Pennies*	1974	7500	47.50	41.00 to 47.50
Annual, Fish Duet*	1975	8000	50.00	50.00
Annual, American Eagle*	1976	8000	60.00	60.00

Lenox pottery was founded in Trenton, New Jersey, in 1889 by Walter Scott Lenox. It was later moved to its present site in Pomona, New Jersey. Lenox entered the limited edition market in 1970 with the introduction of the Edward Marshall Boehm Bird series.

Lenox, Boehm Birds, see also Boehm plates

Lenox Bowl

Patriot	1976			75.00 to 90.00

Lenox Pitcher

Romeo And Juliet	1976		75.00	75.00

Lenox Plates

American Tree, Douglas Fir	1976		60.00	121.00
American Tree, Scotch Pine	1977		60.00	60.00
Boehm, Bird Of Peace, Mute Swan	1972	5000	150.00	154.00 to 375.00
Boehm, Eaglet	1973	6000	165.00	100.00 to 175.00
Boehm, Honor America, Bald Eagle	1976	12000	85.00	85.00
Boehm Birds, Wood Thrush*	1970	Year	35.00	190.00 to 360.00
Boehm Birds, Goldfinch*	1971	Year	35.00	82.50 to 180.00
Boehm Birds, Mountain Bluebird*	1972	Year	37.50	50.00 to 100.00
Boehm Birds, Meadowlark	1973	Year	41.00	48.00 to 90.00
Boehm Birds, Hummingbirds	1974	Year	45.00	49.50 to 75.00
Boehm Birds, Redstarts	1975	Year	50.00	49.50 to 90.00
Boehm Birds, Cardinal*	1976		62.50	62.50
Boehm Birds, Robin	1977	Year	55.00	55.00
Boehm Wildlife, Raccoons	1973	Year	50.00	49.00 to 75.00
Boehm Wildlife, Foxes	1974	Year	52.00	41.00 to 60.00
Boehm Wildlife, Rabbits	1975	Year	58.50	39.99 to 64.00
Boehm Wildlife, Eastern Chipmunk	1976	Year	62.50	56.50 to 62.50
Boehm Wildlife, Beavers	1977	Year		67.50
Boehm Wildlife, Whitetail Deer*	1978	Year	70.00	70.00
States Of Confederacy, Set Of 10	1972	1201	900.00	500.00 to 1000.00

Lenox Tray

Romeo And Juliet	1977		80.00	80.00

Lenox Vases

Belleek, Walter Scott*	1974	5000	250.00	125.00 to 250.00

Lalique, Annual Plate, 1968

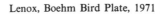
Lenox, Boehm Bird Plate, 1971

Lalique, Annual Plate, 1972

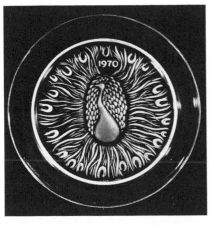

Lalique, Annual Plate, 1969

Lenox, Boehm Bird Plate, 1972

Lalique, Annual Plate, 1970

Lenox, Boehm Bird Plate, 1970

Lihs Lindner, Christmas Plate, 1973

Lihs Lindner, Christmas Plate, 1972

Lalique, Annual Plate, 1971

Lihs Lindner, Easter Plate, 1973

Lihs Lindner, Mother's Day Plate, 1972

Lenox, Plate, Boehm Birds, Cardinal, 1976

Lihs Lindner, Flag Plate, 1973

Lenox, Vase, Belleek, Walter Scott, 1974

Lladro, Plate, Christmas,
Christ Child, 1976

Lincoln Mint, Christmas Plate, 1972, Silver

Lihs Lindner, Mother's Day Plate, 1973

Lenox, Plate, Boehm Wildlife,
Whitetail Deer, 1978

Lincoln Mint, Dali Easter Plate,
1974

Lladro, Christmas Plate, 1972

Title	Issue Date	Number Issued	Issued Price	Current Price
Leyendecker Eggs				
Easter	1976		15.00	14.50 to 15.00
Leyendecker, see also Ridgewood, Royal Cornwall Plates				
Leyendecker Foundation Bells				
Christmas, Santa Loves You	1977	19500	22.50	22.50
Mother's Day, God Bless Mommy	1978	5000	22.50	22.50
Leyendecker Foundation Mugs				
Christmas, Santa Loves You	1977	19500	19.50	19.50
Leyendecker Foundation Plates				
Christmas, Santa Loves You	1977	19500	35.00	35.00
Mother's Day, God Bless Mommy	1978	10000	35.00	35.00

Lihs Lindner limited editions are designed by Mr. Helmut H. Lihs of Long Beach, California, and manufactured by the Lindner Company of Kueps Bavaria, Germany.

Title	Issue Date	Number Issued	Issued Price	Current Price
Lihs Lindner Bells				
Christmas, Drummer Boy	1973	3000	25.00	14.00 to 24.00
Christmas, Girl Caroler	1974	3000	24.00	15.00 to 24.00
Christmas, Sleigh Ride	1975	3000	32.00	32.00
Christmas, Joy Of Christmas	1976		32.00	32.00
Christmas Bell	1977	3000		28.00
Lihs Lindner Plates				
America The Beautiful, Set Of 6	1974	1500	250.00	Unknown
Bicentennial, Freedom Train	1976	1500		Unknown
Bicentennial, Spirit Of America	1976	3500	45.00	45.00
Christmas, Little Drummer Boy*	1972	6000	20.00	65.00 to 80.00
Christmas, We Wish You A Merry Christmas*	1973	6000	25.00	20.00 to 36.00
Christmas, Peace On Earth	1974	6000	25.00	15.00 to 30.00
Christmas, Christmas Cheer	1975	6000	30.00	26.95 to 32.00
Christmas, The Joy Of Christmas	1976	6000	30.00	30.00
Christmas, Have A Holly Jolly Christmas	1977	6000		30.00
Easter, Bunnies*	1973	1500	22.00	18.00 to 45.00
Easter, Springtime	1974	1500	25.00	13.00 to 25.00
Easter, Love For Easter	1975	1500	28.00	15.00 to 28.00
Flag*	1973	3000	60.00	45.00 to 125.00
Golden Spike Centennial, Set Of Two	1974	1500	40.00	35.00 to 40.00
Mother's Day, Mother And Child*	1972	1000	24.00	93.35 to 140.00
Mother's Day, Mother And Child*	1973	2000	24.00	10.00 to 25.00
Mother's Day, A Bouquet For Mother	1974	2000	25.00	14.00 to 30.00
Mother's Day, We Wish You Happiness, Mother	1975	2000	28.00	18.00 to 28.00
Playmates, Timmy And His Best Pal	1976	5000	45.00	45.00
Playmates, Heidi And Her Friend	1977	5000	45.00	45.00
Union Pacific	1972	1500	22.00	16.50 to 25.00
Union Pacific, Big Boy	1973	1500	25.00	16.50 to 25.00
Lihs Lindner Vases				
Christmas, Poinsettia	1972	500	85.00	85.00

Limoges, see Royal Limoges

Limoges, Dali plates, see Puiforcat

The Lincoln Mint of Chicago, Illinois, entered the limited edition field in 1971. Gold, silver, and vermeil plates.

Title	Issue Date	Number Issued	Issued Price	Current Price
Lincoln Mint Bells				
Alice In Daliland, Sterling	1972	5000	200.00	60.00 to 100.00
Christmas, The Carolers, Silver	1977	Year		25.00
Christmas, The Carolers, Gold	1977	Year		35.00
Norman Rockwell, Downhill Daring	1975	Year	25.00	25.00
Thanksgiving, Silver Plate	1977			25.00
Lincoln Mint Plates				
Christmas, Madonna Della Seggiola, Gold Plate	1972	125	150.00	150.00
Christmas, Madonna Della Seggiola, Silver*	1972	3000	125.00	40.00 to 55.00
Dali, Unicorn Dyonisiaque, Gold	1971	100	1500.00	1500.00
Dali, Unicorn Dyonisiaque, Silver	1971	5000	100.00	49.00 to 105.00
Dali, Dyonisiaque Et Pallas Athena, Gold	1972	300	2000.00	2000.00
Dali, Dyonisiaque Et Pallas Athena, Gold Plate	1972	2500	150.00	100.00 to 150.00

Lladro, Christmas Plate, 1971

Lladro, Mother's Day Plate, 1971

Lladro, Mother's Day Plate, 1972

Lladro, Mother's Day Plate, 1973

Title	Issue Date	Number Issued	Issued Price	Current Price
Dali, Dyonisiaque Et Pallas Athena, Silver	1972	7500	125.00	50.00 to 85.00
Dali, Christmas Cross, Gold	1977			35.00
Dali, Christmas, Gold	1977	5000		225.00
Dali, Christmas, Silver	1977	10000		175.00
Dali, Christmas Cross, Silver	1977			25.00
Dali, Easter Christ, Gold Plate	1972	10000	200.00	150.00 to 200.00
Dali, Easter Christ, Silver	1972	20000	150.00	65.00 to 127.00
Dali, Easter Christ, Pewter*	1974		45.00	45.00
Mother's Day, Collies, Silver	1972		125.00	34.95 to 60.00

Lindner Lihs, see Lihs Lindner

Lionel Barrymore, see Gorham

Walt Litt Plates

Title	Issue Date	Number Issued	Issued Price	Current Price
Christmas, Madonna & Child*	1978	1000	200.00	200.00

Lladro Porcelain factory of Tabernes Blanques, Spain, produced its first limited edition Mother's Day plate in 1971. The plates are a combination of bas-relief white bisque with an underglaze blue border. Lladro also produces a large line of limited and nonlimited edition sculptures.

See listing for Lladro in Figurine section

Lladro Plates

Title	Issue Date	Number Issued	Issued Price	Current Price
Christmas, Caroling*	1971	800	27.50	20.00 to 40.00
Christmas, Carolers*	1972	Year	35.00	20.00 to 35.00
Christmas, Boy And Girl	1973	Year	45.00	24.00 to 60.00
Christmas, Carolers	1974	Year	55.00	30.00 to 55.00
Christmas, Cherubs	1975	Year	60.00	65.00
Christmas, Christ Child*	1976	Year	60.00	39.95 to 60.00
Christmas	1977	Year	67.50	67.50
Christmas	1978	Year	80.00	80.00
Mother's Day, Kiss Of The Child*	1971	800	27.50	55.00 to 100.00
Mother's Day, Bird & Chicks*	1972	3500	27.50	20.00 to 42.00
Mother's Day, Mother And Children*	1973	2000	45.00	35.00 to 70.00
Mother's Day, Mother Nursing	1974	Year	45.00	65.00 to 125.00
Mother's Day, Mother & Child	1975	Year	60.00	60.00
Mother's Day, Tender Vigil*	1976	Year	60.00	60.00
Mother's Day, Mother & Daughter	1977	Year	67.50	67.50
Mother's Day	1978	Year	80.00	80.00

Lladro Vases

Title	Issue Date	Number Issued	Issued Price	Current Price
Floral, Blue Vase, 15 3/4 In.		200	900.00	Unknown
Floral, Red Vase, 15 1/4 In.		200	900.00	Unknown
Floral, Tan Vase, 14 3/4 In.		200	900.00	900.00
Paradise		500	800.00	1100.00
Rooster, Floral		500	900.00	1250.00
Vase, Blue & White, 19 1/4 In.		300	900.00	1750.00
Vase, Branches, Dark Blue Branch, 19 1/4 In.		150		1500.00
Vase, Peach Blossoms, 19 1/4 In.		150		1250.00
Vase, Peacocks, 29 1/4 In.		150	1800.00	2000.00
Vase, Three Blossoms, 19 1/4 In.		150		1800.00

Lockhart Bird plates, see Pickard

Lori Bells

Title	Issue Date	Number Issued	Issued Price	Current Price
Christmas	1973	1000	17.50	13.35 to 20.00
Christmas	1974	1000		16.95 to 19.95
Christmas	1975	1000		13.35 to 20.00

Loup, Jean-Paul, see Jean-Paul Loup

Lund & Clausen Plates

Title	Issue Date	Number Issued	Issued Price	Current Price
Astronaut, Moon Landing	1969			4.50 to 10.00
Astronaut	1971			9.00 to 14.00
Christmas, Deer Park	1971		13.50	2.99 to 10.00
Christmas, Stave Church	1972		13.50	8.00 to 13.50
Christmas, Scene	1973			13.50
Mother's Day, Rose	1970			5.00 to 20.00
Mother's Day, Forget-Me-Nots	1971			5.00 to 17.00
Mother's Day, Bluebell	1972			12.50 to 17.00
Mother's Day, Lilies-Of-The-Valley	1973		16.00	16.00

Lundberg Vase

Title	Issue Date	Number Issued	Issued Price	Current Price
School Of Fish		250		195.00

Lladro, Plate, Mother's Day, Tender Vigil, 1976

Walt Litt, Christmas Plate,
Madonna & Child, 1978

Mallek, Christmas Plate, 1972,
Navidad En Mexico

Mallek, Navajo Christmas Plate, 1972

Mallek, Navajo Christmas Plate, 1973

Mallek, Christmas Plate, 1973, Game Bird

Marmot, Plate, Mother's Day,
Ducks, 1976

Mallek, Christmas Plate, 1972, Game Bird

Marmot, Plate, Christmas,
Dutch Sea Village, 1976

Marmot, Plate, Christmas,
Covey Of Quail, 1975

Marmot, Christmas Plate, 1972

Marmot, Mother's Day Plate, 1972

Marmot, Mother's Day Plate, 1973

Marmot, Plate, Mother's Day,
Raccoons, 1975

Title	Issue Date	Number Issued	Issued Price	Current Price

The first Kay Mallek Navajo Christmas plate was made in 1971. The limited edition plaques and plates are designed by contemporary Arizona artists and marketed through Kay Mallek Creations of Tucson, Arizona.

Mallek Mugs

Title	Issue Date	Number Issued	Issued Price	Current Price
Christmas, Game Bird, Gambel Quail	1972		20.00	20.00
Christmas, Game Bird	1973		20.00	20.00

Mallek Plaques

Title	Issue Date	Number Issued	Issued Price	Current Price
Bunnies	1972	500	60.00	60.00
Easter, Chicks In The Nest	1973	500	60.00	60.00
Navajo Thanksgiving	1972	500	60.00	60.00

Mallek Plates

Title	Issue Date	Number Issued	Issued Price	Current Price
A-B-C, Mice	1975	1000	15.00	15.00
A-B-C, Rabbits	1974	1000	15.00	15.00
Amish Harvest Plate	1972	1000	17.00	17.00 to 22.00
Chinese Lunar Calendar, Year Of The Rat	1972	1000	15.00	15.00 to 20.00
Chinese Lunar Calendar, Year Of The Ox	1973	1000	15.00	15.00 to 17.50
Chinese Lunar Calendar, Year Of The Rabbit	1974	1000	15.00	15.00
Christmas, Alaska Canada	1977	1000	15.00	15.00
Christmas, Game Bird, Gambel Quail*	1972	1000	15.00	15.00 to 20.00
Christmas, Game Bird*	1973	1000	15.00	15.00 to 17.00
Christmas, Game Bird, Owl & Cactus	1974	1000	15.00	15.00
Christmas, Game Bird, Chinese Wood Duck	1975	1000	15.00	15.00
Christmas, Game Bird, Wild Turkey	1976	1000	15.00	15.00
Christmas, Game Bird, Mallard	1977	1000	15.00	15.00
Christmas, Game Bird, Canadian Geese	1978	1000	15.00	15.00
Christmas, Navidad En Mexico*	1972	500	15.00	15.00 to 20.00
Kewpie Doll	1976	1000	15.00	9.00 to 15.00
Mexican Christmas	1973	1000	15.00	18.00 to 20.00
Mexican Christmas	1974	1000	18.00	15.00 to 20.00
Mexican Christmas	1975	1000	18.00	20.00
Mexican Christmas	1976	1000	20.00	20.00
Mexican Christmas	1977	1000	20.00	20.00
Mexican Christmas, Christ In The Manger	1972	1000	15.00	15.00
Navajo Christmas, Indian Wise Men, R.Cree*	1971	1000	15.00	200.00 to 250.00
Navajo Christmas, On The Reservation*	1972	2000	17.00	18.00 to 22.50
Navajo Christmas, Hoke Denetsosie*	1973	2000	17.00	18.00 to 20.00
Navajo Christmas, Monument Valley, T.Draper	1974	2000		18.00 to 20.00
Navajo Christmas, Coming Home For Christmas	1975	2000	18.00	18.00 to 20.00
Navajo Christmas, Deer With Rainbow	1976	2000	20.00	20.00
Navajo Christmas, Goat Herders	1977	2000	20.00	20.00
Navajo Christmas, Hogan Christmas	1978	2000	20.00	20.00

Manjundo Company of Kyoto, Japan, was founded in 1772.

Manjundo Plates

Title	Issue Date	Number Issued	Issued Price	Current Price
Chinese Lunar Calendar, Year Of The Rat	1972	5000	15.00	15.00
Chinese Lunar Calendar, Year Of The Ox	1973	5000	15.00	15.00

Marc Chagall plate, see Chagall

The Mark Twain plate series is made by Ridgewood China Co. of Burbank, California.

Mark Twain Plates

Title	Issue Date	Number Issued	Issued Price	Current Price
Huck Finn	1973	15000	45.00	25.00 to 45.00
Life On The Mississippi, Pair, Each	1974	3500		45.00
Tom Gave Up The Brush	1973	15000	45.00	25.00 to 45.00

Marmot Plates

Title	Issue Date	Number Issued	Issued Price	Current Price
Christmas, Polar Bear	1970	5000	13.00	9.00 to 32.00
Christmas, Buffalo	1971	6000	14.00	7.50 to 20.00
Christmas, Boy & Grandfather*	1972	5000	16.00	13.00 to 28.00
Christmas, Snowman*	1973	2000	20.00	10.00 to 34.00
Christmas, Dancing Children	1974	2000	24.00	10.00 to 24.00
Christmas, Covey Of Quail*	1975	2000	30.00	20.00 to 30.00
Christmas, Dutch Sea Village*	1976	2000	40.00	40.00
Father's Day, Stag	1970	3500	12.00	50.00 to 100.00
Father's Day, Horse*	1971	3500	12.50	15.00 to 38.00
Mother's Day, Seal*	1972	6000	16.00	10.00 to 28.00
Mother's Day, Polar Bear*	1973	2000	20.00	70.00 to 140.00
Mother's Day, Penguins*	1974	2000	24.00	16.00 to 30.00

Title	Issue Date	Number Issued	Issued Price	Current Price
Mother's Day, Raccoons*	1975	2000	30.00	18.00 to 30.00
Mother's Day, Ducks*	1976	2000	40.00	40.00
President, George Washington*	1971	1500	25.00	19.95 to 30.00
President, Thomas Jefferson	1972	1500	25.00	20.00 to 30.00
President, John Adams	1973	1500	25.00	25.00

Marquise Commemorative Plates

Preserving Our Heritage, Set Of 3	1975	1000	95.00	95.00

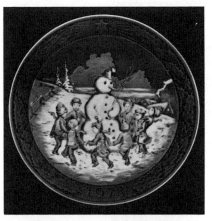

Marmot, Christmas Plate, 1973

The term Mary Gregory glass refers to any glass decorated with a special type of white silhouette figure. Antique Mary Gregory glass was made between 1870 and 1910. The modern limited edition type, introduced in 1973, discontinued in 1976, was made in Czechoslovakia.

Mary Gregory Bells

Christmas	1973	1000	17.50	22.50
Christmas	1975	500		13.35 to 20.00
Christmas, Cranberry	1976	500	21.50	16.50 to 21.50

Mary Gregory Plates

Christmas	1973	1000	55.00	27.50 to 36.65
Christmas	1974	1000	60.00	40.00 to 60.00
Christmas	1975	1000	60.00	40.00 to 60.00
Christmas	1976	500	65.00	65.00
Mother's Day	1973	500	55.00	36.50 to 55.00
Mother's Day	1974	300	60.00	40.00 to 60.00
Mother's Day	1975	300	60.00	40.00 to 60.00
Mother's Day	1976	500	65.00	65.00

Marmot, Mother's Day Plate, 1974

The Meka Company of Copenhagen, Denmark, was started in 1940 by Mr. Kage Meyer. The company produces tableware, jewelry, and trophies. Limited edition spoons were first made in 1966. The spoons are limited to the production of one year.

Meka Spoons

Christmas**	1966	Year	5.00	10.00 to 15.00
Christmas**	1967	Year	5.00	7.50 to 10.00
Christmas**	1968	Year	5.00	6.00 to 7.00
Christmas**	1969	Year	5.00	5.00
Christmas**	1970	Year	6.00	6.00 to 7.00
Christmas**	1971	Year	6.00	6.00
Christmas**	1972	Year	6.00	6.00
Christmas**	1973	Year	6.00	6.00
Christmas**	1974	Year	6.00	6.00
Christmas	1975		6.50	6.50
Christmas	1976		6.50	6.50
Mother's Day**	1970	5000	5.00	15.00 to 20.00
Mother's Day**	1971	5000	5.00	9.00 to 12.00
Mother's Day**	1972	5000	5.00	8.00 to 10.00
Mother's Day**	1973	5000	7.50	7.50
Mother's Day**	1974	5000	7.50	7.50
Mother's Day	1975		8.00	8.00
Mother's Day	1976		8.00	8.00

Marmot, Father's Day Plate, 1971

Marmot, President Plate, 1971

Metawa pewter limited editions are made by the N. V. Metawa Company of Tiel, Holland. Each limited edition piece is marked with the 'Water Gate' hallmark, a symbol used on Dutch pewter since 1647. Limited editions were first made in 1972.

Metawa Plates

Christmas, Ice Skaters	1972	3000	30.00	15.00 to 36.00
Christmas, One-Horse Open Sleigh	1973	1500	30.00	30.00
Christmas, Sailboat	1974		35.00	Unknown

Metropolitan Museum of Art Plates

Treasures Of Tutankhamun	1977	2500	150.00	150.00

Mettlach Plaque

Mother's Day	1978	15000	100.00	100.00

Mettlach Plates

Christmas	1977	15000	175.00	269.00
Christmas, Wisemen	1978	15000	175.00	175.00

Michelsen,
Christmas Fork And Spoon,
1969

Michelsen,
Christmas Fork And Spoon,
1970

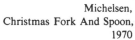

Michelsen,
Christmas Fork And Spoon,
1971

Michelsen,
Christmas Fork And Spoon,
1972

Michelsen,
Christmas Fork And Spoon,
1973

Title	Issue Date	Number Issued	Issued Price	Current Price
Mettlach Steins				
Stein	1977	3000	200.00	200.00

A. Michelsen Silversmiths of Copenhagen, Denmark, was established in 1841. Annual Christmas spoons and forks were introduced in 1910. The spoons and forks are made of enamel and gold plate on sterling silver.

Michelsen Forks

Title	Issue Date	Number Issued	Issued Price	Current Price
Christmas, Star Of Bethlehem	1910			160.00
Christmas, The Infant Christ	1911			160.00
Christmas, Christmas Bells	1912			160.00
Christmas, Christmas Scenery	1913			160.00
Christmas, Christmas Angel	1914			160.00
Christmas, Three Kings Of Cologne	1915			160.00
Christmas, The Madonna	1916			160.00
Christmas, Epiphany	1917			160.00
Christmas, Mistletoe	1918			160.00
Christmas, Peace On Earth	1919			160.00
Christmas, The Mill Of Dybbol	1920			69.00
Christmas, Christmas Boat	1921			69.00
Christmas, Holly	1922			34.00
Christmas, Cathedral In Copenhagen	1923			69.00
Christmas, Sheaf Of Grain	1924			69.00
Christmas, Poinsettia	1925			69.00
Christmas, Organ Pipes	1926			69.00
Christmas, Spire Of Famous Church, Copenhagen	1927			69.00
Christmas, Epiphyllum	1928			69.00
Christmas, Christmas Rose	1929			69.00
Christmas, Christmas In Port	1930			68.00
Christmas, Star Of Bethlehem	1931			68.00
Christmas, Children Around Christmas Tree	1932			68.00
Christmas, Little Match Girl	1933			68.00
Christmas, Holy Night	1934			68.00
Christmas, Kneeling Shepherd	1935			68.00
Christmas, Christmas Candle	1936			68.00
Christmas, Birds In The Christmas Sheaf	1937			68.00
Christmas, Snowberries	1938			68.00
Christmas, Gift-Laden Christmas Tree	1939			68.00
Christmas, Star Of Bethlehem	1940			67.00
Christmas, Mistletoe	1941			67.00
Christmas, Madonna And Child	1942			67.00
Christmas, Dove Of Peace	1943			67.00
Christmas, Hearty Holiday Spirit	1944			67.00
Christmas, Snow Crystals	1945			67.00
Christmas, Holly	1946			67.00
Christmas, Falling Snowflakes	1947			67.00
Christmas, Christmas Ram	1948			67.00
Christmas, Candles Of Advent	1949			67.00
Christmas, Winter Forest	1950			66.00
Christmas, Colorful Christmas	1951			66.00
Christmas, Santa And The Reindeer	1952			66.00
Christmas, The Herald Angels	1953			66.00
Christmas, Coronets	1954			66.00
Christmas, Poinsettia	1955			66.00
Christmas, Snow Flowers	1956			66.00
Christmas, Danish Yule-Nisses	1957			66.00
Christmas, The Wise Men From The East	1958			66.00
Christmas, The Lucia Bride	1959			66.00
Christmas, Winter Solstice	1960			65.00
Christmas, Organ Pipes	1961			65.00
Christmas, Madonna And Child	1962			65.00
Christmas, Santa's Village	1963			65.00
Christmas, Orion	1964			65.00
Christmas, The Christmas Tree	1965			65.00
Christmas, Flight Into Egypt	1966			65.00
Christmas, Splendor Of Yule	1967			65.00
Christmas, A Mother's Heart	1968			65.00
Christmas, Greenlander*	1969			65.00
Christmas, Mr.Snowman's Christmas Tree**	1970			64.00
Chrittmas, Golden Universe*	1971			64.00

Title	Issue Date	Number Issued	Issued Price	Current Price
Christmas, Herald**	1972			64.00
Christmas, Solstice And Family**	1973	Year		64.00
Christmas, Blue Bird	1974	Year	48.00	64.00
Christmas, Shooting Star*	1975	Year	60.00	64.00
Christmas, Snow Crystal	1976	Year	60.00	60.00
Christmas, Winter Rose**	1977	Year	64.00	64.00
Christmas, Solstice**	1978	Year	64.00	64.00
Commemorative, King Christian IX	1898			60.00
Commemorative, Wedding Of Prince Christian	1898			60.00
Commemorative, Four Generations Of Kings	1899			60.00
Commemorative, King Christian IX, Birthday	1903			60.00
Commemorative, Christian IX, Anniversary	1903			60.00
Commemorative, Falcon Of Iceland	1907			60.00
Commemorative, King Christian X, Accession	1912			60.00
Commemorative, Baltic Exhibition	1914			60.00
Commemorative, Constitution	1915			60.00
Commemorative, Reunion Of Denmark And Slésvig	1920			60.00
Commemorative, Silver Wedding, Christian X	1923			60.00
Commemorative, Wedding Of Prince Knud	1933			60.00
Commemorative, Wedding, Prince Frederik	1935			60.00
Commemorative, King Christian X, Anniversary	1937			60.00
Commemorative, King Christian X, Birthday	1940			60.00
Commemorative, King Frederik IX, Birthday	1949			55.00
Commemorative, Princess Margrethe, Birthday	1958			55.00
Commemorative, Anniversary, Frederik, Ingrid	1960			55.00
Commemorative, Princess Anne Marie, Wedding	1964			55.00
Commemorative, Princess Margrethe, Wedding	1967			55.00
Commemorative, Princess Benedikte, Wedding	1968			55.00
Commemorative, Danish Flag, 750th Birthday	1969			55.00
Commemorative, King Frederik IX, Birthday	1969			55.00
Commemorative, Queen Ingrid, Birthday	1970			55.00
Commemorative, Queen Margrethe, Accession	1972			55.00

Michelsen Spoons

Title	Issue Date	Number Issued	Issued Price	Current Price
Christmas, Star Of Bethelhem**	1910			160.00
Christmas, The Infant Christ**	1911			160.00
Christmas, Christmas Bells**	1912			160.00
Christmas, Christmas Scenery**	1913			160.00
Christmas, Christmas Angel**	1914			160.00
Christmas, Three Kings Of Cologne**	1915			200.00
Christmas, The Madonna**	1916			160.00
Christmas, Epiphany**	1917			160.00
Christmas, Mistletoe**	1918			160.00
Christmas, Peace On Earth**	1919			160.00
Christmas, The Mill Of Dybbol**	1920			69.00
Christmas, Christmas Boat**	1921			69.00
Christmas, Holly**	1922			34.50 to 69.00
Christmas, Cathedral In Copenhagen**	1923			69.00
Christmas, Sheaf Of Grain**	1924			69.00
Christmas, Poinsettia**	1925			69.00
Christmas, Organ Pipes**	1926			69.00
Christmas, Spire Of Famous Church**	1927			69.00
Christmas, Epiphyllum**	1928			69.00
Christmas, Christmas Rose**	1929			69.00
Christmas, Christmas In Port**	1930			68.00
Christmas, Star Of Bethlehem**	1931			68.00
Christmas, Children Around Christmas Tree**	1932			68.00
Christmas, Little Match Girl**	1933			68.00
Christmas, Holy Night**	1934			68.00
Christmas, Kneeling Shepherd**	1935			68.00
Christmas, Christmas Candle**	1936			68.00
Christmas, Birds In The Christmas Sheaf**	1937			68.00
Christmas, Snowberries**	1938			68.00
Christmas, Gift-Laden Christmas Tree**	1939			68.00
Christmas, Star Of Bethlehem**	1940			67.00
Christmas, Mistletoe**	1941			67.00
Christmas, Madonna And Child**	1942			67.00
Christmas, Dove Of Peace**	1943			67.00
Christmas, Hearty Holiday Spirit**	1944			67.00
Christmas, Snow Crystals**	1945			67.00

Michelsen, Fork,
Christmas,
Shooting Star, 1975

Michelsen, Christmas Spoons, 1920 - 1929

Moser, Mother's Day Plate, 1971

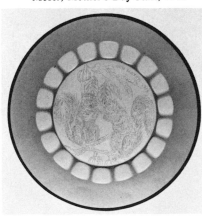

Moser, Mother's Day Plate, 1973

Title	Issue Date	Number Issued	Issued Price	Current Price
Christmas, Holly**	1946			67.00
Christmas, Falling Snowflakes**	1947			67.00
Christmas, Christmas Ram**	1948			67.00
Christmas, Candles Of Advent**	1949			67.00
Christmas, Winter Forest**	1950			66.00
Christmas, Colorful Christmas**	1951			66.00
Christmas, Santa And The Reindeer**	1952			66.00
Christmas, The Herald Angels**	1953			66.00
Christmas, Coronets**	1954			66.00
Christmas, Poinsettia**	1955			66.00
Christmas, Snow Flowers**	1956			66.00
Christmas, Danish Yule-Nisses**	1957			66.00
Christmas, Wise Men From The East**	1958			66.00
Christmas, The Lucia Bride**	1959			66.00
Christmas, Winter Solstice**	1960			65.00
Christmas, Organ Pipes**	1961			65.00
Christmas, Madonna And Child**	1962			65.00
Christmas, Santa's Village**	1963			65.00
Christmas, Orion**	1964			65.00
Christmas, The Christmas Tree**	1965			65.00
Christmas, Flight Into Egypt**	1966			65.00
Christmas, Splendor Of Yule**	1967			65.00
Christmas, A Mother's Heart**	1968			65.00
Christmas, Greenlander**	1969			65.00
Christmas, Mr.Snowman's Christmas Tree	1970			64.00
Christmas, Golden Universe**	1971			64.00
Christmas, Herald**	1972			64.00
Christmas, Solstice And Family**	1973	Year		64.00
Christmas, Blue Birds	1974	Year		64.00
Christmas, Shooting Star	1975	Year		64.00
Christmas, Snow Crystal	1976	Year		60.00
Christmas, Winter Rose**	1977	Year	64.00	64.00
Christmas, Solstice**	1978	Year	64.00	64.00
Commemorative, King Christian IX	1898			60.00
Commemorative, Wedding Of Prince Christian	1898			60.00
Commemorative, Four Generations Of Kings	1899			60.00
Commemorative, King Christian IX, Birthday	1903			60.00
Commemorative, Christian IX, Anniversary	1903			60.00
Commemorative, Falcon Of Iceland	1907			60.00
Commemorative, King Christian X, Accession	1912			60.00
Commemorative, Baltic Exhibition	1914			60.00
Commemorative, Constitution	1915			60.00
Commemorative, Reunion Of Denmark And Slesvig	1920			60.00
Commemorative, Silver Wedding, Christian X	1923			60.00
Commemorative, Wedding Of Prince Knud	1933			60.00
Commemorative, Wedding, Prince Frederik	1935			60.00
Commemorative, King Christian X, Anniversary	1937			60.00
Commemorative, King Christian X, Birthday	1940			60.00
Commemorative, King Frederik IX, Birthday	1949			55.00
Commemorative, Princess Margrethe, Birthday	1958			55.00
Commemorative, Anniversary, Frederik, Ingrid	1960			55.00
Commemorative, Princess Anne Marie, Wedding	1964			55.00
Commemorative, Princess Margrethe, Wedding	1967			55.00
Commemorative, Princess Benedikte, Wedding	1968			55.00
Commemorative, Danish Flag, 750th Birthday	1969			55.00
Commemorative, King Frederik IX, Birthday	1969			55.00
Commemorative, Queen Ingrid, Birthday	1970			55.00
Commemorative, Queen Margrethe, Accession	1972			55.00

Mickey Mouse, see Schmid, Walt Disney

Millous, Pierre, see Cartier

Mingolla Plates

Title	Issue Date	Number Issued	Issued Price	Current Price
Christmas, Enamel On Copper	1973	1000	95.00	149.50 to 275.00
Christmas, Enamel On Copper	1974	1000	110.00	125.00 to 200.00
Christmas, Enamel On Copper	1975	1000		90.00 to 110.00
Christmas, Enamel On Copper	1976	1000	125.00	125.00
Christmas, Enamel On Copper, Childhood Scene	1977	2500	200.00	200.00
Christmas, Porcelain	1974	5000	35.00	17.75 to 30.00
Christmas, Porcelain	1975	5000	35.00	18.50 to 24.50

National Trust, Porcelain Boxes, Set Of 5, 1976

Title	Issue Date	Number Issued	Issued Price	Current Price
Christmas, Porcelain	1976	5000	24.50	24.50
Christmas, Porcelain, Winter Wonderland	1977	5000	65.00	65.00

Miss America, see Ridgewood, Plates

Moppets, see Gorham

Moser, now known as Karlovy Vary Glassworks-Moser of Czechoslovakia, was founded by Kolomon Moser in 1857 at Karlsbad, Czechoslovakia. Moser became famous for enameled art nouveau glass around the turn of the century. Limited edition plates, introduced in 1970, are of copper wheel cut crystal.

Moser Plates

Title	Issue Date	Number Issued	Issued Price	Current Price
Annual, Hradcany Castle, Lavender	1970	400	75.00	450.00 to 599.00
Annual, Karlstein Castle, Pale Green	1971	1365	75.00	55.00 to 140.00
Annual, Old Town Hall	1972	1000	85.00	87.50 to 130.00
Annual, Capricorn	1973	300	90.00	85.00 to 200.00
Mother's Day, Peacocks, Pale Green*	1971	350	75.00	299.00 to 440.00
Mother's Day, Butterflies, Cobalt Blue	1972	750	85.00	120.00 to 240.00
Mother's Day, Squirrels*	1973	200	90.00	84.00 to 100.00

Mueller Plates

Title	Issue Date	Number Issued	Issued Price	Current Price
Christmas, Christmas In The Tyrol	1971	Year	20.00	10.00 to 18.00
Christmas, Christmas Messenger	1972	Year	15.00	15.00
Christmas, Couple Bringing Home Tree	1973	Year	20.00	20.00
Christmas, Family Trimming Tree	1974	Year	25.00	16.00
Christmas, Family On Christmas Morning	1975	Year	27.50	18.35
Christmas, Christmas Fire	1976	Year	28.50	28.50
Christmas, Ice Skating	1977	Year	28.50	28.50

Mueller Steins

Title	Issue Date	Number Issued	Issued Price	Current Price
Christmas, Christmas In The Tyrol	1971	Year	20.00	17.00 to 20.00
Christmas, Christmas Messenger	1972	Year	20.00	17.50 to 22.50
Christmas, Bringing Home Tree	1973	Year	35.00	35.00
Christmas, Decorating The Tree	1974	Year	35.00	35.00
Christmas, Christmas Gifts	1975	Year	35.00	35.00
Christmas, Christmas Fire	1976	Year	37.00	37.00
Christmas, Ice Skating	1977	Year	37.00	37.00
Father's Day, Happy Days	1972	Year	20.00	20.00
Father's Day, Fishing With Children	1974	Year		20.00
Father's Day, Climbing With Children	1975	Year	35.00	35.00
Father's Day, Father & Child	1976	Year		37.00
Father's Day, Jubilation	1977	Year		37.00

N. C. Wyeth, see George Washington Mint

National Trust Boxes

Title	Issue Date	Number Issued	Issued Price	Current Price
Porcelain Boxes, Set Of 5*	1976	2500	600.00	600.00

Navajo Christmas plate, see Mallek

New World, see Seven Seas

Noritake marked porcelain was first made in Japan after 1904. Noritake limited editions were introduced in 1971.

Noritake Bells

Title	Issue Date	Number Issued	Issued Price	Current Price
Christmas, Holly	1972		15.00	8.00 to 18.50
Christmas, Partridge In Pear Tree	1973		15.00	13.35 to 20.00
Christmas, Two Turtle Doves**	1974			12.00 to 18.50
Christmas, Three French Hens	1975		18.00	16.95 to 18.00
Christmas, Four Colly Birds	1976		18.00	17.50
Christmas, Five Golden Rings	1977		18.00	18.00
Christmas, Six Geese Alaying	1978			Unknown
Kissing	1975	5000		25.00

Noritake Cups

Title	Issue Date	Number Issued	Issued Price	Current Price
Mother's Day	1973		15.00	15.00
Mother's Day**	1974	4000	17.50	17.50
Mother's Day, Carnations	1975			20.00
Mother's Day, Forget-Me-Nots	1976			20.00

Noritake Eggs

Title	Issue Date	Number Issued	Issued Price	Current Price
Easter, Bunnies	1971	Year	10.00	38.50 to 79.50
Easter, Easter Lilies	1972	Year	10.00	15.00 to 25.00
Easter, Hen & Chicks*	1973	Year	10.00	10.00 to 22.50

Michelsen, Christmas Spoons, 1940 - 1949

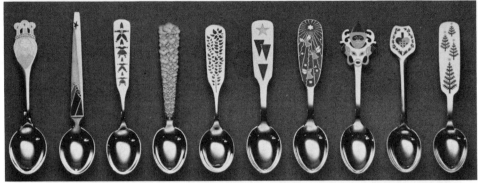

Michelsen, Christmas Spoons, 1950 - 1959

Michelsen, Christmas Spoons, 1960 - 1969

Noritake, Easter Egg, 1973

Norwegian Pewter,
Plate, Christmas, Vestfold,
Norway, 1975

Norwegian Pewter, Plate,
Christmas, Lofoten,
Norway, 1976

Norwegian Pewter,
Plate, Christmas, 1977

Norwegian Pewter,
Plate, Christmas, 1978

Title	Issue Date	Number Issued	Issued Price	Current Price
Easter, Easter Basket	1974	Year	11.00	10.00 to 20.00
Easter, Ducks	1975	Year	15.00	8.00 to 15.00
Easter, Easter Bonnet	1976	Year	15.00	12.95 to 15.00
Easter, Lambs	1977	Year	15.00	15.00
Easter, Daffodils	1978	Year	17.50	17.50

Noritake Hearts

Valentine's Day, Dove And Key	1973	10000	20.00	9.00 to 11.50
Valentine's Day, Come To Me	1974	5000	15.00	13.95 to 17.50
Valentine's Day, Cupid	1975	3500	15.00	15.00
Valentine's Day, Valentine Letter	1976		15.00	15.00
Valentine's Day	1977		15.00	15.00
Valentine's Day, Butterflies	1978		15.00	15.00

Noritake Mugs

Father's Day	1972		20.00	9.95 to 15.00
Father's Day	1973		20.00	11.65 to 20.00
Father's Day**	1974	2500	17.50	13.35 to 20.00
Father's Day	1975		20.00	13.35 to 20.00
Father's Day	1976		20.00	16.50 to 20.00
Mother's Day	1973		16.00	7.00 to 20.00
Mother's Day	1974		17.50	11.65 to 17.50
Mother's Day	1975		20.00	13.35 to 20.00
Mother's Day	1976		20.00	20.00

Noritake Ornaments

Mother's Day, Doe & Fawn	1974	2800	40.00	40.00

Norman Rockwell, see Franklin Mint, Gorham, Rockwell Society, Royal Devon.

Norse Plates, also called Historic Norway, are made in Norway.

Norse Plates

Nidaros Cathedral	1970		12.50	17.50
Wooden Stave Church	1971		12.50	15.00
Gokstad Viking Ship	1972		13.00	19.00
Akershus Castle	1973			18.00
Haakon's Hall	1974			18.00
Norwegian Constitution	1975			18.00
Parliament Building	1976			20.00
Building	1977			20.00

North Dakota Auto Club Plates

Early Morning Hours	1974	500	17.50	17.50
Grassy Butte Post Office	1974	500	17.50	17.50
Country Doctor	1975	500	18.50	18.50
Old School House	1975	500	18.50	18.50

Norwegian Pewter

Christmas, Stave Church At Borgund, Norway	1973	10000	25.00	350.00 to 400.00
Christmas, Telemark, Norway	1974	10000	30.00	40.00
Christmas, Vestfold, Norway*	1975	20000	30.00	40.00
Christmas, Lofoten, Norway*	1976	20000	30.00	35.00
Christmas*	1977	20000	35.00	35.00
Christmas*	1978	20000	37.50	37.50

OMA Plates

Western Series, Bronco Buster	1972	500	100.00	Unknown
Western Series, Chuck Wagon	1972	500	100.00	Unknown
Western Series, Round-Up	1972	500	100.00	Unknown

Orrefors Glassworks, located in the Swedish province of Smaland, was established in 1916. Collector's plates were introduced in 1970.

Orrefors Plates

Annual, Notre Dame Cathedral	1970	Year	45.00	18.00 to 50.00
Annual, Westminster Abbey	1971	Year	50.00	18.00 to 60.00
Annual, Basilica Di San Marco	1972	Year	50.00	38.00 to 50.00
Annual, Cologne Cathedral*	1973	Year	50.00	29.00 to 50.00
Annual, Rue De La Victoire	1974	Year	60.00	28.00 to 50.00
Annual, Basilica Of San Peitro, Rome	1975	Year	85.00	29.00 to 49.50
Annual, Christ Church, Philadelphia	1976	Year	85.00	85.00
Christmas, Three Kings*	1973	6000	35.00	20.00

Orrefors, Christmas Plate, 1973

Orrefors, Annual Plate, 1973

Orrefors, Mother's Day Plate, 1973

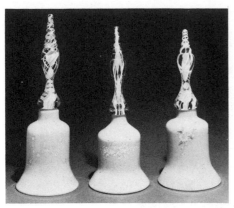

Pairpoint, Bell, French Blue, Decorated, 1975

Picasso, Plate, Tete En Forme D'Horloge

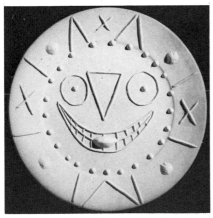

Picasso, Plate, Horloge A La Langue

Picasso, Plate, Visage A La Grille, White

Title	Issue Date	Number Issued	Issued Price	Current Price
Christmas, Shepherds	1974	4000	40.00	28.00 to 35.00
Christmas, No Room At Inn	1975	6000	40.00	40.00
Mother's Day, Flowers For Mother	1971	Year	45.00	22.00 to 65.00
Mother's Day, Mother With Children	1972	Year	45.00	20.00 to 50.00
Mother's Day, Mother And Child*	1973	Year	45.00	28.95 to 50.00
Mother's Day, Mother And Child	1974	5000	55.00	40.00 to 50.00
Mother's Day, Child's First Steps	1975	Year	75.00	34.95 to 60.00
Mother's Day, Children And Puppy	1976	Year	75.00	75.00

Pairpoint limited editions are made by the Pairpoint Glass Company of Sagamore, Massachusetts. Artisans in Glass, Inc. of New York is the distributor of Pairpoint limited editions.

See listing for Pairpoint in Paperweight section

Pairpoint Bells

Title	Issue Date	Number Issued	Issued Price	Current Price
Amethyst, Decorated	1976	100	95.00	115.00
Emerald Green, Decorated	1977	100	110.00	120.00
French Blue, Decorated*	1975	100	95.00	110.00
Peachblow, Decorated	1974	200	95.00	200.00

Pairpoint Bowls

Bicentennial, Paul Revere	1973	150	200.00	200.00

Pairpoint Cups

New Bedford, Crystal	1973	20	700.00	700.00

Pairpoint Goblets

Bicentennial	1973	150	200.00	Unknown

Pairpoint Mugs

Bicentennial	1973	150	100.00	75.00 to 100.00

Pairpoint Urns

Bicentennial	1973	150	250.00	250.00

Palisander plates are made in Denmark. They are made of rosewood with silver inlay.

Palisander Plates

Title	Issue Date	Number Issued	Issued Price	Current Price
Bicentennial	1973	250	50.00	Unknown
Christmas, Red Robin On Holly	1971	1200	50.00	Unknown
Christmas, Flying Geese	1972	1200	50.00	Unknown
Christmas	1973			Unknown
Presidential, George Washington	1971	1000	50.00	Unknown
Presidential, Thomas Jefferson	1972	1000	50.00	Unknown
Presidential, John Adams	1973	1000	50.00	Unknown

Paramount Classics, a division of Paramount International Coin, is producing a series of limited edition art objects by famous artists.

Paramount Classics Porcelain Plates

Jubilee Of Queen Elizabeth**	1977	5000	375.00	400.00

Paramount Classics, Stuart Devlin Goblets

Violet, Sterling And Gold Vermeil**	1976	500	335.00	335.00
Grape Arbour, Sterling & Gold Vermeil**	1977	500	375.00	375.00

Paul Briant, see Briant

Peanuts, see Schmid, Peanuts

Pearl Buck Plates

The Good Earth	1973	10000	37.50	19.95 to 38.00

Pennington Pottery Plates

Ancient Egypt, Trilogy	1978	5000	45.00	45.00

Perillo, see Sango, Pickard, Roman Bronzes

Picasso, see also George Washington Mint, Hamilton Mint

Picasso Medallions, Plaques, Plates

Title	Issue Date	Number Issued	Issued Price	Current Price
Assiette Vallauris	1953	400		Unknown
Bouquet A La Pomme, Blue	1956	400		Unknown
Bouquet A La Pomme, White	1956	400		Unknown
Cavalier Et Cheval, Black Border	1968	100		Unknown
Cavalier Et Cheval, Red Border	1968	100		Unknown
Centaure, Brown On Yellow	1956	100		Unknown

Picasso, Plate, Visage Aux Taches

Title	Issue Date	Number Issued	Issued Price	Current Price
Centaure De Profil	1950	40		Unknown
Centaure, White	1956	100		Unknown
Corrida	1953	200		Unknown
Corrida Aux Personnages	1950	50		Unknown
Danseurs Et Joueur De Diaule	1956	100		Unknown
Danseurs Sur Fond Clair, Black On White	1956	500		Unknown
Danseurs Sur Fond Fonce, White On Black	1956	500		Unknown
Deux Danseurs	1956	450		Unknown
Dormeur	1956	100		Unknown
Faune Cavalier, Blue Outlined Man On White	1956	100		Unknown
Faune Cavalier, White	1956	100		Unknown
Femme A La Chevelure Aux Traits	1950	250		Unknown
Femme Au Chapeau A Fleurs	1964	100		Unknown
Femme Aux Cheveau Defaits	1950	250		Unknown
Femme Aux Cheveux Flous	1964	100		Unknown
Femme Echevelee, Blue, Yellow, White	1963	100		Unknown
Femme Echevelee, White	1963	100		Unknown
Femmes Et Toreador, Rectangular	1968	500		Unknown
Figure Au Triangle	1971	200		Unknown
Figure Aux Courbes	1971	200		Unknown
Grande Tete De Femme Au Chapeau Orne	1964	50		Unknown
Homme Aux Grosses Jambes	1950	250		Unknown
Homme Aux Petits Bras	1950	250		Unknown
Homme Barbu	1949	75		Unknown
Horloge A La Langue*	1956	100		Unknown
Jacqueline Au Chevalet	1956	100		Unknown
Joie De Vivre	1956	100		Unknown
Joueur De Diaule Et Faune	1956	100		Unknown
Joueur De Flute	1951	40		Unknown
Joueur De Flute Et Cavaliers	1956	100		Unknown
Joneur De Flute Et Chevre	1956	450		Unknown
Le Dejeuner Sur L'Herbe	1964	50		Unknown
Le Sein	1955	100		Unknown
Le Verre Sous La Lampe	1964	100		Unknown
Mains Au Poisson, Red Hands	1953	250		Unknown
Mains Au Poisson, White Hands	1953	100		Unknown
Masque Rieur, Black Square	1968	100		Unknown
Masque Rieur, Yellow Dots	1968	100		Unknown
Nature Morte A La Cuiller, Gray	1952	200		Unknown
Nature Morte A La Cuiller, White	1952	100		Unknown
Neptune Clair	1968	100		Unknown
Neptune Fonce	1968	100		Unknown
Oiseau	1955	100		Unknown
Oiseau De Profil	1949	60		Unknown
Oursin Ouvert	1955	100		Unknown
Pecheur A La Ligne	1950	250		Unknown
Personnage De Face	1950	250		Unknown
Personnages Et Cavalier, Rectangular	1968	500		Unknown
Petit Buste De Femme	1964	100		Unknown
Petit Soleil, Rectangular, Color, Black	1969	100		Unknown
Petit Soleil, Rectangular, Color, Orange Border	1969	100		Unknown
Petit Soleil, Rectangular, Color, Yellow Border	1969	100		Unknown
Petit Visage Barbu, Blue Dots	1968	100		Unknown
Petit Visage Barbu, Yellow Dots	1968	100		Unknown
Petit Visage De Peau-Rouge, Green	1968	100		Unknown
Petit Visage De Peau-Rouge, Yellow	1968	100		Unknown
Petit Visage Solaire, Blue	1968	100		Unknown
Petit Visage Solaire, Yellow	1968	100		Unknown
Petite Tete De Femme Couronnee	1964	100		Unknown
Picador	1954	100		Unknown
Picador Et Taureau	1949	40		Unknown
Picador Et Taureau	1959	100		Unknown
Picador Et Taureau, Reversed Date	1953	200		Unknown
Picador Et Taureau, Square	1950	100		Unknown
Picadore Et Taureau, Black Line Border	1953	200		Unknown
Plat Vallauris Avec Faune, Faces In Colors	1956	100		Unknown
Plat Vallauris Avec Faune, White	1956	100		Unknown
Poisson Blanc, Oval	1952	200		400.00
Poisson Chine, Oval	1952	200		Unknown
Poisson De Profil	1955	100		Unknown

Picasso, Plate, Visage Aux Palmes

Title	Issue Date	Number Issued	Issued Price	Current Price
Poisson De Profil, Blue	1951	25		Unknown
Poisson De Profil, Green	1951	50		Unknown
Poisson De Profil, Yellow	1951	25		Unknown
Poisson Fond Blanc	1952	200		400.00
Poisson Fond Noir	1952	100		Unknown
Poisson Fond Roux, Oval	1952	100		Unknown
Profil De Jacqueline	1956	100		1000.00
Profil De Jacqueline Sur Fond Clair, Black	1956	500		Unknown
Profil De Jacqueline Sur Fond Fonce, White	1956	500		Unknown
Profil De Taureau Clair, White, Black Outline	1956	450		Unknown
Profil De Taureau Fonce, Black	1956	450		Unknown
Quatre Danseurs, Black Dancers On White	1956	450		Unknown
Quatre Danseurs, White Dancers On Black	1956	450		Unknown
Quatre Profils, Blue	1949	35		Unknown
Quatre Profils, Turquoise	1949	25		Unknown
Sauterelle Sur Une Branche	1955	100		Unknown
Scenes De Corrida, 8 Plates	1959	50		Unknown
Scenes De Corrida, 8 Plates, Polychrome	1959	50		Unknown
Scene De Plage, Black People	1956	450		Unknown
Scene De Plage, Black People On White	1956	500		Unknown
Scene De Plage, White People On Black	1956	450		Unknown
Scene De Plage, White People On Black	1956	500		Unknown
Scene De Tauromachie	1954	100		Unknown
Scene De Tauromachie, Dark Figures On White	1959	100		Unknown
Scene De Tauromachie, Orange Border	1959	100		Unknown
Scene De Tauromachie, White Outlined Figures	1956	100		Unknown
Sylvette	1955	100		Unknown
Taureau Attaquant	1949	60		Unknown
Taureau En Pied	1954	100		Unknown
Tete D'Homme Aux Cheveux Longs, Black	1968			Unknown
Tete D'Homme Aux Cheveux Longs, Yellow	1968	50		Unknown
Tete De Chevre De Profil, Black Goat	1950	60		Unknown
Tete De Chevre De Profil, Brown	1952	100		Unknown
Tete De Chevre De Profil, Brown Goat	1950	50		Unknown
Tete De Chevre De Profil, Gray Spotted, Oblong	1952	250		Unknown
Tete De Chevre De Profil, Red Orange, Oblong	1952	250		Unknown
Tete De Chevre De Profil, Stem In Mouth	1950	200		Unknown
Tete De Chevre De Profil, Tan	1952	100		Unknown
Tete De Chevre De Profil, White	1952	100		Unknown
Tete De Chevre De Profil, Yellow Head	1952	100		Unknown
Tete De Chouette, Black Border	1968	100		Unknown
Tete De Chouette, Yellow Square	1968	100		Unknown
Tete De Lion, Black	1968	50		Unknown
Tete De Lion, Red	1968	100		Unknown
Tete Au Masque	1956	100		Unknown
Tete De Taureau	1954	100		Unknown
Tete De Taureau	1960	100		Unknown
Tete De Taureau	1956	100		Unknown
Tete En Forme D'Horloge*	1956	100		Unknown
Trois Personnages Sur Tremplin, Black People	1956	500		Unknown
Trois Personnages Sur Tremplin, White People	1956	500		Unknown
Un Poisson	1956	100		Unknown
Vase Au Bouquet Blue	1956	200		Unknown
Vase Au Bouquet Marron	1956	300		Unknown
Visage A La Barbiche, Green	1968	100		Unknown
Visage A La Barbiche, Red	1968	50		Unknown
Visage A La Cravate	1960	100		Unknown
Visage A La Fraise	1971	200		Unknown
Visage A La Grille, Blue, White	1956	100		Unknown
Visage A La Grille, White*	1956	100		Unknown
Visage Au Gros Nez	1963	100		Unknown
Visage Au Masque De Chevrons	1963	100		Unknown
Visage Au Nez Vert, Gray	1968	100		Unknown
Visage Au Nez Vert, White	1968	100		Unknown
Visage Au Nez Pince	1959	100		Unknown
Visage Au Nez Rond	1971	200		Unknown
Visage Au Trait Oblique, Red	1968	100		Unknown
Visage Au Trait Oblique, White	1968	100		Unknown
Visage Au Traits, Red Border	1968	100		Unknown
Visage Au Traits, Yellow Border	1968	100		Unknown

Title	Issue Date	Number Issued	Issued Price	Current Price
Visage Aux Cheveux Boucles, Black, Blue	1968	100		Unknown
Visage Aux Cheveux Boucles, Red	1968	100		Unknown
Visage Aux Feuilles, Blue, Yellow	1956	100		Unknown
Visage Aux Feuilles, White	1956	100		Unknown
Visage Aux Grands Yeux	1960	100		Unknown
Visage Aux Mains	1956	100		Unknown
Visage Aux Palmes*	1956	100		Unknown
Visage Aux Quatre Visages	1971	200		Unknown
Visage Aux Taches*	1956	100		Unknown
Visage Aux Yeux Carres	1959	100		Unknown
Visage Aux Yeux Ronds	1960	100		Unknown
Visage Barbu	1959	100		Unknown
Visage Cubiste	1960	100		Unknown
Visage Cubiste Aux Taches Blanches, Red	1969	100		Unknown
Visage Cubiste Aux Taches Blanches, Yellow	1969	100		Unknown
Visage D'Homme, Black	1968	50		Unknown
Visage D'Homme, Rectangular	1966	500		Unknown
Visage D'Homme, Red	1968	100		Unknown
Visage Dans Assiette Concave	1963	100		Unknown
Visage Dans Un Carre, Blue	1956	100		Unknown
Visage Dans Un Carre, White	1956	100		Unknown
Visage Dans Un Ovale, Black Face	1955	100		600.00
Visage Dans Un Ovale, Blue Face	1955	100		Unknown
Visage Dans Un Ovale, Reddish Face	1955	100		Unknown
Visage De Face	1960	100		Unknown
Visage De Face	1963	100		Unknown
Visage De Face Aux Taches	1965	100		Unknown
Visage De Face, Date Bottom Left	1965	100		Unknown
Visage De Face, Date Bottom Right	1965	100		Unknown
Visage De Face, Date Lower Middle Left	1965	100		Unknown
Visage De Face, Date Lower Middle Right	1965	100		Unknown
Visage De Face, Date Middle Right, Horizontal	1965	100		Unknown
Visage De Face, Date Middle Right, Vertical	1965	100		Unknown
Visage De Face En Creux	1965	100		Unknown
Visage De Faune	1955	100		Unknown
Visage De Faune	1955	150		Unknown
Visage De Faune Tourmente, Blue On White	1956	100		Unknown
Visage De Faune Tourmente, White	1956	100		Unknown
Visage De Femme	1949	150		Unknown
Visage De Femme	1971			Unknown
Visage De Femme Pomone, Gray	1968	50		Unknown
Visage De Femme Pomone, Yellow	1968	100		Unknown
Visage De Trois Quarts	1965	100		Unknown
Visage En Forme D'Horloge	1956	100		Unknown
Visage En Gros Relief	1959	100		Unknown
Visage En Gros Relief	1963	100		Unknown
Visage Geometrique	1956	100		Unknown
Visage Geometrique Aux Traits	1956	100		Unknown
Visage Geometrique, Oval	1956	100		Unknown
Visage Stylise A L'y, Green X	1968	100		Unknown
Visage Stylise A L'y, Yellow & Blue X	1968	100		Unknown
Visage Sur Carton Ondule	1956	100		Unknown
Visage Tourmente, White	1956	100		Unknown
Visage Tourmente, Yellow Border On Black	1956	100		Unknown
Yan Bandeau		500		350.00

Picasso Vases

Title	Issue Date	Number Issued	Issued Price	Current Price
Droit Visage, Terra Cotta, Black		500		300.00
Gothic Aux Points		350		1750.00
Grand Vase Aux Danseurs	1950	25		Unknown
Grand Vase Aux Femmes Nues, Gray, White	1950	25		Unknown
Grand Vase Aux Femmes Nues, Spotted Lady	1950	25		Unknown
Grand Vase Ecossais, White Happy Face, Texture	1956	25		Unknown
Grand Vase Ecossais, White Sad Face, Smooth	1956	25		Unknown
Grand Vase Pekine	1956	25		Unknown
Hibou, Marroon				625.00
Oiseaux Et Poissons	1955	25		Unknown
Personnages Et Tetes, Square	1954	25		Unknown
Vase Aux Chevres	1952	40		Unknown

Pickard, Plate, Bicentennial,
Lincoln, For Depauw

Pickard, Plate, Christmas, Nativity, 1977

Pickard, Plate, Lockhart Birds,
Bald Eagle, 1974

Pickard, Plate, Lockhart,
American Buffalo, 1976

Title	Issue Date	Number Issued	Issued Price	Current Price

Pickard China Studio was established in Chicago by Wilder Austin Pickard in 1898. In 1935, the company opened a china factory in Antioch, Illinois. The current trademark, a lion with fleur-de-lis, was adopted in 1938. The first limited edition plates by Pickard were made in 1970.

Pickard, see also Cowboy Artists

Pickard Bells

Title	Issue Date	Number Issued	Issued Price	Current Price
Christmas, First Noel	1977	3000	75.00	75.00

Pickard Plates

Title	Issue Date	Number Issued	Issued Price	Current Price
Bicentennial, Abraham Lincoln	1976	5000	30.00	30.00
Bicentennial, Lincoln, For Depauw*	1976	5000	30.00	30.00
Bicentennial, Paul Revere	1976			24.50
Christmas, Alba Madonna**	1976	7500	60.00	200.00
Christmas, Nativity**	1977	7500	65.00	90.00 to 100.00
Companion, Perillo, Cubs	1977	5000	40.00	40.00
Companion, Perillo, Mighty Sioux	1978	5000	40.00	40.00
Father's Day, Soccer	1977	Year	16.50	20.00
Queen Victoria	1977	5000	95.00	95.00
Queens Of England*	1977	5000	75.00	110.00
King George III	1977	5000	95.00	95.00
Lockhart Birds, Woodcock* & Ruffed Grouse	1970	2000	150.00	195.00 to 300.00
Lockhart Birds, Green-Winged Teal* & Mallard	1971	2000	150.00	150.00 to 250.00
Lockhart Birds, Mockingbird* & Cardinal	1978	2000	150.00	90.00 to 195.00
Lockhart Birds, Wild Turkey & Pheasant	1973	2000	165.00	120.00 to 215.00
Lockhart Birds, Bald Eagle**	1974	2000	150.00	165.00 to 300.00
Lockhart White-Tailed Deer	1975	2500	100.00	95.00 to 100.00
Lockhart, American Buffalo*	1976	2500	165.00	165.00
Lockhart, Great Horned Owl**	1977	2500	100.00	100.00
Lockhart, American Panther**	1978	2000	175.00	175.00
President, Harry S Truman*	1972	3000	35.00	20.00 to 40.00
President, Abraham Lincoln	1973	5000	35.00	35.00 to 40.00
Renoir, Girl With A Watering Can	1978	5000	50.00	50.00
U.S.Bicentennial Society, Patriots, Set Of 6	1976	2500	750.00	Unknown
Wildlife, American Panther	1978	2000	175.00	175.00

Pierre Millous, see Cartier

The Poillerat Christmas plates, designed by French artist Gilbert Poillerat, are produced by the Atelier d'Art Faure of Limoges, France. The plates are enamel on copper. Poillerat also designs crystal plates and paperweights for Cristal d'Albret.

Poillerat Bird of Peace and Four Seasons plate, see Cristal d'Albret

Poillerat Plates

Title	Issue Date	Number Issued	Issued Price	Current Price
Christmas, Three Kings*	1972	500	350.00	199.00 to 350.00
Christmas, Rose	1973	250	350.00	350.00

The Poole Pottery of Poole, Dorset, England, has produced pottery since 1873. Limited edition plates, which were first made in 1972, are handmade to resemble stained-glass windows.

See listing for Poole in Figurine section

Poole Plates

Title	Issue Date	Number Issued	Issued Price	Current Price
Cathedral, Christ On Cross*	1973	11000	125.00	125.00
Cathedral, Adoration Of Magi	1973	1000	125.00	125.00
Cathedral, Flight Into Egypt	1973	1000	125.00	125.00
Calendar, January, Drinking Wine By The Fire	1972	1000	100.00	60.00 to 150.00
Calendar, February, Chopping Wood	1972	1000	100.00	60.00 to 150.00
Calendar, March, Digging In The Fields	1973	1000	125.00	95.00 to 135.00
Calendar, April, Carrying A Flowering Branch	1973	1000	125.00	95.00 to 135.00
Calendar, May, Hawking	1974	1000	125.00	125.00
Calendar, June, Mowing Hay	1974	1000	125.00	125.00
Calendar, July, Cutting Corn With Sickle	1975	1000	125.00	125.00
Calendar, August, Threshing With Flail	1975	1000	125.00	125.00
Calendar, September, Picking Grapes	1976	1000	125.00	125.00
Calendar, October, Sowing Winter Corn	1976	1000	125.00	125.00
Calendar, November, Gathering Acorns For Pigs	1977	1000	125.00	125.00
Calendar, December, Pig Killing	1977	1000	125.00	125.00

Pickard, Lockhart Bird Plate, 1970,
Woodcock

Pickard, Lockhart Bird Plate, 1971,
Green-Winged Teal

Pickard, Lockhart Bird Plate, 1972,
Mockingbird

Pickard, Plate, Queens Of England, 1977

Pickard, President Plate, 1972

Poillerat, Christmas Plate, 1972

Poole, Cathedral Plate, 1973

Porcelaine De Paris, Plate,
Bridges Of Paris,
Notre Dame De Paris, 1976

Porsgrund, Easter Plate, 1973

Porsgrund, Christmas Plate, 1973

Porsgrund, Deluxe Christmas Plate, 1973

Title	Issue Date	Number Issued	Issued Price	Current Price
Porcelaine de Paris Plates				
Bridges Of Paris, Le Pant Aux Meuniers	1976	5000	42.50	42.50
Bridges Of Paris, Le Pant Neup	1976	5000	42.50	42.50
Bridges Of Paris, Le Petit Chatelet	1976	5000	42.50	42.50
Bridges Of Paris, Notre Dame De Paris*	1976	5000	42.50	42.50
Bridges Of Paris, Place De La Bastille	1976	5000	42.50	42.50
Bridges Of Paris, Quai Aux Fleurs	1976	5000	42.50	42.50
Lao Tse, Set Of 4	1973	300	175.00	160.00 to 175.00

Porcelana Granada plates are made in Columbia, South America. The limited edition Christmas series, begun in 1971, is based on the life of Christ.

Title	Issue Date	Number Issued	Issued Price	Current Price
Porcelana Granada Plates				
Christmas, The Annunciation	1971	10000	12.00	16.00
Christmas, Mary & Elizabeth	1972	6000	12.00	15.00 to 15.50
Christmas, Road To Bethlehem	1973	5000	14.00	15.00 to 15.50
Christmas, No Room At The Inn	1974	5000	15.00	16.00
Christmas, Shepherds In The Field	1975	5000	16.50	16.50
Christmas, The Nativity	1976	5000	17.50	17.50
Christmas, Three Kings	1977	5000	18.00	18.00

Porsgrund, Norway's only porcelain factory, was started in 1887 by Johan Jermiassen. Porsgrund made one of the world's first Christmas plates in 1909 only. The contemporary Christmas plate series was begun in 1968. Mugs were added in 1970.

Title	Issue Date	Number Issued	Issued Price	Current Price
Porsgrund Mugs				
Christmas, Road To Bethlehem	1970	Year	20.00	11.00 to 20.00
Christmas, A Child Is Born	1971	Year	20.00	7.00 to 20.00
Christmas, Hark The Herald Angels	1972	Year	20.00	12.50 to 20.00
Christmas, Promise Of The Saviour	1973	Year	20.00	14.00 to 24.00
Christmas, The Shepherds	1974	Year	20.00	16.00 to 30.00
Christmas, Road To The Temple	1975	Year	19.50	15.95 to 30.00
Christmas, Jesus In The Temple	1976	Year	35.00	19.50 to 35.00
Christmas, The Great Fisherman	1977	Year	38.00	38.00
Father's Day, Cookout	1972	Year	11.00	9.00 to 11.50
Father's Day, Sledding*	1973	Year	11.00	11.00
Father's Day, Wheelbarrow	1974	Year		10.00
Father's Day, Skating	1975	Year		10.00 to 12.50
Father's Day, Skiing	1976	Year	19.50	19.50
Father's Day, Soccer	1977	Year	20.00	20.00
Porsgrund Plates				
Christmas, Christmas Flowers	1909			400.00 to 475.00
Christmas, Church Scene	1968	Year	7.50	85.00 to 180.00
Christmas, Three Kings	1969	Year	10.00	12.00 to 30.00
Christmas, Road To Bethlehem	1970	Year	10.00	5.00 to 15.00
Christmas, A Child Is Born	1971	Year	12.00	8.00 to 20.00
Christmas, Hark The Herald Angels	1972	Year	12.00	8.00 to 20.00
Christmas, Promise Of The Saviour *	1973	Year	12.00	4.50 to 18.00
Christmas, The Shepherds	1974	Year	15.00	7.50 to 18.00
Christmas, Road To The Temple	1975	Year	19.50	19.50 to 20.00
Christmas, Jesus In The Temple	1976	Year	22.00	22.00
Christmas, The Great Fisherman	1977	Year	24.00	24.00
Deluxe Christmas, Road To Bethlehem*	1970	3000	50.00	35.00 to 65.00
Deluxe Christmas, A Child Is Born	1971	3000	50.00	20.00 to 45.00
Deluxe Christmas, Hark The Herald Angels	1972	3000	50.00	35.00 to 50.00
Deluxe Christmas, Promise Of The Saviour*	1973	3000	50.00	30.00 to 50.00
Deluxe Christmas, The Shepherds	1974	3000	50.00	30.00 to 40.00
Deluxe Christmas, Road To The Temple	1975	3000	50.00	50.00
Deluxe Christmas, Jesus In The Temple	1976	3000	80.00	80.00
Deluxe Christmas, The Great Fisherman	1977	3000	80.00	80.00
Easter, Ducks	1972	Year	12.00	7.95 to 18.00
Easter, Birds*	1973	Year	12.00	6.00 to 17.00
Easter, Bunnies	1974	Year	15.00	15.00
Easter, Chicks	1975	Year	19.50	19.50
Easter, Sheep In The Field	1976	Year	22.00	22.00
Easter, Butterflies	1977	Year	24.00	24.00
Father's Day, Father & Son Fishing	1971	Year	7.50	4.00 to 10.00
Father's Day, Cookout	1972	Year	8.00	5.50 to 11.50

Title	Issue Date	Number Issued	Issued Price	Current Price
Father's Day, Sledding	1973	Year	8.00	7.00 to 13.00
Father's Day, Wheelbarrow	1974	Year	10.00	3.00 to 12.00
Father's Day, Skating	1975	Year	12.00	8.50 to 12.50
Father's Day, Skiing	1976	Year	15.00	15.00
Five Year Plate, Fishing Fleet	1970			10.00
Five Year Plate, Stave Church	1975		47.50	47.50
Jubilee, Femboringer	1970	Year	25.00	16.00 to 19.00
Mother's Day, Mare & Foal*	1970	Year	7.50	3.00 to 20.00
Mother's Day, Boy & Geese	1971	Year	7.50	4.00 to 10.00
Mother's Day, Doe & Fawn	1972	Year	8.00	4.00 to 10.00
Mother's Day, Cat & Kittens*	1973	Year	12.00	5.00 to 10.00
Mother's Day, Boy & Goat	1974	Year	10.00	3.00 to 12.00
Mother's Day, Boy And Dog	1975	Year	12.50	7.25 to 12.50
Mother's Day, Cow And Calf	1976	Year	15.00	12.50 to 15.00
Mother's Day, Boy Feeding Chicks	1977	Year	16.50	16.50

Porsgrund, Father's Day Mug, 1973

The Puiforcat Exodus plate was made by La Monnaie de Paris, the official French government mint. Puiforcat porcelain limited editions are made in Limoges, France.

Puiforcat Plates

Dali, Carte A Jouer, Set Of 5	1972	2000	300.00	Unknown
Exodus, Silver	1973	2000	200.00	Unknown

Raggedy Ann and Andy, see Schmid, Raggedy Ann and Andy

Ram limited editions are manufactured by the Ram China Plate Company of Minneapolis, Minnesota.

Ram Plates

Christmas, Boston 500 Series	1973	500	30.00	Unknown
Easter, Boston 500 Series	1973	500	30.00	Unknown
Father's Day, Boston 500 Series	1973	500	30.00	Unknown
Great Bird Heroes, Cher Ami	1973	1000	7.95	Unknown
Great Bird Heroes, The Mocker	1973	1000	7.95	Unknown
Mother's Day, Boston 500 Series	1973	500	30.00	Unknown

Porsgrund, Mother's Day Plate, 1970

Ray Harm Bird plates, see Spode

Reco Plates

Americana, Gaspee, Stuart Devlin, Silver	1972	1000	130.00	110.00 to 150.00
Christmas, Old Mill In Valley	1977	5000	28.00	28.00
Flower Of America, Anemone	1977	1000	135.00	135.00
Four Seasons, Fall	1973	2500	50.00	25.00 to 50.00
Four Seasons, Spring	1973	2500	50.00	25.00 to 50.00
Four Seasons, Summer	1973	2500	50.00	25.00 to 50.00
Four Seasons, Winter	1973	2500	50.00	25.00 to 50.00
Western, The Mountain Man	1974	1000	165.00	165.00
World Of Children, Rainy Day Fun*	1977	10000	50.00	50.00
World Of Children, When I Grown Up	1978		50.00	50.00

Reed & Barton Silversmiths of Taunton, Massachusetts, was established in 1824. Limited edition plates of Damascene silver (a combination of copper, bronze, and silver) were first made in 1970.

Reed & Barton Bells

American Holiday, St.Patrick's Day	1978	5000	19.95	19.95

Reed & Barton Damascene Insculptures

Bicentennial, Declaration Of Independence	1976	200	85.00	85.00
Bicentennial, Spirit Of '76	1976	200	85.00	85.00
Christmas, Morning Train	1976	2500	85.00	85.00
Christmas, Decorating The Church	1977	2500	85.00	85.00
Christmas, General Store	1978	2500	85.00	85.00
Custer's Last Stand, Set Of 3	1977	850	250.00	250.00
Wildlife, Ruffled Grouse	1974	2500	75.00	Unknown
Wildlife, Mallard Ducks	1974	2500	75.00	Unknown
Wildlife, On A Point	1974	2500	75.00	Unknown
Wildlife, Flush'd	1974	2500	75.00	Unknown

Reed & Barton Damascene Plates

Audubon Birds, Pine Siskin*	1970	5000	60.00	35.00 to 100.00
Audubon Birds, Red-Shouldered Hawk*	1971	5000	60.00	20.00 to 60.00
Audubon Birds, Purple Finch	1977	5000	75.00	75.00

Porsgrund, Mother's Day Plate, 1973

Reco, Plate, World Of Children,
Rainy Day Fun, 1977

Title	Issue Date	Number Issued	Issued Price	Current Price
Audubon Birds, Stilt Sandpiper*	1972	5000	60.00	45.00 to 60.00
Audubon Birds, Red Cardinal*	1973	5000	60.00	60.00 to 65.00
Audubon Birds, Chickadee*	1974	5000	60.00	60.00 to 62.50
Audubon Birds, Yellow-Breasted Chat*	1975	5000	65.00	65.00
Audubon Birds, Bay-Breasted Warbler*	1976	5000	65.00	65.00
Chicago Fire			60.00	35.00
Christmas, Partridge*	1970	2500	60.00	125.00 to 175.00
Christmas, We Three Kings*	1971	7500	60.00	37.50 to 75.00
Christmas, Hark The Herald Angels*	1972	7500	60.00	40.00 to 70.00
Christmas, Adoration Of The King*	1973	7500	60.00	50.00 to 65.00
Christmas, Adoration Of The Magi	1974	7500	65.00	65.00
Christmas, Adoration Of Kings*	1975	7500	65.00	65.00
Christmas, Morning Train	1976	7500	65.00	65.00
Christmas, Decorating The Church	1977	7500	65.00	65.00
Christmas, General Store	1977	7500	65.00	65.00
Currier & Ives, Village Blacksmith	1972	1500	85.00	15.00 to 27.50
Currier & Ives, Western Migration	1972	1500	85.00	26.50 to 39.50
Currier & Ives, Oaken Bucket	1973	1500	85.00	85.00
Currier & Ives, Winter In The Country	1973	1500	85.00	90.00 to 110.00
Currier & Ives, Preparing For Market	1974	1500	85.00	85.00
Delta Queen	1972	2500	75.00	40.00 to 75.00
Founding Fathers, Ben Franklin*	1973	2500	65.00	65.00
Founding Fathers, George Washington	1974	2500	65.00	65.00
Founding Fathers, Thomas Jefferson	1975	2500	65.00	65.00
Founding Fathers, John Adams	1976	2500	65.00	65.00
Founding Fathers, John Hancock	1976	2500	65.00	65.00
Founding Fathers, Patrick Henry	1976	2500	65.00	65.00
Kentucky Derby	1972	1000	75.00	75.00
Kentucky Derby, Riva Ridge	1973	1500	75.00	75.00
Kentucky Derby, 100th Running	1974	1500	75.00	75.00
Mission, San Diego De Alcala	1971		65.00	75.00 to 100.00
Mission, Carmel	1972		65.00	60.00 to 75.00
Mission, Santa Barbara	1973	1500	65.00	65.00
Mission, Santa Clara De Asis	1974	1500	65.00	65.00
Mission, San Gabriel	1976	1500	65.00	65.00
Mississippi Queen	1975	2500	75.00	75.00
Russell, Free Trapper	1972	2500	65.00	65.00
Russell, Outpost	1973	2500	65.00	65.00
Russell, Road Runner	1972	1500	65.00	65.00
Russell, Toll Collector	1974	2500	65.00	65.00
Russell, Lewis & Clark	1975	2500	65.00	65.00
Zodiac	1970	1500	75.00	85.00 to 100.00

Reed & Barton Sterling Ornaments

Title	Issue Date	Number Issued	Issued Price	Current Price
Christmas Cross	1971	Year	10.00	15.00 to 29.00
Christmas Cross	1972	Year	10.00	12.00 to 30.00
Christmas Cross	1973	Year	10.00	11.00 to 19.00
Christmas Cross	1974	Year	12.95	12.95
Christmas Cross	1975	Year	12.95	10.95 to 12.00
Christmas Cross	1976	Year	13.95	13.95
Christmas Cross	1977	Year	15.00	15.00
Christmas Cross	1978	Year	16.00	16.00
Christmas Star	1976	Year	8.95	Unknown
Christmas Star	1977	Year	10.00	10.00
Christmas Star	1978	Year	10.75	10.75
Holly Ball	1976	Year	13.95	Unknown
Holly Ball	1977	Year	15.00	15.00
Holly Ball	1978	Year	15.00	15.00
Snowflakes, Pair	1977	Year	10.00	10.00
Snowflakes, Pair	1978	Year	12.00	12.00

Reed & Barton Vermeil Ornaments

Title	Issue Date	Number Issued	Issued Price	Current Price
Christmas Cross	1971	Year	17.50	Unknown
Christmas Cross	1972	Year	17.50	Unknown
Christmas Cross	1973	Year	17.50	Unknown
Christmas Cross	1974	Year	20.00	Unknown
Christmas Cross	1975	Year	20.00	Unknown
Christmas Cross	1976	Year	19.95	Unknown
Christmas Cross	1977	Year	18.50	18.50
Christmas Cross	1978	Year	20.00	20.00
Christmas Star	1976	Year	12.95	Unknown
Christmas Star	1977	Year	12.50	12.50

Reed & Barton, Plate, Audubon Birds,
Yellow-Breasted Chat, 1975

Reed & Barton, Audubon Bird Plate,
1971, Red-Shouldered Hawk

Reed & Barton, Plate, Audubon Birds,
Chickadee, 1974

Reed & Barton, Audubon Bird Plate,
1972, Stilt Sandpiper

Reed & Barton, Plate,
Audubon Birds,
Bay-Breasted Warbler, 1976

Reed & Barton, Christmas Plate, 1970

Reed & Barton, Plate,
Founding Fathers, Ben Franklin, 1976

Reed & Barton, Audubon Bird Plate,
1972, Red Cardinal

Reed & Barton, Christmas Plate, 1971

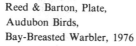

Reed & Barton, Audubon Bird Plate,
1970, Pine Siskin

Title	Issue Date	Number Issued	Issued Price	Current Price
Christmas Star	1978	Year	13.00	13.00
Snowflakes	1977	Year	15.00	15.00
Snowflakes	1978	Year	18.00	18.00
Tree Castles, Large Cube	1977	Year	12.50	12.50
Tree Castles, Small Cube	1977	Year	9.00	9.00
Tree Castles, Peace Prism	1977	Year	12.50	12.50
Tree Castles, Choir	1978	Year	10.00	10.00
Tree Castles, Nativity	1978	Year	10.00	10.00

Rembrandt, see Gorham

Remington Plates

Title	Issue Date	Number Issued	Issued Price	Current Price
Apache Scout, Carnival	1972	750	12.50	25.00
Sioux Chief, Carnival	1973	750	9.50	25.00

Remington, see also George Washington Mint, Gorham

Reuge Bells

Title	Issue Date	Number Issued	Issued Price	Current Price
Bicentennial, Drum & Flag, Battle Hymn	1976	5000	35.00	35.00
Bicentennial, Liberty Bell, God Bless America	1976	5000	35.00	35.00
Bicentennial, Stars And Stripes Forever	1976	5000	35.00	35.00
Christmas, Silent Night	1975	13882	35.00	29.50 to 45.00
Christmas, Madonna, Adeste Fidelis	1976	Year	35.00	35.00
Mother's Day, Dream Of Love	1976	Year	35.00	24.75 to 40.00
Mother's Day, Glockenspiel	1975	5358	35.00	45.00 to 55.00
Mother's Day	1977			35.00
Mother's Day	1978	3000	35.00	26.50 to 35.00
Valentine's Day, Heart Of Love		2500		35.00

Ridgewood, see also Andrew Wyeth, Golf Digest, Halbert,
Mark Twain, Marquise Commemorative, North Dakota Auto Club,
Winslow Homer Plates

Ridgewood Bells

Title	Issue Date	Number Issued	Issued Price	Current Price
Leyendecker New Year's	1977			24.50

Ridgewood Eggs

Title	Issue Date	Number Issued	Issued Price	Current Price
Leyendecker, Easter	1976	1500	14.50	15.00
Leyendecker, Easter	1977	5000	15.00	15.00

Ridgewood Plates

Title	Issue Date	Number Issued	Issued Price	Current Price
American Presentation Guild, Christmas	1977	3000	50.00	50.00
Annual, Miss America	1975			16.75 to 22.50
Bicentennial, Drafting The Declaration	1976		25.00	25.00
Bicentennial, First In War	1974	12500	40.00	40.00
Bicentennial, Signing The Constitution	1976		25.00	25.00
Bicentennial, Signing The Declaration	1976		35.00	35.00
Bicentennial, Spirit Of '76	1976		25.00	25.00
Bicentennial, Washington Crossing Delaware	1976		25.00	25.00
Colonial Heritage Series, Mulberry Plantation			99.00	30.00
Constable, Hay Wain	1976			33.50
Constable, Valley Farm	1976			33.50
Grandma Moses, Annual, Golf Oil Co.	1975	30000	29.90	29.90
Harbor Town Golf Links	1976	2500	50.00	50.00
Leyendecker, Bicentennial, Liberty Bell	1976			31.95 to 35.00
Leyendecker, Bicentennial, Paul Revere	1976		24.50	24.50
Leyendecker, Christmas Morning	1975	10000	24.50	33.00 to 36.00
Leyendecker, Christmas Surprise	1976		16.50	19.50 to 26.50
Leyendecker, Christmas	1977	3000		50.00
Leyendecker, Mother's Day, Apple Pie	1976	5000	24.50	22.50 to 24.50
Leyendecker, Mother's Day, Tenderness	1977	10000	35.00	35.00
Little Traveller	1978	4000	45.00	45.00
Louisiana Collection, Set Of 6	1976	5000		40.00
Russell, Western Series, Set Of 4	1975	15000	65.00	67.50 to 72.50
Trester, Little Men, Come Ride With Me	1976		50.00	50.00
Trester, Little Women, Song Of Spring	1976		45.00	60.00 to 67.00
Trester, Little Women, Sweet Long Ago	1976		45.00	45.00

River Shore Bells

Title	Issue Date	Number Issued	Issued Price	Current Price
Rockwell, Children Series I, 4	1977	15000	120.00	120.00
Rockwell, Children Series II, 4**	1978	15000	140.00	140.00

River Shore Copper Plates

Title	Issue Date	Number Issued	Issued Price	Current Price
Remington, Bronco Buster*	1978	15000	55.00	55.00
Remington, Coming Thru The Rye	1978	15000	55.00	55.00

Reed & Barton, Christmas Plate, 1972

Reed & Barton, Christmas Plate, 1973

River Shore, Copper Plate,
Rockwell By Rockwell, 1977

Reed & Barton, Plate, Christmas,
Adoration Of Kings, 1975

River Shore, Copper Plate, Remington,
Bronco Buster, 1978

River Shore, Copper Plate, Rockwell,
Peace Corps, 1978

Rosenthal, Christmas Plate, 1964

Rorstrand, Christmas Plate, 1973

Rorstrand, Father's Day Plate, 1973

Rorstrand, Mother's Day Plate, 1973

Title	Issue Date	Number Issued	Issued Price	Current Price
Rockwell, Lincoln, No.1**	1976	9500	40.00	160.00
Rockwell, Lincoln, No.2	1977	9500	45.00	60.00
Rockwell By Rockwell**	1977	9500	45.00	45.00
Rockwell, Peace Corps**	1978	9500	45.00	45.00
Rockwell, Spirit Of Lindbergh	1979	9500	45.00	45.00

Rockwell, see Franklin Mint, Gorham, Rockwell Society, Rockwell Museum, Royal Devon

Rockwell Museum Plates

Title	Issue Date	Number Issued	Issued Price	Current Price
Baby's First Step	1978	9900	30.00	30.00

Rockwell Collector's Club Plates

Title	Issue Date	Number Issued	Issued Price	Current Price
Doctor & Doll	1978	Year	14.50	14.50

Rockwell Society Plates

Title	Issue Date	Number Issued	Issued Price	Current Price
Christmas, Scotty Gets His Tree	1974	Year	24.50	57.50 to 85.00
Christmas, Angel With Black Eye	1975	Year	24.50	39.00
Christmas, Golden Christmas	1976	Year	24.50	24.50
Christmas, Toy Shop Window	1977	Year	24.50	24.50
Christmas, The Big Moment	1978	Year	27.50	19.50 to 27.50
Mother's Day, A Mother's Love	1976	Year	24.50	25.00 to 42.00
Mother's Day, Faith	1977	Year	24.50	24.50
Mother's Day, Bedtime	1978	Year	24.50	24.50
Rockwell Heritage, Toy Maker	1977	Year	14.50	14.50
Rockwell Heritage, Cobbler	1978	Year	19.50	19.50

Roman Bronzes Plaques

Title	Issue Date	Number Issued	Issued Price	Current Price
Perillo, Buffalo Hunt	1978	2500	300.00	300.00

Rorstrand, founded in Sweden in 1726, is the oldest porcelain factory in Scandinavia and the second oldest in all of Europe. Rorstrand entered the limited edition market in 1968 with its Christmas plates. Mother's and Father's Day plates were introduced in 1971.

Rorstrand Plates

Title	Issue Date	Number Issued	Issued Price	Current Price
Christmas, Bringing Home The Tree	1968	Year	10.00	300.00 to 520.00
Christmas, Fisherman Sailing Home	1969	Year	10.00	75.00 to 125.00
Christmas, Nils With His Geese	1970	Year	10.00	15.00 to 25.00
Christmas, Nils In Lapland	1971	Year	13.50	18.00 to 20.00
Christmas, Dalecarlian Fiddler	1972	Year	16.00	18.00 to 20.00
Christmas, Farm In Smaland*	1973	Year	16.00	60.00 to 100.00
Christmas, Vadslena	1974	Year	19.00	19.00
Christmas, Nils In Vastmanland	1975	Year	20.00	32.50
Christmas, Welcome To Spring	1976	Year	20.00	20.00 to 30.00
Christmas, Nils In Uppland	1976	Year	20.00	20.30
Christmas	1977	Year	29.50	29.95
Christmas, Nils Holgersson's Journey	1977	Year	29.50	29.50
Father's Day, Father & Child	1971	Year	10.00	10.00 to 18.00
Father's Day, A Meal At Home	1972	Year	10.00	5.50 to 22.50
Father's Day, Tilling Fields*	1973	Year	15.00	15.00
Father's Day, Fishing	1974	Year	18.00	10.00 to 25.00
Father's Day, Fishing	1975	Year	20.00	20.00
Father's Day	1975	Year	20.00	13.00 to 20.00
Father's Day, Ploughing	1976	Year	20.00	20.00
Father's Day, Ploughing With Brunte	1976	Year	20.00	11.00 to 21.00
Father's Day, Ploughing	1977	Year	20.00	20.00
Father's Day, Ploughing	1978	Year	20.00	20.00
Mother's Day, Mother & Child	1971	Year	10.00	10.00 to 20.00
Mother's Day, Shelling Peas	1972	Year	15.00	10.00 to 18.00
Mother's Day, Old-Fashioned Picnic*	1973	Year	15.00	15.00
Mother's Day, Candle Lighting	1974	Year	18.00	10.00 to 18.00
Mother's Day, Pontius On Floor	1975	Year	20.00	10.00 to 21.00
Mother's Day, Flowers For Mother	1976	Year	20.00	2.00
Mother's Day, Apple Picking	1976	Year	20.00	11.00 to 21.00
Mother's Day, Kitchen	1977	Year	27.50	27.50
Mother's Day, Kitchen	1978	Year	27.50	27.50

Rose Kennedy plate, see Caritas

Rosenthal Company of West Germany was founded by Philip Rosenthal, Sr., in 1880. The company made open-stock Christmas plates from 1910 through 1970. All of these molds were destroyed in 1970. Limited edition Christmas plates were initiated in 1971.

Title	Issue Date	Number Issued	Issued Price	Current Price
Rosenthal, see also Hibel, Danbury Mint				
Rosenthal Plates				
Annual, Tapio Wirkkala, Finland	1971	3000	100.00	100.00 to 120.00
Annual, Natale, Sapone, Italy	1972	3000	100.00	100.00 to 120.00
Burgues, Chun Li At The Pond*	1978	5000	100.00	100.00
Burgues, June Dream**	1978	5000	75.00	75.00
Christmas, Winter Peace*	1910			500.00
Christmas, Three Wise Men*	1911			225.00
Christmas, Stardust*	1912			150.00
Christmas, Christmas Lights*	1913			150.00
Christmas, Christmas Song*	1914			275.00
Christmas, Walking To Church*	1915			150.00
Christmas, Christmas During War*	1916			150.00
Christmas, Angel Of Peace*	1917			150.00
Christmas, Peace On Earth*	1918			150.00
Christmas, St.Christopher With Christ Child*	1919			200.00
Christmas, Manger In Bethlehem*	1920			200.00
Christmas, Christmas In The Mountains*	1921			160.00
Christmas, Advent Branch*	1922			160.00
Christmas, Deer In The Woods*	1923			160.00
Christmas, Children In Winter Woods*	1924			160.00
Christmas, Three Wise Men*	1925			160.00
Christmas, Christmas In The Mountains*	1926			160.00
Christmas, Station On The Way*	1927			140.00
Christmas, Chalet Christmas*	1928			140.00
Christmas, Christmas In The Alps*	1929			140.00
Christmas, Group Of Deer Under The Pines*	1930			160.00
Christmas, Path Of The Magi*	1931			140.00
Christmas, Christ Child*	1932			140.00
Christmas, Thru The Night To Light*	1933			100.00
Christmas, Christmas Peace	1934			100.00
Christmas, Christmas By The Sea	1935			100.00
Christmas, Nurnberg Angel	1936			100.00
Christmas, Berchtesgaden	1937			160.00
Christmas, Christmas In The Alps	1938			160.00
Christmas, Schneekoppe Mountain	1939			160.00
Christmas, Marien Church In Danzig	1940			225.00
Christmas, Strassburg Cathedral	1941			225.00
Christmas, Marianburg Castle	1942			275.00
Christmas, Winter Idyll	1943			275.00
Christmas, Wood Scape	1944			275.00
Christmas, Christmas Peace	1945			300.00
Christmas, Christmas In An Alpine Valley*	1946			120.00
Christmas, Dillenger Madonna*	1947			350.00
Christmas, Message To The Shepherds*	1948			300.00
Christmas, Holy Family*	1949			100.00
Christmas, Christmas In The Forest*	1950			120.00
Christmas, Star Of Bethlehem*	1951			200.00
Christmas, Christmas In The Alps*	1952			120.00
Christmas, Holy Light*	1953			120.00
Christmas, Christmas Eve*	1954			120.00
Christmas, Christmas In A Village*	1955			120.00
Christmas, Christmas In The Alps*	1956			100.00
Christmas, Christmas By The Sea*	1957			100.00
Christmas, Christmas Eve*	1958			100.00
Christmas, Midnight Mass*	1959			100.00
Christmas, Christmas In A Small Village*	1960			120.00
Christmas, Solitary Christmas*	1961	2764		200.00
Christmas, Christmas Eve*	1962	2826		100.00
Christmas, Silent Night*	1963	2989		150.00
Christmas, Christmas Market In Nurnberg*	1964	3568		185.00
Christmas, Christmas In Munich*	1965	4075		200.00
Christmas, Christmas In Ulm	1966	3000		200.00
Christmas, Christmas In Reginburg*	1967	5400		120.00
Christmas, Christmas In Bremen*	1968	6400		200.00
Christmas, Christmas In Rothenburg*	1969	8500		120.00
Christmas, Christmas In Cologne*	1970	9000		125.00
Christmas, Christmas In Garmisch*	1971	6000	45.00	70.00 to 100.00
Christmas, Christmas Eve, Franconia*	1972	5000	50.00	58.00 to 85.00
Christmas, Christmas In Lubeck-Holstein	1973	9000	77.00	45.00 to 80.00

Rosenthal, Christmas Plate, 1965

Rosenthal, Christmas Plate, 1967

Rosenthal, Christmas Plate, 1968

Rosenthal, Christmas Plate, 1969

Rosenthal, Plate, Burgues,
June Dream, 1978

Rosenthal, Christmas Plate, 1970

Rosenthal, Christmas Plates

1910	1911	1912

Rosenthal, Christmas Plates

1916	1917	1918

1913	1914	1915

Rosenthal, Christmas Plates

1919	1920	1921

Rosenthal, Christmas Plates

Rosenthal, Christmas Plates

1922	1923	1924

1925	1926	1927

Rosenthal, Christmas Plates

Title	Issue Date	Number Issued	Issued Price	Current Price
Christmas, Christmas In Warzberg	1974	10000	85.00	Unknown
Christmas, Freiburg Cathedral	1975	11000	75.00	Unknown
Christmas, Christmas At Burg Cochem	1976	12000	95.00	100.00
Christmas, Hanover Town Hall	1977	Year	125.00	125.00
Christmas, Winblad, Madonna & Child	1971	4000	95.00	95.00 to 120.00
Christmas, Winblad, King Caspar	1972	4000	100.00	100.00 to 120.00
Christmas, Winblad, King Melchior	1973	4000	100.00	120.00
Christmas, Winblad, King Balthazar	1974		125.00	Unknown
Christmas, Winblad, The Annunciation	1975	15000	195.00	Unknown
Christmas, Winblad, The Herald	1976		195.00	225.00
Christmas, Winblad, Adoration Of The Shepherd	1977		225.00	225.00
Christmas, Winblad, Angel With Harp	1978		275.00	275.00
Crystal, Christmas, Winblad, The Herald	1976		225.00	Unknown
Crystal, Christmas, Winblad	1977		225.00	225.00
Crystal, Christmas, Winblad, Three Kings	1978		225.00	225.00
Falter, Bring Home Pumpkins	1976		70.00	70.00
Falter, Countryside At Harvest Time	1977	5000	70.00	70.00
Falter, An Honest Day's Work	1978	4000	70.00	70.00
Mother's Day, Flowers For Mother	1976	7500	40.00	23.00 to 55.00
Mother's Day, Darcy	1977	7500	50.00	50.00
Mother's Day, A Moment To Reflect	1978	8000	55.00	50.00
Oriental Nights, Winblad, Flutist	1976		50.00	50.00
Oriental Nights, Winblad, Mandolin Player	1977		55.00	55.00
Runci Classics, Springtime	1977	5000	95.00	95.00
Runci Classics, Summertime	1977	5000	95.00	95.00
Trester, Summertime	1975	5000	60.00	60.00 to 80.00
Trester, One Lovely Yesterday	1976	5000	70.00	50.00 to 80.00

Roskild, see Danish Church

Royal Bayreuth Porcelain has been made in Germany since the late nineteenth century. Limited editions were first made in 1972. The popular Sunbonnet Babies plates, made by the factory during the early twentieth century, have been reissued in a limited edition.

Royal Bayreuth Eggs

Easter, Hen & Chicks	1974		15.00	35.00
Easter, Bunnies	1975		15.00	8.00 to 15.00
Easter, Picking Flowers	1976		15.00	15.00
Easter, Girl With Dog	1977		15.00	10.00 to 15.00
Easter, Girl With Chicks	1978	2500	20.00	20.00

Royal Bayreuth Pitcher

Devil & Cards*	1975	1000	75.00	75.00

Royal Bayreuth Plaques

European Songbirds, Set Of 6		2000	210.00	85.00 to 180.00

Royal Bayreuth Plates

Antique American Art, Farmyard Tranquility	1976	3000	50.00	60.00
Antique American Art, Half Dome	1977	3000	55.00	55.00
Christmas, Carriage In The Village*	1972	4000	15.00	50.00 to 75.00
Christmas, Snow Scene	1973	4000	16.50	15.00 to 30.00
Christmas, Old Mill	1974	4000	24.00	15.00 to 33.00
Christmas, Forest Chalet*	1975	4000	24.50	25.00 to 33.00
Christmas, Christmas In The Country	1976	5000	40.00	45.00
Christmas, Peace On Earth	1977	5000	40.00	40.00
Henry, Just Friends	1976	5000	50.00	50.00
Henry, Interruption	1977	4000	55.00	55.00
Mother's Day	1975	5000	25.00	45.00
Mother's Day, Consolation*	1973	4000	16.50	39.00
Mother's Day, Young Americans	1974	4000	25.00	60.00
Mother's Day, Young Americans II*	1978	5000	25.00	69.00
Mother's Day, Young Americans III**	1976	5000	30.00	75.00
Mother's Day, Young Americans IV	1977	4000	50.00	50.00
Mother's Day, Young Americans V	1978	5000	45.00	45.00
Sunbonnet Babies, Set Of 7	1973	15000	120.00	100.00 to 120.00
Sunbonnet Babies, 13 In.	1976	1000	75.00	75.00

Royal Bayreuth Stein

Devil & Cards	1975	2000	50.00	50.00

Royal Berlin-KPM Eggs

Easter	1972	600	60.00	49.00 to 60.00

Rosenthal, Christmas Plate, 1971

Rosenthal, Christmas Plate, 1972

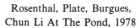

Rosenthal, Plate, Burgues,
Chun Li At The Pond, 1978

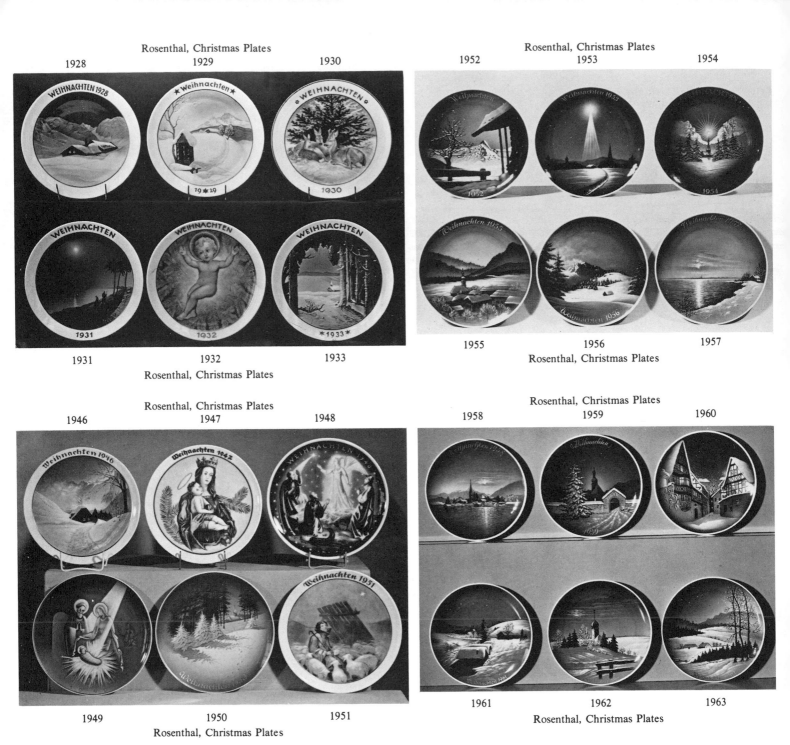

Rosenthal, Christmas Plates

1928   1929   1930

1931   1932   1933

Rosenthal, Christmas Plates

Rosenthal, Christmas Plates

1952   1953   1954

1955   1956   1957

Rosenthal, Christmas Plates

Rosenthal, Christmas Plates

1946   1947   1948

1949   1950   1951

Rosenthal, Christmas Plates

Rosenthal, Christmas Plates

1958   1959   1960

1961   1962   1963

Rosenthal, Christmas Plates

Royal Bayreuth, Christmas Plate, 1972

Royal Bayreuth, Mother's Day Plate, 1973

Title	Issue Date	Number Issued	Issued Price	Current Price
Easter*	1973	500	60.00	55.00 to 89.00
Easter*	1974	350	80.00	60.00 to 99.00
Easter	1975	350	85.00	42.50 to 85.00
Easter	1976	350	95.00	95.00

Royal Berlin-KPM Plaques

Olympic	1972	8000		12.00 to 18.00

Royal Berlin-KPM Plates

Christmas, Heralding Angel*	1974	5000	35.00	17.50 to 35.00
Christmas	1975	5000	40.00	20.00 to 40.00

Royal Canadian Mounted Police, see Bengough

Royal Copenhagen Porcelain Manufactory, Ltd., of Copenhagen, Denmark, was established in 1755. The first commemorative plate was made in 1888. Christmas plates were introduced in 1908, and the first Mother's Day plate was made in 1971. Royal Copenhagen has also produced many special commemorative plates in limited edition over the years.

Royal Copenhagen Bowls

Black-White Moderne	1975		70.00	100.00
Russet-Green Fantasy	1976		70.00	95.00
Bicentennial*	1976	2500	2000.00	2000.00

Royal Copenhagen Eggs

Hieroglyphic	1977		105.00	105.00

Royal Copenhagen Mugs

Year, Large*	1967	Year		165.00
Year, Small*	1967	Year		180.00 to 195.00
Year, Large	1968	Year		25.00 to 27.00
Year, Small	1968	Year		9.00 to 18.00
Year, Large	1969	Year		13.00 to 27.00
Year, Small	1969	Year		12.00 to 15.00
Year, Large	1970	Year		13.00 to 28.00
Year, Small	1970	Year		6.00 to 14.00
Year, Large	1971	Year		12.00 to 30.00
Year, Small	1971	Year		6.00 to 14.00
Year, Large*	1972	Year		35.00
Year, Small*	1972	Year		12.00 to 14.00
Year, Large**	1973	Year	35.00	30.00 to 35.00
Year, Small**	1973	Year	14.50	14.50
Year, Large	1974	Year	35.00	29.95 to 35.00
Year, Small	1974	Year	14.50	14.50
Year, Large	1975	Year	42.50	42.00 to 49.00
Year, Small	1975	Year	18.50	16.00
Year, Large	1976	Year		42.00 to 50.00
Year, Small	1976	Year		18.00 to 50.00
Year, Large	1977	Year	52.00	52.00
Year, Small	1977	Year	22.50	22.50

Royal Copenhagen Plates

Christmas, Madonna & Child*	1908	Year	1.00	900.00 to 1500.00
Christmas, Danish Landscape*	1909	Year	1.00	75.00 to 106.00
Christmas, Adoration Of The Magi*	1910	Year	1.00	70.00 to 110.00
Christmas, Danish Landscape, Sheaf Of Corn*	1911	Year	1.00	80.00 to 135.00
Christmas, Danish Landscape, Small*	1911			2000.00
Christmas, Elderly Couple By Christmas Tree*	1912	Year	1.00	80.00 to 135.00
Christmas, Spire Of Frederik Church*	1913	Year	1.50	80.00 to 125.00
Christmas, Sparrows In Tree*	1914	Year	1.50	75.00 to 115.00
Christmas, Snow-Covered Landscape*	1915	Year	1.50	66.00 to 100.00
Christmas, Angel And Shepherd	1916	Year	1.50	40.00 to 90.00
Christmas, Tower Of Our Saviour's Church	1917	Year	2.00	40.00 to 85.00
Christmas, The Shepherds*	1918	Year	2.00	60.00 to 84.00
Christmas, Shepherds In The Field, Large*	1918	49		Unknown
Christmas, In The Park*	1919	Year	2.00	57.00 to 75.00
Christmas, Mary With Child Jesus	1920	Year	2.00	52.00 to 75.00
Christmas, Marketplace In Aabenraa*	1921	Year	2.00	47.00 to 72.00
Christmas, Three Singing Angels	1922	Year	2.00	47.00 to 75.00
Christmas, Danish Landscape*	1923	Year	2.00	46.00 to 75.00
Christmas, Christmas Star Over The Sea	1924	Year	2.00	59.00 to 75.00
Christmas, Street Scene From Christianshavn*	1925	Year	2.00	53.00 to 70.00

Royal Bayreuth, Plate, Christmas,
Forest Chalet, 1975

Royal Bayreuth, Plate, Mother's Day,
Young Americans II, 1978

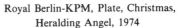

Royal Berlin-KPM, Plate, Christmas,
Heralding Angel, 1974

Royal Copenhagen, Year Mug, 1967, Large, Small

Royal Copenhagen, Bowl, Bicentennial, 1976

Royal Copenhagen, Plate,
Mother's Day, Mermaids, 1976

Royal Copenhagen, Plate,
Christmas, Viback Water Mill, 1976

Title	Issue Date	Number Issued	Issued Price	Current Price
Christmas, View From Christianshavn Canal	1926	Year	2.00	53.00 to 70.00
Christmas, Ship's Boy At The Tiller*	1927	Year	2.00	72.00 to 95.00
Christmas, Vicar's Family On Way To Church	1928	Year	28.00	49.00 to 75.00
Christmas, Grundtvig Church, Copenhagen	1929	Year	2.00	53.00 to 75.00
Christmas, Fishing Boats	1930	Year	2.50	55.00 to 75.00
Christmas, Mother & Child*	1931	Year	2.50	55.00 to 84.00
Christmas, Frederiksberg Gardens With Statue	1932	Year	2.50	55.00 to 75.00
Christmas, Ferry & The Great Belt*	1933	Year	2.50	72.00 to 90.00
Christmas, Hermitage Castle	1934	Year	2.50	67.00 to 112.00
Christmas, Fishing Boat Off Kronborg Castle	1935	Year	2.50	74.00 to 135.00
Christmas, Roskilde Cathedral*	1936	Year	2.50	76.00 to 120.00
Christmas, Christmas Scene In Main Street*	1937	Year	2.50	81.00 to 135.00
Christmas, Round Church In Osterlars*	1938	Year	3.00	142.00 to 240.00
Christmas, Expeditionary Ship In Greenland*	1939	Year	3.00	142.00 to 240.00
Christmas, The Good Shepherd*	1940	Year	3.00	210.00 to 375.00
Christmas, Danish Village Church*	1941	Year	3.00	200.00 to 375.00
Christmas, Bell Tower Of Old Church*	1942	Year	4.00	175.00 to 375.00
Christmas, Flight Of Holy Family To Egypt*	1943	Year	4.00	300.00 to 540.00
Christmas, Typical Danish Winter Scene*	1944	Year	4.00	84.00 to 150.00
Christmas, A Peaceful Motif*	1945	Year	4.00	199.00 to 372.00
Christmas, Zealand Village Church*	1946	Year	4.00	81.00 to 135.00
Christmas, The Good Shepherd*	1947	Year	4.50	104.00 to 210.00
Christmas, Noddebo Church At Christmastime	1948	Year	4.50	67.00 to 120.00
Christmas, Church Of Our Lady*	1949	Year	5.00	79.00 to 130.00
Christmas, Boeslunde Church, Zealand*	1950	Year	5.00	85.00 to 165.00
Christmas, Christmas Angel*	1951	Year	5.00	145.00 to 300.00
Christmas, Christmas In The Forest	1952	Year	5.00	43.00 to 96.00
Christmas, Frederiksborg Castle	1953	Year	6.00	50.00 to 90.00
Christmas, Amalienborg Palace, Copenhagen*	1954	Year	6.00	74.00 to 135.00
Christmas, Fanoe Girl*	1955	Year	7.00	120.00 to 225.00
Christmas, Rosenborg Castle*	1956	Year	7.00	75.00 to 150.00
Christmas, The Good Shepherd*	1957	Year	8.00	74.00 to 90.00
Christmas, Sunshine Over Greenland*	1958	Year	9.00	77.00 to 112.00
Christmas, Christmas Night*	1959	Year	9.00	70.00 to 135.00
Christmas, The Stag*	1960	Year	10.00	78.00 to 150.00
Christmas, Training Ship*	1961	Year	10.00	81.00 to 135.00
Christmas, Little Mermaid At Wintertime	1962	Year	11.00	98.00 to 180.00
Christmas, Hojsager Mill	1963	Year	11.00	41.00 to 60.00
Christmas, Fetching The Christmas Tree*	1964	Year	11.00	40.00 to 60.00
Christmas, Little Skaters*	1965	Year	12.00	35.00 to 60.00
Christmas, Blackbird At Christmastime	1966	Year	12.00	25.00 to 51.00
Christmas, The Royal Oak	1967	Year	13.00	18.00 to 35.00
Christmas, The Last Umiak*	1968	Year	13.00	15.00 to 31.00
Christmas, Geese On Farm	1969	Year	15.00	12.00 to 27.00
Christmas, Cat & Rose*	1970	Year	15.00	10.00 to 25.00
Christmas, Rabbit In Snow*	1971	Year	16.00	10.00 to 22.00
Christmas, Desert	1972	Year	16.00	12.00 to 22.00
Christmas, Going Home For Christmas*	1973	Year	22.00	11.00 to 25.00
Christmas, Winter Twilight	1974	Year	22.00	12.00 to 22.00
Christmas, Marselisborg Castle	1975	Year	27.50	28.50
Christmas, Queen's Palace	1975	Year	27.50	30.00
Christmas, Viback Water Mill*	1976	Year	27.50	36.00
Christmas, Immervad	1977	Year	32.00	32.00
Christmas, Greenland Scenery	1978	Year	35.00	35.00
Mother's Day, American Mother*	1971	Year	13.00	35.00 to 45.00
Mother's Day, Oriental Mother*	1972	Year	13.00	5.00 to 15.00
Mother's Day, Danish Mother*	1973	Year		6.00 to 16.00
Mother's Day, Greenland Mother	1974	Year	16.50	8.00 to 17.00
Mother's Day, Bird In Nest	1975	Year	20.00	21.00
Mother's Day, Mermaids*	1976	Year	20.00	20.00
Mother's Day, The Twins	1977	Year	24.00	24.00
Mother's Day	1978	Year	26.00	26.00
National Parks, Set Of 2	1978	5000	150.00	150.00

Royal Copenhagen Special Commemorative Plates

Title	Issue Date	Number Issued	Issued Price	Current Price
Scandinavian Exhibition In Copenhagen*	1888	1200		Unknown
Golden Wedding, Christian IX & Louise*	1892	1200		Unknown
Silver Wedding, Prince Frederik & Louise*	1894	1200		Unknown
Diploma Of Honor, Women's Exhibition*	1895	13		Unknown
Women's Exhibition In Copenhagen*	1895	1200		Unknown
Wedding, Prince Carl To Princess Maud*	1896	1200		Unknown

Title	Issue Date	Number Issued	Issued Price	Current Price
Wedding, Princess Louise To Friederich*	1896	1200		Unknown
Art And Industry Exhibition In Stockholm*	1897	1200		Unknown
Jutland Farmers Association Exhibition*	1897	1200		Unknown
Odd Fellows Hospital, Dragon & Rapier*	1897	1500		Unknown
Odd Fellows Hospital, St.George & Dragon*	1897	100		Unknown
Stockholm Exhibition, Royal Crown Of Sweden*	1897	100		Unknown
Stockholm Exhibition, Three Wavy Lines*	1897	100		Unknown
Wedding, Princess Ingeborg To Prince Carl*	1897	1200		Unknown
Women's Building In Copenhagen*	1897	1200		Unknown
80th Birthday, Queen Louise*	1897	1200		Unknown
Art Society Of 18th November*	1898	300		Unknown
Industrial Exhibition In Naskov*	1898	500		Unknown
Odd Fellows Hospital, Icelandic Falcon*	1898	2500		Unknown
The Cenotaph On Skamlingsbanken*	1898	1200		Unknown
Tourist Association Of Denmark*	1898	800		Unknown
Wedding, Prince Christian & Alexandrine*	1898	2500		Unknown
25th Anniversary, Wine Merchants*	1898	600		Unknown
50th Anniversary, Slesvig-Holstein War*	1898	850		Unknown
80th Birthday, King Christian IX*	1898	1200		Unknown
Freemason Lodge, Armed Mason*	1899	600		Unknown
Freemason Lodge, Masonic Insignia*	1899	800		Unknown
Odd Fellows, I.O.O.F.*	1899	500		Unknown
Odd Fellows Hospital, Geyser & Dragon*	1899	200		Unknown
Odd Fellows Hospital, Icelandic Volcano*	1899	200		Unknown
Odd Fellows Hospital, Polar Bear	1899	1900		Unknown
Odd Fellows Hospital, Skogafos Waterfall*	1899	200		Unknown
25th Anniversary, Copenhagen Students*	1899	100		Unknown
25th Anniversary, Royal Theatre, Copenhagen*	1899	35		Unknown
50th Anniversary, Battle Of Fredericia*	1899	200		Unknown
50th Anniversary, Olaf Rye*	1899	1000		Unknown
Danish-Norwegian Friendship Association*	1900	50		Unknown
Danish Participation In World Exhibition*	1900	600		Unknown
Glasgow Exhibition*	1901	262		Unknown
Turn Of The Century*	1901	500		Unknown
Vordingborg Exhibition*	1901	455		Unknown
Coronation, King Edward VII Of England*	1902	1000		Unknown
May Day Festival*	1903	500		Unknown
Odd Fellows, 25th Anniversary, Hourglass*	1903	250		Unknown
St.Louis Exhibition*	1903	500		Unknown
Town Hall Of Gentofte*	1903	225		Unknown
40th Anniversary, Christian IX, Closed Edge	1903	1200		Unknown
40th Anniversary, Christian IX, Open Edge*	1903	40		Unknown
Foundation Of Journalists' Association*	1904	300		Unknown
Restoration, Ribe Cathedral*	1904	200		Unknown
25th Anniversary, Danish Teetotallers' Club*	1904	1000		Unknown
750th Anniversary, Bulow Family*	1904	700		Unknown
Copenhagen Agricultural Exhibition*	1905	454		Unknown
Fishery Association*	1905	666		Unknown
Odd Fellows Hospital, Frigate*	1905	300		Unknown
100th Anniversary, Hans Christian Andersen*	1905	800		Unknown
Accession To Throne, King Frederik VIII*	1906	1500		Unknown
Completion Of Frescoes, Viborg Cathedral*	1906	243		Unknown
Coronation, Haakon VII & Maud*	1906	1500		Unknown
Danish Virgin Islands' Church Fund*	1906	300		Unknown
Danish Virgin Islands' Nursing Home*	1906	300		Unknown
Freemason Lodge, 50th Anniversary*	1906	800		Unknown
King Christian IX, Commemorative*	1906	1500		Unknown
40th Anniversary Danish Commercial Travel*	1906	1000		Unknown
Centenary, Fire Of Koldinghus Castle*	1907	600		Unknown
Danish Virgin Islands' Church Fund, Cross*	1907	250		Unknown
Danish Virgin Islands' Day Nursery*	1907	36		Unknown
Fanoe Commemorative*	1907	215		Unknown
Hotel And Restaurant Association*	1907	372		Unknown
Odd Fellows Hospital, Crowned M & Anchor*	1907	430		Unknown
Philatelist Club Stamp Exhibition*	1907	457		Unknown
Saint Canute Cathedral, Odense*	1907	212		Unknown
10th Anniversary, Aarhus Commercial Travel*	1907	300		Unknown
30th Anniversary Red Cross Society*	1907	300		Unknown
50th Anniversary, Agricultural Show*	1907	208		Unknown
250th Anniversary, Battalion*	1907	650		Unknown
250th Anniversary, Royal Lifeguard Regiment*	1907	825		Unknown

Royal Copenhagen, Christmas Plate, 1908

Royal Copenhagen, Christmas Plate, 1909

Royal Copenhagen, Christmas Plate, 1910

Royal Copenhagen, Year Mug, 1972, Large, Small

Royal Copenhagen, Christmas Plate, 1911

Royal Copenhagen, Christmas Plate, 1911, Small

Royal Copenhagen, Christmas Plate, 1912

Royal Copenhagen, Christmas Plate, 1913

Title	Issue Date	Number Issued	Issued Price	Current Price
Freemason Lodge, St.Clemens*	1908	331		Unknown
Freemason Lodge, St.Clemens, Lamb On Rock*	1908	29		Unknown
Journalists' Association, Ballet Dancer*	1908	250		Unknown
American Exhibition In Aarhus*	1909	396		Unknown
Congress For Raw Material Testing*	1909	25		Unknown
Danish Expedition To Greenland, Dogsleds*	1909	341		Unknown
Danish Expedition To Greenland, Eskimo*	1909	315		Unknown
Danish Expedition To Greenland, Two Men*	1909	5		Unknown
Danish Expedition To Northeast Greenland*	1909	642		Unknown
Danish Relief Mission To Messina*	1909	1107		Unknown
Freemason Lodge, St.Andrew*	1909	127		Unknown
Freemason Lodge, St.Andrew, Oval*	1909	28		Unknown
Mutual Aid Society Of Maribo County*	1909	238		Unknown
National Exhibition, Aarhus*	1909	1460		Unknown
Preservation Of Frigate Jylland, Large*	1909	18		Unknown
Preservation Of Frigate Jylland, Small*	1909	496		Unknown
Princess Marie Commemorative*	1909	2756		Unknown
Wedding, Prince Harald & Helena*	1909	1653		Unknown
Zoological Garden, Copenhagen*	1909	392		Unknown
Danish Women's Club, Defense Of Denmark*	1910	2423		Unknown
First Flight From Copenhagen To Malmo*	1910	251		Unknown
Welfare, Duchess Of Hessen*	1910	480		Unknown
West Indian Church And Kindergarten Fund*	1910	251		Unknown
Bishop Thomas Skat Rordam Commemorative*	1911	205		Unknown
Carlsberg Research Laboratories*	1911	200		Unknown
Castle Ruin Lindos On Rhodos Island*	1911	143		Unknown
Centenary, Carlsberg Brewery*	1911	575		Unknown
Coronation, King George V Of England*	1911	1936		75.00
Danish Commercial Travelers' Building*	1911	812		Unknown
Granary Of Carlsberg	1911	135		Unknown
Neptune Fountain, Frederiksborg Castle	1911	158		Unknown
Palmhouse, Botanical Gardens In Copenhagen	1911	137		Unknown
Peristyle At Carlsberg	1911	161		Unknown
Racing Boat Club, Copenhagen	1911	174		Unknown
Restoration Of Frederiksborg Castle	1911	194		Unknown
Royal Danish Society Of Sciences & Letters	1911	125		Unknown
200th Anniversary Danish Postal Service	1911	492		Unknown
1000th Anniversary, Conquest Of Normandy	1911	131		Unknown
Castle Of Kalmar, Sweden	1912	125		Unknown
Copenhagen Fishery Exhibition*	1912	291		Unknown
Copenhagen Rifle Corps*	1912	375		Unknown
Coronation, King Christian X & Alexandrine*	1912	2179		100.00
Danish Virgin Islands' Charity*	1912	424		Unknown
Danish Women's Club, Defense Of Denmark*	1912	1677		Unknown
Granting Of Municipal Charter, Herning*	1912	285		Unknown
King Frederik VIII Commemoration*	1912	1975		Unknown
Saint Canute Cathedral, Swans*	1912	490		Unknown
Scene From The Beach At The Skaw*	1912	139		Unknown
50th Anniversary Old People's Home*	1912	399		Unknown
150th Anniversary Royal Hussar Regiment*	1912	359		Unknown
Cathedral Of Our Lady, Copenhagen*	1913	163		Unknown
25th Anniversary, Danish Tourist Association*	1913	573		Unknown
70th Anniversary, Tivoli Gardens*	1913	626		Unknown
500th Anniversary, Landskrona, Sweden*	1913	120		Unknown
Baltic Exhibition*	1914	265		Unknown
Charity, Queen's Christmas Fund*	1914	599		Unknown
Scene Of Frankfurt Am Main*	1914	1107		Unknown
50th Anniversary, Battle Of Dybbol*	1914	2814		Unknown
50th Anniversary, Victory At Helgoland*	1914	1761		Unknown
70th Birthday, Queen Alexandra Of England*	1914	929		Unknown
Charity, World War I, St.George & Dragon*	1915	2123		Unknown
Meeting Of Scandinavian Kings In Malmo*	1915	3610		Unknown
San Francisco Exhibition*	1915	557		Unknown
San Francisco Exhibition, California*	1915	179		Unknown
San Francisco Exhibition, Landscape*	1915	1197		Unknown
25th Anniversary, Haand I Haand Insurance*	1915	421		Unknown
100th Anniversary, Army Cadet Academy*	1915	683		Unknown
Denmark Association, Landscape*	1916	1044		Unknown
Odd Fellows, Good Samaritan*	1916	890		Unknown
Actors' Association, Olaf Poulsen*	1917	765		Unknown

Royal Copenhagen, Christmas Plate, 1914

Royal Copenhagen, Christmas Plate, 1922

Royal Copenhagen, Christmas Plate, 1919

Royal Copenhagen, Christmas Plate, 1923

Royal Copenhagen, Christmas Plate, 1915

Royal Copenhagen, Christmas Plate, 1918

Royal Copenhagen, Christmas Plate, 1925

Royal Copenhagen, Christmas Plate, 1921

Royal Copenhagen, Christmas Plate, 1927

Royal Copenhagen, Christmas Plate, 1918,
Large

Royal Copenhagen, Christmas Plate, 1931

Royal Copenhagen, Christmas Plate, 1940

Royal Copenhagen, Christmas Plate, 1938

Royal Copenhagen, Christmas Plate, 1941

Royal Copenhagen, Christmas Plate, 1933

Royal Copenhagen, Christmas Plate, 1936

Royal Copenhagen, Christmas Plate, 1942

Royal Copenhagen, Christmas Plate, 1939

Royal Copenhagen, Christmas Plate, 1943

Royal Copenhagen, Christmas Plate, 1937

Royal Copenhagen, Christmas Plate, 1944

Royal Copenhagen, Christmas Plate, 1951

Royal Copenhagen, Christmas Plate, 1949

Royal Copenhagen, Christmas Plate, 1954

Royal Copenhagen, Christmas Plate, 1945

Royal Copenhagen, Christmas Plate, 1946

Royal Copenhagen, Christmas Plate, 1955

Royal Copenhagen, Christmas Plate, 1950

Royal Copenhagen, Christmas Plate, 1956

Royal Copenhagen, Christmas Plate, 1947

Royal Copenhagen, Christmas Plate, 1957

Royal Copenhagen, Christmas Plate, 1965

Royal Copenhagen, Christmas Plate, 1961

Royal Copenhagen, Christmas Plate, 1968

Royal Copenhagen, Christmas Plate, 1958

Royal Copenhagen, Christmas Plate, 1959

Royal Copenhagen, Christmas Plate, 1970

Royal Copenhagen, Christmas Plate, 1964

Royal Copenhagen, Christmas Plate, 1971

Royal Copenhagen, Christmas Plate, 1960

Title	Issue Date	Number Issued	Issued Price	Current Price
Coast Artillery Association, Fortress*	1917	511		Unknown
Danish Commercial Travelers, Zealand*	1917	174		Unknown
Odd Fellows, Men Greeting Each Other*	1917	587		Unknown
Red Cross Society, Denmark, Nurse*	1917	360		Unknown
70th Birthday, Empress Dagmar Of Russia*	1917	2359		Unknown
Corporation Of Publicans, Copenhagen*	1918	600		Unknown
Founding Of Mercantile Navy Museum, Kronborg*	1918	1435		Unknown
Odd Fellows Foundling Home, Moses*	1918	1325		Unknown
Odd Fellows, 25th Anniversary Roskilde Lodge*	1918	352		Unknown
Odd Fellows, 40th Anniversary*	1918	1570		Unknown
40th Anniversary, Army Supply Corps*	1918	603		Unknown
50th Anniversary, City Of Esbjerg	1918	417		Unknown
100th Anniversary, Birth Of Christian IX*	1918	3063		Unknown
Odd Fellows, Centenary, Blacksmith*	1919	1500		Unknown
Peace Plate*	1919	3488		Unknown
Reunification With Slesvig, Landscape*	1919	5054		Unknown
Reunification With Slesvig, Queen Thyra*	1919	4411		Unknown
40th Anniversary, Danish Teetotallers' Club*	1919	157		Unknown
Memorial, Scandinavian Soldiers, World War I*	1920	802		Unknown
Odd Fellows, 25th Anniversary Ansgar Lodge*	1920	592		Unknown
35th Anniversary, Aarhus Fire Brigade*	1920	367		Unknown
50th Birthday, King Christian X*	1920	2601		Unknown
100th Anniversary, Copenhagen Students' Club*	1920	1229		Unknown
Silver Wedding, Haakon VII & Maud*	1921	606		Unknown
Wedding, Princess Margrethe & Rene*	1921	1124		Unknown
Charity, Home For Children, Bethlehem*	1922	866		Unknown
Civic Association Of Frederiksberg*	1922	634		Unknown
Freemason Lodge, St.John, Iceland, Harbor*	1922	300		Unknown
200th Anniversary, Danish Theatre*	1922	577		Unknown
25th Anniversary, Portland Cement Works*	1923	368		Unknown
40th Anniversary, Home For Children*	1923	397		Unknown
Odd Fellows, 25th Anniversary, Lighthouse*	1924	337		Unknown
First Flight, Copenhagen To Tokyo*	1926	212		Unknown
Frigate Jylland*	1926	1903		Unknown
25th Anniversary, Royal Danish Auto Club*	1926	670		Unknown
50th Anniversary, Artisans' Guild, Hjorring*	1926	443		Unknown
600th Anniversary, Municipal Charter, Skive*	1926	617		Unknown
200th Anniversary, Nibe's Municipal Charter*	1927	114		Unknown
B & W Shipbuilding Company, Copenhagen*	1928	158		Unknown
Christiansborg Castle, Copenhagen*	1928	121		Unknown
Prince Valdemar & Marie's Benevolent Fund*	1928	232		Unknown
50th Anniversary, Botanical Gardens*	1928	1214		Unknown
20th Anniversary, Copenhagen Rifle Corps*	1929	169		Unknown
150th Anniversary, Royal Copenhagen*	1929	216		Unknown
150th Anniversary, Royal Copenhagen, Seascape*	1929	1815		Unknown
Freemason Lodge, Copenhagen*	1930	324		Unknown
10th Anniversary, Reunification Of Slesvig*	1930	1175		Unknown
50th Anniversary, Order Of Good Templar*	1930	304		Unknown
Silver Wedding, Frederik IX & Ingrid*	1960			Unknown
200th Anniversary, Royal Hussar	1962		10.00	40.00 to 55.00
Virgin Islands Commemorative	1967		12.00	25.00 to 35.00
Frankfurt Am Main	1968			25.00 to 35.00
150th Anniversary, City Of Frederikshavn*	1968			Unknown
Apollo 11	1969		15.00	10.00 to 15.00
Danish Flag*	1969			20.00 to 30.00
Mill Dybbol	1970			20.00 to 25.00
King Frederik IX	1972		22.00	20.00 to 22.00
Olympics	1972		25.00	25.00 to 30.00
Royal Copenhagen Bicentennial	1975		30.00	30.00
Olympics	1976		29.50	29.50
United States Bicentennial	1976		35.00	35.00
Birth Of H.C.Orsted	1977		35.00	35.00
Electromagnetism	1977		35.00	35.00
Captain Cook, Cook Landing	1978		37.50	37.50

Royal Cornwall Plates

Title	Issue Date	Number Issued	Issued Price	Current Price
Golden Age Of Cinema, The King	1978	19500	45.00	45.00
Granget, Fledgling	1978	5000	60.00	60.00
Granget, Voices Of Spring	1978	5000	60.00	60.00
Granget, Warmth	1978	5000	60.00	60.00
Granget, We Survive	1978	5000	60.00	60.00

Royal Copenhagen, Christmas Plate, 1973

Royal Copenhagen, Mother's Day Plate, 1971

Royal Copenhagen, Mother's Day Plate, 1972

Royal Copenhagen, Mother's Day Plate, 1973

Royal Copenhagen,
Scandinavian Exhibition In Copenhagen,
1888

Royal Copenhagen, Wedding,
Princess Louise To Friederich, 1896

Royal Copenhagen,
Women's Exhibition In Copenhagen, 1895

Royal Copenhagen,
Art And Industry Exhibition In Stockholm,
1897

Royal Copenhagen,
Golden Wedding,
Christian IX & Louise, 1892

Royal Copenhagen,
Silver Wedding,
Prince Frederik & Louise, 1894

Royal Copenhagen,
Jutland Farmers Association Exhibition,
1897

Royal Copenhagen, Wedding,
Prince Carl To Princess Maud, 1896

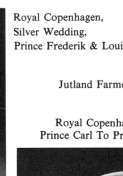

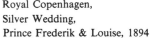

Royal Copenhagen,
Odd Fellows Hospital,
Dragon & Rapier, 1897

Royal Copenhagen,
Diploma Of Honor,
Women's Exhibition, 1895

Royal Copenhagen, Odd Fellows Hospital,
St.George & Dragon, 1897

Royal Copenhagen,
Art Society Of 18th November, 1898

Royal Copenhagen,
Women's Building In Copenhagen, 1897

Royal Copenhagen,
Industrial Exhibition In Naskov, 1898

Royal Copenhagen, Stockholm Exhibition,
Royal Crown Of Sweden, 1897

Royal Copenhagen, Stockholm Exhibition,
Three Wavy Lines, 1897

Royal Copenhagen,
Odd Fellows Hospital,
Icelandic Falcon, 1898

Royal Copenhagen,
80th Birthday, Queen Louise, 1897

Royal Copenhagen,
The Cenotaph On Skamlingsbanken,
1898

Royal Copenhagen, Wedding,
Princess Ingeborg To Prince Carl,
1897

Royal Copenhagen,
Tourist Association Of Denmark, 1898

Royal Copenhagen, Freemason Lodge,
Masonic Insignia, 1899

Royal Copenhagen, 80th Birthday,
King Christian IX, 1898

Royal Copenhagen, Odd Fellows,
I.O.O.F., 1899

Royal Copenhagen, Wedding,
Prince Christian & Alexandrine, 1898

Royal Copenhagen, 25th Anniversary,
Wine Merchants, 1898

Royal Copenhagen, Odd Fellows Hospital,
Geyser & Dragon, 1899

Royal Copenhagen, Freemason Lodge,
Armed Mason, 1899

Royal Copenhagen, Odd Fellows Hospital,
Icelandic Volcano, 1899

Royal Copenhagen, 50th Anniversary,
Slesvig-Holstein War, 1898

Royal Copenhagen,
Odd Fellows Hospital,
Skogafos Waterfall, 1899

Royal Copenhagen,
Danish Participation In World Exhibition,
1900

Royal Copenhagen, 50th Anniversary,
Olaf Rye, 1899

Royal Copenhagen,
Glasgow Exhibition, 1901

Royal Copenhagen, 25th Anniversary,
Copenhagen Students, 1899

Royal Copenhagen, 25th Anniversary,
Royal Theatre, Copenhagen, 1899

Royal Copenhagen,
Turn Of The Century, 1901

Royal Copenhagen,
Danish-Norwegian Friendship Association,
1900

Royal Copenhagen,
Vordingborg Exhibition, 1901

Royal Copenhagen, 50th Anniversary,
Battle Of Fredericia, 1899

Royal Copenhagen, Coronation,
King Edward VII Of England, 1902

Royal Copenhagen,
Foundation Of Journalists' Association,
1904

Royal Copenhagen,
Town Hall Of Gentofte, 1903

Royal Copenhagen, Restoration,
Ribe Cathedral, 1904

Royal Copenhagen,
May Day Festival, 1903

Royal Copenhagen, Odd Fellows,
25th Anniversary, Hourglass, 1903

Royal Copenhagen, 25th Anniversary,
Danish Teetotallers' Club, 1904

Royal Copenhagen, 40th Anniversary,
Christian IX, Open Edge, 1903

Royal Copenhagen, 750th Anniversary,
Bulow Family, 1904

Royal Copenhagen,
St.Louis Exhibition, 1903

Royal Copenhagen,
Copenhagen Agricultural Exhibition,
1905

Royal Copenhagen, Coronation,
Haakon VII & Maud, 1906

Royal Copenhagen, Accession To Throne,
King Frederik VIII, 1906

Royal Copenhagen,
Danish Virgin Islands' Church Fund,
1906

Royal Copenhagen,
Fishery Association, 1905

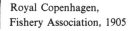

Royal Copenhagen,
Odd Fellows Hospital,
Frigate, 1905

Royal Copenhagen,
Danish Virgin Islands' Nursing Home,
1906

Royal Copenhagen, Completion Of Frescoes,
Viborg Cathedral, 1906

Royal Copenhagen, Freemason Lodge,
50th Anniversary, 1906

Royal Copenhagen, 100th Anniversary,
Hans Christian Andersen, 1905

Royal Copenhagen, King Christian IX,
Commemorative, 1906

Royal Copenhagen,
Hotel And Restaurant Association,
1907

Royal Copenhagen,
Danish Virgin Islands' Day Nursery, 1907

Royal Copenhagen,
Odd Fellows Hospital,
Crowned M & Anchor, 1907

Royal Copenhagen,
40th Anniversary Danish Commercial Travel,
1906

Royal Copenhagen, Centenary,
Fire Of Koldinghus Castle, 1907

Royal Copenhagen,
Philatelist Club Stamp Exhibition,
1907

Royal Copenhagen,
Fano Commemorative, 1907

Royal Copenhagen,
Saint Canute Cathedral,
Odense, 1907

Royal Copenhagen,
Danish Virgin Islands' Church Fund,
Cross, 1907

Royal Copenhagen, 250th Anniversary,
Royal Lifeguard Regiment, 1907

Royal Copenhagen,
Danish Expedition To Greenland,
Dogsleds, 1909

Royal Copenhagen,
American Exhibition In Aarhus, 1909

Royal Copenhagen,
Danish Expedition To Greenland,
Eskimo, 1909

Royal Copenhagen,
Freemason Lodge, St.Clemens, 1908

Royal Copenhagen,
Freemason Lodge, St.Clemens,
Lamb On Rock, 1908

Royal Copenhagen, Danish Expedition
To Northeast Greenland, 1909

Royal Copenhagen,
Congress For Raw Material Testing, 1909

Royal Copenhagen,
Danish Expedition To Greenland,
Two Men, 1909

Royal Copenhagen,
Journalists' Association,
Ballet Dancer, 1908

Royal Copenhagen,
Danish Relief Mission To Messina,
1909

Royal Copenhagen,
Preservation Of Frigate Jylland,
Small, 1909

Royal Copenhagen, Freemason Lodge,
St.Andrew, Oval, 1909

Royal Copenhagen,
Princess Marie Commemorative, 1909

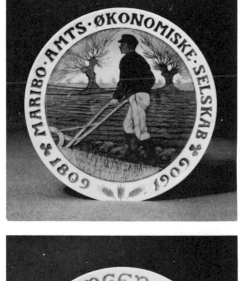

Royal Copenhagen, Freemason Lodge,
St.Andrew, 1909

Royal Copenhagen,
Mutual Aid Society Of Maribo County,
1909

Royal Copenhagen, Wedding,
Prince Harald & Helena, 1909

Royal Copenhagen,
Preservation Of Frigate Jylland,
Large, 1909

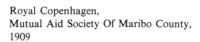

Royal Copenhagen, Zoological Garden,
Copenhagen, 1909

Royal Copenhagen,
National Exhibition, Aarhus, 1909

Royal Copenhagen,
Danish Women's Club,
Defense Of Denmark, 1910

Royal Copenhagen,
Bishop Thomas Skat Rordam
Commemorative, 1911

Royal Copenhagen, Carlsberg Brewery, 1911

Royal Copenhagen, Coronation,
King George V Of England,
1911

Royal Copenhagen, First Flight
From Copenhagen To Malmo,
1910

Royal Copenhagen, Welfare,
Duchess Of Hessen, 1910

Royal Copenhagen,
Danish Commercial Travelers' Building,
1911

Royal Copenhagen,
Castle Ruin Lindos On Rhodos Island,
1911

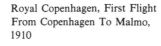
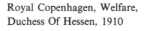

Royal Copenhagen,
Carlsberg Research Laboratories, 1911

Royal Copenhagen, West Indian Church
And Kindergarten Fund, 1910

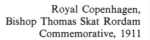

Royal Copenhagen,
Copenhagen Fishery Exhibition, 1912

Royal Copenhagen,
King Frederik VIII Commemoration,
1912

Royal Copenhagen, Danish Women's Club,
Defense Of Denmark, 1912

Royal Copenhagen,
Saint Canute Cathedral, Swans, 1912

Royal Copenhagen,
Copenhagen Rifle Corps, 1912

Royal Copenhagen,
Coronation, King Christian X & Alexandrine,
1912

Royal Copenhagen,
Scene From The Beach At The Skaw,
1912

Royal Copenhagen,
Granting Of Municipal Charter, Herning, 1912

Royal Copenhagen,
50th Anniversary Old People's Home,
1912

Royal Copenhagen,
Danish Virgin Islands' Charity, 1912

Royal Copenhagen,
150th Anniversary Royal Hussar Regiment,
1912

Royal Copenhagen, Charity,
Queen's Christmas Fund, 1914

Royal Copenhagen, 500th Anniversary,
Landskrona, Sweden, 1913

Royal Copenhagen,
Scene Of Frankfurt Am Main, 1914

Royal Copenhagen,
Cathedral Of Our Lady,
Copenhagen, 1913

Royal Copenhagen, 25th Anniversary,
Danish Tourist Association, 1913

Royal Copenhagen, 50th Anniversary,
Battle Of Dybbol, 1914

Royal Copenhagen, Baltic Exhibition, 1914

Royal Copenhagen, 50th Anniversary,
Victory At Helgoland, 1914

Royal Copenhagen, 70th Anniversary,
Tivoli Gardens, 1913

Royal Copenhagen, 10th Anniversary,
Aarhus Commercial Travel, 1907

Royal Copenhagen, 70th Birthday,
Queen Alexandra Of England, 1914

Royal Copenhagen, 30th Anniversary,
Red Cross Society, 1907

Royal Copenhagen, Charity,
World War I, St.George & Dragon, 1915

Royal Copenhagen, 50th Anniversary,
Agricultural Show, 1907

Royal Copenhagen, 250th Anniversary,
Battalion, 1907

Royal Copenhagen,
Meeting Of Scandinavian Kings In Malmo, 1915

Royal Copenhagen, San Francisco Exhibition, 1915

Royal Copenhagen, 100th Anniversary,
Army Cadet Academy, 1915

Royal Copenhagen, Actors' Association,
Olaf Poulsen, 1917

Royal Copenhagen,
Denmark Association, Landscape, 1916

Royal Copenhagen,
Coast Artillery Association, Fortress,
1917

Royal Copenhagen,
San Francisco Exhibition, Landscape,
1915

Royal Copenhagen, 25th Anniversary,
Haand I Haand Insurance, 1915

Royal Copenhagen,
Danish Commercial Travelers,
Zealand, 1917

Royal Copenhagen, Odd Fellows,
Good Samaritan, 1916

Royal Copenhagen, Odd Fellows,
Men Greeting Each Other, 1917

Royal Copenhagen,
San Francisco Exhibition, California, 1915

Royal Copenhagen, Red Cross Society,
Denmark, Nurse, 1917

Royal Copenhagen, 40th Anniversary,
Army Supply Corps, 1918

Royal Copenhagen,
Odd Fellows Foundling Home, Moses, 1918

Royal Copenhagen, 100th Anniversary,
Birth Of Christian IX, 1918

Royal Copenhagen, 70th Birthday,
Empress Dagmar Of Russia, 1917

Royal Copenhagen,
Founding Of Mercantile Navy Museum,
Kronborg, 1918

Royal Copenhagen, Odd Fellows,
25th Anniversary Roskilde Lodge, 1918

Royal Copenhagen, Odd Fellows,
40th Anniversary, 1918

Royal Copenhagen, Odd Fellows,
Centenary, Blacksmith, 1919

Royal Copenhagen,
Corporation Of Publicans,
Copenhagen, 1918

Royal Copenhagen, Year Mug, 1973, Large

Royal Copenhagen, Year Mug, 1973, Small

Michelsen, Christmas Spoons,
1910 - 1919 Left To Right

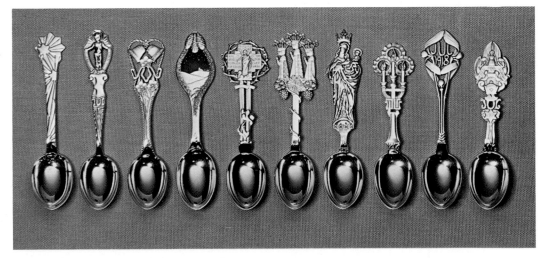

Michelsen, Christmas Spoons,
1920 -1929 Left To Right

Michelsen, Christmas Spoons,
1930 -1939 Left To Right

Michelsen, Christmas Spoons,
1940 - 1949 Left To Right

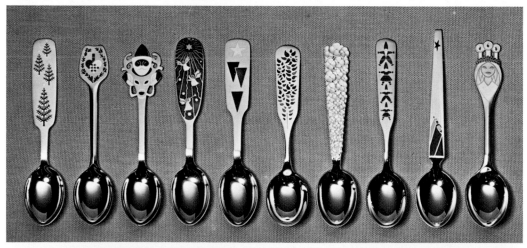

Michelsen, Christmas Spoons,
1950 - 1959 Left To Right

Michelsen, Christmas Spoons,
1960 - 1969 Left To Right

Georg Jensen, Christmas Spoon,
1971, Cherry Blossom

Michelsen, Christmas Fork And Spoon, 1972

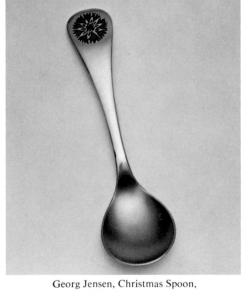

Michelsen, Christmas Fork And Spoon,
1973

Michelsen, Christmas Spoon, 1971

Michelsen, Christmas Fork And Spoon, 1974

Georg Jensen, Christmas Spoon,
1972, Cornflower

Georg Jensen, Christmas Spoon, 1973,
Corn Marigold

Michelsen, Christmas Fork And Spoon,
1970

Ispanky, Abraham

Ispanky, Dragon, Emerald

Ispanky, Love Letters

Ispanky, Maid Of The Mist

Boehm, Brown Pelican

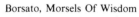

Borsato, Morsels Of Wisdom

Boehm, Mute Swans (Bird Of Peace)

Boehm, E.M.Boehm Orchid Centerpiece

Boehm, Hooded Mergansers

Boehm, Canadian Warbler, Fledgling

Boehm, Rufous Hummingbirds

Lenox, Boehm Wildlife Plate, 1973, Racoons

Lenox, Boehm Bird Plate, 1970, Wood Thrush

Lenox, Boehm Bird Plate, 1971, Goldfinch

Rosenthal, Christmas Plate, 1973

Wheaton Village, Paperweight,
Bicentennial Floral, Clear, 1976

Wheaton Village, Paperweight,
Bicentennial Floral, Blue, 1976

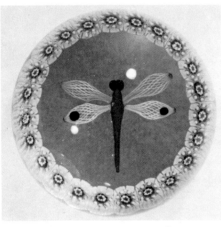

Perthshire, Paperweight, Dragonfly

Perthshire, Paperweight, Dahlia

Gorham, Paperweight, Egg, 1978

Pairpoint,
Red, White And Blue Crown Paperweight

Pairpoint, Faceted Red Rose Paperweight

Pairpoint, Peachblow Bell, 1973

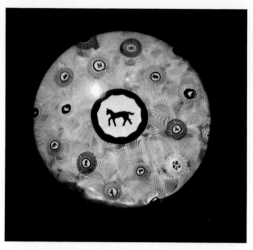

Baccarat, Gridel Horse

Baccarat, Millefiori, Regular

Baccarat, Harry S. Truman, Overlay

Baccarat, Complex Flower

Baccarat, Gridel Squirrel
Baccarat, Millefiori, Concentric

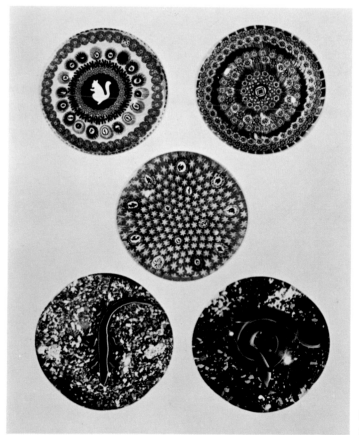

Baccarat, Carpet Ground
With Zodiac Signs

Royal Bayreuth, Christmas Plate, 1973

Baccarat, Salamander
Baccarat, Snake

Royal Bayreuth, Sunbonnet Babies Plates

River Shore, Bell, Rockwell, Children Series II, 4, 1978

Burgues, Spirit Of Freedom, Equus Caballus, Color, 1976

Royal Copenhagen,
Peace Plate, 1919

Royal Copenhagen, 35th Anniversary,
Aarhus Fire Brigade, 1920

Royal Copenhagen, Memorial,
Scandianavian Soldiers,
World War I, 1920

Royal Copenhagen, 50th Birthday,
King Christian X, 1920

Royal Copenhagen,
Reunification With Slesvig,
Landscape, 1919

Royal Copenhagen, 40th Anniversary,
Danish Teetotallers' Club, 1919

Royal Copenhagen, 100th Anniversary,
Copenhagen Students' Club, 1920

Royal Copenhagen, Odd Fellows,
25th Anniversary Ansgar Lodge, 1920

Royal Copenhagen, Silver Wedding,
Haakon VII & Maud, 1921

Royal Copenhagen,
Reunification With Slesvig,
Queen Thyra, 1919

Royal Copenhagen,
Wedding Princess Margrethe & Rene,
1921

Royal Copenhagen, 40th Anniversary,
Home For Children, 1923

Royal Copenhagen, 200th Anniversary,
Danish Theatre, 1922

Royal Copenhagen, 25th Anniversary,
Lighthouse, 1924

Royal Copenhagen, Charity,
Home For Children, Bethlehem, 1922

Royal Copenhagen,
Civic Association Of Frederiksberg,
1922

Royal Copenhagen, First Flight,
Copenhagen To Tokyo, 1926

Royal Copenhagen, 25th Anniversary,
Portland Cement Works, 1923

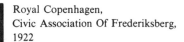

Royal Copenhagen,
Frigate Jylland, 1926

Royal Copenhagen, Freemason Lodge,
St.John, Iceland, Harbor, 1922

Royal Copenhagen, 50th Anniversary,
Artisans' Guild, Hjorring, 1926

Royal Copenhagen, 50th Anniversary,
Botanical Gardens, 1928

Royal Copenhagen,
B & W Shipbuilding Company,
Copenhagen, 1928

Royal Copenhagen, 25th Anniversary,
Royal Danish Auto Club, 1926

Royal Copenhagen,
Christiansborg Castle, Copenhagen, 1928

Royal Copenhagen, 600th Anniversary,
Municipal Charter, Skive, 1926

Royal Copenhagen, 20th Anniversary,
Copenhagen Rifle Corps, 1929

Royal Copenhagen,
Prince Valdemar & Marie's
Benevolent Fund, 1928

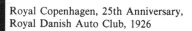

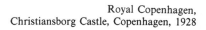

Royal Copenhagen, 150th Anniversary,
Royal Copenhagen, 1929

Royal Copenhagen, 200th Anniversary,
Nibe's Municipal Charter, 1927

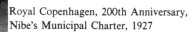

Royal Copenhagen, 150th Anniversary,
Royal Copenhagen, Seascape, 1929

Royal Copenhagen, Silver Wedding,
Frederik IX & Ingrid, 1960

Royal Copenhagen, Freemasons' Lodge,
Copenhagen, 1930

Royal Copenhagen, 50th Anniversary,
Order Of Good Templar, 1930

Royal Copenhagen, 150th Anniversary,
City Of Frederikshavn, 1968

Royal Copenhagen, 10th Anniversary,
Reunification Of Slesvig, 1930

Royal Copenhagen, Dannebrog,
Danish Flag, 1969

Royal Delft, Christmas Plate, 1973
10 Inch   7 Inch

Title	Issue Date	Number Issued	Issued Price	Current Price
Royal Crown Derby of England was established as the Derby factory in 1750. The name Royal Crown Derby was used after 1890. Current limited editions were introduced in 1969.				
See listing for Royal Crown Derby in Figurine section				
Royal Crown Derby Bells				
Investiture Of The Prince Of Wales	1969	500	45.00	Unknown
Royal Crown Derby Boxes				
Queen's Silver Jubilee	1977	25	1300.00	1300.00
Royal Crown Derby Cups & Saucers				
British Birds, Common Sandpiper	1972	50	150.00	Unknown
British Birds, Dipper	1972	50	150.00	Unknown
British Birds, Lapwing	1972	50	150.00	Unknown
British Birds, Mallard	1972	50	150.00	Unknown
British Birds, Oystercatcher	1972	50	150.00	Unknown
British Birds, Tufted Duck	1972	50	150.00	Unknown
Royal Crown Derby Dessert Plates				
Clarence	1977	500	80.00	80.00
Derbyshire Landscapes, Beeley Brook	1972	50	225.00	Unknown
Derbyshire Landscapes, Dove Holes	1972	50	225.00	Unknown
Derbyshire Landscapes, Dovedale	1972	50	225.00	Unknown
Derbyshire Landscapes, Edale Head	1972	50	225.00	Unknown
Derbyshire Landscapes, Edenser	1972	50	225.00	Unknown
Derbyshire Landscapes, Haddon Hall	1972	50	225.00	Unknown
Derbyshire Landscapes, Lathkil Dale	1972	50	225.00	Unknown
Derbyshire Landscapes, Milldale	1972	50	225.00	Unknown
Derbyshire Landscapes, Nether Bridge	1972	50	225.00	Unknown
Derbyshire Landscapes, Stanton Moor	1972	50	225.00	Unknown
Derbyshire Landscapes, Stoney Middleton	1972	50	225.00	Unknown
Derbyshire Landscapes, Wolfscote Dale**	1972	50	225.00	Unknown
Royal Crown Derby Trays				
Five Petal	1977	1500	50.00	50.00
Royal Crown Derby Vases				
Kedleston Vase	1973	125	290.00	Unknown
St. Leger	1976	50	1547.00	Unknown

Royal Delft,
Ambassador Plate, 1973

Royal Delft,
Ambassador Mug, 1973

Royal Delft of Holland, also known as De Porceleyne Fles, has been making delftware for over 300 years. Christmas plates were introduced in 1915. No plates were made between the years 1942 and 1954. Contemporary limited editions were started in 1968.

Title	Issue Date	Number Issued	Issued Price	Current Price
Royal Delft Mugs				
Ambassador*	1973	4500	45.00	Unknown
Royal Delft Plates				
Ambassador*	1973	4500	75.00	Unknown
Apollo 11				Unknown
Bicentennial, George Washington	1976	2500	325.00	325.00
Christmas	1915	Year		Unknown
Christmas	1916	Year		Unknown
Christmas	1917	Year		Unknown
Christmas	1918	Year		Unknown
Christmas	1919	Year		Unknown
Christmas	1920	Year		Unknown
Christmas	1921	Year		Unknown
Christmas	1922	Year		Unknown
Christmas	1923	Year		Unknown
Christmas	1924	Year		Unknown
Christmas	1925	Year		Unknown
Christmas	1926	Year		Unknown
Christmas	1927	Year		Unknown
Christmas	1928	Year		Unknown
Christmas	1929	Year		Unknown
Christmas	1930	Year		Unknown
Christmas	1931	Year		Unknown
Christmas	1932	Year		Unknown
Christmas	1933	Year		Unknown
Christmas	1934	Year		Unknown

Royal Delft, Easter Plate, 1973

Royal Delft, Father's Day Plate, 1973

Royal Delft, Mother's Day Plate, 1973

Royal Delft, Valentine's Day Plate, 1973

Royal Doulton, Plate, Ports Of Call,
Montmartre, 1978

Royal Doulton, Plate,
Neiman, Columbine, 1977

Title	Issue Date	Number Issued	Issued Price	Current Price
Christmas	1935	Year		Unknown
Christmas	1936	Year		Unknown
Christmas	1937	Year		Unknown
Christmas	1938	Year		Unknown
Christmas	1939	Year		Unknown
Christmas	1940	Year		Unknown
Christmas	1941	Year		Unknown
Christmas	1955	Year		Unknown
Christmas	1956	Year		Unknown
Christmas	1957	Year		Unknown
Christmas	1958	Year		Unknown
Christmas	1959	Year		Unknown
Christmas	1960	Year		Unknown
Christmas	1961	Year		Unknown
Christmas	1962	Year		Unknown
Christmas	1963	Year		Unknown
Christmas	1964	Year		Unknown
Christmas	1965	Year		Unknown
Christmas	1966	Year		Unknown
Christmas	1967	Year		Unknown
Christmas, Schreierstoren, 10 Inch	1968	Year		Unknown
Christmas, Walmolen Mill, 7 Inch	1968	Year		Unknown
Christmas, Mill Near Gorkum, 7 Inch	1969	Year		Unknown
Christmas, Old Church In Dordeckt, 10 Inch	1969	Year		Unknown
Christmas, Cathedral In Veere, 10 Inch	1970	Year		Unknown
Christmas, Mill Near Haarlem, 7 Inch	1970	Year		Unknown
Christmas, Canal Scene In Utrecht, 10 Inch	1971	Year	60.00	Unknown
Christmas, Towngate Of Zierkee, 7 Inch	1971	Year	40.00	Unknown
Christmas, Church Of Edam, 10 Inch	1972	Year	70.00	Unknown
Christmas, Towngate At Elburg, 7 Inch	1972	Year	40.00	Unknown
Christmas, Towngate Of Amersfoort, 7 Inch	1973	Year	50.00	Unknown
Christmas, Weigh Office In Alkmaar, 10 Inch	1973	Year	75.00	Unknown
Christmas, 10 In.	1974			110.00
Easter, Dutch Palm Sunday Cross*	1973	Year	75.00	Unknown
Easter	1974	1000	85.00	Unknown
Father's Day, Fisherman & Son Of Volendam	1972	Year	40.00	Unknown
Father's Day, Looking At The Zuider Zee*	1973	Year	50.00	Unknown
Father's Day	1974	1000	65.00	Unknown
Hamilton Set, 12 Months	1978	6000	600.00	600.00
Mother's Day, Mother & Daughter Of Volendam	1971	Year	35.00	Unknown
Mother's Day, Women Of Hindeloopen	1972	Year	40.00	Unknown
Mother's Day, Marken Villagers*	1973	Year	50.00	Unknown
Olympic	1972	Year		Unknown
Pilgrim Fathers	1970	Year		Unknown
Valentine's Day*	1973	Year		Unknown
Valentine's Day	1974	1000	85.00	Unknown

Royal Devon plates are made by Gorham Company. The Rockwell series began in 1975.

Royal Devon Plates

Title	Issue Date	Number Issued	Issued Price	Current Price
Rockwell, Christmas, Downhill Racing	1975	Year	24.50	43.00
Rockwell, Christmas, The Christmas Gift	1976	Year	24.50	19.50 to 24.50
Rockwell, Christmas, The Big Moment	1977	Year	27.50	27.50
Rockwell, Mother's Day, Doctor & Doll	1975	Year	23.50	60.00
Rockwell, Mother's Day, Puppy Love	1976	Year	24.50	29.00
Rockwell, Mother's Day, The Family	1977	Year	24.50	24.50
Rockwell, Mother's Day, Mom's Day Off	1978	7500	27.50	27.50
Rockwell, Tom Sawyer	1976	10000	27.50	Unknown
Stillwell-Weber, Winter Winds	1978	7500	32.50	32.50

The Doulton Porcelain factory was founded in 1815. Royal Doulton is the name used on pottery made after 1902. A series of limited edition commemorative and special wares was made during the 1930s. Modern limited edition Christmas plates and mugs were first made in 1971. Royal Doulton also makes a line of limited edition porcelains.

See listing for Royal Doulton in Figurine section

Royal Doulton Commemorative & Special Wares

Title	Issue Date	Number Issued	Issued Price	Current Price
Regency Coach Jug*	1931	500		550.00
George Washington Jug*	1932	1000		225.00 to 275.00

Royal Doulton,
Regency Coach Jug, 1931

Royal Doulton,
George Washington Jug, 1932
(front view)

Royal Doulton,
Drake Jug, 1933

Royal Doulton,
Shakespeare Jug, 1933

Royal Doulton, Treasure
Island Jug, 1934

Royal Doulton, Three
Musketeers Loving Cup, 1936

Royal Doulton, Plate, Chen-Chi,
Imperial Palace, 1977

Royal Doulton, Plate, Mother's Day,
Lucia And Child, 1977

Royal Doulton, Plate,
I Remember America,
Lovejoy Bridge, 1978

Royal Doulton, Plate, Flower Garden,
Poet's Garden, 1977

Royal Doulton, Plate, Mother's Day,
Sayuri & Child, 1974

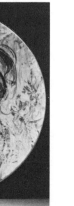

Royal Doulton, Plate,
Ports Of Call, Venice, 1977

Royal Doulton, Plate, Christmas,
Christmas In Holland, 1976

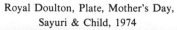

Royal Doulton,
Dickens Jug, 1936

Royal Doulton,
Village Blacksmith Jug, 1936

Royal Doulton, Elizabeth II
Coronation Loving Cup, 1953

Royal Doulton, Edward VIII
Coronation Loving Cup,
Small, 1937

Royal Doulton, George VI
Coronation Loving Cup, 1937

Royal Doulton, Plate,
Flower Garden,
Country Bouquet,
1978

Royale, Easter Ornament,
1973

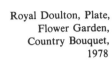

Royal Doulton,
Edward VIII Coronation
Loving Cup, Large, 1937

Royal Doulton, Plate,
Flower Garden,
Spring Harmony, 1975

Royal Doulton, Plate,
Flower Garden,
Dreaming Lotus, 1976

Royal Doulton, Tankard, Christmas,
Ghost Christmas Present, 2nd, 1977

Royal Doulton, Mayflower Loving Cup, 1970

Royal Doulton, Plate, Mother's Day,
Kristina & Child, 1975

Royal Doulton, Plate,
Christmas,
Christmas In Norway,
1975

Title	Issue Date	Number Issued	Issued Price	Current Price
Captain Cook Jug	1933	350		Unknown
Drake Jug*	1933	500		550.00
John Peel Loving Cup	1933	500		400.00
Shakespeare Jug*	1933	1000		250.00 to 300.00
Tower Of London Jug	1933	500		250.00 to 300.00
Apothecary Loving Cup	1934	600		Unknown
Guy Fawkes Jug	1934	600		400.00
Pied Piper Jug	1934	600		750.00
Treasure Island Jug*	1934	600		550.00
King George & Mary Silver Wedding Loving Cup	1935	1000		Unknown
Nelson Loving Cup	1935	600		Unknown
Dickens Jug*	1936	1000		750.00
Three Musketeers Loving Cup*	1936	600		250.00 to 300.00
Village Blacksmith Jug*	1936	590		550.00
Edward VIII Coronation Loving Cup, Large*	1937	2000		485.00
Edward VIII Coronation Loving Cup, Small*	1937	2000		165.00
George VI Coronation Loving Cup*	1937	2000		165.00
Elizabeth II Coronation Loving Cup*	1953	2000		Unknown
Charles Dickens Loving Cup	1970	500	285.00	285.00
Mayflower Loving Cup*	1970	500	285.00	285.00

Royal Doulton, Plate,
Christmas,
Christmas In Poland,
1977

Royal Doulton Plaques

Title	Issue Date	Number Issued	Issued Price	Current Price
Christmas, Christmas Carol	1972	13000	37.50	35.00 to 40.00
Christmas	1973		37.50	37.50

Royal Doulton Plates

Title	Issue Date	Number Issued	Issued Price	Current Price
American Tapestries, Sleigh Bells**	1978	10000	70.00	70.00
All God's Children, A Brighter Day	1978	7500	60.00	60.00
Chen-Chi, Garden Of Tranquility	1976	15000	70.00	70.00
Chen-Chi, Imperial Palace*	1977		75.00	75.00
Christmas, Bone China, Winter Fun	1977		25.00	25.00
Christmas, Bone China, Victorian Girl	1978		25.00	25.00
Christmas, Christmas In England	1972	11000	35.00	35.00 to 40.00
Christmas, Christmas In Mexico	1973	15000	37.50	37.50
Christmas, Christmas In Bulgaria	1974	15000	40.00	40.00
Christmas, Christmas In Norway*	1975	15000	45.00	47.00
Christmas, Christmas In Holland*	1976	15000	50.00	60.00
Christmas, Christmas In Poland*	1977	15000	50.00	50.00
Christmas, Christmas In America	1978	15000	55.00	55.00
Flower Garden, Spring Harmony*	1975	15000	60.00	66.00
Flower Garden, Dreaming Lotus*	1976	15000	65.00	70.00
Flower Garden, Poet's Garden*	1977	15000	70.00	70.00
Flower Garden, Country Bouquet*	1978	15000	70.00	70.00
I Remember America, Pennsylvania*	1977	15000	70.00	70.00
I Remember America, Lovejoy Bridge**	1978	15000	70.00	70.00
Kate Greenaway, Almanack	1978	Year	25.00	25.00
Log Of Dashing Wave, Sailing With Tide	1976	15000	65.00	70.00
Log Of Dashing Wave, Running Free*	1977	15000	65.00	70.00
Log Of Dashing Wave, Rounding Horn**	1978	15000	70.00	70.00
Mother's Day, Colette & Child	1973	15000	40.00	400.00 to 500.00
Mother's Day, Sayuri & Child*	1974	15000	40.00	105.00 to 140.00
Mother's Day, Kristina & Child*	1975	15000	50.00	80.00 to 130.00
Mother's Day, Marilyn & Child	1976	15000	55.00	75.00 to 100.00
Mother's Day, Lucia And Child*	1977	15000	55.00	55.00 to 75.00
Mother's Day	1978	15000	55.00	55.00
Neiman, Harlequin	1974	15000	50.00	75.00
Neiman, Pierrot	1976	15000	60.00	65.00
Neiman, Columbine*	1977	15000		70.00
Neiman, Punchinello**	1978	15000	70.00	70.00
Ports Of Call, San Francisco	1975	15000	60.00	66.00
Ports Of Call, New Orleans	1976	15000	65.00	70.00
Ports Of Call, Venice*	1977	15000	70.00	70.00
Ports Of Call, Montmartre*	1978	15000	70.00	70.00
Valentine, Victorian Boy And Girl	1976	Year	25.00	25.00
Valentine, Heart & Flowers	1977	Year	25.00	25.00

Royal Doulton, Plate, I Remember America,
Pennsylvania, 1977

Royal Doulton Tankards

Title	Issue Date	Number Issued	Issued Price	Current Price
Christmas, Cratchit & Scrooge	1971	13000	35.00	35.00 to 54.00
Christmas, Carolers	1972	15000	37.50	37.50 to 42.00
Christmas, Solicitation	1973	15000	40.00	40.00
Christmas, Marley's Ghost	1974			45.00

Royal Doulton, Plate, Log Of Dashing Wave,
Running Free, 1977

Royal Worcester, Plate, Porcelain, Bicentennial,
Independence, 1976

Royal Worcester, Plate, Porcelain, Dorothy
Doughty, Blue-Winged Sivas & Bamboo, 1976

Royal Worcester, Plate, Porcelain,
Fabulous Birds, II, 1977

Royal Worcester, Bicentennial Plate, 1972

Title	Issue Date	Number Issued	Issued Price	Current Price
Christmas, Ghost Christmas Past	1975			47.50
Christmas, Ghost Christmas Present	1976			60.00
Christmas, Ghost Christmas Present, 2nd*	1977			50.00
Christmas, Ghost Christmas Present, 3rd	1978			55.00
Royal Limoges Plates				
Christmas, Les Santons De Noel	1972	5000	25.00	20.00 to 25.00
Christmas, Three Wise Men	1973	5000	25.00	25.00
Christmas, Three Wise Men	1974	10000		23.00

Royal Tettau was established in Germany in 1794. It is parent company to Royal Bayreuth. Limited editions were first made in 1971.

Title	Issue Date	Number Issued	Issued Price	Current Price
Royal Tettau Plates				
Christmas, Carriage In The Village	1972		12.50	Unknown
Christmas	1973		13.50	13.50
Papal, Pope Paul VI	1971	5000	100.00	Unknown
Papal, Pope John XXIII	1972	5000	100.00	Unknown
Papal, Pope Pius XII	1973	5000	100.00	Unknown

The Royal Worcester Porcelain Factory, of Worcester, England, was founded under the name of Worcester, in 1751. The name was changed to Royal Worcester in 1862. Limited edition plates, in both pewter and porcelain, were first introduced in 1972. Limited edition porcelains have been made since the 1930s.

See listing for Royal Worcester in Figurine section

Title	Issue Date	Number Issued	Issued Price	Current Price
Royal Worcester Plaques				
Mother-Child	1976	500	1150.00	1150.00
Queen Elizabeth II	1977	1000	875.00	875.00
Royal Worcester Plates, pewter				
American History, Washington's Inauguration	1977	1250	65.00	65.00
Annual, Road Winter	1974	5000	59.50	40.00 to 60.00
Annual, Old Grist Mill	1975	2500	59.50	60.00
Annual, Winter Pastime	1976	1500	59.50	62.00
Annual, Home To Thanksgiving	1977	500	59.50	59.50
Birth Of Nation, Boston Tea Party*	1972	10000	45.00	140.00 to 400.00
Birth Of Nation, Paul Revere	1973	10000	45.00	40.00 to 60.00
Birth Of Nation, Concord Bridge	1974	10000	50.00	30.00 to 50.00
Birth Of Nation, Declaration Of Independence	1975	10000	65.00	65.00
Birth Of Nation, Crossing Delaware	1976	10000	65.00	65.00
Royal Worcester Plates, porcelain				
Audubon, Warbler & Jay	1977	5000	150.00	150.00
Audubon, Kingbird & Sparrow	1978	5000	150.00	150.00
Bicentennial, Independence*	1976	10000	150.00	100.00 to 150.00
Chinoiserie, Bishop Sumner	1977		65.00	65.00
Dorothy Doughty, Redstarts & Beech*	1972	2000	125.00	140.00 to 195.00
Dorothy Doughty, Myrtle Warbler & Cherry*	1973	3000	175.00	100.00 to 250.00
Dorothy Doughty, Blue-Grey Gnatcatcher	1974	3000	195.00	185.00 to 195.00
Dorothy Doughty, Blackburnian Warbler	1975	3000	195.00	235.00
Dorothy Doughty, Blue-Winged Sivas & Bamboo*	1976	3000	195.00	165.00 to 195.00
Dorothy Doughty, Paradise Whydah	1977	3000	195.00	195.00
Dorothy Doughty, Bluetits	1978	3000	200.00	195.00
Fabulous Birds, I	1976	10000	65.00	65.00
Fabulous Birds, II*	1977	10000	65.00	65.00
Royal Worcester Spoons				
Annual*	1965	Year	27.50	20.00 to 35.00
Annual*	1966	Year	27.50	20.00 to 35.00
Annual*	1967	Year	27.50	35.00
Annual*	1968	Year	27.50	20.00 to 35.00
Annual*	1969	Year	27.50	20.00 to 35.00
Annual*	1970	Year	27.50	35.00
Annual*	1971	Year	27.50	35.00
Royale Ornaments				
Easter Rabbit, Decorated	1972	200	85.00	60.00 to 100.00
Easter Rabbit, White	1972	2500	20.00	16.00 to 23.00
Easter Rabbit, Decorated	1973	200	85.00	55.00

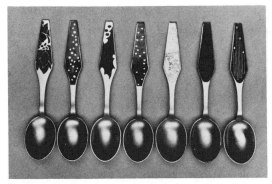

Royal Worcester, Christmas Spoon, 1965 - 1971

Royal Worcester,
Dorothy Doughty Plate, 1972

Royale, Christmas Plate, 1969

Royale Worcester, Dorothy Doughty Plate, 1973

Royale, Game Plate, 1973

Royale, Christmas Plate, 1973

Royale, Bird Plaque, 1973

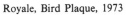

Royale, Mother's Day Plate, 1970

Royale, Father's Day Plate, 1974

Royale, Mother's Day Plate, 1973

Royale, Mother's Day Plate, 1974

Royale, Plate, Mother's Day, Koala Bear, 1977

Royale, Plate, Christmas, Sledding, 1977

Title	Issue Date	Number Issued	Issued Price	Current Price
Easter Rabbit, White*	1973	2000	20.00	20.00
Royale Plaques				
Baltimore Orioles	1972	500	200.00	200.00 to 215.00
Bird	1974		200.00	200.00
Goldfinches	1975	150	250.00	250.00
Mother's Day, Birds, Blue	1976	350	350.00	350.00
Scarlet Tanagers*	1973	350	200.00	230.00 to 260.00
Royale Plates				
Apollo, Landing On The Moon	1969	2000	30.00	25.00
Christmas, Christmas Fair*	1969	6000	12.00	45.00 to 100.00
Christmas, Mass At Kalundborg Church	1970	10000	13.00	10.00 to 17.00
Christmas, Snow On Rooftops	1971	8000	15.00	10.00 to 24.00
Christmas, Elks In Winter	1972	8000	16.00	17.00 to 30.00
Christmas, Christmas Dawn*	1973	6000	18.00	14.00 to 22.00
Christmas, Village At Christmas	1974	5000	22.00	12.00 to 22.00
Christmas, Feeding Time	1975	5000	26.00	13.00 to 26.00
Christmas, Christmas At Seaport	1976	5000	27.50	25.00 to 28.00
Christmas, Sledding*	1977	5000	30.00	30.00
Father's Day, Sailing Ship	1970	5000	13.00	5.00 to 25.00
Father's Day, Man Fishing	1971	5000	13.00	3.00 to 20.00
Father's Day, Mountain Climber	1972	5000	16.00	8.00 to 20.00
Father's Day, Camping	1973	4000	18.00	12.00 to 25.00
Father's Day, American Bald Eagle*	1974	2500	22.00	12.00 to 25.00
Father's Day, Regatta	1975	2500	26.00	18.00 to 26.00
Father's Day, Hunting Scene	1976	2500	27.50	20.00 to 27.50
Father's Day, Fishing*	1977	2500	30.00	30.00
Game, Setters Pointing Quail	1972	500	180.00	180.00 to 250.00
Game, Fox*	1973	500	200.00	150.00 to 300.00
Game, Osprey	1974	250		125.00 to 250.00
Game, California Quail*	1975	250	265.00	265.00
Goldfinch	1974	150		125.00 to 250.00
Mother's Day, Swan & Brood*	1970	6000	12.00	25.00 to 85.00
Mother's Day, Deer	1971	9000	13.00	12.00 to 20.00
Mother's Day, Rabbits	1972	9000	16.00	12.00 to 20.00
Mother's Day, Owl*	1973	6000		12.00 to 40.00
Mother's Day, Duck & Ducklings*	1974	5000	22.00	10.00 to 22.00
Mother's Day, Lynx	1975	5000	26.00	10.00 to 26.00
Mother's Day, Woodcock & Young	1976	5000	27.50	25.00 to 27.00
Mother's Day, Koala Bear*	1977	5000	30.00	30.00
Tufted Titmouse	1975	150		265.00

See listing for Royale Germania Crystal in Paperweight section

Royale Germania Crystal Goblets

Title	Issue Date	Number Issued	Issued Price	Current Price
Annual, Green	1972	500	160.00	105.00 to 220.00
Annual, Blue	1973	300	180.00	120.00 to 180.00
Annual, Topaz	1974	300	200.00	133.00 to 200.00
Annual, Amber	1975	300	250.00	250.00

Royale Germania Crystal Plates

Title	Issue Date	Number Issued	Issued Price	Current Price
Annual, Orchid, Blue*	1970	600	200.00	425.00 to 600.00
Annual, Cyclamen, Red	1971	1000	200.00	110.00 to 310.00
Annual, Silver Thistle, Green	1972	1000	250.00	155.00 to 310.00
Annual, Tulip, Lilac*	1973	600	275.00	180.00 to 320.00
Annual, Sunflowers, Topaz*	1974	500	300.00	150.00 to 300.00
Annual, Snowdrops, Amber	1975	350	450.00	450.00
Mother's Day, Roses, Red	1971	250	180.00	350.00 to 550.00
Mother's Day, Elephant, Green	1972	750	180.00	120.00 to 250.00
Mother's Day, Koala Bear, Lilac*	1973	600	200.00	115.00 to 230.00
Mother's Day, Squirrels, Topaz*	1974	500	240.00	160.00 to 240.00
Mother's Day, Swan, Amber*	1975	350	350.00	350.00

Ruffin, see Fairmont

Runci, see Rosenthal

Russell, Charles, see Antique Trader, Ridgewood

Ruthven Bird plates, see Hutschenreuther

Sabino Plates

Title	Issue Date	Number Issued	Issued Price	Current Price
Annual, King Henry IV & Maria De Medici	1970	1500		45.00 to 75.00
Annual, Milo Of Crotona	1971	500		50.00 to 75.00
Annual	1972			80.00 to 120.00

Royale Germania, Annual Plate, 1970

Schumann, Christmas Plate, 1971

Royale Germania,
Mother's Day Plate, 1974

Royale Germania, Annual Plate, 1973

Royale, Plate, Father's Day, Fishing, 1977

Royale Germania, Annual Plate, 1974

Royale Germania, Plate,
Crystal, Mother's Day, Swan, Amber, 1975

Royale, Plate, Game, California Quail, 1975

Royale Germania, Mother's Day Plate, 1973

Title	Issue Date	Number Issued	Issued Price	Current Price
Salvador Dali, see Daum, Lincoln Mint, Puiforcat				
Sango Plates				
Christmas, Spark Of Christmas	1974	5000	25.00	25.00 to 32.00
Christmas, Christmas Eve In The Country	1975	5000	27.50	20.00 to 27.50
Christmas, Madonna & Child	1976		25.00	25.00
Christmas, Undesired Slumber	1976	7500	25.00	25.00
Christmas, Togetherness	1977	5000	25.00	25.00
Living American Artist, Sweethearts, Rockwell	1976	10000	30.00	20.00 to 32.00
Living American Artist, Apache Girl, Perillo	1977	5000	35.00	35.00
Living American Artist, Natural Habitat	1978	5000	40.00	40.00
Mother's Day, Spring Delight	1976	7500	20.00	20.00
Mother's Day, Broken Wing	1977		25.00	25.00
Santa Clara Plates				
Christmas, The Christmas Message	1970	10000	12.00	12.00 to 20.00
Christmas, Three Wise Men	1971	10000	12.00	10.00 to 25.00
Christmas, Children In The Woods	1972	10000	12.00	12.00 to 40.00
Christmas, Archangel	1973	5000	25.00	32.00 to 50.00
Christmas, Spirit Of Christmas	1974	10000	25.00	25.00
Christmas, Christmas Eve	1975	10000	27.50	25.00
Christmas, Madonna & Child	1976	5000	25.00	25.00
Mother's Day, Mother & Child	1971	10000	12.00	5.00 to 10.00
Mother's Day	1972	12000	12.00	5.00 to 10.00
Sarna Bells				
Bicentennial				125.00 to 150.00
Christmas	1974	4000		30.00 to 50.00
Christmas	1975	4000		20.00 to 50.00
Christmas	1976	3000	17.50	17.50
Christmas	1977			33.00
Sarna Plates				
Christmas, Over The Bridge	1974	5000	20.00	13.00 to 20.00
Christmas, Village Square	1975	5000	20.00	13.00 to 20.00
Christmas	1976	3000	17.50	17.50
Christmas	1977	3000	25.00	25.00

Sawyer plates, see George Washington Mint

Hummel Schmid limited editions are made in West Germany for exclusive distribution by Schmid Brothers in the United States. Permission to reproduce the works of Berta Hummel on limited edition items was granted to Schmid Brothers by Victoria Hummel, mother of the artist, in 1971.

Title	Issue Date	Number Issued	Issued Price	Current Price
Schmid Bells, Disney				
Christmas, Caroling	1975	Year		10.00
Christmas, Building A Snowman	1976	Year		10.00
Christmas, Mickey Is Santa	1977	Year		10.00
Mother's Day, Pluto And Friends	1977	Year	13.00	13.00
Mother's Day, Flowers For Bambi	1978	Year	13.00	13.00
Schmid Bells, Hummel				
Christmas, Angel With Flute	1972	20000	15.00	36.95 to 60.00
Christmas, Silent Night*	1973		15.00	9.50 to 22.50
Christmas, Guardian With Child	1974		17.50	9.50 to 17.50
Christmas, Christmas Child	1975	Year	18.95	13.00 to 22.95
Christmas, Children With Donkey	1976	Year	22.50	14.00 to 22.50
Christmas, Herald Angel	1977	Year	25.00	25.00
Christmas, Heavenly Trio	1978	Year	27.50	27.50
Mother's Day, Afternoon Stroll	1978	Year	27.50	27.50
Schmid Bells, Peanuts				
Bicentennial	1976		10.00	9.00 to 13.00
Christmas, Snoopy And Santa	1975		10.00	7.95 to 10.00
Christmas, Woodstock's Christmas	1976		10.00	10.00
Christmas, Deck The Dog House	1977		10.00	10.00
Christmas, Filling The Stocking	1978		13.00	13.00
Mother's Day, Dear Mom	1977		13.00	13.00
Schmid Bells, Raggedy Ann and Andy				
Bicentennial	1976	Year	10.00	7.95 to 13.00
Christmas, Decorating The Tree	1977	Year	10.00	10.00

Title	Issue Date	Number Issued	Issued Price	Current Price
Christmas, Checking The List	1978	Year	15.00	15.00
Mother's Day, Flowers For Mom	1977	Year	13.00	13.00
Mother's Day, Hello Mom	1978	Year	13.00	13.00
Schmid Cups, Hummel				
Child's, Child's Rest	1973	Year	10.00	7.99 to 13.50
Child's, Bumblebee	1974	Year	10.00	6.50 to 13.00
Child's, Christmas Child	1975	Year	10.00	11.00 to 15.00
Child's, Devotion	1976	Year	10.00	10.00 to 15.00
Child's, Moonlight Return	1977	Year	15.00	15.00
Schmid Ornaments, Disney				
Christmas, Caroling	1975	Year	6.00	3.85
Christmas, Building A Snowman	1976	Year	4.50	4.50
Christmas, Mickey Is Santa	1977	Year	4.50	4.50
Christmas, Night Before Christmas	1978	Year	4.50	4.50
Schmid Ornaments, Hummel				
Christmas, Guardian Angel	1974	Year	4.00	3.50 to 4.00
Christmas, Child	1975	Year	4.00	2.50 to 4.50
Christmas, Children With Donkey	1976	Year	4.50	4.50
Christmas, Herald Angel	1977	Year	4.50	4.50
Christmas, Heavenly Trio	1978	Year	4.50	4.50
Schmid Ornaments, Raggedy Ann and Andy				
Raggedy Ann Skates	1976	Year	4.50	4.50
Decorating The Tree	1977	Year	4.50	4.50
Checking The List	1978	Year	4.50	4.50
Schmid Plates, Bugs Bunny				
Mother's Day	1977	Year	13.00	13.00
Schmid Plates, Disney				
Christmas, Sleighride	1973	Year	10.00	125.00
Christmas, Decorating Tree	1974	Year	10.00	65.00
Christmas, Caroling	1975	Year	10.00	10.50 to 12.50
Christmas, Building A Snowman	1976	Year	13.00	13.00
Christmas, Down The Chimney	1977	Year	13.00	13.00
Fiftieth Anniversary	1978	Year	25.00	25.00
Mother's Day, Flowers For Mother	1974	Year	13.00	33.00
Mother's Day, Snow White, Seven Dwarfs	1975	Year	13.00	16.00 to 25.00
Mother's Day, Minnie Mouse	1976	Year	13.00	13.00
Mother's Day, Pluto And Friends	1977	Year	13.00	13.00
Mother's Day, Flowers For Bambi	1978	Year	15.00	15.00
Schmid Plates, Hummel				
Christmas, Angel In Christmas Setting	1971	Year	15.00	16.00 to 45.00
Christmas, Angel With Flute*	1972	20000	15.00	10.00 to 35.00
Christmas, Silent Night*	1973	Year	15.00	25.00 to 75.00
Christmas, Guardian Angel	1974	Year	25.00	15.00 to 24.00
Christmas, Christmas Child	1975	Year	25.00	13.75 to 25.00
Christmas, Children With Donkey	1976	Year	27.50	13.75 to 27.50
Christmas, Herald Angel	1977	Year	27.50	27.50
Christmas, Heavenly Trio	1978	Year	32.50	32.50
Mother's Day, Playing Hooky*	1972	Year	15.00	10.00 to 30.00
Mother's Day, Fishing	1973	Year	15.00	28.00 to 60.00
Mother's Day, The Bumblebee	1974	Year	25.00	12.00 to 34.50
Mother's Day, Message Of Love	1975	Year	25.00	12.00 to 25.00
Mother's Day, Devotion For Mother	1976	Year	27.50	13.75 to 37.50
Mother's Day, Devotion	1976	Year	27.50	28.50 to 37.50
Mother's Day, Moonlight Return	1977	Year	37.50	37.50
Mother's Day, Afternoon Stroll	1978	Year	32.50	32.50
Schmid Plates, Peanuts				
Christmas, Woodstock Pulling Snoopy's Sled*	1972	20000	10.00	22.50 to 48.00
Christmas, Snoopy*	1973		10.00	40.00 to 75.00
Christmas, Christmas At Fireplace	1974		10.00	45.00 to 75.00
Christmas, Woodstock's Christmas	1975		12.00	8.35 to 12.50
Christmas, O Christmas Tree	1976	10000	12.00	10.50 to 12.00
Christmas, Deck The Dog House	1977		13.00	13.00
Christmas, Filling The Stocking	1978		13.00	13.00
Mother's Day, Linus With Rose*	1972	15000	10.00	15.00 to 26.50
Mother's Day, Snoopy & Woodstock*	1973	8000	10.00	20.00 to 35.00

Peanuts, Christmas Plate, 1972

Peanuts, Mother's Day Plate, 1973

Peanuts, Mother's Day Plate, 1972

Peanuts, Christmas Plate, 1973

Selandia, Christmas Plate, 1972

Selandia, Christmas Plate, 1973

Selandia, Plate, Christmas,
Star Over Bethlehem, Unsigned, 1975

Seven Seas, Christmas Plate, New World,
1970

Title	Issue Date	Number Issued	Issued Price	Current Price
Mother's Day, Snoopy Carrying Flag With Heart	1974		10.00	30.00 to 55.00
Mother's Day, Snoopy Kissing Lucy	1975		12.50	9.40 to 14.95
Mother's Day, Linus And Snoopy	1976		13.00	13.00
Mother's Day, Dear Mom	1977		13.00	13.00
Mother's Day, Thoughts That Count	1978		15.00	15.00
Valentine	1977		13.00	13.00
Schmid Plates, Raggedy Ann and Andy				
Bicentennial	1976	Year	13.00	9.00 to 13.50
Christmas	1975	Year		10.50 to 25.00
Christmas	1976	Year	13.00	9.00 to 13.00
Christmas, Decorating The Tree	1977	Year		13.00
Christmas, Checking The List	1978	Year	15.00	15.00
Mother's Day	1976	Year	13.00	19.50 to 32.00
Mother's Day, Flowers For Mom	1977		13.00	13.00
Mother's Day, Hello Mom	1978		15.00	15.00
Schmid Steins, Hummel				
Father's Day, Metal Top, 10 In.	1977		37.00	37.00
Schumann Plates				
Christmas, Snow Scene*	1971	10000	12.00	Unknown
Christmas, Deer In Snow	1972	15000	12.00	Unknown
Christmas	1973	5000	12.00	Unknown
Christmas, Church In Snow	1974	5000		Unknown
Christmas, Fountain	1975	5000		Unknown
Composer, Mozart				Unknown
Scottish Plates				
Annual, Edinburgh	1972	2500	25.00	25.00
Sebring Heritage Plates				
Father's Day	1971	Year	12.50	5.00 to 7.00
Father's Day	1972	Year	12.50	5.00 to 7.00
Fourth Of July	1971	Year	12.50	5.00 to 7.00
Mother's Day	1971	Year	12.50	5.00 to 7.00
Mother's Day	1972	Year	12.50	5.00 to 7.00

Selandia Pewter Company of Norway, makers of domestic pewter ware, introduced its first limited edition pewter plate in 1972. The first 200 plates of each series are signed by the artist.

Title	Issue Date	Number Issued	Issued Price	Current Price
Selandia Plates				
Christmas, On The Way To Bethlehem, Signed	1972	250	100.00	100.00
Christmas, On The Way To Bethlehem, Unsigned*	1972	4750	30.00	10.00 to 29.00
Christmas, Three Wise Men, Signed	1973	200	100.00	100.00
Christmas, Three Wise Men, Unsigned*	1973	4750	35.00	29.00
Christmas, Shepherds In The Field, Signed	1974	200	100.00	Unknown
Christmas, Shepherds In The Field, Unsigned	1974	4800	35.00	Unknown
Christmas, Star Over Bethlehem, Signed	1975	200	100.00	Unknown
Christmas, Star Over Bethlehem, Unsigned*	1975	4800	35.00	Unknown
Christmas, Christ Is Born, Signed	1976	200	100.00	100.00
Christmas, Christ Is Born, Unsigned	1976	4800	40.00	40.00
Seven Seas Plates				
Christmas, New World, Holy Family*	1970	3500	15.00	Unknown
Christmas, Traditional, I Heard The Bells*	1970	4000	15.00	Unknown
Christmas, New World, Three Wise Men	1971	1500	15.00	Unknown
Christmas, Traditional, O Tannenbaum	1971	4000	15.00	Unknown
Christmas, New World, And Shepherds Watched	1972	1500	18.00	Unknown
Christmas, Traditional, Deck The Halls	1972	1500	18.00	Unknown
Christmas, O Holy Night	1973	2000	18.00	Unknown
History, Landing On The Moon, No Flag	1969	2000	13.50	Unknown
History, Landing On The Moon, With Flag	1969	2000	13.50	Unknown
History, Year Of Crisis	1970	4000	15.00	Unknown
History, First Vehicular Travel	1971	3000	15.00	Unknown
History, Man's Final Trip To The Moon	1972	2000	15.00	Unknown
History, Peace	1973	3000	15.00	Unknown
Mother's Day, Girl Of All Nations	1970	5000	15.00	Unknown
Mother's Day, Sharing Confidences*	1971	1400	15.00	Unknown
Mother's Day, Scandinavian Girl*	1972	1600	15.00	Unknown
Mother's Day, All American Girl*	1973	1500	15.00	Unknown
Passion Play	1970	2500	18.00	Unknown

Title	Issue Date	Number Issued	Issued Price	Current Price

Shenango China Company, of New Castle, Pennsylvania, was founded in 1905. It is presently a division of Interpace Corporation. Two series of limited edition Christmas plates were made to be given away as premiums to customers. The first was based on Dickens' Christmas Carol and was made from 1949 through 1961. No plate was made in 1951. The second series, based on Twelve Days of Christmas, was started in 1964 and continued until 1975. The plates were free so there is no issue price information. In 1937, a series of 12 limited edition American Legion Auxiliary plates was produced to raise funds for the Indianapolis branch of the American Legion. The edition numbers of these plates are not known.

Seven Seas, Christmas Plate, Traditional, 1970

Shenango Plates

Title	Issue Date	Number Issued	Issued Price	Current Price
Christmas, Dickens	1949	Year		Unknown
Christmas, Dickens	1950	Year		Unknown
Christmas, Dickens	1952	Year		Unknown
Christmas, Dickens	1953	Year		Unknown
Christmas, Dickens	1954	Year		Unknown
Christmas, Dickens	1955	Year		Unknown
Christmas, Dickens	1956	Year		Unknown
Christmas, Dickens	1957	Year		Unknown
Christmas, Dickens	1958	Year		Unknown
Christmas, Dickens	1959	Year		Unknown
Christmas, Dickens	1960	Year		Unknown
Christmas, Dickens	1961	Year		Unknown
Christmas, Twelve Days	1964	3300		Unknown
Christmas, Twelve Days	1965	3300		Unknown
Christmas, Twelve Days	1966	3300		Unknown
Christmas, Twelve Days	1967	3300		Unknown
Christmas, Twelve Days	1968	3300		Unknown
Christmas, Twelve Days	1969	3300		Unknown
Christmas, Twelve Days	1970	3300		Unknown
Christmas, Twelve Days	1971	3300		Unknown
Christmas, Twelve Days	1972	3300		Unknown
Christmas, Twelve Days	1973	3300		Unknown
Christmas, Twelve Days	1974	3300		Unknown
Christmas, Twelve Days	1975	3300		Unknown

Seven Seas, Mother's Day Plate, 1971

Shuler, see Kurz

Silver City Plates

Title	Issue Date	Number Issued	Issued Price	Current Price
Christmas, Winter Scene	1969			Unknown
Christmas, Water Mill	1970			Unknown
Christmas, Skating Scene	1971			Unknown
Christmas, Logging In Winter	1972			Unknown
Christmas	1973			Unknown
Independence Hall	1972		13.50	Unknown

Skelton, see Fairmont

L. E. Smith Glass Company of Mt. Pleasant, Pennsylvania, was founded in the early 1900s. Limited edition carnival glass plates were first made in 1971. A series of pewter and silver plates is made by Wendell August Forge for the Smith Glass Company.

Seven Seas, Mother's Day, 1972

Smith Glass, see also Wendell August Forge

Smith Glass Plates

Title	Issue Date	Number Issued	Issued Price	Current Price
Coin, Morgan Silver Dollar	1971	5000	10.00	Unknown
Kennedy, Carnival*	1971	2500	10.00	Unknown
Lincoln, Carnival	1971	2500	10.00	Unknown
Jefferson Davis, Carnival	1972	5000	11.00	Unknown
Robert E.Lee, Carnival	1972	5000	11.00	Unknown

Southern Landmark plate, see American Commemorative Council

Spencer, Irene, see Gorham, Fairmont

Spode Works, located in England's Staffordshire district, was founded in 1776 by Josiah Spode. Spode formed a partnership with William Copeland, whose descendants now manage the Spode factory. Limited edition Christmas plates were introduced in 1970. The firm is now Royal Worcester Spode, Inc.

Seven Seas, Mother's Day Plate, 1973

Spode Hammersley Bells

Title	Issue Date	Number Issued	Issued Price	Current Price
Annual, Singing Angels*	1971	Year	25.00	32.50

Smith Glass, Kennedy Plate, 1971

Spode Hammersley,
Bicentennial Bell, 1973

Spode, Bell, Annual, Singing Angels,
1971

Title	Issue Date	Number Issued	Issued Price	Current Price
Annual, Famous Buildings	1972	Year	25.00	32.50
Annual, Three Kings	1973	Year	25.00	Unknown
Annual, Adoration	1974	Year	31.50	32.50
Annual, A-Skating Go*	1975	Year	31.50	32.50
Annual, Ebb-Tide*	1976	Year	35.00	35.00
Bicentennial, The Sound Of Liberty*	1973	15000	25.00	25.00 to 30.00
Bicentennial, Gauntlet	1974	15000	25.00	20.95 to 25.00
Bicentennial, Destiny	1975	15000	25.00	19.95 to 25.00
Bicentennial	1976	15000	25.00	15.00 to 35.00
Annual	1977	Year	35.00	35.00
Annual	1978	Year	35.00	35.00

Spode Loving Cups

European Community	1972	500	245.00	245.00

Spode Plates

Charles Dickens	1970	5000		35.00 to 70.00
Christmas, Twelve Days Of Christmas	1970	Year	35.00	20.00 to 35.00
Christmas, In Heaven The Angels Singing*	1971	Year	35.00	15.00 to 25.00
Christmas, I Saw 3 Ships A-Sailing*	1972	Year	35.00	13.00 to 35.00
Christmas, We Three Kings	1973	Year	35.00	35.00 to 65.00
Christmas, Deck The Halls	1974	Year	35.00	22.00 to 35.00
Christmas, Christmas Tree*	1975	Year	45.00	21.00 to 45.00
Christmas, Good King Wenceslas*	1976	Year	45.00	25.00 to 45.00
Christmas, Holly & Ivy	1977	Year	45.00	45.00
Cutty Sark	1970			35.00 to 50.00
European Community	1973	5000	59.00	50.00 to 60.00
Imperial Plate Of Persia	1971	10000	125.00	65.00 to 150.00
Mayflower	1970			100.00
Peace, Cecil Benton	1970			6.00 to 15.00
Ray Harm Birds, Set Of 12	1972		350.00	400.00 to 650.00
Winston Churchill	1968		150.00	50.00 to 100.00

St. Louis Gateway Arch plate, see Stix, Baer & Fuller

Stanek Plates

Moon Landing	1969			Unknown
Mayflower*	1972	60		Unknown
Santa Maria*	1972	60		Unknown
Eagle	1973	400	250.00	Unknown

Sterling America limited editions, introduced in 1970, are made of sterling on crystal. Two Christmas plate series are made.

Sterling America Plates

Christmas, Customs, England*	1970	2500	18.00	10.00 to 16.00
Christmas, 12 Days, Partridge*	1970	2500	18.00	9.00 to 25.00
Christmas, Customs, Holland*	1971	2500	18.00	9.00 to 25.00
Christmas, 12 Days, Turtle Doves*	1971	2500	18.00	20.00 to 25.00
Christmas, Customs, Norway*	1972	2500	18.00	13.00 to 20.00
Christmas, 12 Days, Three French Hens*	1972	2500	18.00	13.00 to 20.00
Christmas, Customs, Germany	1973	2500	20.00	13.00 to 20.00
Christmas, 12 Days, Four Colly Birds	1973	2500	20.00	24.00
Christmas, Customs, Mexico	1974	2500		24.00
Christmas, 12 Days, Five Gold Rings	1974	2500	24.00	20.00 to 24.00
Christmas, 12 Days, Six Geese	1975	2500	24.00	24.00
Christmas, 12 Days, Seven Swans	1976	2500		24.00
Mother's Day, Mare, Foal*	1971	2500	18.00	18.00 to 25.00
Mother's Day, Horned Owl*	1972	2500	18.00	18.00 to 20.00
Mother's Day, Raccoons*	1973	2500	20.00	20.00
Mother's Day, Deer	1974	2500	20.00	13.00 to 20.00
Mother's Day, Quail	1975	2500	24.00	24.00
Mother's Day	1976		10.00	10.00

Stieff limited edition pewter plates are made by Stieff Silversmiths of Baltimore, Maryland.

Stieff Plates

Bicentennial, Declaration Of Independence	1972	10000	50.00	25.00 to 50.00
Bicentennial, Betsy Ross	1974	10000	50.00	50.00
Bicentennial, Crossing The Delaware*	1975	10000	50.00	50.00
Bicentennial, Serapio & Bon Homme*	1976	10000	50.00	50.00

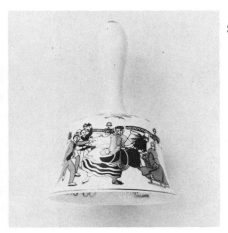

Spode, Annual, Bell, A-Skating Go, 1975

Spode, Plate, Christmas, Christmas Tree, 1975

Spode, Christmas Plate, 1972

Spode, Plate, Christmas,
Good King Wenceslas, 1976
Spode, Bell, Ebb-Tide, 1976

Spode, Christmas Plate, 1971

Stanek, Mayflower Plate

Stieff, Plate, Bicentennial,
Serapio & Bon Homme, 1976

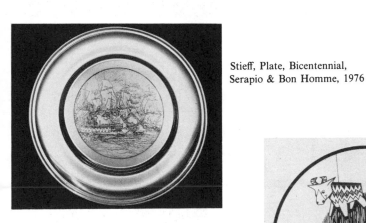

Sterling America, Plate, Christmas,
Customs, Mexico, 1974

Stieff, Plate, Bicentennial,
Crossing The Delaware, 1975

Stanek, Santa Maria Plate

Sterling America,
Christmas Plate, Customs, 1970

Sterling America,
Christmas Plate, Customs, 1971

Sterling America,
Christmas Plate, Customs, 1972

Sterling America,
Christmas Plate, 12 Days, 1970

Sterling America,
Christmas Plate, 12 Days, 1971

Sterling America,
Christmas Plate, 12 Days, 1972

Sterling America, Mother's Day Plate, 1971

Sterling America, Mother's Day Plate, 1973

Stromberg, Crystal State Flower Plate

Sterling America, Mother's Day Plate, 1972

Svend Jensen, Plate, Mother's Day,
Daisies For Mother, 1974

Svend Jensen, Plate, Mother's Day,
Complete Gardener, 1976

Svend Jensen, Plate, Christmas,
Ugly Duckling, 1975

Svend Jensen, Plate, Christmas,
Snowman, 1977

Svend Jensen, Plate, Mother's Day,
Dreams, 1978

Svend Jensen, Plate, Mother's Day,
Surprise For Mom, 1975

Svend Jensen, Plate,
Mother's Day, Little Friends, 1977

Svend Jensen, Plate, Christmas,
Snow Queen, 1976

Svend Jensen, Plate, Christmas,
The Oak Tree, 1978

Svend Jensen, Christmas Plate, 1971

Svend Jensen, Christmas Plate, 1972

Svend Jensen, Christmas Plate, 1974

Svend Jensen, Mother's Day Plate, 1971

Title	Issue Date	Number Issued	Issued Price	Current Price

The St. Louis Gateway Arch plate was produced for Stix, Baer & Fuller, a St. Louis department store, by Reed & Barton. The plate is made of damascene silver.

Stix, Baer & Fuller Plates

Title	Issue Date	Number Issued	Issued Price	Current Price
St. Louis Gateway Arch	1972	1000	75.00	Unknown

Stromberg Glassworks of Sweden was founded in 1876. Limited edition plates and mugs are hand blown and cut.

Stromberg Mugs

Title	Issue Date	Number Issued	Issued Price	Current Price
Annual, Aztec	1968			40.00 to 60.00
Annual, Moon Craft	1969			30.00 to 50.00
Annual, Jingo Ji	1970			9.00 to 16.00
Annual, Freden	1971			16.00
Annual, Olympiad	1972			16.00
Annual, Brotherhood	1973		30.00	30.00
Annual, Statement	1977		45.00	45.00

Stromberg Plates

Title	Issue Date	Number Issued	Issued Price	Current Price
Crystal State Flower, Each*		250	35.00	25.00 to 40.00

Studio di Volteradici, see Volteradici

Stuart Devlin, see Reco

Stumar Bells

Title	Issue Date	Number Issued	Issued Price	Current Price
Christmas, Drummer Boy	1976	10000	14.50	14.50
Christmas, Joyful Expectations*	1977	10000	14.50	14.50

Stumar Plates

Title	Issue Date	Number Issued	Issued Price	Current Price
Charioteer	1978	5000	54.00	54.00
Christmas, Angel	1970	10000	8.00	12.00 to 300.00
Christmas, The Old Canal	1971	10000	8.00	7.00 to 25.00
Christmas, Countryside	1972	10000	8.00	7.00 to 22.00
Christmas, Friendship	1973	10000	10.00	12.00 to 21.00
Christmas, Making Fancy*	1974	10000	10.00	12.00 to 20.00
Christmas, Preparation	1975	10000	10.00	12.00 to 20.00
Christmas, Drummer Boy*	1976	10000	10.00	12.00 to 20.00
Christmas, Joyful Expectations*	1977	10000	19.50	19.50
Egyptian Trilogy	1977	5000	45.00	45.00
Mother's Day, Flower Garden	1971	10000	8.00	7.00 to 10.00
Mother's Day, Mother With Child	1972	10000	8.00	7.00 to 10.00
Mother's Day, Mother Quilting	1973	10000	10.00	7.00 to 10.00
Mother's Day, Mother At Cradle	1974	10000	10.00	10.00
Mother's Day, Mother Baking	1975	10000	10.00	10.00
Mother's Day, Mother Reading	1976	10000	10.00	10.00
Mother's Day, Mother Comforting Child*	1977	10000	19.00	19.00
Mother's Day, Tranquility*	1978	10000	19.50	19.50

Svend Jensen of Denmark entered the limited edition field with Christmas and Mother's Day plates in 1970. The plates are limited to the year of production. Desiree Porcelain Company of Denmark produces the plates.

Svend Jensen Plates

Title	Issue Date	Number Issued	Issued Price	Current Price
Christmas, Hans Christian Andersen's House	1970	20136	14.00	100.00 to 200.00
Christmas, The Little Match Girl*	1971	Year	15.00	32.50 to 78.00
Christmas, Little Mermaid*	1972	22122	16.50	30.00 to 39.00
Christmas, The Fir Tree	1973	Year	20.00	30.00 to 37.00
Christmas, Chimney Sweep*	1974	Year	22.00	30.00 to 38.00
Christmas, Ugly Duckling**	1975	22000	27.50	18.00 to 27.50
Christmas, Snow Queen**	1976	25000	27.50	19.00 to 27.50
Christmas, Snowman*	1977	25000	29.50	29.50
Christmas, The Oak Tree**	1978			27.50
Easter	1976		50.00	50.00
Mother's Day, A Bouquet For Mother	1970	13740	14.00	60.00 to 200.00
Mother's Day, Mother's Love*	1971	14310	15.00	24.00 to 39.00
Mother's Day, Child In Arms*	1972	11018	16.50	27.00 to 36.00
Mother's Day, Flowers For Mother*	1973	11000	20.00	27.00 to 38.00
Mother's Day, Daisies For Mother*	1974	11000	22.00	25.00 to 37.00

Title	Issue Date	Number Issued	Issued Price	Current Price
Mother's Day, Surprise For Mom*	1975	15000	27.50	21.00 to 27.50
Mother's Day, Complete Gardener*	1976	20000	27.50	16.00 to 27.50
Mother's Day, Little Friends*	1977	20000	29.50	33.00
Mother's Day, Dreams*	1978	Year	32.00	32.00

Tapestry plate, see Haviland & Parlon

Texas Ranger, see WNW Mint

Svend Jensen, Mother's Day Plate, 1972

Tirschenreuth limited edition plates, introduced in 1969, are made by the Porzellanfabrik Tirschenreuth of Germany. The factory was founded in 1856.

Tirschenreuth Plates

Title	Issue Date	Number Issued	Issued Price	Current Price
Christmas, Homestead*	1969	3500	12.00	Unknown
Christmas, Church	1970	3500	12.00	Unknown
Christmas, Star Of Bethlehem	1971	3500	12.00	Unknown
Christmas, Elk Silhouette	1972	3500	13.00	Unknown
Christmas	1973			Unknown

Towle Silversmiths of Newburyport, Massachusetts, was established by William Moulton in 1664. Towle limited edition ornaments were first issued in 1971. Plates followed in 1972.

Towle Ornaments

Title	Issue Date	Number Issued	Issued Price	Current Price
Christmas, Medallion	1971	Year	10.00	50.00 to 90.00
Christmas, Medallion	1972	Year	10.00	45.00
Christmas, Medallion	1973	Year	10.00	13.00
Christmas, Medallion	1974	Year	15.00	15.00
Christmas, Medallion	1975	Year	15.00	15.00
Christmas, Medallion	1976	Year	15.00	15.00
Christmas, Medallion	1977	Year	15.00	15.00

Svend Jensen, Mother's Day Plate, 1973

Towle Plates

Title	Issue Date	Number Issued	Issued Price	Current Price
Christmas, Wise Men, Sterling*	1972	2500	250.00	125.00
Valentine's Day, Silver Plate, 6 1/2 In.	1972		10.00	10.00
Valentine's Day, Silver Plate, 6 1/2 In.	1973		10.00	10.00

Trester, Lorainne, see Ridgewood, Rosenthal, Kaiser

Ukranian Bells

Title	Issue Date	Number Issued	Issued Price	Current Price
Bell	1974	1000	27.50	27.50
Bell	1975	1000	35.00	35.00

Ukranian Easter eggs are designed by Ukranian artist Ostap Kobycia. They are made of wood.

Ukranian Eggs

Title	Issue Date	Number Issued	Issued Price	Current Price
Easter	1974	500	12.50	Unknown
Easter	1975	1500	16.00	16.00
Easter	1976	1500	16.00	16.00

Tirschenreuth, Christmas Plate, 1969

Ulmer Keramic Plates

Title	Issue Date	Number Issued	Issued Price	Current Price
Christmas, Peace On Earth	1971		15.00	2.00 to 11.00
Christmas, Let Us Adore Him	1972		15.00	2.00 to 11.00

U. S. Historical Society Plates

Title	Issue Date	Number Issued	Issued Price	Current Price
Annual	1977	5000	60.00	60.00
Annual	1978	10000	75.00	75.00

Towle, Christmas Plate, 1972

Val St.Lambert Cristalleries of Belgium was founded by Messieurs Kemlin and Lelievre in 1825. Limited editions were introduced in 1968.

Val St. Lambert Plates

Title	Issue Date	Number Issued	Issued Price	Current Price
American Heritage, Pilgrim Fathers*	1969	500	200.00	Unknown
American Heritage, Paul Revere's Ride	1970	500	200.00	Unknown
American Heritage, Washington On Delaware*	1971	500	225.00	Unknown
Old Masters, Rubens & Rembrandt*	1968	5000	50.00	Unknown
Old Masters, Van Dyke & Van Gogh	1969	5000	50.00	Unknown
Old Masters, Da Vinci & Michelangelo	1970	5000	50.00	Unknown
Old Masters, El Greco & Goya	1971	5000	50.00	Unknown
Old Masters, Reynolds & Gainsborough	1972	5000	50.00	Unknown
Rembrandt	1970		25.00	Unknown

Stumar, Plate, Mother's Day,
Tranquility, 1978

Stumar, Plate, Christmas,
Making Fancy, 1974

Stumar, Plate, Christmas,
Drummer Boy, 1976

Stumar, Plate, Bell, Christmas,
Joyful Expectations, 1977

Stumar, Plate, Bell, Mother's Day,
Mother Comforting Child, 1977

Val St.Lambert,
American Heritage Plate, 1969

Val St.Lambert, American Heritage Plate,
1971

Val St.Lambert, Old Masters Plates, 1968

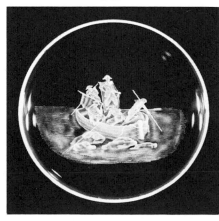

Veneto Flair, Plate, Dog, Doberman, 1974

Title	Issue Date	Number Issued	Issued Price	Current Price

Veneto Flair plates are designed and manufactured by Vincente Tiziano in Northern Italy. Creative World is the U. S. distributor for Veneto Flair. The first limited edition faience plate was produced in 1970.

Veneto Flair, see also Carlo Monte, Creative World, Fontana, Pearl Buck

Veneto Flair Bells

Title	Issue Date	Number Issued	Issued Price	Current Price
Christmas, Pine Cones*	1973	2000	25.00	55.00 to 90.00
Christmas, Bell And Ball	1974	2000	25.00	40.00
Christmas, Tree	1975	2000	30.00	30.00
Christmas, Candle	1976	2000	25.00	30.00
New Year's, Winter Scene	1977	2000	30.00	30.00

Veneto Flair Candlesticks

Title	Issue Date	Number Issued	Issued Price	Current Price
Chalet	1975	7500	15.00	15.00
Landscape	1976	7500	17.50	17.50
Yellow	1977	7500	18.00	18.00
Pink	1978	7500	22.00	22.00

Veneto Flair Eggs

Title	Issue Date	Number Issued	Issued Price	Current Price
Easter, Lily, White	1975	7500	17.50	19.50
Easter, Apple Blossom, Blue	1976	7500	17.50	17.50
Easter, Daisies, Yellow	1977	7500	17.50	17.50
Easter, Pink	1978	7500	17.50	17.50

Veneto Flair, Plate, Four Seasons,
Summer, Plated, 1974

Veneto Flair Plates

Title	Issue Date	Number Issued	Issued Price	Current Price
Bellini, Madonna	1970	500	37.50	395.00 to 500.00
Bird, Owl	1972	2000	35.00	50.00 to 85.00
Bird, Falcon	1973	2000	37.50	25.00 to 40.00
Bird, Mallard Duck	1974	2000	45.00	30.00 to 45.00
Cat, Persian	1974	2000	40.00	30.00 to 45.00
Cat, Siamese	1975	2000	45.00	25.00 to 45.00
Cat, Tabby*	1976	2000	45.00	35.00 to 45.00
Christmas, Three Kings	1971	1500	55.00	125.00 to 200.00
Christmas, Three Shepherds*	1972	2000	55.00	41.00 to 60.00
Christmas, Nativity*	1973	2000	55.00	25.00 to 55.00
Christmas, Angel	1974	2000	55.00	30.00 to 55.00
Christmas Card, Christmas Eve	1975	5000	45.00	34.00 to 55.00
Christmas Card, Old North Church	1976	5000	45.00	45.00
Christmas Card, Log Cabin*	1977	5000	50.00	50.00
Christmas Card, Dutch Christmas	1978	5000	50.00	50.00
Dog, German Shepherd*	1972	2000	37.50	40.00 to 75.00
Dog, Poodle	1973	2000	37.50	40.00
Dog, Doberman*	1974	2000	40.00	25.00 to 40.00
Dog, Collie	1975	2000	45.00	30.00 to 45.00
Dog, Dachsund	1976	2000	45.00	35.00 to 45.00
Easter, Rabbit	1973	2000	50.00	65.00 to 95.00
Easter, Chicks	1974	2000	50.00	25.00 to 50.00
Easter, Lamb	1975	2000	50.00	20.00 to 50.00
Easter, Composite	1976	2000	70.00	40.00 to 55.00
Four Seasons, Fall, Plated	1972	2000	75.00	30.00 to 75.00
Four Seasons, Fall, Sterling	1972	250	125.00	25.00 to 75.00
Four Seasons, Spring, Plated	1973	2000	75.00	60.00 to 75.00
Four Seasons, Spring, Sterling	1973	250	125.00	100.00 to 125.00
Four Seasons, Winter, Plated*	1973	2000	25.00	Unknown
Four Seasons, Winter, Sterling	1973	250	125.00	100.00 to 125.00
Four Seasons, Summer, Sterling	1974	250	125.00	100.00
Four Seasons, Summer, Plated*	1974	2000	75.00	60.00
Goddess Diana	1974	500	75.00	75.00
Goddess Of Pomona	1973	500	75.00	75.00
La Belle Femme, Lily	1978	9500	70.00	70.00
Last Supper, First Scene*	1972	2000	100.00	24.00 to 50.00
Last Supper, Second Scene*	1973	2000	70.00	30.00 to 50.00
Last Supper, Third Scene	1974	2000	70.00	Unknown
Last Supper, Fourth Scene	1975	2000	70.00	Unknown
Last Supper, Christ	1976	2000	70.00	70.00
Mosaic, Justinian	1973	500	50.00	25.00 to 65.00
Mosaic, Pelican	1974	1000	50.00	40.00 to 55.00
Mosaic, Theodora	1977	500	50.00	50.00
Mother's Day, Madonna	1972	2000	55.00	50.00 to 140.00

Veneto Flair, Plate, Cat, Tabby, 1976

Veneto Flair, Plate,
Christmas Card, Log Cabin, 1977

Veneto Flair, Christmas Plate, 1972

Vernonware, Christmas Plate, 1971

Veneto Flair, Plate, Mother's Day,
Daughter & Doll, 1975

Veneto Flair, Plate, Christmas,
Nativity, 1973

Veneto Flair, Four Seasons Plate,
1973, Winter

Veneto Flair, Last Supper Plate,
Scene 1

Veneto Flair, Dog Plate, 1972

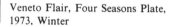

Veneto Flair, Bell, Christmas,
Pine Cones, 1973

Veneto Flair, Wildlife Plate, 1973

Veneto Flair, Last Supper Plate,
Scene 2

Title	Issue Date	Number Issued	Issued Price	Current Price
Mother's Day, Madonna	1973	2000	55.00	22.00 to 70.00
Mother's Day, Mother & Child	1974	2000	55.00	22.00 to 55.00
Mother's Day, Daughter & Doll*	1975	2000	45.00	30.00 to 50.00
Mother's Day, Son & Daughter	1976	2000	55.00	55.00
Mother's Day, Crib Scene	1977	2000	50.00	50.00
Mother's Day, Cherub Flowers	1978	5000	45.00	45.00
Valentine's Day, Silver	1973	2000	135.00	50.00 to 65.00
Valentine's Day, Valentine Boy	1977	3000	45.00	45.00
Valentine's Day, Valentine Girl	1978	3000	45.00	45.00
Wildlife, Deer	1971	500	45.00	300.00 to 400.00
Wildlife, Elephant	1972	1000	37.50	100.00 to 125.00
Wildlife, Puma	1973	2000	37.50	30.00 to 35.00
Wildlife, Tiger*	1974	2000	37.50	30.00 to 40.00

Veneto Flair Ornaments

Title	Issue Date	Number Issued	Issued Price	Current Price
Holly & Evergreen, Pair	1975	10000	12.50	8.00 to 12.00
Bell & Ball, Pair	1976	10000	15.00	30.00
Candle & Lantern, Pair	1977	10000	17.00	10.00

Veneto Flair Steins

Title	Issue Date	Number Issued	Issued Price	Current Price
Castle On Lake, Blue*	1976	3000	60.00	Unknown
Landscape, Yellow	1977	3000	70.00	70.00
Landscape, Pink	1978	3000	70.00	70.00

Vernonware is a division of Metlox Potteries of Manhattan Beach, California. The limited edition plates, introduced in 1971, are hand-painted bas-relief with a Della Robbia border.

Vernonware Plates

Title	Issue Date	Number Issued	Issued Price	Current Price
Christmas, Partridge In A Pear Tree*	1971	10000	15.00	45.00 to 60.00
Christmas, Jingle Bells	1972	12000	17.50	8.00 to 20.00
Christmas, The First Noel	1973	10000	20.00	10.00 to 35.00
Christmas, It Came Upon....	1974	10000	20.00	16.00 to 22.00
Christmas, O Holy Night	1975	10000	20.00	10.00 to 25.00
Christmas, Hark The Herald....	1976	10000	20.00	25.00
Christmas, Away In The Manger	1977	10000	30.00	30.00

Viletta, see also American Academy of Arts

Viletta Plates

Title	Issue Date	Number Issued	Issued Price	Current Price
Christmas, Joy To The World	1970		10.00	Unknown
Christmas, Hark The Herald Angels Sing	1971		10.00	Unknown
Christmas, Silent Night	1972		10.00	Unknown
Christmas, Shepherds Watch	1973		10.00	Unknown
Clara & Nutcracker	1978	Year	19.50	19.50
Disneyland's Betsy Ross	1976	3000	15.00	Unknown
Disneyland's Crossing The Delaware	1976	3000	15.00	Unknown
Disneyland's Signing The Declaration	1976	3000	15.00	Unknown
Disneyland's Spirit Of '76	1976	3000	15.00	Unknown
First Light	1977	2200	40.00	Unknown
Patriots Of American Bicentennial	1977	15000	37.00	Unknown
Charlie Chaplin	1978	5000	35.00	35.00
Neighbor's Pony	1978	5000	45.00	45.00

Villeroy and Boch, see Mettlach

Vogel Pewter Candles

Title	Issue Date	Number Issued	Issued Price	Current Price
Candle	1976	Year	50.00	50.00

Vogel Pewter Plates

Title	Issue Date	Number Issued	Issued Price	Current Price
Christmas*	1975	Year		45.00
Christmas*	1976	Year		40.00 to 50.00
Mother's Day*	1976	Year		30.00 to 40.00

Dante di Volteradici plates are made of cast alabaster.

di Volteradici Plates

Title	Issue Date	Number Issued	Issued Price	Current Price
Grand Opera Series, Rigoletto	1976	Year	35.00	35.00
Grand Opera Series, Madam Butterfly	1977	Year	35.00	35.00
Grand Opera Series, Carmen	1978	Year	40.00	40.00
Pensive Madonna	1977	Year	45.00	45.00

Walt Disney, see Schmid, Disney

Veneto Flair, Stein, Castle On Lake, Blue, 1976

Vogel Pewter, Plate, Christmas, 1975

Vogel Pewter, Plate, Christmas, 1976

Vogel Pewter, Plate, Mother's Day, 1976

Wedgwood, State Seal Compotier,
Benjamin Franklin & Pennsylvania, 1972

Wedgwood, Calendar Plate, 1971

Wedgwood, Calendar Plate, 1972

Wedgwood, Calendar Plate, 1973

Title	Issue Date	Number Issued	Issued Price	Current Price
The Washington Mint of Beachwood, Ohio, was organized in 1970.				
Limited edition silver plates were issued in 1972.				

Washington Mint, see also George Washington Mint

Washington Mint Plates

Title	Issue Date	Number Issued	Issued Price	Current Price
Last Supper, Sterling	1972		125.00	Unknown

Waterford Vases

Title	Issue Date	Number Issued	Issued Price	Current Price
Magi	1971	250	1200.00	Unknown
Ten Commandments	1972	250	1400.00	Unknown

Wedgwood was established in Etruria, England, by Josiah Wedgwood in 1759. The factory was moved to Barlaston in 1940. Wedgwood is famous for its Jasperware, Basalt, and Queensware, all produced in the eighteenth century. These wares are still used by Wedgwood for its limited editions, introduced in 1969.

See listing for Wedgwood in Figurine section

Wedgwood Candlesticks

Title	Issue Date	Number Issued	Issued Price	Current Price
Triton			1725.00	1725.00

Wedgwood Compotiers

Title	Issue Date	Number Issued	Issued Price	Current Price
State Seal, B.Franklin & Pennsylvania, Pair*	1972	5000	20.00	15.00 to 20.00
State Seal, Thomas Jefferson & Virginia, Pair	1972	5000	20.00	15.00 to 20.00
State Seal, J.Hancock & Massachusetts, Pair**	1973	5000	20.00	15.00 to 20.00
State Seal, J.Witherspoon & New Jersey, Pair	1973	5000	20.00	20.00
State Seal, P.Livingston & New York, Pair**	1973	5000	20.00	15.00 to 20.00
State Seal, Ceasar Rodney & Delaware, Pair	1974	5000	20.00	20.00
State Seal, J.Bartlett & New Hampshire, Pair	1974	5000	20.00	20.00
State Seal, J.Hewes & North Carolina, Pair	1975	5000	20.00	20.00
State Seal, Lyman Hall & Georgia, Pair	1975	5000	20.00	20.00
State Seal, Samuel Chase & Maryland, Pair	1975	5000	20.00	20.00
State Seal, E.Rutledge & South Carolina, Pair	1976	5000	20.00	20.00
State Seal, R.Sherman & Connecticut, Pair	1976	5000	25.00	25.00
State Seal, S.Hopkins & Rhode Island, Pair	1976	5000	25.00	25.00

Wedgwood Eggs

Title	Issue Date	Number Issued	Issued Price	Current Price
Easter, Dove Of Peace	1977	Year	25.00	25.00
Easter, The Heron	1978	Year	28.00	28.00

Wedgwood Goblets

Title	Issue Date	Number Issued	Issued Price	Current Price
Three Color Jasper	1976	200	1750.00	1750.00

Wedgwood Mugs

Title	Issue Date	Number Issued	Issued Price	Current Price
Bicentennial, Jasper	1976	500	600.00	600.00
Bicentennial, Queen's Ware	1976	5000	100.00	100.00
Christmas, Picadilly Circus	1971	Year	40.00	13.00 to 25.00
Christmas, St.Paul's Cathedral	1972	Year	40.00	20.00 to 40.00
Christmas, Tower Of London	1973	Year	40.00	50.00
Christmas, House Of Parliament	1974	Year	45.00	40.00 to 60.00
Christmas, Tower Bridge	1975	Year	50.00	35.00 to 55.00
Christmas, Hampton Court	1976	Year	55.00	55.00
Christmas, Westminster Abbey	1977	Year	55.00	55.00
Christmas, Horse Guards	1978	Year		Unknown

Wedgwood Plaques

Title	Issue Date	Number Issued	Issued Price	Current Price
Beloved Of Enchantress	1977	250	600.00	600.00
Lord Of Diadems	1977		700.00	700.00
Fairyland Luster	1977		1500.00	1500.00
Frightened Horse	1977	250	1500.00	1500.00
Lord Of Two Lands	1977		1500.00	1500.00
St.Paul's	1977	250	900.00	900.00

Wedgwood Plates

Title	Issue Date	Number Issued	Issued Price	Current Price
Apollo	1969		30.00	10.00 to 20.00
Bicentennial, Boston Tea Party	1972	5000	30.00	26.00 to 45.00
Bicentennial, Battle Of Concord	1973	5000	30.00	30.00 to 65.00
Bicentennial, Paul Revere**	1973	5000	30.00	25.00 to 40.00
Bicentennial, Across The Delaware	1975	5000	45.00	50.00 to 70.00
Bicentennial, Declaration Is Signed	1976	5000	45.00	45.00
Bicentennial, Victory At Yorktown	1976	5000	45.00	45.00
Bicentennial, Jasper, Independence Hall	1976	10000	85.00	95.00
Bicentennial, Pair	1976	5000	175.00	175.00

Title	Issue Date	Number Issued	Issued Price	Current Price
Bicentennial Scene	1976		85.00	85.00
Blossoming Of Suzanne, Innocence	1978	15000	60.00	60.00 to 120.00
Calendar, Cherubs At Play*	1971	Year	12.00	10.00 to 20.00
Calendar, Animal Carnival*	1972	Year	12.00	3.00 to 22.00
Calendar, Bountiful Butterfly**	1973	Year	12.00	5.00 to 20.00
Calendar, Heraldic**	1974	Year	12.00	12.00
Calendar, Children's Games	1975	Year	15.00	15.00 to 35.00
Calendar, Robin	1976	Year	19.00	25.00
Calendar, Tonatiuh	1977	Year	30.00	30.00
Calendar, Samurai*	1978	Year	30.00	30.00
Child's Day, American, The Sandman*	1971	Year	7.95	15.00
Child's Day, The Tinder Box**	1972	Year	7.95	15.00
Child's Day, Emperor's New Clothes	1973	Year	9.00	10.00 to 20.00
Child's Day, Ugly Duckling	1974	Year	10.00	6.00 to 15.00
Child's Day, Little Mermaid*	1975	Year	11.00	12.00
Child's Day, Hansel & Gretel	1976	Year	11.00	12.50 to 15.00
Child's Day, Rumpelstiltskin	1977	Year	15.00	15.00
Child's Day, Frog Prince	1978	Year	15.00	15.00
Christmas, Windsor Castle*	1969	Year	25.00	122.00 to 250.00
Christmas, Trafalgar Square*	1970	Year	25.00	75.00
Christmas, Picadilly Circus*	1971	Year	30.00	10.00 to 45.00
Christmas, St.Paul's Cathedral*	1972	Year	35.00	17.00 to 35.00
Christmas, Tower Of London**	1973	Year	40.00	20.00 to 45.00
Christmas, Houses Of Parliament	1974	Year	40.00	20.00 to 45.00
Christmas, Tower Bridge*	1975	Year	45.00	25.00 to 50.00
Christmas, Hampton Court	1976	Year	50.00	53.00
Christmas, Westminster Abbey	1977	Year	55.00	55.00
Christmas, Horse Guards	1978	Year		Unknown
Indian, Chief Black Hawk, Black Basalt	1972	500	275.00	275.00
Jasper Trophy Plate, Bicentennial	1976	200	1250.00	1250.00
Mother's Day, Mother's Little Angel*	1971	Year	20.00	10.00 to 25.00
Mother's Day, Seamstress*	1972	Year	20.00	15.00 to 25.00
Mother's Day, Baptism Of Achilles	1973	Year	25.00	10.00 to 25.00
Mother's Day, Domestic Employment	1974	Year	30.00	10.00 to 30.00
Mother's Day, Mother & Child	1975	Year	35.00	15.00 to 35.00
Mother's Day, Spinner*	1976	Year	35.00	17.00 to 35.00
Mother's Day, Leisure Time	1977	Year	35.00	35.00
Mother's Day, Swans & Cygnets	1978	Year	40.00	40.00
Olympics	1972	Year		15.00 to 20.00
Presidents	1977		400.00	400.00
Williamsburg State Seal, Set Of 13*	1977		375.00	375.00

Wedgwood Vases

Three Color	1977	200	1200.00	1200.00
Portland			8000.00	8000.00

Wellings Mint Plates

Annual, St.Urbain, Gold	1971		100.00	Unknown
Annual, St.Urbain, Sterling	1971		100.00	40.00 to 45.00
Annual, On The River, Sterling	1972		125.00	25.00 to 40.00
Mother's Day, Sterling	1972		125.00	25.00 to 45.00

Wendell August Forge produces silver and pewter limited edition plates for the L. E. Smith Glass Company of Mount Pleasant, Pennsylvania.

Wendell August Forge Plates

Christmas, Caroler, Bronze	1974	2500	25.00	Unknown
Christmas, Caroler, Pewter	1974	2500	30.00	Unknown
Christmas, Christmas In Country, Bronze	1975	2500	30.00	Unknown
Christmas, Christmas In Country, Pewter	1975	2500	35.00	Unknown
Christmas, Lamplighter, Bronze	1976	2500	35.00	Unknown
Christmas, Lamplighter, Pewter	1976	2500	40.00	Unknown
Christmas, Covered Bridge, Bronze	1977	2500	40.00	40.00
Christmas, Covered Bridge, Pewter	1977	2500	45.00	45.00
Great Moments, Columbus, Pewter	1971	5000	40.00	Unknown
Great Moments, Columbus, Silver	1971	500	200.00	Unknown
Great Americans, JFK, Pewter	1971	5000	40.00	20.00
Great Americans, JFK, Silver*	1971	500	200.00	175.00
Great Americans, Lincoln, Pewter	1972	5000	40.00	Unknown
Great Americans, Lincoln, Silver	1972	500	200.00	Unknown

Wedgwood, Plate, Calendar, Samurai, 1978

Wedgwood, Child's Day Plate, 1971

Wedgwood, Plate, Child's Day,
Little Mermaid, 1975

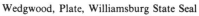

Wedgwood, Plate, Williamsburg State Seal

Wedgwood, Child's Day Plate, 1972

Wedgwood, Mother's Day Plate, 1972

Wedgwood, Christmas Plate, 1972

Wendell August Forge,
Great Americans Plate, 1971, Silver

Wedgwood, Christmas Plate, 1969

Wedgwood, Christmas Plate, 1970

Wedgwood, Plate, Christmas,
Tower Bridge, 1975

Wedgwood, Mother's Day Plate, 1971

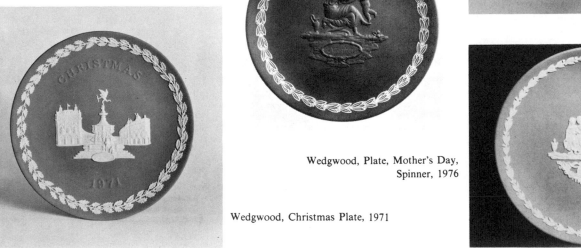

Wedgwood, Plate, Mother's Day,
Spinner, 1976

Wedgwood, Christmas Plate, 1971

Title	Issue Date	Number Issued	Issued Price	Current Price
Great Moments, Landing Of Pilgrims, Pewter	1972	5000	40.00	Unknown
Great Moments, Landing Of Pilgrims, Silver	1972	500	200.00	Unknown
Great Moments, First Thanksgiving, Pewter	1973	5000	40.00	Unknown
Great Moments, First Thanksgiving, Silver	1973	500	200.00	Unknown
Great Moments, Patrick Henry, Pewter	1974	5000	40.00	Unknown
Great Moments, Patrick Henry, Silver	1974	500	200.00	Unknown
Great Moments, Paul Revere, Pewter	1975	5000	45.00	Unknown
Great Moments, Paul Revere, Silver	1975	500	200.00	Unknown
Great Moments, Signing Of Declaration, Pewter	1976	5000	50.00	Unknown
Great Moments, Signing Of Declaration, Silver	1976	500	200.00	Unknown
Peace, Doves, Silver*	1973	2500	250.00	Unknown
Wildlife, On Guard, Aluminum	1977	1900	35.00	35.00
Wildlife, On Guard, Bronze	1977	1500	45.00	45.00
Wildlife, On Guard, Pewter	1977	1500	55.00	55.00
Wildlife, On Guard, Silver	1977	100	250.00	250.00
Wildlife, Thunderbird, Aluminum	1978	1900	40.00	40.00
Wildlife, Thunderbird, Bronze	1978	1500	50.00	50.00
Wildlife, Thunderbird, Pewter	1978	1500	60.00	60.00
Wildlife, Thunderbird, Silver	1978	100	250.00	250.00
Wings Of Man, Columbus' Ships, Pewter	1971	5000	40.00	Unknown
Wings Of Man, Columbus' Ships, Silver*	1971	500	200.00	Unknown
Wings Of Man, Conestoga Wagon, Pewter	1972	5000	40.00	Unknown
Wings Of Man, Conestoga Wagon, Silver	1972	500	200.00	Unknown

Wendell August Forge, Peace Plate, 1973

Westminster Collectible Plates

Trick Or Treat	1976		38.50	38.50

Westmoreland Glass Company of Grapeville, Pennsylvania, was established in 1889. Limited edition plates, introduced in 1972, are hand-painted in gold on black glass.

Wendell August Forge,
Wings Of Man Plate, 1971, Silver

Westmoreland Plates

Christmas, Holy Birth*	1972	2500	35.00	Unknown
Christmas, Manger Scene	1973	3500	35.00	Unknown
Christmas, Gethsemane*	1974	1500	35.00	35.00
Christmas, Christ Is Risen*	1975		45.00	45.00

Wheaton Industries of Millville, New Jersey, was established in 1888. The firm made hand-blown and pressed glassware. Wheaton now makes all types of containers for industry, as well as many collectors' bottles. Limited edition plates were first made in 1971.

Wheaton Commemorative Plates

Presidential, Adams	1971	9648	5.00	5.00 to 7.00
Presidential, Eisenhower	1971	8856	5.00	5.00 to 7.00
Presidential, Hoover	1971	10152	5.00	5.00 to 7.00
Presidential, Kennedy	1971	11160	5.00	5.00 to 7.00
Presidential, Lincoln**	1971	9648	5.00	5.00 to 7.00
Presidential, Madison	1971	9504	5.00	5.00 to 7.00
Presidential, Monroe	1971	9792	5.00	5.00 to 7.00
Presidential, Roosevelt, F.D.	1971	9432	5.00	5.00 to 7.00
Presidential, Taft	1971	9648	5.00	5.00 to 7.00
Presidential, Van Buren	1971	9576	5.00	5.00 to 7.00
Presidential, Washington**	1971	10800	5.00	5.00 to 7.00
Presidential, Wilson	1971	8712	5.00	5.00 to 7.00

Westmoreland, Christmas Plate, 1972

Westmoreland, Plate,
Christmas, Gethsemane, 1974

White House of the Confederacy limited edition plates were commissioned by the Trustees of the White House of the Confederacy. The plates are made by Lenox.

White House of the Confederacy Plates

Confederacy Collection, Set Of 10	1972	1000	900.00	900.00 to 1000.00

Winblad Plate, see Rosenthal

Winslow Homer plates, see U.S. Bicentennial Society

Worcester, see Royal Worcester

World Wild Life Collection Plates

Tiger Banquet	1978	6000	50.00	50.00

Wyeth, Andrew, see Andrew Wyeth

Wyeth, James, see Franklin Mint

Wyeth, N. C., see George Washington Mint

Westmoreland, Plate, Christmas,
Christ Is Risen, 1975

Title	Issue Date	Number Issued	Issued Price	Current Price
Zenith, located in Gouda, Holland, is one of the original delft potteries. Limited editions are produced in both blue and green delft. Fourteen different birthday plates are made each year, representing each day of the week, for both boys and girls.				
Zenith Eggs				
Easter, Blue Delft*	1972	750		35.00 to 55.00
Easter, Green Delft	1973	750	60.00	45.00 to 60.00
Zenith Jars				
Aalborg	1978	350	32.50	32.50
Zenith Plates				
Anniversary, Autumn	1973	500	45.00	Unknown
Anniversary, Spring	1973	500	45.00	Unknown
Anniversary, Summer	1973	500	45.00	Unknown
Anniversary, Winter	1973	500	45.00	Unknown
Annual Greetje, Gretel Tending Geese, Green*	1973	750	60.00	Unknown
Birthday, Boy*	1973	3000	15.00	Unknown
Birthday, Girl*	1973	3000	15.00	Unknown
Hans Brinker, Green Delft*	1972	500	60.00	Unknown
Hans Brinker, Green Delft	1973	750	60.00	Unknown

Zolan, see American Academy of Arts

Zenith, Birthday Plate, 1973, Boy

Zenith, Birthday Plate, 1973, Girl

Zenith, Hans Brinker Plate, 1972

Zenith, Annual Greetje Plate, 1973

Zenith, Easter Egg, 1972